I0824772

METROPOLITANS

Also by A. M. Gittlitz

I Want to Believe: Posadism,
UFOs and Apocalypse Communism

METROPOLITANS

New York Baseball, Class Struggle, and the People's Team

A. M. Gittlitz

Astra House New York

Copyright © 2026 by A. M. Gittlitz
All rights reserved. Copying or digitizing this book for storage, display, or distribution in any other medium is strictly prohibited.

For information about permission to reproduce selections from this book, please contact permissions@astrahouse.com.

Astra House
A Division of Astra Publishing House
astrahouse.com
Printed in the United States of America

Library of Congress Cataloging-in-Publication Data is available upon request.
ISBN: 978-1-6626-0300-6

First edition
10 9 8 7 6 5 4 3 2

Design by Alissa Theodor
The text is set in Warnock Pro
The titles are set in Franklin Gothic Std

Dedicated to the memories of New Breed martyrs Mickey Schwerner, Andrew Goodman, James Chaney, and Jeffrey Glenn Miller

CONTENTS

METROPOLITANS

INTRODUCTION

"When people ask me if I'm a baseball fan," *Simpsons* voice actor Hank Azaria proudly proclaims, "I say, 'No. I'm a Mets fan.' There's a difference."

The goal of this book is to understand the nature of this difference—to use the Mets' tragic, comic, and chaotic history to rip open the dead skin of our nation's tight-stitched pastime, allowing an alternate history of America, and the sport's most profound truths, to unfurl.

As such, I hope readers with no interest in baseball will read on. This will not be a typical sports book, dense with obscure statistics, textual play-by-plays of obscure championship innings, and hagiographic polemics about the perversions of profit motive that nostalgically pretend the sport can be made *great again*—because this is neither a book about greatness nor baseball. It's about the New York Mets.

When I first met the Mets at the age of six, it was like walking into Springfield, Bluffington, or Weinerville. A section of the parking lot outside Shea Stadium had been converted to a Nickelodeon amusement park, a daily saturnalia in which characters from *Rugrats* and *Rocko's Modern Life* punished parents with cream pies and buckets of orange slime. The action was little different inside the Technicolor coliseum, where men in comics-inspired uniforms and their miserable adult fans groaned through nine innings of indignity while a baseball-man hybrid cheered the jubilant audience of wild children. Later that year, when the fed-up players went on strike and the season was canceled, I shrugged and flipped the channel back to SNICK.

Born nine months after the team's last championship in 1986, I had as little concern for the standings as how well Doug Funnie or Bart Simpson might perform on their SATs. I watched each game to laugh at the bizarre names of players like Butch Huskey and Bernard Gilkey, with little higher aspiration than flagging them down for an autograph as if they were Disneyland fur characters. I chanted and shrieked giddily for the occasional homer or come-from-behind rally, loving the Mets equally if they won or lost.

As I got a little older, the Mets, under roguish coach Bobby Valentine, cohered into scrappy competitors to the achromatic team from the Bronx. My dad's bile rose for the perennial champions as it did for Rudy Giuliani or Newt Gingrich, a dynamic I grew to understand as the halls of my Westchester middle school filled with Jeter tees. The most chauvinistic Yankees supporters were the same bullies that hurled fries and slurs toward my friends' lunchtime *Magic: The Gathering* tournaments. The better the Yankees did, the more my black cap and Piazza jersey became like the non-sequitur Hot Topic shirts of my geeky gang—a signifier of weakness, weirdness, or queerness, worn with pride in the face of constant taunts of *Mets Suck!*

My fandom hardened with preteen angst. During my teenage descent into the punk and anarchist counterculture, I became fully convinced the Mets were the team of a downtrodden underworld of artists and radicals, with the Yankees representing the contemptible dominant ideology of New York's financial elite, its conservative law-and-order mayor, and his villainous army of police. I now cared deeply about the World Series—if the Mets could beat the Yankees, I thought, the wretched of the Earth had a chance of finally putting all the oppressors in their place.

The cruelest aspects of the rivalry softened after the decisive 2000 Subway Series, and my baseball fandom likewise dulled during my maturation into an antiwar protester, Wall Street Occupier, and ally of the Movement for Black Lives. But each time these movements came and went, the Mets were always there to offer bittersweet consolation. Once I embraced my partisanship anew, I began studying the franchise between games with the materialist methods I picked up during years in the struggle. To my surprise, I learned how close my youthful caprice had come to the team's historic truth.

The Mets debuted in 1962 as one of the sole survivors of a politically progressive war on baseball. Branch Rickey, famous for inventing the farm system and integrating the Dodgers, created his outlaw Continental League to force the majors to expand its territory throughout the Americas as an effort to counter Yankees dominance and win youth away from brutally telegenic football.

When the outlaw league was defeated by the Senate's affirmation of the majors' monopoly, New York's bureaucrat-in-chief, Robert Moses, and his deep-state lawyer, William Shea, salvaged its unnamed New York team. A final triumph of the city's New Deal restructuring, the city built a stadium to serve as a link between the inner-city proletarian *cosmopolis*—the deindustrializing abyss that swallowed the Dodgers and Giants in 1957—and the middle-class suburbs of Westchester and Long Island, where many of their fans had fled. The city planners named the team to honor this combination of these diverging worlds into a massive unitary *metropolis*.

Through hip marketing appealing to the populist spite against the corporate profiteering that sold the teams out west, leaving only the elitist Yankees behind, the Mets were craftily branded as an *anti-team*. They were terrible by all prior standards, and yet the overmatched journeymen, colorfully dressed in pop-art-inspired threads, mysteriously attracted more and more ironic enthusiasm each game. This New Breed of sports fan came to games in wacky outfits, smuggling snarky signs dedicated to the struggling players, and converted their frustrations into the first *Let's go [team]* chant to cheer them on.

By the end of the season, they boasted both the worst record in baseball history, and a massive, loyal, and enthusiastic fan base rivaling Babe Ruth's Yankees and Jackie Robinson's Dodgers. They were almost equally atrocious in 1964, and yet handily outdrew the Yankees—and would continue to do so for over a decade. Why, aside from irony, the sports establishment wondered, were Mets fans so *true to the orange and blue*? How did they maintain their passion? What were they hoping for? What *meaning* could they derive from certified *losers*?

Reflecting on other sixties' countercultural explosions, feminist rock critic Ellen Willis had called Woodstock "a marketing scheme that got out of control and succeeded through the sheer will of the crowd."[1] *Metsomania* reflected a similar dynamic. By restoring the blue-collar Brooklyn Dodgers and once-anti-capitalist New York Giants, and combining these nostalgic brands with the beatnik-like rants of sarcastic manager Casey Stengel, instinctively antiauthoritarian youth identified with the brand and made it their own. The populist reappropriation represented a tradition of New Yorkers, described by city historian Andy Battle, "to take what capitalism has created and use it wrongly."[2] They were playing a very different game: one that finds meaning not in winning, but in satirizing baseball as a representation of liberal democracy's egalitarian pretensions. During these awful six years, the New Breed did not flock to the Polo Grounds and Shea Stadium to see baseball; they came to see the Mets.

Then came the unprecedented players' strikes of the spring of '68, and a little later, the guerrilla offensive of the Mets' miracle championship run in October '69. Much of the New Breed had become the New Left, deepening their identification with baseball's youngest team of fellow youth-movement dropouts—rebel athletes, connected to the libertine culture of free love and free expression, who explicitly told the press they considered their odds-defying campaign part of the movement against the war in Vietnam and for racial equality. A swarm of Yippies, hippies, and hipsters merged with the players on the Shea field after each series clinch in riots reminiscent of the jovial "Pentagon Levitation" in October 1967, or the millenarian Winter Palace–storming in Moscow fifty years prior. When the World Series was clinched, an anonymous Yippie of the Chicago 8 hailed their victory as a blow against the Yankee imperialism of the "Amerikkkan League," and Wall Street was mobbed with a peace-sign-gesturing crowd larger than the one that welcomed the *Apollo 11* astronauts back to EARTH a few weeks prior. Belief was widespread among peaceniks, Black radicals, astrologers, anarchists, and acid futurists alike that a quasi-cosmic force was moving society away from the rotten bourgeois order to a new era of total freedom. The Tet Offensive, Woodstock, Stonewall, and the Miracle Mets provided equal confirmatory signs of this coming messianic Age of Aquarius, in which *the last shall be first.*

This story of the Mets' intersections with the New Left could have been enough for a book in itself—the Mets, as a baseball team that existed specifically as a social-progressive force, counteracting the apolitical posture of the capitalist sports establishment.

But this story, I found as I researched baseball's political history, stretched back much further.

The Mets were not, in fact, New York's newcomer junior team, but its oldest. They were established in 1880, *twenty-three years prior* to the Yankees, by visionary hipster Jim Mutrie, and John Day, an agent of the Tammany Hall political machine that controlled the city's Democratic Party through its working-class vote. Together, they created the Metropolitan Club—the first team called the Mets—as a populist and philanthropic endeavor, marketed specifically to *the people.*

Gilded Age confrontations between classes were meant to play out harmlessly between the proletarian Mets and their aristocratic sibling-team, the Gothams, at their shared Tammany-built Polo Grounds ballpark. But the underdogs proved themselves far too powerful. Their stunning run to the *first* World Series in 1884 inspired a torchlit parade of thousands of fans celebrating the Mets' first miracle that proved all-too reminiscent of the militant workers' marches spreading across the country. The teams' financiers abruptly ended the experiment, selling the best Mets off to the Gothams, rebranded as New York's Giants, and the upstart Brooklyn Bridegrooms, later the Dodgers.

These teams continued 1884's momentum, finally meeting in a proto–Subway World Series in 1889. Owners and sportswriters again played up the regional rivalry between WASPish Brooklyn and bohemian Manhattan. But off the field, the ex-Met core of both teams, inspired by the insurgent workers' movement, had helped organize the first players' union. Days after the series ended, they announced their joint secession from capitalist baseball into the worker-run Players' League.

Baseball's robber barons crushed the uprising after one season, reestablishing the National League as a singular monopolistic trust. What remained of the original Mets vanished, as did their offspring *people's teams,* the Giants and Dodgers, sixty-seven years later. With millions of cheers suddenly quieted, and the shrieks of New York's political machine breaking down along lines of race and class becoming all too audible, a Frankenstein-like stitch-up of all three deceased teams, electrified with neo-Tammany populism, reanimated the monstrous Mets to fill the void.

A singular spirit, then, runs through the 1880 Mets, the Giants and Dodgers until 1957, the 1962 Mets, and the team today. This book's second section employs the quasi-mystical approach of a *fan history* to analyze the significance of this transmigratory soul in a way that approaches the archetypical categories of psychologist Carl Jung—tortured heroes eternally journeying in the Yankees' kingly shadow; the iconoclastic trickster profaning baseball traditionalism; and the Luciferian temptation to gain forbidden knowledge through a bite of the Home Run Apple.

Communion of these ideals in our collective unconscious is the essence of all fandom—an unceasing vibration of collective meaning coursing beneath the corporate uniforms of players and parishioners. Scorecard empiricism alone cannot capture the paranormal dimension of the 1969 Mets black-cat witchery, the mass psychosis of field-stormings at Shea, the mantra-manifested pennant of 1973, the paratrooper invasion and between-the-legs comeback of the 1986 World Series, the surreal showdown between pitches of the Piazza–Clemens duel that led to the tragic loss in the 2000 Subway Series, the Nietzschean superhero fantasies surrounding the 2015 pennant run, or the homosocial synergy of the 2024 team nicknamed the Gay Grimace Mets.

The book's first section establishes the foundation for this spiritual fan history through a historical materialist reading of the emergence of baseball and its New York people's teams. This method, developed by Karl Marx and Friedrich Engels, argues that historical spirit does nothing on its own—it is the result of individuals, players, fans, executives, and politicians, pursuing their own aims in the context of reproducing their societies. All wealth, culture, and consciousness is the result of the production process, dominated in the capitalist era by constant struggle between the interests of the business-owning bourgeoisie and their laborers, the working class. Owners seek to maximize profits by controlling labor costs while attracting more fans, and athletes strive for higher earnings and autonomy over their bodies, working conditions, and game integrity. Most everything about the game, from its inception to the present day, is often best explained by analyzing these competing interests—pitch clocks, injury epidemics, shifting racial composition, booming free agent contracts, team identities, and even uniform colors.

The oft-repeated saying that "baseball was made for kids, and grown-ups only screw it up," for instance, hints at not only the game's postbellum professionalization and commodification into big business, but its origins in Manhattan during the early United States' class formation. As the nation began to industrialize and Wall Street's financial power grew, a new class of worker was born in its labyrinthine office towers that desired physical exertion suitable for their singular position between the workers and capitalist elite. Around 1837, this emerging middle class escaped their dark towers to the parks of Midtown and the idyllic fields of New Jersey to begin the experiments that would transform a folk game, mainly played by children, into the legalistic sport we know today. With its turn-based structure, their neurosis as a class between worlds, equally envious and resentful of the libidinal physicality of the workers below them, and the chaste technical prowess of the capitalist elite above, formed the game's core tension—constant showdowns between a mechanistic defense, resembling a factory production line, and violent, club-wielding offense, seeking to run free through its works for a climactic return to the safety of home.

As the middle class grew, so too did "the New York Game." The northeast craze expanded nationally in the Union camps of the Civil War, and became federally designated as *America's Pastime* shortly after. The solidification of class structure during the Reconstruction era transformed the game of middle-class social clubs into a commercial spectacle, played by professional athletes earning wages from the price of admission to their enclosed fields. These upwardly mobile workers, too, found the perfect artistic medium to express their dual desires to stabilize industrial wealth creation, and destroy the consolidating power of the bourgeoisie in a manner both peaceful and well remunerated.

According to Marxist historian and cricketer C. L. R. James, it is no coincidence professional baseball emerged when it did. He noted that Europe's democratic revolutions of 1848, the emancipation of enslaved Black Americans and Marx and Engels' founding of the International Workingmen's Association in 1864, and establishment of the Paris Commune in 1871, neatly coincided with the first golf Open Championship in 1860, the establishment of the English Football Association and international cricket competitions in 1863, and the first professional baseball teams in 1869. Not since the Olympic Games of democratic Greece, and the invention of tragic and comic theater that developed out of them, had competitive spectacle emerged on such mass scale, because, James concluded, the "same public that wanted sports and games so eagerly wanted popular democracy too."[3]

No matter how much the elites who standardized and professionalized these sports wanted to reserve the game for a narrow, genteel fan base, they remained dependent on inspiring the passions of the masses to fill their ever-more-capacious cathedral-like ballparks. In the early twentieth century, this contradiction turned the game into an entertainment business rivaling all others—an allegorical stage play in which working-class players and fans improvise cathartic meaning upon American capitalism's mythic level playing field. It is "a game that's played in the mind that comes out of the body," Mets pitcher Bill Pulsipher once asserted—a passive-aggressive drama representing the neurosis of modern life fractured between thought and action, individual and collective, technological discipline and primal force, city and country, work and play.[4]

At the negative core of baseball's dialectical ballet lies the tortured soul of freedom entrapped in mechanical banality. This romantic understanding of the game as a structured unfolding of class tension offers both visions of escape, and relief from the cruelty of the sport's luxury-box and front-office conception. While most fans have a tendency to imitate their own bosses to deride players as spoiled brats when they slump or rebel, they do not show up to the stadium in shirts and jerseys celebrating owners like Hal Steinbrenner and Steve Cohen, because most understand it is the team that earns the trophies, and not the executives who hired them. Our cheers of *Let's Go Mets*, Roger Angell wrote in 1962, are really thus "yells for ourselves," representing this recognition that the players are workers engaged in a bizarre workplace that resembles our own, because it, in fact, *is* our own.[5]

Leftists, however, have often agreed with the framing of professional sports as contemptible products of bourgeois hegemony. As C. L. R. James studied the significance of this historic conjuncture between the emergence of international class struggle and mass athletic spectacle, the leader of his international movement, Leon Trotsky, chastised him that "workers were deflected from politics by sports." Fellow Bolshevik Maxim Gorky similarly denounced professional sports as a bourgeois ploy to "produce cannon fodder for imperialist wars."[6] A century later, leftist commentator Noam Chomsky grumbled that radio callers displayed deep knowledge and passion for the minutiae of local teams while being, he presumed, deeply ignorant of America's endless wars.[7] To these critics, modern sports are not the enlightened theatrical games of ancient Greece, but the propagandistic bread-and-circus spectacles of imperial Rome.

I cannot argue that the derision toward what some leftists call *sportsball* is wholly unfounded. America sunk toward genocidal fascism as I completed this book between 2024 and 2025, and yet on countless evenings, as brave comrades blockaded streets and occupied universities hoping to grind the war machine to a halt, I sat staring at a laptop screen divided between my manuscript and a pirated SNY stream. The Mets' success or failure in these games, and whether or not I stood for the national anthem at Citi Field, changed nothing about the world or my role within it. My insistence on watching, however, provided a convenient excuse for staying out of trouble.

And like many of the great heroes of the revolutionary counterculture, the Mets have moved decisively into the core of the establishment after their seemingly millenarian 1969 miracle. Among the highest-paid and most profitable teams since the Reagan era, by the aughts they represented so much capital investment that their Bernie Madoff–funded Ponzi-scheme business model became central to the worst financial crisis since the Great Depression.

In the dismal aftermath of that collapse, billionaire hedge-fund manager Steve Cohen arrived as a Bonapartist savior. A representative of the cunning criminality of the financial oligarchy, Cohen has since roiled the baseball establishment by frequently being the top bidder on star contracts, fielding a 2023 roster with the largest payroll of all time, and making Juan Soto the highest-paid athlete in history in 2025.

But even Cohen's bailout billions have not drowned the Mets' populist character. Far from emerging as an answer to the Yankees' invincibility, they still appear to be scrappy and often outmatched rebels. Their players remain at the vanguard of the labor struggles within baseball, and social justice struggles around race, class, and sexuality outside it. Their fans, too, are still the same demographic of the New Breed—a predominantly middle-class composition of young radicals and hipsters, and their nostalgic parents. While they can no longer be said to be true underdogs, their embodiment of these epochal contradictions of culture and economy only makes them all the more a perennial people's team, or, at least, "the main character of baseball," as the *Batting Around* podcast described them in 2023.[8]

And while baseball is no longer the most overtly political sport—basketball has stolen that trophy, much to the detriment of baseball's ratings and relevance—its fandom remains, compared to our sham democracy, a far more popular and authentic political undertaking. Overattention to sports may be stupefying, but throughout the summer of 2024, as the antiwar protests were crushed, a more contrived competition took prominence—the elections. Nothing makes us dumber than the electoral spectacle that turns millions of Americans into such fans of the plutocratic parties that they fill their lawns and plaster their bumpers with the names of their favorite cronies.

Following James, sports historian Tony Collins theorized mass athletic spectacle, on the other hand, as ripe with *deep politics*—so "tightly woven into the political culture of the commonplace that its politics appeared to be invisible."[9] The greatest moments in baseball history, the ones on which this book will focus, were when these deep-political truths were comically and tragically revealed during the people's team phases of the Giants, Dodgers, Yankees, and Mets. The time-markers of these politically charged seasons produce a legible history of the expanding and contracting contours of America's class struggle, just as the history of forests can be gleaned in the warped tree rings visible in each shard of broken bat.

As the book moves toward the present in its third section, I shift slightly from the methods of Marxism and fan history toward a more subjective sketch of the contemporary Mets and their fans. Many of these later chapters were scribbled at dozens of games at Citi Field during the 2024 season, as the Gay Grimace Mets went from a spring laughingstock to the postseason's final four. With the Mets in their element, I meditated on the activity of the players and the stadium experience, and recorded conversations in tailgates and the stands with fans patient enough to entertain my THC gummy–influenced existential queries: What are we thinking and doing when we watch the Mets? What are they trying to tell us? What do the Mets *mean*?

The answers painted a picture of a tortured paradox familiar to leftists. We cling to a franchise that we know is likely doomed, racing toward defeat again and again in hopes for an October revolution that may never arrive. I have watched the rise and fall of the anti-globalization movement, and the Subway Series defeat of 2000; the impotence of the antiwar and immigrant-rights movements, and the late-season heartbreaks of *Los Mets* from 2006 to 2008; the brutal suppression of the dignity-demanding Occupy Wall Street and Black Lives Matter movements, and the flaccid postseason defeats of 2015 and 2016; and two far-right regimes bookending the proletarian uprising of 2020, and the late-season collapse of 2023.

What explains our willingness, as sports fans or politicos, to rush, like so many Charlie Browns, toward humiliation again and again? Roger Kahn, the great scribe of the Brooklyn Dodgers, described this worldview as the "choke hypothesis"—in which our emotional attachment to something is always shadowed by superstitious certainty that a catastrophic error, injury, or total collapse is inevitable.[10] Cultural critic and long-suffering Cubs fan Lauren Berlant developed the parallel theory of *cruel optimism*. This "might involve food, or a kind of love," they wrote in 2011, "it might be a fantasy of the good life, or a political project. . . . These kinds of optimistic relation[s] are not inherently cruel. They become cruel only when the object that draws your attachment actively impedes the aim that brought you to it initially."[11]

Neither Kahn nor Berlant argued for us to sever these attachments. Joining the triumphalist Bleacher Creatures of Yankee Stadium or the

MAGA movement will do little good, because the apocalyptic horizon of late-stage capitalism has made this nihilistic phenomenon pervasive. Instead, they argue the recognition of optimism's toxic dynamics presents the opportunity to reevaluate our desires, find new ways of relating to our hopes and fears for the future, and enact radical alternatives. This will be the book's concluding mission—to provide a strategy for breaking cruel optimism's cycle in which Mets fans and partisans of a truly free, egalitarian society alike are trapped.

We will either leave the metropolitan labyrinth of baseball-man hybrids, levitating fruit, and bat-chucking ogres having discovered baseball's deep political truths, or remain forever enclosed in the occult horrors of this mystifying urban carnival. Either way, we will journey, giddy as our inner-child fans on the 7 train, passing the working-class neighborhoods and scrapyards of Queens, through the neo-Ebbets facade and into Citi Field, entering its concrete passageways lined with colorful merchandise and screens, awaiting with every swift step emergence to the sunlit field, New York City in its totality on the horizon behind us.

PART I

THE PEOPLE'S TEAMS (1776–1962)

The apparently uncontrolled surge of moral delinquency in our great cities is more or less directly the result of misused leisure. Leisure is wonderful in creative hands. It accounts for great architecture, great paintings, and great music. People who can be masters of their own time have given us great literature and great artistic blessings of all kinds. . . . A great American historian has said that it is just too bad that the history of nations could not have been written judging a people from their play at games rather than from their indulgence in wars.

—Branch Rickey, The American Diamond

Cricket is a gentle pastime . . . played and applauded in a conventional, decorous and English manner. Base Ball is an Athletic Turmoil, played and applauded in an unconventional, enthusiastic and American manner.

The founder of our National Game became a Major General in the United States Army! The sport had its baptism when our country was in the preliminary agonies of a fratricidal conflict. . . . Base Ball, I repeat, is War!

—Albert Spalding, America's National Game

Chapter 1

THE METS

This forenoon the Brigade went thro the Manouvers . . . excersisd in the afternoon[,] in the intervals playd at base.
—Valley Forge, April 7, 1778

This first known recording of baseball play in the Americas, in the journal of Continental Army ensign George Ewing, is perfectly suited for the honorific the sport earned nearly a century later: America's *pastime.* Arriving with the spring thaw, it is an annual promise for many months of free play with friends in sprawling meadows as a reprieve from monotonous toil and winter. All of life's harshness, whether it be the cruelty of one's boss, drill instructor, or the tyrant King George, was sublimated into the battle between hitter and pitcher, defense and offense, with all fear of death in battle, poverty, or humiliation of one's ideals reduced to the harmless matter of runs and outs.

But in the context of the rest of Ewing's journal, the game's more radical populist character is also revealed. He was one of the thousands of plebeian farmers, workers, artisans, and immigrants who joined the

Continental Army and played baseball, while their colonial patrician generals, Washington and Knox, separately played the British game of cricket. More than a new nation, the United States of America they were fighting for would level the social playing field by guaranteeing the natural right for all men, everywhere created equal, to pursue happiness as they saw fit. The consciousness of that class difference between Ewing's comrades and the elite circle of officers can be further read into his account of what happened once darkness cut play short: His bunkmates, perhaps still riled from the game, set the tail of their superior's horse on fire as a rebellious prank.

More class tension emerged within the camp three weeks later when news arrived that Spain and France had recognized a free United States. Ewing's comrades broke into a mass celebration on May Day, erecting maypoles and parading around the camp with one of their own dressed as the folk hero King Tammany—the Lenape chief who struck a diplomatic accord with their settler ancestors. At nightfall, the revelers marched toward the generals' quarters demanding their homage to the folk saint as well, "but just as they were descending the hill to the house," Ewing wrote, "an Aid met them and informd them that the Genl was Indisposd and desird them to retire which they did with the greatest decency and regularity."

The postrevolutionary class divide between baseball-playing soldiers and cricket-playing officers deepened with the formation of the Society of Cincinnati, an elite network of Continental Army commanders, bankers, and proponents of a strong central government. The rank-and-file veterans answered by creating a populist Tammany Society, committed to the revolution's libertarian ideals. In their dual Independence Day celebrations, Cincinnati members held refined banquets, while Tammany's "braves" (for whom Atlanta's baseball team is named) staged raucous street festivals with artillery fire and pyrotechnics.

Patriotic unity further crumbled when the US sided with Britain against the French Revolution, as Tammanyites defended the Jacobins by publicly guillotining aristocratic effigies. The conflict turned violent when Cincinnati founder Alexander Hamilton was pelted with stones while giving a speech in New York for his opposition to revolutionary democracy, in the US and abroad. The fundamental irreconcilability of American class divisions was ultimately sealed in blood when Tammany's Aaron Burr killed Hamilton in their 1804 duel on the Hudson shore.

The shaken parties represented by these dueling frontmen retreated from the brink of civil war toward a republican balance from then on. The elite Federalists consolidated commercial power, while New York's amok-running mobs mandated the populist Democrats, headquartered in Tammany Hall, to check the rapacious gentry through negotiation. Tammany's revolutionary levelers traded their Phrygian caps for the oversized suits of populist mayors, cutting deals between immigrant-enclave strongmen and finance lobbyists at town hall meetings, or behind the curtains of luxe lounges. Political blood sport dulled on this razor-edged stage to a simultaneously brutish and elegant ballet not unlike "the New York Game" soon to be developed in the Elysian Fields of Jersey City, just a few paces from the clearing where Burr pitched his fatal fastball.

Emerging in Midtown parks during the 1830s, the Manhattan version of baseball was the sporting equivalent of Tammany's new political order, created by the emerging middle class as a reprieve from urban contradiction. Its progenitors were a subculture of Manhattan doctors, lawyers, accountants, and paper-pushers—men who worked on Wall Street during the day and lurked in Bowery brothels and bars at dusk. Restless between the worlds of yacht races and bare-knuckle boxing, these sheet-balancing Bartlebys turned to the folk game as a vitalistic escape from their office-tower dungeons, and the emasculation of being derided by the ringside rabble as *the fancies*—shortened in proletarian patois to *fans.* Like the Valley Forge warriors, their game was a medium to assert independent agency, subconsciously expressing their unique identity crisis of being caught in between the worlds above and below them which they admired and despised in equal measure. Evoking both the defensive impulses of the elite, and the overburdened's violent desire to strike, it became a form of artistic physical therapy for this neurosis—an opportunity to sweat, slide, and run freely and equally together with their fellows in the fields of new frontiers.

Bosses and builders alike catcalled these dandies playing a child's game in Madison Square Park, much as they would the contemporary dodgeballers and pickleballers of hipster Brooklyn. How pretentious it must have looked to see the traditional violent pegging (hitting the runner with the ball) replaced with force-outs (tossing the ball ahead of the runner to the base), or the carriage-spoke clubs and lumpy feather-sack balls smoothed into cylindrical-sanded bats and artfully sewn spheres. But the game's advancement, and the fellowship forged by their experimental exercise, served sufficient recompense for the slights. "We played for fun and health," baseball founder William Wheaton recalled, "and won every time."[12]

Only when a financial crisis and bread riots broke out in 1837 did they ferry to a more tranquil laboratory across the Hudson River. The Elysian Fields amusement park and recreation area was the grounds of founding father John Stevens, a retreat for the affluent to socialize in seclusion from Manhattan's chaotic streets. In the idyllic fields, the hobbyists transformed into the utopian Knickerbocker social club (satirically named after a slur for the old-moneyed Dutch). Influenced by the Owenite and Fourierist communism advocated by Horace Greeley's republican *Tribune*, they managed themselves democratically, selecting ad-hoc teams to play games whose results were never more important than the communal pot of chowder they shared whenever an arbitrarily decided winning score was reached.

The Elysian Fields became crowded with copycat clubs as the commercial economy recovered and the middle class expanded the next decade. To ensure their sport's refined sociality remained sacred, the Knicks asserted themselves as the game's guarantors, distributing their rulebook that squeezed all the wildness of the folk game into their polished diamond. They at last dropped their prohibition on competitive exhibitions between clubs in 1845, under the condition they be monitored for adherence to their rulebook and logged on an official scorecard. This match, which the Knicks lost to the unknown "New York Nine" 23–1 in four innings, is today recognized as the first in the annals of "modern baseball" for having achieved a narrative permanence allowing it to be *put in the books*.

Soon, "the New York Game" broke Elysian Field containment to spread throughout the northeast. A Knick-established umbrella organization, the National Association of Base Ball Players (NA), democratically managed qualifying clubs with friendly schedules and occasional public exhibitions. Most New Yorkers, however, still assumed the game a hipster exuberance that would fade, much like the then-failing utopian communes.

But simultaneously, much of the NA's ranks registered with a new formation dedicated to bringing their reforms to national political power—the Republican Party. Unlike the Southern-linked Tammany Democrats, these were abolitionists who saw the expansion of slavery into the westward territories as pure regression. When their candidate,

Abraham Lincoln, won the 1860 presidential election, the Southern states seceded, and the turn-of-the-century social peace was shattered.

As New York's white working class erupted into anti-Black pogroms against the draft, the NA's Republican pioneers enlisted as clerks and officers to defend the Union. They taught soldiers New York baseball as a way to keep them away from gambling, boozing, and other forms of mischief, and were stunned at how well baseball could discipline the conscripted underclass soldiers on a level that barking orders and blowing bugles could not. Even Confederate prisoners of war who initially perceived the Yankee game as a form of torture in time came to love that aspect of their captivity. Four years later, thousands of veterans marched home from the battlefield singing a paean to the martyred abolitionist John Brown, while daydreaming of bringing home the new game they learned between battles.

"From the rocky coast of Maine to the Golden Gate of California, from upstart Chicago to the reconstructed states of Dixie, a baseball mania swept the land," George B. Kirsch wrote. Baseball's postwar boom became a unifying symbol of how the fractured Union would heal. In 1865, President Andrew Johnson invited members of the NA to discuss how the government could support baseball as its ranks swelled from the hundreds of clubs forming in every corner of the country, its westward territories, and Canada. Freedmen organized Black teams and trained to join the NA. Soldiers sent to the Kansas plains to exterminate Comanche Indians kept up with the game in between their scalping expeditions. Even a Ku Klux Klan team, presumably playing without hoods, beat a group of "carpetbagger" Reconstruction agents in the first recorded game in Fayetteville, Tennessee.[13]

The explosion of baseball team-building occurred at pace with vigorous organizing of the first mass unions. Dedicated to renewing America's revolutionary egalitarianism, they demanded the democratic franchise extend into the workshops and factories as well. Their central demand was the eight-hour workday, which would permit a third of their lives not dedicated to sleep and wage-labor to be spent pursuing happiness. Many of the thousands who won that luxury chose to spend their new free time organizing for greater political autonomy for their class. Many others spent it playing the game now officially declared *America's pastime.*

William "Boss" Tweed, the all-powerful Tammany sachem who effectively ran the city in the 1860s, steered municipal resources toward the latter. He sponsored the Mutuals club, founded by firefighters of the Mutual Hook and Ladder Company in 1857, and slowly replaced its amateur ranks with hand-chosen workers. As Tweed took full control of the club, he awarded the ringers no-show city jobs so they could focus solely on strengthening their athletic skills. By the mid-sixties, New Yorkers swarmed to the first enclosed ballpark, the Union Grounds in Williamsburg, Brooklyn, actually *paying* to see the Tammany-branded squad look like the Harlem Globetrotters as they embarrassed a whole nation of the dandy NA's hobbyist Washington Generals.

Tammany's professional model rapidly generalized throughout the NA, fracturing its middle-class amateur old guard with a new breed of wage-earning athletes. A decisive moment came in 1867, when the Pythians, an amateur Black team of Radical Republican ex-Union soldiers from Philadelphia, applied to join the association. The NA's white Philadelphia club had sponsored them, opening the door to dozens of idealistic amateur Black and lower-class teams to rejuvenate the sport's traditional social and anti-commercial pretenses.

African Americans had played baseball in New York since at least the 1850s, with the first known game between Black teams taking place between the Henson Base Ball Club from Jamaica, Queens, and the Unknowns of Weeksville, Brooklyn, in 1859. During the war, the heroic Black regiments played baseball enthusiastically. Eleven of those regiments had been recruited by Philadelphia abolitionist and Pythians founder Octavius Catto, who had seen how important the image of Black soldiers fighting for the Union had been for the cause of accepting African Americans as patriotic citizens. Catto transitioned to baseball after the war, believing the national pastime should be integrated along with the army and voter rolls. But after some debate, the NA's conclusion cemented the old guard's inability, mirrored by the collapse of Reconstruction and continued failure to integrate the nascent labor movement, to keep the Civil War's egalitarian fire burning—the Pythians' application was declined to avoid "political discussions."[14]

The NA's apolitically framed segregation foreshadowed it splitting between its amateur and professional teams in 1871, and the death of player-run baseball altogether. While the amateurs continued to play mostly for free at unenclosed fields, the professionals treated the game as a business, albeit one controlled by the workers themselves through a guild-like structure. But the decision to keep their ranks white also declared idealism taboo. After four seasons, professional baseball was perceived not as an exercise in worker autonomy, but a free-market mania, patronized predominantly by lumpen hooligans and gambling addicts, in which every player and umpire was constantly for sale to rival teams or bookies.

With respectable and moneyed fans preferring the legitimacy of amateurism, revenues shrank, and baseball's small bourgeoisie of grounds owners and club investors moved to rein in the chaos.[15] In 1875, Chicago pitcher and sporting goods merchandiser Albert Spalding and White Stockings owner William Hulbert launched a coup of strong-arm buyouts to seize the professional association. The clubs were immediately corporatized. The players, forced to sign contracts reserving them to their clubs unless traded or fired, were stripped of any say in their rosters, rules, schedules, or identity. New York's Tammany populism was counteracted with models of Protestant discipline. Owners hired spies to follow the players and ensure they weren't drinking, gambling, or organizing against their new bosses. Alcohol and Sunday games were banned—two measures to prevent working-class rabble from sullying the reputation of baseball among a desired high class of clientele. Independent circuits were forced into farm-like peonage to the new premier league, and the few Black players who had managed to make their way onto progressive rosters were banished for good. The new monolithic monopoly called itself the National League (NL).

As the lone New York team in the NL, Tammany Hall's Mutuals now appeared a crumbling civic monument. Barely able to compete with the concentrated talent of their disciplined opponents, they were eliminated from contention for the league's championship flag—the "pennant"—long before the final weeks of the 1876 season. When the ashamed players declined to embark on their final road trip, a liberty tolerated in the days when the players ran the sport themselves, they were labeled truant workers, and summarily expelled from the league.[16]

For the next four years, baseball in the city reverted to its amateur origins. The development was welcome to much of the working class, who despised the National League like any other industrial trust in the early Gilded Age. Tens of thousands had gathered in Tompkins Square Park in 1877 under the Workingmen's Association banner as part of a nationwide workers' uprising. Rejecting industrial monopolization, and the immense inequality that came with it, they demanded a cooperative economic system.

The police and National Guard forces crushed the movement, constructing imposing armories at urban flash points shortly after as a warning against future challenges to capitalism. One of these fortresses rose on the Union Grounds in Williamsburg where the Mutuals had once played.

Hoping to appease the still-simmering rage of immiserated workers in the aftermath of the rebellion, the triumphant robber barons refashioned themselves as philanthropists. They funded parks, museums, schools, hospitals, libraries, and athletic clubs. Among them were plenty of Tammany financiers with blank checks reserved specifically for anyone who could restore the Democrats' claim to populism by bringing a National League team to New York.

John Day, a tobacco merchant, pitcher, and Tammany agent, was their man for the task. In the years following the Mutuals' disappearance, he combed the amateur baseball nines of Manhattan and Brooklyn for talent, only to find many didn't care much for the capitalist vision of baseball or for developing the skills necessary to compete at an NL level. And those who did, like Day himself, simply lacked the talent.

In 1880, help arrived on a penny-farthing from Connecticut in the form of quintessential *dude* Jim Mutrie. Dudes were the hipsters of the late nineteenth century, famous for their self-satirical voluminous top hats, tails, canes, monocles, slicked-back hair, and absurd mustaches curled stiff with wax. The fanciful self-mythologizer introduced himself to Day during the game that day as baseball's Johnny Appleseed. He had taught Union soldiers to play on Boston Common, and traveled the postwar semipro leagues as a journeyman ringer, coach, and manager. Most recently, he told Day, he had been hired to manage an up-and-coming team in New Haven. But during his first game he decided the modest rural settings no longer suited his aspirations. After the last out, he hopped on his bike and rode toward New York, where he dreamed of converging unknown talent from Androscoggin to White Plains into the great metropolis's new people's team.

The fateful encounter of Day and Mutrie (rumored to have been arranged by a member of the aging amateur-era old guard[17]) resulted in the incorporation of the Metropolitan Exposition Company (MEC). Its sole venture was the Metropolitan Baseball Club—a name referring to the five boroughs and their periphery, as opposed to the Manhattan *cosmopolis* known simply as "New York." They combined urban amateur nines with regional semipro prospects into a barnstorming squad renowned for their major-league aspirations and unflagging passion for play. They rapidly became the most prolific semipro team in history, recording 151 games in 1881 and 162 in 1882, with a remarkable record of 201–136–7. Against amateur and college teams they were unbeatable, and they bested NL teams in about a third of their exhibitions. Tammany's municipal populism and Mutrie's suburban hipster millenarianism rapidly synthesized into the talk of baseball—an underdog team nicknamed by their passionate, traveling fan base *the Mets.*

With MEC's concept proven, Tammany money poured in. A spending spree followed that swelled the Mets' core with veteran and prospect remnants from the Rochester Hop Bitters, Buffalo Bisons, and the NL's defunct Troy Trojans. By early 1883, the now suspiciously large all-star squad broke ground on Manhattan's first ballpark. Its location would be a muddy field north of Central Park, still derided as the Polo Grounds after the aristocratic equestrian sport's failed importation from Britain. In ironic testament to baseball's unrivaled patriotic and interclass appeal, MEC kept the name as well.

The National League bosses, once glad to have rid themselves of degenerate Tammany influence six years prior, now looked on in envy. The Philadelphia, St. Louis, and Louisville clubs had dropped from the NL shortly after the Mutuals, reducing the NL to a six-team, predominantly Midwestern circuit, and imperiling their claims to be the nation's premier baseball business. Especially suffering from a lack of New York's gate receipts and legitimacy, the NL now *needed* Tammany's Mets.

But when NL owners invited the Mets to join their elite circle for the 1883 season, they stridently declined. Mutrie announced they would instead join the American Association. The new league, organized by brewers and saloon-owners to move product to baseball's underclass of fans who streamed to and from neighboring bars during dry NL games, was derided by the puritanical NL owners as the "beer and whiskey league." Mutrie, personally fond of drinking with his players, imagined his *people's team* more at home in this outlaw circuit catering specifically to the working class, where admission was half that of the NL, and games were played on Sunday, the only day most workers had off.

The sporting press suspected there was more to "Truthful James" Mutrie's populist decision than he was letting on—and Day confirmed MEC's wider ambitions days later. The Mets were cleaved in half, with their best players moved to a new luxury-branded National League team catering to the tastes of Manhattan's cosmopolitan elites. He called them the Gothams, adapted from the backhanded nickname for Manhattan by Washington Irving in a text describing the city's dual character as "the most charming, pleasant, polished, and praiseworthy city under the sun," and "most shockingly ill-natured and sarcastic, and wickedly given to all manner of backsliding."[18]

Polo Grounds was expanded to suit the dialectic. A luxurious double-decker grandstand with a separate entrance for the carriage-riding class was built around the Gothams' Fifth Avenue side, while the Mets' hoi polloi would enter through a Sixth Avenue gate to cram into a shoddier set of bleachers surrounding a second-rate, rough-cut diamond. Simultaneous games would allow Gothams fans, who often called the team simply "New York," to buy booze from the Metropolitans' wing of the grounds, with the thin canvas fence separating the fields heightening the natural rivalry between the distinct fanbases.[19]

This business-minded plan to unleash and harmlessly divert the pent-up desire for class war came not a moment too soon. As thousands of workers swarmed downtown on May Day to protest sinking wages and longer hours in the aftermath of the crushed 1877 rebellion, a faction of whom carried images of the recently deceased Karl Marx, 15,000 packed the Polo Grounds for Opening Day. The exuberant, cross-class crowd sat astride former president Ulysses S. Grant and Tammany and Wall Street bigwigs to see the Gothams, in white shirts emblazoned with the seal of New York, triumph over the Boston Beaneaters. Eleven days later, as the ranks of the Knights of Labor and Central Labor Union swelled, a modest working-class crowd of 3,000 watched the Mets' debut. In dudely polka-dotted blue-and-white shirts and dark-blue stockings, they were blown out by the Philadelphia Athletics 11–4.[20]

Although an inferior brand, the Mets' offbeat roster allowed them to retain their cult following. Their ace was "Smiling" Tim Keefe, son of an Irish carpenter who quit the family trade for baseball after he was stiffed on a job in 1877. He came into his own on the Mets, leading the AA in strikeouts in 1883, and striking out nearly the same number in 1884 to end the season with a 2.25 ERA and 37 wins. Behind him was Jack Lynch, praised by the *New York Clipper* as "effective and puzzling" for his mastery of "mystery pitches." Their star hitter was "Big" Dave Orr, a Queens stonemason and proto-Ruth who weighed 250 pounds and topped the AA in batting average and RBIs. Not far behind Big Dave in batting was third baseman "Dude" Esterbrook of Staten Island, another flamboyant hipster with a romantic philosophy of sport as a provider of eternal youth: "If a man, no matter how old, behaved like a boy, played in the street, walked eight or ten miles a day, and took plenty of exercise, he could live to be one hundred and fifty."[21]

Mutrie's men went on to play well at home, but suffered on the road to end with a 54–42 record ranking in the middle of the AA standings. The Gothams' season, however, proved a far greater disappointment. They finished sixth of eight, with a losing record and middling attendance.

Believing the dual-team strategy that should have doubled attendance to have actually divided it, Day moved the Mets from the Polo Grounds to a new park a few blocks east. With its half-built stands atop an industrial landfill surrounded by immigrant slums and toxic fume-spewing factories, fans and players called the new park "The Dump." Play there was so frequently interrupted by buried trash emerging onto the diamond that Jack Lynch cautioned new infielders not to "go down for a grounder and come up with Malaria."[22]

Low attendance, and Day's sudden disinterest, rapidly put the Mets on the verge of bankruptcy. Mutrie, however, refused to be spiritually defeated by the humiliating conditions. Nighttime guerrilla raids on the clubhouses of the Gothams' posh NL opponents supplemented their depleted budget with stolen equipment that kept them battling up the ranks of the AA. The hearts of New Yorkers were definitively recaptured in the final month of the 1884 season, when the Mets went 17–3–3 to occlude the Louisville Eclipse and poke past the Columbus Buckeyes. When the Mets clinched New York's first pennant, some reported their torchlit victory parade swelling into the thousands.[23]

Mutrie celebrated the victory with an audacious challenge to the National League champion Providence Grays: come to New York for an interleague championship series. The Grays initially dismissed the invitation with aristocratic disdain, claiming the Mets stood no chance against any NL squad. Once Mutrie's relentless provocations finally goaded them into accepting, a spectacular humiliation indeed followed. The Metropolitans, perhaps taking the Dude's wisdom too literally, "played like children"[24] during the noncompetitive three-game sweep.

The press, either seeking to diminish the rout, or mock New York's historic pretension as the global capital, hailed Providence as "World Champions" of baseball's first "World Series."[25]

Meanwhile, another mediocre season in 1884 from the Gothams convinced Day to ditch the dual-league strategy. Even with the added revenue from lager and ale, the profitability gap of the American Association's smaller seating capacities and half-price tickets made the miracle Mets appear more show stealer than loss leader. Esterbrook and Keefe were transferred back to the Polo Grounds, with Mutrie retained as the NL team's new manager. The rest of the Mets were sold to ferry entrepreneur Erastus Wiman as a promotion for his real estate interests in the developing neighborhoods of Staten Island. The AA champs were quickly forgotten on that lesser key of the metropolitan archipelago, but the deal paid off handsomely for MEC. Now the lone team in towering Manhattan, Mutrie rechristened the NL's new all-star squad baseball's "Giants."

Under their new identity, the team maintained their elite caliber, placing second in their thrilling 1885 NL debut, while broadening franchise appeal to working-class Mets devotees in the bleachers or picnicking on the surrounding bluffs. Newspapers from the Giants' first season implied this new diversity by quoting fans of various backgrounds in Irish and African American vernacular. Introduction of a "Ladies Day" promotion further expanded the ranks of Giants fans—proving so successful that men often found the best seats already taken by women spectators.[26]

Most Giants fans, however, came to see their maverick superstar, John Montgomery "Monte" Ward. A visionary on the field, Ward revolutionized baseball by introducing innovations like the pitcher's mound, intentional walk, pitchout, and cut-off throw. Ward was equally dynamic between games—studying law at Columbia by night and leading the Giants on excursions to mingle in the downtown counterculture. He wrote that these new friends soon accompanied them back uptown for games: "lawyers and litterateurs, Bohemians of every class, clerks, merchants, and day jobbers. You can see them any day at the Polo Grounds, mixed up together in the most democratic fashion."[27]

The sordid crowd was precisely what the NL magnates had feared when they allowed New York back into their ranks. But the Giants were now perennial top drawers, and their owners reveled in their irreplaceability. "Who are the people?" an emboldened Mutrie yelled through a megaphone parading the stands before games. The fans yelled back the Giants' slogan: *"We Are the People!"*

To the owners and most of the fans, the slogan was an assertion of the cross-class, cross-cultural New York identity embodied by the team. So long as ballplayers were relatively well-off artisans (paid two to four times that of the average factory worker), all differences between the audience could be overcome as they jeered underperformers who could be cut to lower leagues or nonathletic work, or cheered for those who deserved to rise to more prominent status within the sport. The most successful athletes could even start their own offseason businesses—often taverns, buzzing with patrons hoping to share a mug with their favorite star. So long as the balance held, baseball served as a spectacle exhibiting the American dream of class mobility, and a powerful legitimizer for Tammany's politicians as forward-thinking mediators between classes.

The players, however, grew to have a different understanding of the *We Are the People* slogan. In his study sessions at Columbia, Monte Ward turned his attention to labor law, discovering the league's contracting practice that "reserved" a player to a single team for life was a blatantly illegal scheme to monopolize athletic labor-power. While a manufacturing worker had the right to quit their factory and pursue higher wages elsewhere, a baseball player could only hope to be traded or sold to a more benevolent franchise.

The NL owners' 1885 collusion to further limit top salary to $2,000 was the worst affront yet to the Giants' star-studded roster. Inspired by the cooperationist ideals of the Knights of Labor, Ward organized his teammates into the core of the sport's first union: the Brotherhood of Professional Base Ball Players. Slugger Jim O'Rourke became their great orator, proselytizing worker power to visiting players. Tim Keefe, who had moonlighted as an accountant and sporting-goods entrepreneur, became union secretary. Ex-teamster Buck Ewing and Brooklynite veteran Mickey Welch also enthusiastically joined their ranks. To them, *the People* no longer referred to New Yorkers as a whole, but the players and their worker fans *against* the political establishment and big capitalist trusts like the National League.

Mutrie and Day quickly defied their fellow owners to appease Ward and O'Rourke with exceptional salaries, but their stars' resolve only grew stronger as Brotherhood ranks expanded. In 1886, Ward penned a polemic for *Lippincott's Monthly Magazine* arguing ballplayers were not the privileged dandies the press usually made them out to be, but something more akin to the itinerant toilers roving between company towns. Their lives were an exhausting slog of training and travel, marred by the ever-present threats of career-ending injuries, micromanaging owners and their Pinkerton spies, and the cruel heckles of sycophantic "baseball cranks," whom he distinguished from ordinary fans as *fiends*. "With the loss of sleep and the fatigue of the games," he concluded, "we lose all appreciation of the interesting and the beautiful."[28]

Radicalization continued as the Brotherhood came under deeper influence from the insurgent mayoral campaign of the egalitarian economist

Henry George and the United Labor Party in 1887. Renewing calls for the cooperative economic model defeated in the uprising a decade prior, the coalition sought to establish labor as an independent political force, capable of checking the power of capital, and ultimately winning equal distribution of all land and social wealth. Flexing the Brotherhood's muscle, Keefe designed a new raven-black uniform for the Giants to wear at the Polo Grounds, perhaps a nod to the flags ubiquitous in the revived worker movement's confrontational demonstrations.

By the end of the year, a *New York Clipper* survey had revealed the majority of players now understood themselves as permanent members of the working class, and Ward issued the Brotherhood's first demands to the league.[29] Their central cause was limiting contractual reservation to five years, at which point players would be able to reenter the market as *free agents* and sign to another team.

This modified reserve system is more or less how the major leagues operate today—but it would not be won for another ninety years. Day and Mutrie's allowance of extra salary to Ward and O'Rourke had catalyzed the entire mess, their fellow owners believed, and granting any further concession, no matter how reasonable, would only inspire the players to ask for more.[30]

The most steadfast anti-unionist among the owners was the league's dominant figure, the Chicago White Stockings' Albert Spalding. He had been something like the Ward of his generation—an innovative ace pitcher with the deep political belief that baseball's advancement influenced the course of American society. But as he became a successful sporting goods entrepreneur, Spalding came to identify less with his fellow ballplayers than his bosses. He became the key ballplayer in the ownership coup that established the National League, buying his way into their ranks soon after with the fortune he earned as its exclusive supplier of balls and bats. That success turned him into the most fervent ideologue of big capital among his fellow owners, pushing them to consolidate into a strong and efficient trust capable of profiting from every game from sandlot to stadium. Essential to the task was suppression of all competition from other leagues, equipment suppliers, and, of course, the self-organization of their player-workers.

But Ward knew the Brotherhood had an advantage over workers at the steel or mining trusts. While manufacturing depended on deskilling workers and making them interchangeable, the NL had to hire from the narrow pool representing the *best* ballplayers in the country. And while striking miners, steelworkers, or rail-workers could be forced back to work at the barrel of a gun, baseball crowds already prone to riot against umpires or opposing players would undoubtedly explode at the sight of National Guardsmen marching their heroes to the field with bayonets.

As the 1888 season approached, the Brotherhood ordered its members not to sign their contracts. This collectivization of the "holdout" tactic, once only available to irreplaceable stars like Ward, forced the NL to compromise. The salary cap was adjusted to allow many of the Brotherhood large raises, and the reserve law was codified in standard contracts—something Ward believed would provide fertile ground for a legal challenge.

A season of peace followed in which Brotherhood ranks expanded again on the basis of their modest victory; their Polo Grounds clubhouse-headquarters becoming even more alluring as the Giants rose to first in the National League during the summer. When Spalding's second-place White Stockings visited New York in August, their showdown appeared to be a proxy battle between opposing views of the game's labor relations. In a dramatic gesture to demonstrate to his union-skeptical opponents why players' rights were worth fighting for, Ward orchestrated a post-game excursion downtown to Wallack's Theatre. The evening's climax arrived when celebrated actor DeWolf Hopper honored both teams by delivering the first public performance of poet Ernest Thayer's new "Ballad of the Republic"—a poem known best today as "Casey at the Bat."

The booming voice of Hopper transported the packed house to the bottom of the ninth inning in mythical Mudville. The home team, trailing 4–2, makes two quick outs. With stands emptying, two consecutive hits by slumping players bring the crowd roaring back to life as their champion, Casey, makes his showboating stroll to the plate. Two consecutively called strikes transform the jubilation to near violence—*"Kill him! Kill the umpire!"* the crowd howls. Held in check only by Casey's steadying hand, a decisive third pitch flies. The poem's purview widens to survey an America where citizens elsewhere bask at carefree picnics, before snapping back to a Mudville devastated by Casey's catastrophic *whiff.*

The Giants and their foes, whose game had ended in similar fashion by that exact score hours prior, were moved to tears. Each had been in Casey's shoes before, carrying all the neuroses of the stands on their backs to earn a living. The hope and fear of the game, the aspiration and humiliation, the victory and the choke, the players now realized, were parts of a larger tragedy, politically and artistically equaling Aeschylus or Shakespeare, that the players wrote and performed themselves. The profit-obsessed owners were blind to the importance of this drama, and foolish for ignoring the riot-quelling mercy of Casey. The White Stockings returned to Chicago as the Brotherhood's newest recruits.

While "Casey at the Bat" painted a negative vision of society descending into anarchy without baseball's tranquilizing effect, Edward Bellamy's science fiction novel *Looking Backward*, published that same year, revived the bygone utopianism of baseball's amateur-era origins. The narrative relates the vision of a time traveler recently returned from the year 2000, a future in which citizens enjoy shortened workdays and retirement at forty-five—all made possible by the nation's pooled resources and the efforts of a highly disciplined, democratic "industrial army." Hunger, crime, prisons, and worker riots become things of the past once the common good replaces profit. Sports, too, remain central in the futuristic society, still enjoyed on the mass scale provided by the National League, but with a communal spirit lost since the Elysian Fields: "The professional sportsmen, which were such a curious feature of your day, we have nothing answering to," says Dr. Leete, the time traveler's guide:

> "nor are the prizes for which our athletes contend money prizes, as with you. Our contests are always for glory only. The generous rivalry existing between the various guilds, and the loyalty of each worker to his own, afford a constant stimulation to all sorts of games. . . . The demand for 'panem et circenses' preferred by the Roman populace is recognized nowadays as a wholly reasonable one. If bread is the first necessity of life, recreation is a close second, and the nation caters for both."[31]

Looking Backward became a massive hit, outselling *Uncle Tom's Cabin*, *Ben-Hur*, and all other American novels by the end of the century. Readers organized themselves into "Nationalist Clubs" dedicated to creating the world envisioned by Bellamy. These groups had a similar, although more patriotic and utopian, proposal to the cooperationist workers' movement—artisans and workers pooling their talent and money to create self-managed workshops that would, Edwin G. Burrows and Mike Wallace wrote in their New York history *Gotham*, "preserve republican traditions of mutuality, and still survive in the larger free market economy."[32]

New York's chapter was headed by Civil War hero Abner Doubleday, who decades later would be apocryphally credited with inventing baseball. While that story was a Mutriesque myth, his Nationalist movement directly provided the Brotherhood with a new gameplan: to make the socialist sci-fi vision of guild-based competitive sport a reality.

The Giants continued organizing and playing with revolutionary fervor through the rest of the 1888 season, winning the pennant, and giving New York its first world championship over the St. Louis Browns. The Brotherhood's flagship team now topped the game both on the field and in the balance sheets, having drawn a record 305,000 fans, with a rumored profit of $55,000.[33] The momentum propelled them toward the greater prize for their class in the looming winter confrontation with the magnates. "The novelty of being Champions of the World has died out," the *Sporting News* reported a week after the win, "and nothing but politics is at present talked of."[34]

The Brotherhood's power peaking, Spalding extended a flattering invitation to their leader. He announced a world baseball tour, where his White Stockings would play an all-star team, captained by Ward, in exhibitions in England, Italy, France, Australia, New Zealand, India, and Egypt. Ward likely knew he was aiding his enemy's international business expansion, but the trip would be a massive story in the United States, raising his status to equal Spalding as the game's world-renowned star. In the weeks before the owners' winter meeting, Ward and Spalding set sail.

When the tour arrived to play the sandlots of Giza, news reached Ward of treachery back home. The owners had reversed all previous agreements in his absence, and agreed on a new "classification scheme" that would crush the union. Pay would be adjusted to position, further dividing players in their workplace. The scheme's grading system for both on-field performance and off-field activities provided a starker threat: severe financial penalties for arguing with umpires, drinking after the game, and, presumably, organizing with the Brotherhood.

On the bitter journey home, Spalding assured a fuming Ward that the reports must have been exaggerated, and all would be resolved stateside. Once Ward reassembled with the Brotherhood, however, the owners returned to stonewalling. The season was too near to reverse course, Spalding now said, and the matter could only be discussed after the 1889 World Series.

The blindsided Brotherhood promised to strike on Fourth of July in response. As baseball's most profitable weekend approached, the sports press played up the confrontation like any other heated team rivalry. But when Independence Day arrived, the players ominously appeared on field without incident.

Ward had ordered team representatives to instead assemble ten days later—the anniversary of the storming of the Paris Bastille—to announce the Giants' secret plan for their own baseball revolution. No longer content to negotiate for bigger cages and longer chains, the Brotherhood would break free from the NL en masse at the end of the season. With help from the broader workers' movement, they would work day and night to build new ballparks and resume the 1890 season as a new "Players' League" (PL), organized on the cooperationist model, and retaining the majority of NL players, and the top tier of the increasingly formidable AA. The other majors, if they even managed to field full teams, would be deserted of fans, and the radical truism of radical unionists would be proven on America's biggest stage: the bosses needed them, but they did not need the boss.

Ward, however, made a notable exception for his own employers. While the Brotherhood and MEC had their differences, Mutrie was still considered one of the boys, and players qualified Day as far more personable than any other league owner. Once Ward confided in them, the duo signaled their support by reregistering MEC as the generic "New York Base Ball Club"—a move designed to prevent another team from taking the field with the Giants' common "New York" nickname. Spalding demanded an explanation when the Giants came to Chicago in September, but Mutrie declined to meet.

MEC's apparent defection was in reality a strategic hedge. While Mutrie and Day likely sympathized with their players over Spalding, they were not about to throw away the booming business they had built over the past decade to wild-eyed rebellion. The Giants were playing with revolutionary fervor during their tight pennant race, however, and they had seen how their closest competitors in Boston fought with far less passion due to their owners' threats against affiliation with the Brotherhood. With the AA's Brooklyn Bridegrooms gliding toward a pennant, the moment Day and Mutrie had dreamed of since the creation of the Gothams and Mets was on the horizon: an all–New York World Series. Once the championship revenue was secured, they could safely reveal which side the "New York Base Ball Club" would join.

The Brooklyn Bridegrooms had earned their nickname both from their players' playboy reputations, and from owner Charles Byrne's adaptation of MEC's method of buying failing teams and folding them into their Brooklyn roster. The Mets had been the latest shotgun-wedding bride; Byrne had bought the Staten Island exiles in 1888, bringing Darby O'Brien, Paul Radford, Bill Holbert, Al Mays, and "Big" Dave Orr to Brooklyn, and dismissed the rest. While the Mets were no more, their ex-players rekindled the miracle spirit of 1884 that season to give the Bridegrooms their first pennant and a chance for revenge against their old Manhattan bosses.

Attempting to milk the rivalry for all it was worth, Day and Byrne planned the series as an expansive best-of-eleven contest. As spring darkened to fall, the Brooklyn underdogs began slowing the pace of play each time they squeaked out a lead in hopes of cancellation due to rain or darkness. Day charged unsportsmanlike behavior in the press. Byrne shot back with allegations of cheating. The sorry spectacle only diminished attendance and enthusiasm as the series plodded along. In one of these dismal games, a Giants crank started a baseball tradition during the seventh inning when he attempted to rouse the cold and bored fans by ordering them to jump up and "stretch for luck!"

Even when the Giants were finally victorious after nine games, the pathetic rivalry between the owners continued as the united players of both teams made their last-minute preparations. Ward announced the Players League to the press a few days later. The baseball insurrection had begun.

Construction started immediately on new parks and rosters for PL teams in Boston, Chicago, Philadelphia, Pittsburgh, Cleveland, Buffalo, Brooklyn, and—once Mutrie and Day pledged fealty to Spalding—Manhattan. While the other PL teams had chosen new names—like the Monte Ward–managed Ward's Wonders, of Brownsville, Brooklyn—Ewing, Keefe, and O'Rourke answered MEC's betrayal by keeping the name Giants, and pledging to build their park as close to the Polo Grounds as possible.

Dozens of other committees were formed to handle rules, contracts, disputes, and finances. To assure the league was completely self-reliant, every player was expected to chip in funds. It wasn't long before this idealistic financing scheme ran up against the harsh reality of real estate—to break ground on their new parks, they would need wealthy backers. When a search for purely altruistic donors to provide no-strings-attached land fell short as well, Ward began to vet landed investors for sympathy toward the PL's mission of revenue sharing and player control, and their capability to withstand the costly battle to come.

He found his first angels in Cleveland streetcar magnate Albert L. Johnson, a former minority owner of the defunct NL Cleveland Blues, and his brother Tom, a politician aligned with Henry George. The siblings began evangelizing about the PL to their wealthy peers, tempering fears of its socialist ideals with a pitch that the players' communitarian spirit—so evident in the Giants' back-to-back championships—would generate unprecedented excitement and profits in ways the staid National League never could.

Among those sold on the pitch was Edward B. Talcott. Once dubbed the "boy wonder of Wall Street," the heir to a banking and cotton fortune purchased the majority of the PL Giants, and worked out a lease with James Coogan, owner of the hilly area directly across 155th Street where Day had rebuilt the Polo Grounds a year prior. In a further sign of the PL's confidence, schedules were matched to the NL so every game would directly conflict. When opening day came, Brotherhood Park stood directly across from the Polo Grounds, forcing fans to stand between the two towering Giants, each flying their own 1888 and 1889 championship pennants, and literally choose which side they were on.

With the NL and AA largely fielding teams of journeymen scabs, most fans went to the proud and sturdily built Brotherhood parks to see their beloved NL and AA defects. Throughout the league, the Giants' *We Are the People* slogan was waved on banners by union workers parading to Opening Day, where opposing players embraced before the games and called each other *comrade*. The final score for New York's competing Opening Days was NL: 4,600, PL: 12,000, with other PL teams outdrawing by similar margins nationwide.

In a year of continued unrest from the cooperationist labor movement, in which the Knights of Labor formed the United Mine Workers in Ohio, the Brotherhood of Locomotive Firemen initiated a railway strike in New York, and a wave of carpenter's strikes demanding the eight-hour day formed the United Brotherhood of Carpenters, game attendance remained high through the early part of the season. While "the carriage set still rode to Day's Giants' games," David Stevens wrote in his biography of Ward, "the PL Giants had a large blue-collar turnout."[35]

The PL featured fan-friendly higher-scoring games, thanks to the livelier balls engineered by Keefe to replace the "dead-ball" preferred by owners to depress players' value through lowering their offensive stats. The potential for a corresponding increase in fan aggression was diverted by outfield flags for each team that could be ceremonially captured. Every PL game, won or lost, was celebrated as another victory for their common task—proving a fraternal working class was capable of both running the US economy, and restoring its revolution's egalitarian Declaration.

Spalding, too, recognized the baseball war had become a national referendum on the "irrepressible conflict between labor and capital"—one he was certain his class would win. While the PL was correct that the NL needed its star-power to profit, their idealism for worker autonomy had relied on outside investment, and he foresaw the PL suffering the same collapse as the previous player-run leagues. "Base Ball depends for results upon two interdependent divisions," he wrote, "the one to have absolute control and direction of the system, and the other . . . the actual work of production."[36]

Rather than await their inevitable collapse, Spalding's war commission worked to hasten it—deploying spies, courting investors, and tempting stars with bonuses and immunity from reprisals if they returned. Few players accepted these offers to betray their new teams and the passionate working class fans filling PL parks.

But as the season went on, these fans began to see the PL was not as radical as advertised. Spalding's depiction of the PL as "hot-head anarchist[s] out to overthrow the established business of baseball" had given much of the Brotherhood cold feet, much as the bomb allegedly thrown by anarchists toward police lines during the 1886 Haymarket riot in Chicago fractured the workers' movement. The Knights of Labor and the American Federation of Labor had purged their anarchists and socialist wings in response, and the Brotherhood sought further distance by refusing affiliation with either organization. When PL play began, many of these fraternalist fans were additionally dismayed to find the league courted NL profits and exclusivity with fifty-cent admission, bans on alcohol, and Sunday off-days. Despite their rhetoric, the players still dreamed the PL would maintain their wages at a higher level than union artisans because, baseball labor historian Robert P. Gelzheiser wrote, "most players never wanted to view themselves as jobbers."[37]

As the radical pretenses that drew early mass enthusiasm dissolved, the PL appeared merely an oddball alternative. Many fans returned to the American Association's cheaper, rowdier games, or the generally superior facilities of the NL. And while the PL ultimately outdrew the NL 913,000 to 853,000 in cities where the two teams were in direct competition, divided attendance caused deep revenue losses for all three leagues.[38] Some PL clubs were forced to cut wages by the end of the summer, sending many of its players back into the waiting arms of their old clubs, protected from bankruptcy by the NL's ample war chest.

Wall Street wunderkind Talcott became the first financier to defect that summer, agreeing in a backroom deal with Mutrie and Day to merge the teams back into the NL the next season. He had been so offended by the PL's unprofitability that he agreed to do so under the sole condition that the duo would never again entertain their workers' demands. Dude Mutrie abided, and Day assured: "The capitalists on both sides will do the negotiating. The players will have to do what they are told to do."[39]

The rest of the PL's major backers met Spalding behind the players' backs after the season. The experiment had been a failure, he told them. Only the champion Boston club had turned a profit as the PL lost an estimated $125,000 in the oversaturated baseball market. The Brotherhood's new requests for significant reinvestment would defer returns, already reduced by profit sharing, even further into the future. Only the NL held sufficient reserves to last, he reminded them, before offering the same deal as Talcott: The established leagues would buy their shares and ballparks, and dissolve the three leagues back into two.

Ward always knew this devil's offer would come, and had hoped the capitalists he had so carefully vetted for benevolence would refuse. Instead, they accepted unanimously.

The Brotherhood had been played. The investors were never partisans of cooperationist utopia; they had either only liked the theory on paper, or merely said so as a ruse to win favor with organized labor as they developed areas around ballparks built on or around their land investments in the developing urban peripheries. "It occurred to me there was a chance for a good investment if I could get grounds on a streetcar line owned by my brother and myself," Albert Johnson later explained. "Visions of millions of dollars of profit loomed in front of my eyes."[40]

The Brotherhood organized a desperate postseason fundraising barnstorm to save the league. The futile hat-passing turned all the more tragic when Ward's Wonders star "Big" Dave Orr—who had led the PL with a .371 batting average and 124 RBIs—suffered a career-ending stroke during one benefit contest in rural Pennsylvania. Simultaneously, a rowdy crowd attending a Yale vs. Princeton football match at the Wonders' park in Brownsville stomped the grandstand until it collapsed. Realizing all that remained of the PL was scrap, the Brotherhood admitted defeat, and officially dissolved as well.

The reunified Giants ceremoniously opened their 1891 season at Brotherhood Park, purchased by the NL Giants and rechristened Polo

Grounds III—the same field onto which the Mets would be reborn seventy years later. "Tim Keefe and the Giants who had been in the PL queued up along the left-field line," Stevens wrote, "the Giants who had stayed in the NL appeared on the right-field line. . . . The defectors and union stalwarts rushed together as a symbol of fraternalism and embraced."[41]

Throughout American labor history, similar heartwarming scenes of defeated workers burying all resentment for their scabbing counterparts to carry on their labors are common. Far less examples can be found of workers, in the course of their rebellion, reaching toward the class factions below them in common struggle, with the understanding that a victory for one would be a victory for all. The Brotherhood's inability to identify "the People" with this broader working class—including the manual laborers who helped build their parks and stuffed their cotton baseballs—cost them the only demographic numerous enough to sustain the PL. Had these militant fans been centered, the baseball war might have evolved into class war, fortified to resist strikebreaking with strategic counterattacks of proletarian sabotage on the NL's armories. Instead, Stevens wrote, the Brotherhood "wasn't trying to kill the NL or the AA, just co-exist."[42]

The Nationalist Clubs of Doubleday and the United Labor Party of Henry George met a similar fate. After George's narrow loss in the 1886 election, the movement went astray from establishing a revolutionary "new party," Burrows and Wallace wrote in *Gotham*, contenting itself to be "a new element to be bid for by the old parties."[43] Progressive Republican Teddy Roosevelt took some, Tammany's Democrats took the rest, and the radicals in the labor movement slowly collapsed back to the political margins.

The PL had also failed, politically and tactically, by refusing to break the color barrier. Just three years before the revolt, Ward had invited

George Stovey, unquestionably the best pitcher among Black teams, and rumored to be the best in history, to join the Giants during their pennant-race with the White Stockings. Spalding had prevented the move on the grounds that segregated play was an immutable law of baseball. The PL had the opportunity to demonstrate otherwise, either as proof of their radical egalitarian vision for America, or at least as a solution to their late-season player shortage.[44] But fearing non-white players would harm attendance, historian Robert B. Ross speculated, no known attempt was made.[45]

The ongoing segregation set baseball and the rest of the labor movement back decades. The *Sporting Life* reported a year after the PL's defeat that "in no other business in America is the color line so finely drawn as in baseball," and "an African who attempts to put on a uniform and go in among a lot of white players is taking his life in his hands."[46] It would be half a century until the integrationist CIO returned the American working class to an offensive footing, and ten more years from there before Jackie Robinson and Willie Mays took the field at the sold-out Polo Grounds, decisively proving that Black stars dramatically *increase* turnout through the excitement and success they bring their teams. The generation of Black ballplayers who followed, including Donn Clendenon and Cleon Jones of the reincarnated Mets, would further demonstrate how the unceasing demand of Black workers for equality and dignity pushes the class struggle forward—finally winning the Brotherhood's initial crusade against the contractual tyranny of the baseball bourgeoisie.

After managing the Giants for a final season to a respectable third-place finish, Mutrie and Day—still reeling from their wartime struggles—found themselves outmaneuvered by Spalding. He used their feigned interest in the rival league to justify orchestrating a hostile takeover by

Talcott, who promptly restored the purely upscale Gothams branding to the Giants. When the National League absorbed the American Association to become baseball's sole major circuit, the pair were fully shut out. Broke and blacklisted, the former partners sought work in the upstate minors. Years later, Mutrie's fall from grace was complete. Discovered selling secondhand newspapers aboard the Staten Island Ferry, he was offered a position as a mere ticket-taker at the Polo Grounds where he had once reigned.[47]

Charles Byrne hired Ward to manage the Bridegrooms, who had earned a spot in the expanded postwar NL. After two seasons, he returned to the Giants, retiring shortly after to fight for players' rights full-time as a lawyer.

Dude Esterbrook played a final season for Brooklyn in 1891, before being cut from the team to make room for the influx of displaced AA talent. He likewise set out wandering the country on foot in search of a team that would take him, only to find the eccentricities that made him beloved in New York proved bothersome elsewhere. Once he had walked to New Orleans and back without finding a club to keep him, his brother offered to take him upstate to unwind. En route, it was revealed their destination was a mental hospital. Esterbrook perished by leaping off the moving train in an attempt to escape.[48]

Chapter 2

YANKEE INSURRECTOS

In its brief existence, the Players' League laid the tracks on which the twentieth century violently arrived.

Overexpansion of the baseball industry proved a prelude for overproduction crises in rail, agriculture, and finance. When a stock market crash in 1893 sent unemployment soaring up to 35 percent in industrial areas, the capitalists emulated the National League's method of dealing with the ensuing economic chaos and unrest. War was declared on labor organizations, and failing corporations, banks, and farms were swallowed into ever-larger trusts, protected in America's densifying urban industrial centers by Tammany-aligned political machines.

Amid this depression in 1896, the Mets briefly reappeared at the Brotherhood-built, Tammany-stolen Polo Grounds. Like the

1884 Mets, they were a farm team branded as the working-class alternative to the big-league Giants beloved by Vanderbilts, Whitneys, and Paynes.

The second Mets were not as inspiring as their predecessors, however. The project was identified with the Giants' despised new owner, Andrew Freedman. One of Tammany's wealthiest young real estate agents, he had earned a reputation among fans as a pretentious hobbyist who frequently assaulted sportswriters and umpires when he didn't get his way. Fellow owners also loathed Freedman, who openly plotted against their internal democracy by demanding the National League be narrowed into a singular trust, over which he would preside as its Gilded-Age robber baron. He was the most hated man in baseball, described by historian Bill James as "George Steinbrenner on Quaaludes with a touch of Al Capone."[49]

When the brash magnate stormed the field during a summer Mets game to argue with an umpire, the low-drawing sequel was axed from their minor circuit, and never played again. The expulsion made Freedman even more megalomaniacal. Understanding that the Giants' huge profits at home and on the road floated the entire industry, he sold off his star roster, vowing to tank the prestigious team, and by extension the National League, until he got his way. Concessions came as the century turned. Four NL teams were cut so its best players could join the Giants and restore their elite status. By 1902, Freedman had decisively displaced Spalding as the NL's most powerful magnate, and was poised to seize full control of baseball.

Then, suddenly, a rebel battalion from the south appeared atop a hill overlooking the Polo Grounds. They called themselves the Highlanders, but earned an ironic nickname from New Yorkers referencing the slur used against progressive Northerners by the British and Confederates in America's dual revolutions. The colloquial title had such sticking power that the team became officially known as the Yankees.

More than just cheeky appropriation, the Yankee moniker referenced the perceived threat the new team, and the renegade league that fielded them, posed to Tammany Hall. For a century, Tammany had earned its Democratic Party voting base by absorbing arriving immigrants as a counterpower to the waspy "Old Yankee" city administrations that represented big capital. When the 1890s depression perilously reduced conditions for second-generation immigrants and new arrivals alike, many dwellers of crowded tenements turned away from Tammany and toward either progressive Republicans like Teddy Roosevelt—trust-busting opponents of the Gilded Age behemoths and the regional Tammany network—or the small labor movement slowly recomposing itself after the previous decades' defeats.

The early Yankees fit the trend on both ends. Many of the team's players were members of a new union formed in 1900 to claw back some of the National League's unchecked dominance over baseball labor-power. When Freedman refused to acknowledge the union's demands, its ranks defected to a new circuit that was baseball's answer to progressive Republicanism—the American League (AL).

The AL was the creation of Ban Johnson, a Cincinnati sportswriter banned from major-league parks for blaming the chaos of the 1890 Players' League revolt on NL greed. He spent the next decade in baseball's Midwest underworld, organizing a new circuit to restore puritanical respectability to the game. Like Teddy Roosevelt, he branded himself a "benevolent autocrat" who would protect the people from the anarchy of the market, represented by Freedman's rapacious NL power grab, and the anarchy of the underclass, represented by Tammany's multicultural voting base and the frequent riots of unruly fans and players against umpires.

Johnson found investors to restore the teams cut from the AA and NL into the American League. Scores of NL defectors filled the new rosters, lending prestige to the upstart circuit that promised to engage with their union fairly. With attendance surging through 1902, Johnson announced his Baltimore Orioles franchise would move to the NL's New York stronghold as the league's vanguard force against its flagship Giants.

Freedman worked the Tammany machine to stop the AL advance through the offseason. Every time Johnson found a spot for the Orioles to land, city bureaucrats promptly canceled the lease by claiming a road or streetcar would cut through the infield were their ballpark ever built.

But with Tammany losing legitimacy as antitrust Republicans surged to power, a younger wing understood their Gilded Age machine was breaking down and would need to adapt to the new "Progressive Era." Among them was original Mets financier Joseph Gordon, who secured Johnson a rocky hilltop plot in Washington Heights in exchange for making the Orioles, soon rebranded the Highlanders, then Yankees, Tammany's new populist baseball project. They were to be an underdog answer to the blue-blooded Giants, similar to the manufactured Mets-Gothams rivalry two decades prior.

Glenn Stout described the deal in his book *Yankees Century*: "Gordon's Tammany backers treated the new team like any other immigrant. In exchange for help in finding lodging and gainful employment, Tammany would sponsor the new arrival. All Tammany wanted in return was the equivalent of the immigrant's vote—undying loyalty and a percentage of the paycheck."[50]

The Yankees' flag-waving Opening Day marked a new order for American politics and baseball alike. Tammany's insurgent progressives soon defeated its conservative wing to recuperate its straying voter base, and

Freedman's play for full control of the sport was foiled by owners outraged by his failure to prevent the AL's incursion. Peace was declared between the leagues with a new bicameral government known as *organized baseball.*

Johnson proved himself a far more capable hegemon than his predecessors, commanding unchecked control over the American League owners and the sport by proxy, and crushing the players' union he had once courted. Alluding to Nicholas II's defeat of the 1905 Russian Revolution through the creation of democratic structures over which he held ultimate control, the magnates hailed Johnson as "Czar of Baseball."

The Giants were at first the only holdouts to the new regime, refusing in 1904 to play the AL pennant-winners in the restored World Series tradition. But as years passed, the autonomy Johnson had granted to the Yankees as an operation of the Tammany underworld led to an increasingly profitable truce.

Gordon had installed two Tammany agents into Yankees ownership: Frank Farrell, a millionaire criminal who managed hundreds of backroom-casinos and speakeasies; and one of his regular customers, William Devery, the New York Police Department Chief whose motto, when it came to Farrell's illegal operations, was: "Hear, see, and say nothin'. Eat, drink, and pay nothin'."[51] Farrell pampered the Yanks like his racehorses, and bet on them just as freely, as Devery turned a blind eye to the team of drunks, spitballers, gamblers, brawlers, and cheaters. For their patrolman-like complicity, Devery gave the team its interlocking NY logo, which first appeared on the Tiffany & Company–minted NYPD Medal of Valor.

Discipline on the team was "nonexistent," Stout wrote, a reputation that sent an unruly herd of black sheep fans, eschewed by the rest of the respectable American League, to flock up Hilltop. Unthreatened after years of middling performance, the Giants invited the Yankees and their loyal rowdies to descend to the Polo Grounds as their tenant in 1913. Rebuilt in the municipal-philanthropic grandeur of the City Beautiful movement characteristic of the Progressive Era, the Polo Grounds once again housed both an underdog team for the underclass, and a championship squad for the elite. This class contradiction, just as it had two decades prior, would take only a few years to explode.

Around the time of the Yankees' move to the Polo Grounds, Tammany quietly seized New York's third team as well.

Brooklyn had been known as the "City of Churches," a conservative rural expanse dominated by WASPs. After reluctant incorporation into godless New York City at the turn of the century, Brooklyn's population boomed from the overflow of immigrant workers crowded-out from Manhattan's dense tenements. A tangle of commuter rails transported workers on ever-longer and more cramped commutes to the industrial centers of the riverfront and Manhattan, causing an epidemic of brutal deaths for those not swift enough to avoid the oncoming iron behemoths. The Brooklyn team earned a new and lasting nickname from this added danger of proletarian life—the Trolley Dodgers.

Although the Manhattan machine had seized its municipal autonomy, proud Brooklynites still hoped their mere borough could one day surpass its towering neighbor. Among them was Charles Ebbets, who worked his way up from Bridegrooms ticket-taker to Dodger ownership motivated by making Brooklyn's NL team the Giants' perennial rival.

Adapting the "syndicate ball" of buying up and consolidating failing teams pioneered by his predecessors Byrne, Day, Mutrie, and Freedman, Ebbets assembled winning Dodger teams until his stars' defection to the AL in 1902. Hoping a capacious new ballpark could make them financially competitive again, he applied the same strategy to real estate, covertly buying plots of an immigrant slum in Flatbush called

"Pigtown" through shell companies. Once the last parcel was acquired, he revealed his stunning designs for a ballpark more modern than the Polo Grounds—an art-deco facade leading to a double-decker covered grandstand, supported by Roman columns, towering over a marble rotunda, lit by a custom baseball-themed brass chandelier.[52]

But when it came time to break ground, Ebbets ran into the same obstacle that Johnson had a decade prior. The only way for construction to begin was to cut a deal with the Brooklyn Trust Company, a Tammany bank. Reluctantly, he handed over half of team ownership to get the park built.

The machine stayed a silent partner as Ebbets remained in charge of the club, which would play the rest of its years in Brooklyn at the park bearing his name. Sepia-toned photos of the first game at Ebbets Field, an exhibition against the Yankees in 1913, show thirty thousand gruff white faces above starched white shirts, women dressed in elaborate church hats and finery, and some children in Victorian school caps. As the working-class districts of Manhattan rapidly spilled over into vast Brooklyn, subsequent snapshots reveal Ebbets filling with riverfront laborers in blue khakis and flat caps, with the poorest perched in Bedford Avenue's outfield trees for a free glimpse into the melting pot.

The park's infamously close quarters encouraged raucous shouting matches between fans of different ages, origins, and walks of life. These conversations carried over to saloons, stoops, and stickball games, and merged into a common dialect of Brooklynese, an English patois inflected by Yiddish, Italian, Gaelic, and baseball idiom. Like the mostly uncompetitive team, the dialect became a national joke. A Broadway or Radio City comedian had only to utter *youse guys* to slip into the recognizable caricature, an act translated to the ballpark by workers imitating the German foremen who admonished them as *bummlers* (loafers) by jeering *ya bum ya!* at the greatest athletes alive.

This was an American dream of classless community, where labor was play, and the highest value produced was collective pride. "Until stadium lights made night baseball possible, the only way for the stands to be filled was with people who were skipping work or school," Brooklyn taxi driver John Garvey recalled. "Baseball was, for many years, the place where the refusal of work went to enjoy itself."[53]

Under Tammany's oversight, New York baseball was highly profitable, but the working-class rowdiness of Dodgers and Yankees fans the populists encouraged could only be tolerated by Czar Johnson for so long.

At a 1912 game, Johnson watched a Yankees fan berate Detroit star Ty Cobb with racial slurs, prompting the Tiger to leap into the stands toward the man, who had lost both of his hands to a printing press, knock him down, and stomp on his head with his spiked cleats. When a horrified Johnson suspended Cobb, AL rosters rallied to his defense. Many of the players had bought into Johnson's law-and-order patriotism, but the indignity of tolerating heckling fans broke their patience. A league-wide strike was threatened, and Cobb's punishment was reversed.

The greatest victory the players had seen since the Brotherhood came as American labor returned to nationwide strength. The Lawrence textile strike, the Triangle Shirtwaist Factory disaster, the Paterson silk strike, and the Ludlow massacre against miners swelled the ranks of the anarchist and socialist-influenced Industrial Workers of the World (IWW) and the stridently apolitical American Federation of Labor (AFL) into the millions. Following the trend, ex-Yankee Dave Fultz, veteran of the turn-of-the-century union exploited by Johnson, organized the revolt against Cobb's suspension into the Players' Fraternity (PF)—the third attempt at a players' union dedicated to overturning the reserve clause and restoring player control to baseball.

For its first few years, the PF, like the Brotherhood before it, sought respectability by declining direct affiliation with either wing of the labor movement. This mattered little to Johnson, who refused all negotiation with the organization. The emergence of a new circuit in 1914, the Federal League (FL), gave the Fraternity some leverage with renewed threats of defection. Johnson promised lifetime bans for any such transgression, now claiming the NL and AL deserved their immutable monopoly on baseball labor. Fultz and the FL sued organized baseball for this clear violation of antitrust law, and seemed confident about their odds as the case made its way to the court of the Roosevelt-appointed trust-busting federal judge Kenesaw Mountain Landis.

Landis, however, had a soft spot for Johnson's vision of America's pastime. He agreed that organized baseball was an ideal American institution—a collective of small businesses, dedicated to the public good, that must be shielded from the incursions of big capitalist combines and union anarchy. Unable to honestly rule against the FL, however, Landis declined to issue his decision for as long as possible. The Federal League died during the delay in 1916.

With nowhere to run, the Fraternity took a more militant stance. Players were instructed to refuse to sign their contracts, not report the next season, and halt major-league play for as long as it took to win power within its now judicially protected monopoly. This *general strike* tactic, popularly advocated in the US by the IWW, would topple one czar in 1917—just not the one running organized baseball.

Radicalized by the senseless imperial war in Europe, Russian soldiers deserted by the thousands in February 1917, joining industrial strikers and women rioting for bread in the cities until the aristocracy crumbled. The Russian Revolution scrambled the international balance of power, freeing German soldiers to march toward the United States' Western-imperial allies. Mobilization began as Opening Day approached, spreading a jingoistic war fever that viewed the workers' movement as defeatists aligned with Lenin and Trotsky. Flaming the "Red Scare," Judge Landis locked up over a hundred organizers of the IWW for opposing the war—an opening salvo to years of nationwide raids on union offices and deportations of foreign-born organizers.

Already labeled an "outlaw baseball anarchist" in the press, Fultz, fearing any allegiance with the antiwar IWW, turned to the more respectable American Federation of Labor for support.[54] The AFL signaled support of the ballplayers only a year prior, but the patriotic craft union declined to take action against America's game during wartime. The strike was called off, the Players' Fraternity dissolved, and Fultz enlisted in the army.

With the workers in retreat, capitalists tightened the screws on labor in mines, factories, and ballfields alike. At Comiskey Park, not far from Landis's Chicago courtroom, players on the Cubs and Red Sox, insulted by postseason pay cuts, refused to emerge from their clubhouse to play the 1918 World Series. Johnson went to negotiate, telling the players, including Boston's star pitchers Babe Ruth and Carl Mays, that their wildcat action insulted the boys fighting in France—to no avail. Only when fans started heckling the strikers as *Bolsheviki* and *traitors* did they finally take the field.[55]

While the Red Scare decisively crushed the organized player rebellion, small-scale resistance to organized baseball still brewed within the clubhouses in 1919.

White Sox owner Charles Comiskey, Johnson's most loyal lieutenant, informed his players that they were now responsible for their own laundry. They protested the additional pay cut by wearing dirty uniforms all season, earning them the nickname among fans and press as the "Black Sox."

The name took on its infamous meaning once eight players were revealed to have accepted bribes from bookies to throw the 1919 World Series. When the scandal broke in the press, Johnson charged that a shadowy cabal of New York gamblers had bought off the players as part of a broader effort to corrupt the game, and American society as a whole. The press backed him up, and the Black Sox were permanently blacklisted.

Another workplace action in Boston that season, however, proved a crisis that Johnson's reign would ultimately not survive. Red Sox stars Babe Ruth and Carl Mays, still fuming from their treatment in the previous World Series and by management in general, launched individual strikes against the reserve clause—Ruth by refusing to pitch in favor of switching to the outfield, and Mays by walking off the mound mid-game, refusing to play for the team ever again.

Johnson was powerless to penalize Ruth's disobedience as he turned from one of the game's greatest pitchers to its greatest hitter—slugging more home runs than anyone before as an everyday player. Mays's desertion, too, proved difficult to remedy. The Red Sox owner, New York Broadway magnate Harry Frazee, pleaded with Johnson to let him trade Mays to the Yankees, whose new beer-baron owner, Jacob Ruppert, desperately needed to make the team competitive with Prohibition on the horizon. Johnson refused—not only would the transfer reward player indiscipline, but he saw the New York–based affinity between Frazee and Ruppert as an extension of the conspiracy to destroy America via its beloved pastime.

The Czar's paranoia only deepened when a Tammany-aligned New York Supreme Court judge permitted Frazee to trade Mays, a precedent that green-lit the sale of Ruth to the Yankees after the season. Bent on crushing the Red Sox-Yankees alliance—dubbed by the press the *Insurrectos* in reference to the anti-imperialist revolts spreading across the peripheries of America's globalizing empire—Johnson conspired with Giants owner Charles Stoneham to evict the Yankees from the Polo Grounds, and expel them from the sport entirely.

The greatness of Mays and Ruth in pinstripes made the scheme impossible. Mays won twenty-six games in 1920, and the bizarre dimensions of the Polo Grounds, with its home-run-friendly "short porch" in right field, built by the Players' League Giants to encourage high-scoring games thirty years prior, seemingly designed exactly for Ruth. He shattered his previous-season's all-time home run record with an incredible 54.

At last, baseball had its own climactic, stylish, game-stopping play like a goal in soccer or hockey; a touchdown in football; or, decades later, the slam dunk in basketball. New multitudes of Yankees fans even cheered Ruth's misses, Stout wrote: "He didn't give a damn if he struck out, and neither did the fans. The next best thing to seeing Ruth strike out was to see him swing and miss, his body twisting and sometimes falling to the ground as a collective 'aah' spread through the stands."[56]

The Yankees became easily the top-drawing team in New York that year—beating their grounds-mate Giants by 360,000 fans. Now wealthy and unevictable, Ruppert loaned Frazee the cash to buy Fenway Park as a backup field to protect both Insurrecto teams from elimination.

The Ruthian revolution continued to spread in 1921. Ballparks filled wherever the Yankees played as Ruth batted .378 and shattered his home run record again with an unimaginable 59. Only one other *team* had ever hit so many in a season pre-Ruth.

The shift in baseball's fan demographic from gentlemanly middle-class to home-run-happy workers and lumpenproletariat spread to Yankees games nationwide. German, Irish, and Italian immigrants flocked to see Ruth, the brawling, boozing, and promiscuous product of a Baltimore Catholic reform school, raised in the intense poverty of the 1890s speaking Pennsylvania Dutch. There was also a significant influx of Black fans to see Ruth: Harlem's new residents fleeing the poverty and Klan terror of the South. It was no coincidence, rumors among them went, that the player from the northeast's Blackest city, whose reform school nickname was "Niggerlips," and whom opponents sought to drive out of the game on the basis of his alleged Black ancestry, played the game with power, grace, and ingenuity unmatched by any white player before him or since.

The diverse happenings at the Yankees' Polo Grounds games, Johnson's cronies began to argue, was further proof of a Judeo-Bolshevik conspiracy. These lies, revived in the "Curse of the Bambino" myth after the Red Sox 1986 World Series loss to the Mets, were traced by Glenn Stout to a series of columns run in the *Dearborn Independent* titled "The Peril of Baseball—'Too Much Jew.'" Frazee, as a New York cosmopolitan, was secretly a Jew, the Henry Ford–owned paper alleged. And as a Jew, he had obviously plotted with a shadowy racketeering network, led by a Jewish-controlled faction of Tammany Hall and gangster Arnold Rothstein, to fix the 1919 World Series. Not content with mere enrichment, the cabal's alleged alliance with the Bolsheviks and the IWW sought nothing less than the destruction of white supremacy through its greatest achievements—America, capitalism, and baseball.[57] The vulgarity of Ruth's home runs, and the unrespectable types they attracted, was a clear extension of this scheme.

Johnson's anti-Semitic campaign mirrored the rise of the Klan to mass movement in the twenties, and the widespread eugenic theories that sought to purify the American race. Columbia University researchers insisted in *Popular Science Monthly,* for instance, that the Bambino's numbers were the result of a genetic superiority in vision, hearing, and nerves.[58] Ruth consistently rejected both narratives in populist style, defiantly befriending Black and Jewish ballplayers and entertainers, and deflecting any claims he was some sort of Übermensch by consistently asserting that "few great batters are born, the rest are made. There is absolutely no scientific reason why every ball player shouldn't be a good hitter."[59]

Ruth's populism soon defeated Czar Johnson, just as the Russian czar's *Protocols of the Elders of Zion* forgery was ultimately rejected by the Russian Revolution. The Yankee insurrection had made them baseball's most profitable franchise, with other AL teams ditching nineteenth-century small ball to encourage its players to attract Ruth's demographic by swinging for the fences. At the end of the 1920 season, owners across leagues punished Johnson's failed counterinsurgency by installing a new nonowner commissioner to more effectively manage their factional disputes, protect their legal monopoly, and control their players. Their choice was the judge who had neutralized Fultz's Fraternity and the IWW—Kenesaw Mountain Landis.

As Landis unified the owners and asserted himself as a new strongman against the players, the Ruthian revolution continued below. The Yankees captured their first pennant in 1921, at last facing the Giants for an all-NYC World Series. Gate receipts neared $1 million as each game was completely sold out, many to speculators who resold those tickets for an unprecedented ten dollars. Before the broadcast era, an overflow of ten thousand fans packed Madison Square Garden for each game to watch a scoreboard representing the plays sent downtown via telegraph. While the Giants triumphed, there was no doubt which side New Yorkers were on. The Yankees were baseball's new *people's team.*

After the 1921 World Series, Ruth embarked on a barnstorming tour—a prohibited practice of paid exhibition games through small-town America, often scandalously played against Black teams. Landis demanded the tour be canceled, but Ruth defied threats of suspension by invoking his right as a worker to make money however he pleased. A new players' union emerged to defend Ruth, who began musing about quitting the Yankees to start a renegade player-run team. But once again, Ruth was derided in the press as a greedy communist aligned with the blacklisted Black Sox who were connected to the new initiative, so he took a payout from his Yankees bosses to end the tour.

With labor peace and their most profitable asset secured, the Yankees began construction of a massive new ballpark in the South Bronx. Visible from miles away, Yankee Stadium would be an ageless Greco-Roman pantheon built from Thomas Edison's marble-like Portland concrete, dwarfing the municipal chintz of the Giants' sunken Polo Grounds directly across the Harlem River.

Workers filled the neoclassical palace for its inaugural 1923 season, its three copper-frieze adorned tiers seating fifty-eight thousand fans—a number that often pushed upward to seventy thousand. The stadium's outfield walls replicated the Polo Ground's Ruth-friendly distances, and New Yorker teammates like slugger Lou Gehrig and ace Waite Hoyt learned to hit and pitch to its unique dimensions for further advantage. These stars, and their continued identification with the city and common people everywhere, transformed baseball into a populist mass spectacle surpassing Broadway and equalling Hollywood. Only mass gatherings during major moments of labor unrest had convened so many workers together to cheer for the heroes of their class.

Although Ruth had ended a decade of labor unrest by siding with his bosses in the moment when organized baseball was most vulnerable to a new players' revolt, his about-face only deepened his all-American appeal.

He was loved for being a common man, who drank, fucked, and loved baseball—a hero of a working class, who, retaining a healthy skepticism of official representatives in the labor movement, was happy to share a now-illicit beer with coworkers and management alike. While America would never have a political Lenin, Ruth served as his athletic equivalent.

The Yankees went on to triumph over the Giants in the World Series that year—the first of twenty-seven championships, leading all American sports franchises. Outdrawn and overshadowed by Yankee Stadium, the Giants and Dodgers ceased winning pennants after the next season, supplanted by a new National League dynasty in St. Louis built by Cardinals manager, ex-Yankee catcher, and future architect of baseball integration and the 1962 Mets, Branch Rickey.

When Rickey took over the Cardinals in 1917, they were a low-drawing, mediocre franchise identifiable only by their uniforms' esoteric shade of red. With a conservatism equal to Johnson, his religious passion for baseball rebranded the team around the songbird, inspired by an image of the Holy Spirit that appeared to him in a Missouri church. The Cardinals would win nine pennants and four championships in his two decades at the helm.

The Cardinals' transfiguration, however, was less the result of divine intervention than Rickey's recognition that Ruthian prowess came from training as much as talent. Applying that principle to a ruthless modern adaptation of the "syndicate ball" pioneered by Mutrie, Day, Freedman, and Ebbets, Rickey broke ground on baseball's first *farm system*.

Taking advantage of the post–World War I economic slowdown, Rickey bought up failing semipro circuits in Texas, where thousands of unemployed youths were eager to accept meager bonuses and poverty wages in exchange for professional coaching and dreams of a big-league career. The method of scouts scouring the country for the rare, largely self-trained, and potentially freethinking "arm-behind-the-barn" talent, like pro-labor stars Honus Wagner and Babe Ruth, was replaced by "signing players cheaply," Rickey said, and watching them "ripen into money."[60]

With unmatched revenue from annual success at their ballpark, the Yankees became the top buyer of the Cardinals' excess players. The crop fueled a virtuous cycle: Pennant races and championships kept massive Yankee Stadium full, with profits poured into acquiring better players in the offseason, which led to more championships. Between 1923 and 1930 the Yankees generated $2.6 million in profit.[61]

Ruth's Yankees became the definitive phenomenon of Roaring Twenties optimism. America's rapid economic recovery and stock-market boom appeared equally unstoppable. Small-scale manufacturing and agriculture consolidated, with Henry Ford's assembly-line method positioning workers like ballplayers to increase productivity fivefold. Cars and consumer goods became affordable to the average worker, who now lived in electrified homes with radios that began to feature broadcasts of major-league games. Cities became the new population centers of a country that was once mostly rural, with Manhattan surpassing London to become the world's largest metropolis—a futuristic city of elevated trains, highways, monumental skyscrapers, and beautiful baseball stadia.[62]

Wall Street's mystical faith that America was entering a utopian phase of prosperity for all trickled down to the working class in the Roaring Twenties. Political conflicts sparked by turn-of-the-century urbanization now appeared solved. Strikes dropped 80 percent, representing industrial workers' "apparent satisfaction," labor historian Robert H. Zieger wrote, with "the ability of commercial corporatism to provide not only basic necessities but an expanding array of entertaining, even liberating, artifacts and opportunities [that] threatened to turn unions into musty anachronisms."[63]

A few decades prior, Friedrich Engels had commented on this idiosyncratic, apolitical, and endlessly optimistic character of Americans in a letter to a German comrade preparing for a mission to New York to organize workers in Ruppert's breweries.[64] The pure bourgeois origins of the United States, he warned, had imbued its working class with what he elsewhere described as "backwardness of thought"—a belief that Manifest Destiny and unfettered economic development would raise the entirety of its deserving ranks to the middle class.[65,66] The polemic held decades later, as the US achieved no equivalent to the worker uprisings of Russia, Germany, Egypt, Italy, or Mexico, and no mass labor parties or militant unions with the power to demand a social safety net for food, healthcare, or housing in exchange for temporary peace between the classes.

Seizing on the quietude, bosses increased wages just 1 percent as productivity skyrocketed. The conservative Supreme Court upheld verdicts against Black and leftist organizers, ruled picketing illegal, and overturned laws passed for the eight-hour day, minimum wage for women, and regulations on child labor.

But as the boom continued, speculation on future growth made American capitalism appear as omnipotent and clairvoyant as Ruth. One story held that during a critical late-career World Series at bat at Wrigley Field, Ruth, angered by the racist heckles of his Cubbie opponents, pointed to center field before hitting a home run precisely to that spot.

As with all other legends of his supernatural powers, Ruth dismissed the called-shot story as pure fantasy: "I never knew anybody could tell you ahead of time where he was going to hit a baseball. When I get to be that kind of fool, they'll put me in the booby hatch."[67] Wall Street and the American capitalist class, however, knew no such humility.

Chapter 3

BUMS

In the same letter where Friedrich Engels complained of Yankee workers' Ruthian optimism and political backwardness, he predicted Americans would, at some point, make up for lost time: "Once the Americans get started, it will be with an energy and volume compared with which we in Europe shall be mere children."[68]

Remarkably, the peak of this offensive would begin, in stereotypically American fashion, on a baseball diamond.

The economic boom and its roar of optimism peaked in the final months of 1929, bursting the market bubble and sending stocks plunging. Americans murmured ominously as they shuffled off the field of fantasy into the bitter reality of the Great Depression. The company unions and boss-granted benefits on which many had relied disappeared overnight as factories were shuttered, mortgages failed, and farms went broke. The homeless population climbed into the millions. In New York, where the poverty pandemic began on Wall Street, the unemployed sold apples on every street corner in a desperate attempt to survive.

Within a couple years of the crisis, the bums began to organize. Itinerant worker hobos, the unemployed, and veterans awaiting their service bonuses organized to march on government buildings demanding work, food, shelter, and benefits. The Communist Party organized thousands of them into Unemployment Councils, based on the strategies of the IWW and the Bolsheviks in the late 1910s. They took their tent-encampment *Hoovervilles* to DC, forcing President Hoover himself to disperse them with military force. A wave of militant strikes followed, filling the ranks of the American Federation of Labor (AFL). New York Democrat Franklin Delano Roosevelt was catapulted to the presidency, with the ongoing worker unrest pushing him to establish welfare, work programs, and legislation guaranteeing the right to unionize.

In the spring of 1936, an even more massive strike wave began during a semipro ballgame in Akron, Ohio. The teams were composed of workers from two local rubber factories who had enthusiastically supported Roosevelt and joined the AFL. But they quickly became disillusioned with the union's role as impartial mediators with capital. Bureaucratic conciliations had sped up factory lines, making their jobs exponentially more dangerous, disciplined, and exhausting. "We used to work eight hours and feel fine when the quitting whistle blew," one Akron worker complained. "Now we work six hours and are dead-tired."[69]

When the workers took the field that day, they discovered the assigned umpire was a coworker widely despised for siding with their bosses. The crowd sarcastically cheered for the AFL and Roosevelt as players sat down on the field in protest, refusing to play until the umpire was switched out for someone from their ranks.[70]

Shortly afterward, a dispute broke out at one of their factories between a supervisor and a dozen workers who had attended the game. Knowing their union would be of no help, and feeling empowered by their victory on the field, they sat down on the factory floor as the players had on the diamond. "There was much laughter through the works," wrote labor historian Louis Adamic. "'Oh boy, oh boy! Just like at the ball game, no kiddin'."

Every minute the workers sat cost the company hundreds of dollars, and within an hour, Adamic wrote, "the dispute was settled—full victory for the men!"[71]

Brilliant in its simplicity, the novel tactic Akron workers called the "sit-down strike" spread through the region, and then the country. Instead of leaving the factory en masse, a small group could effectively hold the machines hostage, giving them a chance to talk, share grievances, strategize, and organize their rank-and-file committees until their demands were inevitably met. Freed of the top-down mediations of the AFL, the workers were now able to fight not only about survival issues like wages and hours, but for democratic workplaces and unions that recognized the value of after-work "pastimes" as the source of a meaningful and dignified life.

A new radical mass union formed from the alliance of the sit-down committees and Communist-affiliated immigrant-worker organizations, the Congress of Industrial Organizations (CIO). Boasting over four million members, it was twenty-six times larger than the IWW had been at its 1917 peak, and replaced the protectionist craft unionism of the AFL with a broader industrial unionism crossing professional and cultural divides. "It is a people's movement," CIO literature proclaimed. "It does not ask questions of race or color or creed or origin."[72]

The movement reframed the American dream as now achievable through solidarity instead of individualist rank climbing. America's pastime, too, was a central reference point. New York organizer Jack Kroll encouraged CIO members to "talk politics with our neighbors just as we discuss the latest news or baseball scores."[73] An antidiscrimination pamphlet assured white workers that their Black colleagues were much like them—working each day for secure food and shelter for their families, with enough left over to "make a contribution to the Church . . . go to a movie, or to a baseball game."[74]

Engels' prophecy had been fulfilled not a moment too soon for American radicals who sought to align the United States with the Soviet Union as fascism spread across Europe. The Communist Party became baseball-loving patriots almost overnight, campaigning for FDR's reelection under the slogan "Communism is Twentieth Century Americanism," and adding a sports section to their *Daily Worker* newspaper in 1935.

Section editor and Dodgers fanatic Lester Rodney had fought the party's aversion to sports as a distraction to class struggle for years. He had noticed many workers and youth only bought papers to read coverage of their favorite teams, and sought to connect labor's momentum with the day-to-day developments in the standings and stands alike. "Are these 'bad elements'?" Rodney wrote in one column defending the sports obsession of the rowdy Ebbets crowd to skeptical readership. "Many are workers who have so identified themselves with their team that they cannot sleep or eat when the team loses. The leanness of American life under capitalism drives them to this fever."[75]

When it came to the players, however, organizers found the seismic shift had left baseball's labor relations remarkably intact. Many veteran athletes considered themselves lucky to collect a stable paycheck as they watched crowds dwindle during the Depression. And those who might have wanted to seize the class militancy spreading across the industrialized North found that most of their younger teammates were conservative Southerners who believed unions and the New Deal were communist plots to destroy America.

The prevalence of this reactionary demographic and attitude among players in the thirties was another product of Branch Rickey's farm system. The modern method of player development had trained prospects in not only pitching, fielding, and hitting but in the ideology of the owners, as well. Organized baseball's blatantly illegal business model should be protected from all antitrust and labor law, Rickey often evangelized, because it was America's secular church, gathering the communal spirit of many faiths and creeds for a common patriotic goal. Although it was a collective effort, the success of a team was powered by the entrepreneurial determination of individual players, honed by the civic-minded owners who gifted the game to the people by the thousands in their grand cathedrals. Because the constitution banned the United States from selecting an official religion, he argued, it must protect baseball instead.

Players were promoted both for their skill and their obedience to this dogma. The indoctrination system transformed the Cardinals into the most stridently conservative franchise in the thirties, and a similar transformation was underway in the Bronx. In 1932, the Ruth-rich Yankees hired the equally conservative Connecticuter scout George Weiss to adapt and improve upon Rickey's model to cement their status as America's premier sporting franchise. Weiss developed the "Yankee mold"—training players from youth to play to the unique dimensions of the "House that Ruth Built," while replacing Ruth's proletarian charm with genteel pretension, superiority, serious competitiveness, clean grooming, and a prohibition on cursing, intoxication, and any whiff of Black culture. This image, Weiss's biographers Burton and Benita Boxerman wrote, became as "important to the club as their logo and pinstripes."[76]

After four years of decline at the end of the Ruth era, the elite people's team of the twenties reemerged in 1936 with a new crop of players, forged in the conservative mold, as the *team of the elite.* When the Giants faced the Yankees in the World Series that year, Lester Rodney's *Daily Worker* headline sided with the once Gilded Age Manhattan team: *Giants Power Threatens Yankees.*[77]

The Dodgers meanwhile had become a distant afterthought to the drama in Manhattan and the Bronx. The Depression had hit Brooklyn hardest, with an emptied Ebbets Field reduced to the status of the Hooverville shantytowns lining the shuttered worksites along the East River. Its team, too, appeared so much like hapless hobos that they were colloquially derided during the Depression with the Brooklynese slur *Dem Bums.*

Continued bumbling sank the franchise into such infamy during the late thirties' New Deal–fueled economic recovery that away-game attendance tanked everywhere they trainhopped. Since the death of Charles Ebbets in 1925, ownership had been divided between two feuding groups—his Brooklynite heirs and the Tammany bank that owned their park. The paralyzing stalemate gave way as the struggling Ebbets family went into debt during the Depression, and the bank, which used its extensive political, financial, and real-estate network to make fortunes on such foreclosures, took full control of the franchise.

In 1938, Branch Rickey's protégé, Larry MacPhail, was hired to modernize the Dodgers as Weiss had done for the Yankees. Wacky manager Casey Stengel was swiftly replaced with the hard-boiled Cardinal Leo

Durocher, and Tammany funds, greatly expanded thanks to New Deal projects built on their expanded real estate holdings, poured in to formalize the Dodgers' first farm system.

But unlike Yankee Weiss, MacPhail's rebuild did not seek bygone bourgeois respectability. He instead branded the Dodgers explicitly as a product of the New Deal—an outstretched hand to their working-class crowd, described by historian Carl Prince as including "Jews committed to socialist labor-oriented Zionism and trade unionism; radicalized Italian families militantly pro-union, many still mourning the injustice done [to the anarchists] Sacco and Vanzetti a generation before."[78] Ebbets Field was updated with expanded seats, a colorful new paint job, and lighting so jobbers could attend night games. The humorous DIY band of fans calling themselves the *Sym-Phony* was supplemented with the innovation of a baseball organist trolling umpires with "Three Blind Mice" after questionable calls. A barely cogent Babe Ruth was hired as third-base coach, and, in another sign of the consumer base the team hoped to attract, the Depression-era uniform experiments with green and red were ditched for a workman-blue collar and cap in 1939.

Most significantly, the Dodgers' subculture was for the first time expanded past the boundaries of Brooklyn by broadcasting games on the radio. Fearing a reduction in ticket sales, the other New York teams had resisted consistent broadcasts, but MacPhail had seen the magic of sportscaster Red Barber in Cincinnati and thought his innovative turns of phrase and neologisms would blend well with Brooklynese. New Dodgers fans sprung up in isolation around the hundred-mile broadcast range of WHN 1050 AM, a station previously known for its community-oriented programming and nighttime jazz. Joel Oppenheimer of Yonkers, a Westchester County city bordering the Bronx's northern edge, recalled: "I mean, here I was a Dodger fan in a town full of Yankees and Giants rooters. A Royal Crown drinker in a town full of Pepsi and Coke drinkers. A guy who was interested in poems in a town full of louts. . . . It was the loner's way of going against the tide."[79]

The subcultural fandom merged with the resurgent labor movement and the hegemonic radicalism of Brooklyn's working-class immigrant enclaves to make the ascendant Dodgers baseball's most proletarian-coded team. The militant IWW, in the years before being crushed by baseball's Commissioner Landis, had championed the itinerant hobo as a proletarian icon—and now Dodgers fans did the same with the Brooklynese-spouting bum. The caricature parodied by radio comedians as a shorthand for mocking the Depression's dispossessed became the team's mascot in an era before mascots—a similarly ironic figure, Mr. Met, was introduced as baseball's first in 1964.

Connecting the poverty around the stadium to the bottom-barrel franchise, *New York World-Telegram* political cartoonist Willard Mullin first portrayed the Dodgers as this grotesque hobo, his obese face blackened by soot and stubble. "The 'Bum' was never meant to denigrate the lowly," Prince wrote. "It represented at heart a lingering Depression mentality that exalted the virtue that it wasn't what you had that mattered, but how you looked at things. In this way, it was a Dodger-focused, widely understood symbol of working-class pride."[80]

The Bum was drawn digging through their trash for up-and-coming stars, and, as they climbed to third in 1939 and second in 1940, crashing the upscale smoking room of baseball's elite exclaiming, *Oh—excuse me! I musta got inta th' wrong jernt!*

The next season, the Dodgers thumbed their way past Rickey's Cardinals to top the National League for the first time in twenty-one years. Brooklyn celebrated the pennant as if they had won a war of independence. A sixty-thousand-strong parade at Grand Army Plaza celebrated the "miracle Dodgers"—a mass of self-described *bums* united under a *Daily Worker*–esque banner: "Murder the Yanks."[81]

After splitting the first two World Series games, Joe DiMaggio, an immigrant-son and heir of the Gehrig and Ruth dynasty, broke a shutout in the eighth inning of game three to put the Yankees back on top. In game four, Dodgers catcher Mickey Owen dropped the final strike of the game, allowing a four-run rally. The demoralization continued into game five, in which the Yankees took the winning lead on another wild pitch. Unfazed by the Dodgers' inability to move beyond their daffy past, the battalion of bums issued their perennial threat that the underdogs would soon have their day: *Wait 'til next year.*

In St. Louis, Rickey observed the rapid rise of blue-collar Brooklyn with a mix of admiration and envy. His farm system had made the Cardinals into the NL's first dynasty, but now the model was generalizing throughout baseball, tightening the labor market's widened net. He now felt trapped by the conservatism of his invention—the strident segregation of the Southern system only further tangling the market's worst snag: the exclusion of Black athletes.

While insiders knew the claim that Black players couldn't compete with whites was a myth—Negro League stars like Josh Gibson and Satchel Paige excelled in barnstorming games—the real reason for the prohibition's unchallenged continuity was deeper. The racial division of labor allowed bosses to exploit Black workers in dangerous and intensive industries like steel, auto manufacturing, meatpacking, and mining to a degree organized white workers would not accept for themselves. While the sports industry reaped only small profits from the rent low-waged Black teams paid to play in their ballparks, it was essential for the overall economic stability of the country that they preserve an unchallenged image of white supremacy. A parallel example could be seen in the film industry, where Black actors like Hattie McDaniel were primarily given roles as obsequious servants, like in 1939's *Gone with the Wind.* If Black entertainers and athletes took lead roles, the bourgeoisie feared, it might inspire demands for equality in workplaces nationwide, upending the economic order of race and class.

Such events were underway in New York, where many of the millions of Black Southerners fleeing racial terror and seeking work had moved to neighborhoods surrounding the Polo Grounds and Ebbets Field. Many found jobs in integrated shops where the CIO grew stronger each year, with others rallying militant boycotts and marches in Harlem for equal opportunities in housing and hiring.

One faction of this movement took the fight to sports. A coalition of sportswriters from Black newspapers like Joe Bostic of *People's Voice* and Communists like Rodney at the *Daily Worker* lobbied the white press to publish statistics of Black leagues, and for major-league teams to give Black players tryouts. Fearing labor and racial unrest from fans and players, the magnates were committed to resisting these demands for as long as they could.

Agreeing that baseball was far too "profound" for communists to understand, it was only Rickey who had the guile to devise a plan that would integrate the game without challenging the entirety of America's racial hierarchy.[82] He essentially agreed with the CIO's view that workplace integration would improve society by deepening the labor pool while depleting white America's fear of Black revolt. Racism could thus be solved through "American methods" instead of class struggle. If he could develop a few model Black ballplayers, as talented as they were respectable non-agitators, the net would unfurl, and Rickey would haul the first catch.

"You have two years to stay ahead of your competition when you come up with a new idea in baseball," Rickey often said.[83] But the plan would never fly in Jim Crow St. Louis, where any talk of integration was a cardinal sin. He instead turned his attention to the heart of the melting pot—Brooklyn—where he had a standing offer to become president of the Brooklyn Dodgers.

MacPhail's free-rein experimentation had earned a passionate, diverse community that reveled in novelty and dreamed of escaping the shadow of the Giants and Yankees. Their leftism, too, was a plus—more than any other team, Brooklyn fans were cognizant of the fascist turn in Europe, and believed the advance of an antiracist labor movement its patriotic antidote. The postwar order would have to wrestle with the competing visions of a segregated America's liberal democracy against egalitarian Communist dictatorship. By breaking the color barrier, he would prove the virtue of American capitalism by creating a new *people's team* to restore the pre-Depression, class-blind American dream.

Shortly after the 1942 season, Japan bombed the US Navy at Pearl Harbor, Hitler declared war on the United States, and the global war on fascism arrived. MacPhail enlisted, and Rickey took over his Montague Street office as the Dodgers' new president. He immediately cut aging veterans from the payroll, with that money steered toward army-like recruitment ads in boys' magazines inviting those too young for the draft to attend nationwide Dodgers tryout camps. For the first time, this recruitment drive extended to Latin America, the Negro Leagues, and even Japanese internment camps. "If we win the war," he explained to Dodgers trustee George McLaughlin, "it will be worth it. If we lose the war, what difference does it make?"[84]

The federal government pursued the same strategy in 1941. The Harlem boycott struggle threatened to build to a national scale when union leader A. Philip Randolph called for a March on Washington demanding the federal government open defense industry jobs to African Americans in 1941. With the government desperate for wartime labor, Randolph's demands were met, and the march was averted.

The next year, organized baseball appeared to be headed toward similar concessions when the White Sox and Pirates finally allowed tryouts for a handful of Black players. Among them was twenty-three-year-old Jack Roosevelt Robinson. He was the son of sharecroppers from Georgia, whose older brother, Mack, had competed in the 1936 Berlin Olympics alongside Jesse Owens and made the Black world proud by outpacing Hitler's Aryan dashers. At UCLA, Jackie excelled in collegiate football, basketball, swimming, tennis, track, and golf. "He's worth $50,000 of anybody's money," White Sox manager Jimmy Dykes admitted after seeing his performance. "He stole everything but my infielders' gloves."[85]

That Robinson and the others seen that day ended up unsigned was largely due to the Communists' role in the effort, but also because the tryouts were "a charade," Robert Burk wrote, "to reject them on dubious grounds that they simply did not measure up to white standards."[86]

Robinson was called up to the army days after his tryout. He further proved his baseball skills by playing in a training-camp exhibition game between Negro Leaguers and white major-league draftees. Shortly after, he became among the first Black soldiers to publicly protest segregated conditions by refusing an order to sit in the back of an army bus. Covered by the integrationist press, the action and subsequent court-martial made him a household name in Black America. "I had learned that I was in two wars," he told the largest Black daily newspaper in the country, the *Pittsburgh Courier*, "one against a foreign enemy, the other against prejudice at home."[87]

To sell the war effort to African Americans, the *Courier* expanded Robinson's concept of "two wars" into the promise of a "Double Victory"—the defeat of fascism worldwide would mean the end of racism in the United States. But as the first Black soldiers returned, they found their status as second-class citizens had not changed. War veteran Robert Bandy, for instance, was shot by a white police officer in a Harlem hotel in 1943 after he witnessed the officer roughing up a Black woman in the lobby. Hours of rioting followed, with shops that price gouged and refused to hire Black people its main targets.

New York City's government hopped on the integrationist trend to quell the unrest. Communist city council members Peter V. Cacchione of Brooklyn and Benjamin Davis of Harlem pushed a resolution demanding baseball's integration and picketed the major-league parks with photos of Black soldiers killed or injured in combat holding signs reading: "GOOD ENOUGH TO DIE FOR THEIR COUNTRY BUT NOT GOOD ENOUGH TO PLAY ORGANIZED BASEBALL." New York's New Deal mayor Fiorello La Guardia supported parallel legislation promising penalties for bigoted employers, and formed a sports commission of the city's major-league owners to develop a plan for their compliance.

After buying into Dodgers ownership, Rickey enthusiastically joined La Guardia's commission, only to find little sincere interest among his fellow New York magnates. Giants owner Horace Stoneham and the Yankees' Del Webb—whose construction company had built one of the internment camps scouted by Rickey—both knew, so long as the committed segregationist Landis was commissioner, any contract for a Black player would be voided. But by joining the commission, they could demonstrate their commitment to antiracist legislation with confidence that nothing would actually change.

An identical feigned interest prevailed when baseball owners heard an appeal at their 1943 winter meetings from the foremost advocate of sports integration, Paul Robeson. The actor, singer, athlete, and outspoken leftist had smashed numerous color lines, including being the first Black All-American player for the Rutgers collegiate football team in 1915. Robeson continued breaking color barriers on the stage and screen into the forties, making him the most famous Black man in America, heroized then much like Jackie Robinson is today. Unable to deny Robeson's request to ask in person that they earnestly continue tryouts for Black players, they politely applauded his appeal, thanked him for coming, and ignored everything he had said.

Rickey navigated between conservative baseball owners and leftists like Robeson by allying with *Courier* editor Wendell Smith and other liberal integrationists. They produced a full theory of bourgeois integration drawn from sociologists Gunnar Myrdal and Frank Tannenbaum. Myrdal argued equality could be achieved by showing how segregation denied Blacks the "American creed" of opportunity. Rickey biographer Lee Lowenfish wrote that his copy of former IWW militant Tannenbaum's *Slave and Citizen*, filled with notes applying its conclusions to baseball, became "as valuable a source book in race relations as his black loose-leaf notebook of player information had been during his Cardinals days."[88]

Kenesaw Mountain Landis's death the next year provided the best opportunity yet for the experiment to begin. But Rickey knew that for the new commissioner to break tradition, he would have to offer up a Black player who could demonstrate he was not just a place-filler for the wartime labor shortage. The right man would be capable of playing on a major-league level, while maintaining a nonthreatening demeanor to white fans and owners—a family-oriented, non-drinking Christian, with the ability to "turn the other cheek" repeatedly after every inevitable slap of racism or professional disrespect. The candidate who best checked all the boxes was the honorably discharged Jackie Robinson, and after seeing his stunning athletic abilities firsthand at a tryout, Rickey invited Robinson to his office for a lengthy trial by fire. After three hours of simulated racial and physical abuse, Robinson passed Rickey's final test by proving he had "the courage *not to fight.*"

Robinson was signed to play for the Dodgers' Montreal affiliate for the 1946 season. Racism in the Northeast-based International League was less than what it would have been in the Southern circuits, although threats and heckles were common, as was the expectation from teammates that Black ballplayers were more entertainers than athletes. The Negro Leagues had been perceived as a quasi-minstrel show for its use of Harlem Globetrotters–like comic theatrics to attract a wide variety of fans. The Indianapolis team, for example, earnestly branded themselves the Clowns.

Once among white players, however, the reputed minstrelsy of Negro League play faded, and its brilliance became clear. The Black game, James S. Hirsch wrote, "placed greater emphasis on speed, creativity, and daring, for it was designed to explicitly entertain fans at a time when organized entertainment was limited."[89] Glenn Stout wrote of Robinson's use of these skills in his debut season: "Instead of waiting for something to happen, he made it happen himself by dropping a bunt, stealing a base, or testing an outfielder's arm as he stretched a single into a double." The well-worn lie that Blacks could not compete was definitively disproven as Negro League vet Don Newcombe, signed shortly after Robinson, posted 14 wins, 4 losses, and a 2.21 ERA that season, and Robinson's .349 batting average and 40 stolen bases made him the widely acknowledged best player in the minors.

But the owners' deeper concern that integration was a Trojan horse for labor militancy only became more salient in 1946. Baseball saw its first surge in labor organizing in over twenty years when a massive strike wave, fueled by ten million returning servicemen, spread through steel, auto, and meatpacking plants to show players how industry-wide action could result in major pay increases. With their wartime-frozen wages now below the average worker's, some defected to play in Mexico, while others joined Boston labor lawyer Robert Murphy's CIO-affiliated American Baseball Guild, demanding a minimum salary, arbitration, benefits, and an end to the reserve clause. The movement gained traction, particularly with Murphy's beloved Boston Braves, as well as the Pirates in Pittsburgh, where steelworker strikes had been strongest.

When owners refused to negotiate, Murphy called for the Pirates to strike on June 7. Fearing success, the commissioner sent an FBI agent to dissuade players. He promised that organized baseball would create a new labor committee, chaired by Larry MacPhail, at which they would have a seat at the table to draft a new standard contract. The players voted in favor of what Murphy called "the most barefaced attempt to form a company-dominated union that I have ever seen."[90]

A few minor concessions at the meeting on pay, pensions, and service time was enough to get even the most militant reps to drop the reserve-clause issue for the foreseeable future. Nor did the players voice dissent on the owners' near consensus on the "Negro Question" of elevating Robinson to the majors. Rickey's Montreal experiment was naive, the report found, and drummed up by the "social-minded" who "know little about baseball." Integration would kill the Negro Leagues, an important revenue stream for owners like MacPhail who rented out Yankee Stadium to the Black Yankees, with integration in the stands threatening even worse losses: "The preponderance of Negro attendance in parks such as the Yankee Stadium, the Polo Grounds, and Comiskey Park," MacPhail's report concluded, "could conceivably threaten the value of Major League franchises owned by these clubs."[91]

Because only Rickey had voted against MacPhail's findings, the magnates were confident new commissioner Happy Chandler would understand the report as a mandate to void the Black Dodgers' contracts. But Chandler, now sympathetic to Rickey's sociological screeds after seeing the performances of Robinson and Newcombe, and knowing that New York's antidiscrimination legislation would make integration inevitable, happily signed the contracts when they passed his desk before the 1947 season.

With the segregationist owners outmaneuvered, the same clubhouse network that had nearly unionized baseball the previous season quietly organized an early-season *hate strike* against their new Black teammates.

Led by the Dodgers' Alabamian player-rep Dixie Walker, nicknamed the People's Choice (or *Peeple's Cherce* in Brooklynese), the effort to bar Black Dodgers from the field began with a petition circulated at the white Dodgers' hotel room in Panama City ahead of their first exhibition match with Robinson in the lineup. Outfielder Carl Furillo recalled: "Some of the older players . . . came over to me and said they had this petition to keep the nigger off the team, and I should sign it. They said if I didn't sign it the niggers would have my job. I signed it."

If the petition failed to move the front office, the Dodgers vowed to strike. And if that failed, and Robinson was still on the roster for the regular season, Walker and the other player reps prepared a general strike across the National League for Opening Day. The Cubs, Phillies, Cardinals, and even the CIO-curious Pirates had signed on.[92]

Such hate strikes had been common occurrences during WWII. On dozens, possibly hundreds, of occasions, union workers broke their no-strike pledges to walk out or sit down in protest of the integration of factory floors in the auto, arms, and shipping industries—sometimes over issues as petty as the promotion of a couple of Black workers.[93] While many organizers of these actions were Klansmen or other types of ideological racists, their mass support was often motivated by a sense that integration threatened what Marxist historian W. E. B. Du Bois termed the "wages of whiteness." These were the higher pay, better neighborhoods, and other social incentives given to white workers to keep them loyal to their bosses, for fear of being reduced to the poverty of the Black underclass.

The CIO formed hundreds of antidiscrimination committees to respond to the hate strikes on class terms—the divide-and-conquer racialism was all a bosses' ploy to reduce wages and rights overall, and only through solidarity were bigger gains possible. Rickey's esoteric sociological theories about the American dream would be useless in comparison.

Leo Durocher, however, was able to speak their language. "I'm the manager of this ball club," he told the pajama-clad Dodgers at an early-morning team meeting, "and I'm interested in one thing. Winning. I'll play an elephant if he can do the job, and to make room for him I'll send my own brother home." Robinson, he continued, would improve the team and "put money in your pockets and money in mine."[94] Anyone who had a problem with Robinson could write a letter to Rickey asking to be traded, he added. As for the petition, he suggested they could "wipe their ass" with it.

Furillo recalled how Durocher's speech had broken many of the players' anxiety. "Nobody could compare with Jackie, and it didn't take me long to realize he was going to help me feed my family. Salaries weren't all that big in those days and I wasn't going to make a big fuss over what color a player was if he was helping me win."[95]

As Walker watched his teammates side with Durocher and Robinson, he wrote to Rickey asking to be traded. He continued to be cold to Robinson as he awaited an answer.

The same dynamic played out through the rest of the season. Opposing teams plotted their hate strikes, management intervened, and the racism transformed to heckles, beanballs, and injurious slides. With Robinson vowed to pacifism, the abuse turned to his teammates. "Hey, you carpetbaggers," one Philly yelled, "how's your little reconstruction period getting along?" Even their family members became targets, as Gil Hodges's wife Joan recalled: "Jackie Robinson came to bat, we applauded and one of the Philadelphia players turned around and started yelling at us, 'Hey, are you going to sleep with him?' My face just got red and my Italian blood boiled."[96]

Daily incidents like these solidified the club in defense of their cheek-turning teammate. With Robinson's clubhouse isolation broken in May, he began hitting the way he had in Montreal. The Dodgers climbed from fifth place to second by July, and Robinson batted nearly .500 in September to put the Dodgers five games over the Cardinals to win the 1947 pennant. After six long waits 'til next year, Brooklyn finally had their Subway Series rematch.

A league record of 1.8 million people had come to Ebbets that season, outdrawing every other team besides the Yankees. The Dodgers set the all-time record for road attendance as well, with 1.9 million powering the NL's gate receipts past the AL's larger stadiums for the first time in years. *Time* magazine estimated Robinson had single-handedly sold at least 100,000 tickets—representing new African American fans, racist whites rooting against Robinson, and those who just wanted to see the phenom for themselves.[97] "Jackie's nimble, Jackie's quick, Jackie makes the turnstiles click," sang the sports press.[98] A year after Larry MacPhail had sworn Black players could not compete and would hurt attendance, he begged Rickey to play the entire series at massive Yankee Stadium, and split the doubled ticket sales.

Rickey declined the offer. No amount of money could outweigh the Ebbets Field advantage of the Brooklyn faithful, now prouder of their team than ever before. They fought back from a two-game deficit in Flatbush to even the series, splitting the next two before losing game seven in an undramatic denouement. Robinson fielded without error in the series, batted .304 and tortured the Yanks whenever on the basepaths—but otherwise appeared less an experiment than just another beloved Dodger *bum*. While the Yankees remained dynastic, their Ruthian revolution had been matched.

With the color barrier broken, the St. Louis Browns and Indians added Black players Larry Doby, Hank Thompson, and Willard Brown to their rosters in July 1947, and dozens of more prospects and Negro League vets were signed and prepared to appear on major-league rosters that offseason. In 1949, sixty years since their foiled attempt to field George Stovey, the Giants became the second New York team to break the color barrier by elevating Monte Irvin.

As their thrilling and brilliant play continued to fill ballparks past attendance records and earn press accolades, the effect spread to other sports. Levi Jackson was named captain of the Yale football team, and Earl Lloyd became the first Black player in the National Basketball Association with the Washington Capitols in 1950.

A nationwide poll of Little Leaguers at the end of the forties voted Robinson and DiMaggio their favorite players, their likenesses immortalized in a boom of souvenir icons and dolls. One group of Robinson-loving radical youth formed in the neighborhood bordering Flatbush, the Brownsville Boys Club. Founded by socialist teenagers, the BBC greeted the arrival of Black housing projects in their Jewish enclave by encouraging interracial games, conflict mediation sessions, and group outings to Ebbets. They countered the postwar Little League trend by building an autonomous youth movement under the slogan "No Adult Control," rapidly becoming not only a powerful organizer for pickup sports, but a political force. They sought to weed out crime and racism by calling for decent ballfields and basketball courts, affordable housing, and quality schools. Non-white youth were promoted to leadership positions, uniting with the group's founders around the philosophy of "better understanding through working and playing together."[99]

And just as Paul Robeson had helped popularize football among Black youth, Robinson's heroics inspired a new generation to seek careers in baseball nationwide. Among them was future Met Ed Charles, who remembered the scene following a Dodgers exhibition game in his native Daytona Beach, Florida:

> Everybody in our part of town wanted to see him. Old people and small children, invalids and town drunks all walked through the streets. Some people were on crutches, and some blind people clutched the arms of friends, walking slowly to that ball park to sit in the segregated section. We watched him play that day and finally believed what we had read in the papers, that one of us was out there on the ball field. When the game was over, we kids followed Jackie as he walked with his teammates to the train station, and when the train pulled out, we ran down the tracks listening for the sounds as far as we could. And when we finally couldn't hear it any longer, we ran some more and finally stopped and put our ears to the tracks so we could feel the vibrations of the train carrying Jackie Robinson.[100]

While Ruth had embraced his man-of-the-people role, Robinson frequently avoided these crowds by reluctantly lowering the shades on the Dodgers' railcar. "He was the kind of man who had to make his presence felt," Don Newcombe said. "Like a boiler he could not keep it all inside him."[101] But Rickey had sworn Robinson to three years of silence on political subjects, fearing explosive comments on the ongoing racism in the stands, clubhouses, and front offices might send the experiment off-rail.

Certain he was on their side, Ebbets Field's growing population of leftists anxiously awaited the day Robinson would be permitted to speak freely. Bolstered by the popularity of the Soviets after their heroism during the war, and the influx of New Deal–loving Black workers supporting Robinson, these fans had roundly booed anticommunist congressman Richard Nixon when Rickey honored him before a 1947 World Series game at Ebbets. And when pro-union Dixie Walker repented for his preseason agitations, they were quick to accept his apology.

The progressivism of the Dodgers' fan base having already served his purposes, however, Rickey moved to shift the team's culture to the right. He traded the penitent team rep Walker away after the World Series, and worked tirelessly to steer the team's new superstar into the conservative camp. Robinson already believed Rickey had contributed more to the Black cause than any white man since Abraham Lincoln, and patiently listened, like thousands of white ballplayers in Rickey's farm systems before him, to the gospel that anyone calling for more player control of the game had "avowed communist tendencies," and must "deeply resent the continuance of our national pastime."[102] And even if Northern Democrats were more vocal about civil rights than their Republican counterparts, Rickey asserted the party was too chaotically split between the overzealous radicalism of the CIO and their firmly segregationist Dixiecrat wing to change anything. The GOP's platform of gradual cultural and economic integration by "American methods"—guided by an enlightened bourgeois vanguard—seemed a far more plausible route to equality.

Robinson had been so thoroughly persuaded by 1949 that the gag order was lifted early. Rickey now encouraged him to speak out on a major racial political issue dividing the country—the antiwar sentiments of Robinson's forerunner and early advocate, Paul Robeson.

An anti-Robeson hysteria had swept the country that year after he gave a speech at a Paris peace conference criticizing US policies, expressing solidarity with the Soviet Union, and vowing that Black people would not fight a war against communism. The House Un-American Activities Committee (HUAC), a Nixonite project that had long desired to take down the beloved athlete and entertainer in an anticommunist show trial, saw an opportunity to exploit the controversy. Having previously ignored the KKK as an "old American institution," HUAC knew that securing testimony from Robinson against Robeson could help legitimize their crusade and further marginalize the Black workers' movement and antiwar left.

Robeson quickly sent a letter urging Robinson to refuse the invitation. The Paris quotes were false, he wrote, and his true sentiment was that Black people everywhere want to live in peace. Robinson at first agreed, feeling like he didn't know enough about "Communism or any other political-ism."[103] But Rickey, an enthusiastic supporter of HUAC, teamed up with his coterie of centrist Black writers and organizers to beg Robinson to consider the danger of Robeson's words to the integrationist cause.[104] Testifying, they told him, would mark another courageous step in their plan of proving African Americans equal to whites, not only in athletics, but in patriotism.

Bulbs flashed as Robinson entered the previously secretive hearings, now proudly opened to the media. Seated before the Senate, Robinson acknowledged the possibility that Robeson was misquoted, praised his past activism and achievements, and defended his right to be a communist. The baritone went astray, Robinson continued, by claiming to speak for Black Americans in a divisive "siren song sung in bass" that harmed race relations just as they appeared to be healing. "We can win our fight without the Communists," he concluded, "and we don't want their help."

The statement appeared on front pages across the country. The *New York Times* praised Robinson's performance as if it were a game where he had had "four hits and no errors."[105]

Robeson's career would never recover. He was blacklisted from Hollywood and his passport canceled, preventing him from making a living performing outside the country. His albums were taken out of stores, and his sports achievements were removed from record books. His concert forty miles north of New York City that summer in Peekskill, a fundraiser for a new civil rights organization challenging the centrism of the NAACP, turned into a racist riot. Hundreds of veterans, unorganized racists, and local cops converged into a mob that attacked performers and the union crowd, burned crosses, and lynched Robeson in effigy.

Robinson's laundering of HUAC and the subsequent riot marked the beginning of a new Red Scare. Communists, antiwar activists, and their sympathizers were given the same treatment as Robeson—fired from government posts, blacklisted from Hollywood and the press, and banned from the labor movement. Its militants neutralized, the CIO's radical edge dulled to resemble the apolitical business-unionism of the AFL so closely that the two merged in 1955. The player reps of MacPhail's pseudo–players' union were likewise placated from launching further action against their owners until the mid-sixties.

Rickey could celebrate his own "double victory" of integrating baseball (making the Dodgers the best and most profitable team in the league) and using Robinson's heroism as a weapon against the left. Ebbets began hosting routine celebrations for returning soldiers from the widely unpopular genocidal war against communism in Korea, and continued to welcome the once-reviled Nixon, alongside Douglas MacArthur and other far-right figures, as honored guests.[106] Despite their unparalleled

unparalleled left-wing fan base, Carl Prince wrote the franchise became "more consistently anticommunist than any other professional team of that Cold War decade."[107]

But with Robinson's Dodgers perennial pennant contenders for the foreseeable future, Ebbets leftists were satisfied at having chosen the most progressive team and tuned out the jingoism and anti-worker maneuvers behind the scenes. Politics returned to a meaningless diversion to what truly mattered to them—the game itself, in which ceremonial first pitches don't count.

Chapter 4

MEADOWLARKS

Few who have gazed from Shea's or Citi's upper decks upon the tangled horizon of scrap shops and garages imagine the greasy industrial zone having any history worth remembering. But before his death in 2022, the last surviving Willets Point resident Joseph Ardizzone described it as somewhere once utopian.

His family was one of the dozens of Italians and Romani to homestead the narrow meadows between Flushing Bay and the vast dump immortalized by Fitzgerald as the "valley of ashes" during the Depression. His days were spent herding goats, feeding chickens, and tending gardens fertile from the heat of smoldering trash.[108] He hunted rabbits, muskrats, and pheasants through lush woods and swamps chirping with frogs, owls, and meadowlarks. At twilight he joined community games of bocce ball, or adventured with his siblings among the detritus of a metropolis still distant on the horizon.[109]

Then came the World of Tomorrow—New York's 1939 World's Fair. The amusement park would display an altogether different utopia of automated farms and factories in its Ford pavilion, stopless traffic in its GM pavilion, and consumer telephone and television technology in the RCA and AT&T pavilions. At the fair's center was the municipally-funded Democracity, America's answer to the totalitarian German, Italian, and Soviet pavilions, in which New York emerged the skyscraper heart of a regional megacity, surrounded by concentric rings of freeway-linked green spaces and suburban "Pleasantvilles," with a highway-enclosed Flushing Meadows its central polis.

Preparation for the fair's construction was the first massive leap toward the realization of this futurist sprawl. To Democracity's master builder Robert Moses, Willets Point wasn't a community but an impediment, no different from the corrupt Tammany clubhouses he'd spent decades methodically dismantling. The New Deal's 1937 Housing Act handed him the weapon he'd long coveted: a surge of federal funds to bust Tammany's grip on unions and neighborhood organizations. With La Guardia's backing, Moses declared the remaining strongholds "slums"—a designation that legally justified their seizure and demolition. Among the few to keep their land, the Ardizzones watched their Eden razed by an army of Works Progress Administration workers, laboring year-round, day and night, by the light of barrel fires to turn the junkyards and homesteads into an artificial landscape of lakes, canals, and plantings.[110] The surrounding wilderness was leveled entirely for the next quarter-century of modernist constructions: the Grand Central Parkway, LaGuardia Airport, a second World's Fair *Futurama* in 1964, and Shea Stadium. The draining and paving of Flushing Meadows, Ted

Steinberg wrote in his ecological history of New York, *Gotham Unbound*, was "the most significant landscape change in this corner of the planet" since the Ice Age's thaw.[111]

Democracity drew closer with the end of World War II. America became the industrial powerhouse of the war-ruined world, with New York its manufacturing center. The GI Bill guaranteed employment, affordable education, and low-cost suburban mortgages for millions of returning veterans. Moses championed this swelling middle class by building hundreds of parks and roads linking city and suburbia in brutalist grandiosity, becoming "a figure larger than life, almost mythical," Robert Caro wrote, "shrouded in the mist of his own legends, a Paul Bunyan of Public Works, a John Henry of Highways."[112]

His displacement of Tammany near complete, Moses assembled a new power structure in New York that political scientist Richard M. Flanagan called the Plebiscitary Mayoralty—an authoritarian technocracy of New Deal populists and unelected power brokers who manufactured consent for their initiatives through mass media in a "direct, unmediated relationship between the mayor and citizens."[113] Willets Point, the primordial swamp that spawned this new governmental brood, remained central to the project. Moses envisioned it as the recreative center of the bureaucratic dictatorship. The new Central Park for the decentered city would be based on Copenhagen's Tivoli Gardens, a nineteenth-century funfair funded by the Danish king for its architect's promise that "when the people are amusing themselves, they do not think about politics."[114]

A century prior, Tammany's development of professional baseball spectacles played a similar role in its legitimation apparatus. Moses, however, had always seen the sport as a vulgar, profit-seeking scheme to hypnotize the rabble in place of more civic recreative pursuits like swimming, track, or other friendly competitions between amateur citizens' teams on well-regulated municipal fields. But as the contradictions of his creative destruction accumulated through the fifties, he began to understand why Tammany had created the Mets in the first place, and establishing a new people's team steadily rose to his top priority.

Baseball had emerged after the war among America's most powerful cultural products for promoting its unchallenged global hegemony. On hundreds of "little America" army bases dotting the globe, soldiers taught the sport to locals as base radio stations broadcast major-league games. The Yankees toured the ruins of occupied Japan, and Branch Rickey's image of a colorblind and progressive America was touted in State Department literature promoting Robinson as an all-American hero in decolonizing African nations. Serving as carrot to the atomic bomb's terrifying stick, this propaganda implied the capitol of the new superpower was not Washington's Pentagon, but Yankee Stadium and Ebbets Field.

New York's trifecta of baseball dominance was completed in 1951, when the Giants rose to top the major leagues astride the Yankees and Dodgers. Their transition from sepia-toned afterthought came with the arrival of Leo Durocher in Harlem. Fired as Dodgers manager by Rickey following a one-year ban over a public feud with Yankees GM Larry MacPhail, Durocher convinced conservative Giants boss Horace Stoneham to sign and elevate Black prospects Hank Thompson and Monte Irvin in 1949.[115] When the Giants surged to third in the NL that year, Durocher pushed Stoneham to sign teenage prospect Willie Mays.

"My eyes almost popped out of my head when I saw a young colored boy swing the bat with great speed and power, and with hands that had the quickness of a young Joe Louis throwing punches," Giants scout Ed Montague recalled after seeing high-schooler Mays hit batting practice for the first time with the Birmingham Black Barons in 1948. "This was the greatest young ballplayer I had ever seen in my life."[116] Willie Mays's explosive bat, incredible outfield range, and cannon-like arm had drawn interest from the Red Sox, Indians, Pirates, Braves, Yankees, and Dodgers. These teams, however, either refused to integrate (like the Yankees) or feared breaking an unwritten rule against fielding too many Black players. When Durocher finally talked Stoneham into bringing Mays to the Giants in 1951, the impact was immediate. The team, two games under .500 before his arrival, won twenty-five of their next thirty-eight. Mays homered off Warren Spahn in his Polo Grounds debut, and continued to dominate as the Giants erased a thirteen-game midsummer deficit, tying the Dodgers to force a dramatic playoff series.

The two National League teams had battled bitterly all season, the hottest rivalry in sports inflamed fiercely with the hard-boiled and vindictive ex-Dodger Durocher now incandescent in black and orange. After splitting the first two playoff games, diehards of both teams chaotically mingled throughout the Polo Grounds stands as they had for decades to watch the decisive game three on October 3. And now they were joined by exponentially more spectators—the series served as the first pilot of a four-year project of laying coaxial cable coast-to-coast so presidential addresses and the World Series could be seen live on the nation's sixteen million television sets.

The tiebreaker, elevated to the importance of national news and geopolitics, became by far the most simultaneously watched event in human history. Ratings in New York were near total that afternoon—90 percent of all TVs tuned in to NBC to watch Don Newcombe and Sal Maglie's pitchers' duel.[117] Millions of more fans in storefronts, warehouses, bars, bedrooms, prison cells, hospitals, and army bunks across the world listened to the play-by-play on the radio, with the Spanish-language broadcast rhapsodizing Los Gigantes across Mexico, the Caribbean, and South America.[118] When Robinson singled home Pee Wee Reese in the first, the pain and pleasure of New Yorkers coursed through the global collective conscience.

With the two teams locked in a 1–1 tie in the seventh inning, only the politicians and bureaucrats in DC sweated the news that the Soviets had accomplished their first successful nuclear test two weeks prior, because President Truman's press conference at 3:27 that afternoon had not been deemed worthy to interrupt the broadcast. Seeking solace now that their superweapon, so excessively displayed in the holocausts of Hiroshima and Nagasaki, pointed back to the US from across the Iron Curtain, the humbled senators recessed to their chambers to watch the Dodgers pull away with a 4–1 lead in the top of the eighth.

Durocher's taunts of *choker* failed to phase Newcombe until the bottom of the ninth. Three consecutive hits put the tying runs on base, sending Westchester native Ralph Branca from the dugout in relief to face the Giants' home-run leader, Staten Island slugger Bobby Thomson. "Branca throws," Giants' sportscaster Russ Hodges told the free world before the second fastball. "Here's a long drive. It's gonna be, I believe . . . The Giants win the pennant! The Giants win the pennant! The Giants win the pennant! The Giants win the pennant!"[119]

Milliseconds later came "the most tumultuous blowing of automobile horns throughout the metropolitan area since V-E Day," the Associated Press reported. "All over the city people are coming out of their houses," Don DeLillo wrote in *Pafko at the Wall,* the finest work of baseball fiction since "Casey at the Bat." "This is the nature of Thomson's homer. It makes people want to be in the streets, joined with others, telling others what has happened, those few who haven't heard—comparing faces and states of mind."[120]

As Thomson rounded the bases, his ball lost in the throngs, fans storming the field, trash raining down, and Branca weeping on the clubhouse steps, he recalled only thoughts of local spite—his pride in beating Brooklyn.[121] Stunned shrieks from open windows citywide transformed into a cacophony of weeping, radio-smashing, and hysteric revelry. One

Dodgers fan's heart stopped in a Far Rockaway laundromat. Another—Midtown deli worker, pitching prospect, and future Mets owner Fred Wilpon—severed the tip of his pinkie as he distractedly operated a meat slicer.[122]

Julius Rosenberg despaired in his upstate prison cell. The Communist Party member was awaiting execution after being convicted of espionage for convincing his brother-in-law, a GI at the Oak Ridge laboratory managed by Yankees pitcher Johnny Murphy during his war hiatus, to pass information on uranium enrichment and nuclear bomb production to the Soviets. "Gloom of glooms," he wrote to his wife Ethel, also convicted in the affair, "the dear Dodgers lost. . . . And now I'm rooting for the Giants to lick the Yankees."[123]

But there would be no comparable emotion for the Yankees' routine put-down of the Giants the next week. No pennant or World Series had ever been clinched with a walk-off home run before, and each since could only chase Thomson's triumph, Branca's tragedy, and the latest and largest universally shared *moment*. Like FDR's announcement of the bombing of Pearl Harbor before it, and the assassinations of American leaders and terrorist attacks to come, everyone would be able to report where they were, what they were doing, and how they felt when they heard what papers dubbed the "Shot Heard 'Round the World"—a Brooklynese version of the name for the first volleys of the American Revolution at Concord, the Confederate shots at Abner Doubleday's position in Fort Sumter that began the Civil War, or the assassination of the Austrian archduke in Sarajevo that kick-started World War I.

Thomson's sneaky little blast, the product of Durocher's own complex sign-stealing system, had given a suddenly bipolar world a taste of the bitter new Cold War reality of sudden crises and earth-shattering finales. John Steinbeck envied the high-modernist climax of "the best game I or anyone ever saw." A young Jack Kerouac lost himself in a creative mania: "I trembled with joy and couldn't get over it for days and wrote poems about how it is possible for the human spirit to win after all!"[124] Among sportswriters, perhaps only Red Smith recognized the severity of this conjuncture of sports and the global social order in his column for the next morning's *New York Herald Tribune*. "Now it is done," he wrote. "Now the story ends. And there is no way to tell it. The art of fiction is dead. Reality has strangled invention. Only the utterly impossible, the inexpressibly fantastic, can ever be plausible again."[125]

Truman's announcement of nuclear Cold War foretold the acceleration of history to creation and destruction on untold scales. Nuclear power would move mountains and rivers to build thousands of new metropolises for millions, while men, strapped to intercontinental ballistic missiles pointed skyward, would escape Earth's orbit to look down on our home as a singular ball, itself now smashable. And yet, the forty-kiloton detonation in the Kazakh desert was an unheard tree fall compared to "Thomson's Blast," headlining alongside or *above* "Stalin's Bomb" in most newspapers.[126] Perhaps the human spirit, too, could make a similar Giant comeback from a geopolitical order hurtling toward total ruin.

The shot, it would turn out, was not the announcement of a permanent golden age of New York supremacy in baseball and all other spheres that many had hoped, but a premature peak before rapid descent.

Outside baseball's fortresses of optimism, the utopian technocratic designs of the mechanical-megalopolis Democracity steadily broke down each year. The gains of the 1946 strike wave were rolled back dramatically as the Red Scare ejected militancy from the workers' movement. Wages were frozen, rent control removed, and subway fare tripled, as the purchasing power of the dollar plummeted.[127] Factories packed up their machinery, fired their workers, and escaped on Moses's highways to regions lacking both baseball bragging and labor rights. Thousands of white New Yorkers followed, cutting the economic ladder's rungs behind them.[128]

The crisis first appeared to the baseball world as something like a demonstration of fans outside the park before each game. This crowd, growing in number and anger each season, was composed of a new faction of baseball's middle-class fan base—former straphangers, whose new way of life extended the proletarian pastime of trolley-dodging into the basis of a new lifestyle that avoided mass transit altogether as a proud symbol of their elevated social mobility—*the motorist*.

The ex-urbanites found themselves circling in ever-longer and more frustrating spirals around the ballparks, built in the mass-transit era without sufficient parking lots. And on their nighttime marches back to their cars through the ghettoization the "runaway factories" and their own "white flight" had left behind, many resolved to boycott. "Why knock myself out," one Long Island–relocated Dodgers fan interviewed by the *New York Post* put it, "when all I have to do is have the wife bring out the slippers, tune in the twenty-one-inch screen and relax with some of my favorite brew."[129]

Whether these fans were progressives or bigots mattered little, because Robert Moses *was* a racist. Impediments to the movement of the lower classes, particularly Blacks and Latinos, were hidden everywhere in his public works. His roads to Jones Beach were cut with low-clearance highways to prevent access by inner-city buses. His public pools were maintained at temperatures in white neighborhoods he theorized too low for Black visitors. His housing projects, built to accommodate the dwellers of cleared slums, were explicitly designed and located according to racial demographics. Petty crime was the inevitable result of the unemployment, declining tax revenues, and slashed funding left behind. Middle-class New Yorkers were happy to ignore deindustrialization and systemic racism, but game by game, the parking crisis revealed its festering rot.

For a time, the annual prizefights between the three teams served as a cover. Fans tuned in as the Dodgers outpaced the Giants to take the pennant in 1952 and 1953, only to lose to the Yankees in the World Series both years. They watched the Giants take the pennant and topple the Yankees in 1954. Then it was the Dodgers' turn, finally claiming their first world championship when they beat the Yanks in 1955. The consecutive triumphs implied the balance of power shifting away from the metropolis's baseball elites and toward its underdog popular front, self-identified as the *National League Town*. "Far into the night rang shouts of revelry in Flatbush," John Drebinger wrote in the *Times*. "Brooklyn at long last has won a world series and now let someone suggest moving the Dodgers elsewhere!"[130]

The ominous comment acknowledged that, just four years after Thomson's shot, baseball's golden bandage could no longer cover, let alone heal, the city's social and economic wounds. Attendance decline had been particularly bad for the Giants, whose Harlem home was notoriously Blacker and offered even less street parking than Flatbush. Despite their pennants and a championship in 1954, the Giants reported only a $400,000 profit since 1947, compared to $3.5 million each for the Dodgers and Yankees.[131] "There is no longer a chance to survive here," Stoneham told the press as the decline worsened. With the Dodgers' profitability dependent on the Giants rivalry, the murmurs whispered doom for Ebbets Field as well. When asked to consider the agony a move would cause the National League Town's youth, Stoneham countered: "I feel bad about the kids but I haven't seen many of their fathers lately."[132]

Rickey had hoped that integration could attract a new base of upwardly-mobile non-white fans in these neighborhoods. But as the fifties progressed, the colorblind and apolitical pretenses of this strategy were revealed to be woefully insufficient in challenging the economic basis of racial segregation.

So, too, were the antiracist movements of the forties an insufficient counter to the Red Scare and Plebiscitary Mayoralty. Blacklists and bureaucracy killed or captured the interracial unions, community groups, leftist academia, and all other political movements fighting for true racial and economic equality. Among the casualties was the Robinson-inspired Brownsville Boys Club. After years of organizing interracial baseball leagues, Ebbets outings, and conflict mediation groups to ease the tensions of the demographic shift around Flatbush, the group was courted by clothing retailer turned councilman Abe Stark. Known for his HIT SIGN, WIN SUIT advertisement at Ebbets Field, the self-styled populist offered to help secure funding for their autonomous community center under the condition that the stridently youth-led organization would allow him and other city officials to oversee their finances. By 1953, a convenient budget shortfall allowed Stark's board to fire the BBC's remaining idealists, replacing them with social workers. The center was sold to the Department of Recreation the next year, who promptly replaced the social workers with parks employees and police. BBC's founders left for universities and whiter neighborhoods after the defeat, completing the process of turning their egalitarian socialist vision of "better understanding through working and playing together" into, historian Wendell Pritchett concluded, little more than "an engine of upward mobility for its predominantly white clientele."[133]

Black uninterest in the sport whites had left behind was exacerbated by the racism of the sports press. Celebrations of Black stars' athletic gifts often came with condescending slights against their intellect—a treatment most pronounced in descriptions of Willie Mays. While he was intelligent and articulate in his Alabama vernacular, he shied away from the press due to initial struggles with the business-minded patois of Northern whites. Durocher spoke for him, hiding Mays's distaste for discriminatory practices like segregated accommodations and denials of lucrative signing bonuses. When faced with racist taunts or aggressive pitches, he brushed himself off and returned to play. The stoicism that allowed the press to paint him as an idiot savant during his early years, Mays later reflected, came from his acceptance of the paternalistic "programming" of media and coaches as a survival strategy.[134]

Jackie Robinson, however, shed much of his own programming after Walter O'Malley bought Branch Rickey's Dodgers stake in 1951. Though he remained a Nixon-supporting Republican, Robinson embraced his role as the Black ballplayers' unofficial spokesman, consistently challenging racism from owners, opponents, coaches, fans, hotels, and the commissioner's office to become the most outspoken player since Ruth. With most teams still located in the North and Midwest, Florida's spring training camps became the central focus of his integrationist campaign. Conditions steadily improved there through the decade as Robinson galvanized Black players and allies to coordinate actions against sundown-town discrimination with similar tactics to Dr. Martin Luther King Jr. and Rosa Parks' 1955 Montgomery bus boycott.

Much of the baseball world, however, wrote off Robinson's complaints by arguing that he should be grateful for the tolerance and high pay he received—even though his salary topped out at $47,000, compared to over $100,000 for Stan Musial, Ralph Kiner, and Ted Williams the same year.[135] Journalists and owners, including Walter O'Malley, wished he would be more like the seemingly childish Mays, or Robinson's teammate Roy Campanella, who criticized King's emerging Civil Rights Movement as "pressing too far, too fast."[136]

The first major *whitelash* against Robinson came after he called out Yankee prejudice in a 1952 TV interview. While the AL standard-bearer had remained popular with Black fans since the days of Ruth, the South Bronx maintained suburban serenity through the decade, and the franchise protected their marbled legacy, and slowed integration throughout the AL, by refusing to elevate their few Black prospects out of the minor leagues. For pointing this out, Dick Young and other sports journalists chastised Robinson for uppityness, as GM George Weiss boasted behind the scenes: "I will never allow a black man to wear a Yankee uniform. . . . Box-holders from Westchester don't want that sort of crowd."[137]

A season after Robinson's denunciation, Black Yankees fans circulated a pamphlet in the stands asking: "Why can't the Yankees provide a democratic atmosphere? . . . More democracy by the hiring of Negro ballplayers will ensure better quality of baseball." The Yankees had missed Mays due to their racism, and some of the team, including manager Casey Stengel, urged the elevation of Vic Power, an Afro–Puerto Rican leading the minors with a .350 batting average. Weiss stuck to his bigotry nonetheless, anonymously telling the press that Power didn't fit into the "Yankee mold" due to his showboating style of play and history of dating white women.[138]

The Yankees became one of the last teams to break the color barrier in 1955 with catcher Elston Howard. Unlike Power or Robinson, Howard didn't object to slights like the nickname Eight Ball, and seemed only to take offense at questions about his athleticism, like when Stengel complained to the press: "When I finally get a nigger, I get the only one that can't run."[139] When Howard was sent back to the minors shortly after his first appearance, the *Chicago Defender* reported further disillusionment among Black fans: "All up and down [Harlem's] Seventh Ave., all you can hear is 'I told you so.'"[140]

In 1956, the hangover year after Brooklyn's climactic championship over the Yankees, racial tension in the inner city pushed declining gate receipts for the Giants and Dodgers past the point of no return. The slumping revenues, their owners determined, meant they would need to either build new ballparks in their respective boroughs' white enclaves, or follow the runaway factories escaping New York.

Stoneham eyed Midtown for a triple-decked, 110,000-seat arena with new subway lines and a 20,000-spot parking lot for the Giants above the westside railroad tracks. O'Malley likewise unveiled a model for a 100,000-seat geodesic-domed stadium, designed by the futurist architect Buckminster Fuller, in Fort Greene. While Stoneham's proposal gained little momentum, O'Malley advanced the Dodger Dome through the political machine. Having worked his way to ownership through the Tammany bank that owned the Dodgers as a foreclosure lawyer during the Depression, he proposed the city use its slum-clearing power of eminent domain to seize fifteen acres of Fort Greene's deteriorating meat market. Although a private enterprise, the new stadium's parking facility would serve the public year-round, he said. Ebbets Field could be turned into a new housing project, and the Brooklyn Dodgers, a public institution deserving preferential treatment, would be saved.

But the use of "public interest" to reshape the city had shifted dramatically since O'Malley's Tammany days—that power now belonged to Robert Moses alone. After investigating the proposal, Moses wrote O'Malley that Fort Greene was impractical, offering a cheaper location in Brownsville instead. When O'Malley refused to move to the now nearly entirely Black neighborhood, the Moses-loving press depicted O'Malley's preference for white and costly Fort Greene as a sign of pure greed, and his geodesic aspirations a symptom of mania. Moses closed the matter by writing that the Dodgers were *not* a public concern at all, and he should buy his own land.[141]

With the backroom horse-trading and shell-corporation land acquisitions that had built Ebbets Field and the Polo Grounds no longer feasible, the owners began secretly plotting a joint exodus. Under the cover of Dodger dominance in 1956, O'Malley bought the Cubs' minor-league Angels of Los Angeles, where Mayor Norris Poulson eagerly offered to do everything for him Moses would not. His choice of land would be condemned to build a city-subsidized three-hundred-acre stadium with ample parking that would belong to him, along with the oil and mineral wealth below the surface. Poulson joked O'Malley could even "sleep with my wife once a week."[142]

Stoneham's initial plan was to move to the sprawling Twin Cities of Minneapolis and St. Paul, where the Giants owned a minor-league team and territorial rights.[143] But because the rivalry between the two NL teams had been a crucial source of revenue, O'Malley pressured Stoneham to coordinate a move with him to booming California instead. Two major-league teams on the West Coast would cut down on travel costs, and there was a lucrative cable broadcasting venture in the works that would syndicate Giants and Dodgers games to the teams' old fans, preserving much of their established revenues while making the owners even richer.

The Dodgers won the pennant that year, losing to the Yankees in a thrilling seven-game World Series that included Robinson's final game. The success rebounded attendance to nearly their forties numbers, but immediately after, O'Malley announced Ebbets's days were numbered. He had sold Brooklyn's secular cathedral to a real estate developer planning to build a housing project upon the field in 1960. The move west was nearly set in stone when play began their next season, but trying to make Moses the scapegoat, O'Malley told the press that if the city still refused to provide a replacement, 1957 would be the Dodgers' last year in Brooklyn.

Feigning surprise, Stoneham added that the Giants would be doomed without the Dodgers, forcing them to leave the city as well.

As angry letters and telegrams flooded City Hall, Moses finally understood that the widespread desperation to save the National League teams could be either a decisive blow to the Plebiscitary Mayoralty's power, or an opportunity to complete his life's work. Visions of a Colosseum-like municipal ballpark, surrounded by highways and rising above the rusting pavilions of the 1939 World's Fair, flashed before his eyes. It would be the bayside crown of his Democracity, attracting up to one hundred thousand motorist fans from the city and suburbs to justify the completion of his "true" Central Park across the street, the *people's Versailles*: Robert Moses Park. Not only could the owners have their futuristic ballpark, Moses responded in the press, but the city would more than triple the public subsidies O'Malley had requested and *build it for them* in Willets Point.[144]

In a final attempt to save face, O'Malley pinned his suit with the slogan of the fan movement inspired by comedian Phil Foster's schmaltzy song: "Let's Keep the Dodgers in Brooklyn." Queens was not suitable, he argued, because hordes of Giants and Yankees fans lay in wait across Flushing Bay to rob the Dodgers of home field advantage. But few could believe his threatened 2,500-mile move was still merely a leverage tactic following Stoneham's July announcement that the Giants were going to San Francisco. By the time O'Malley inked the LA deal weeks later, he had become the greatest loser of the triangular blame game.

While the archaic Giants represented a fading memory of Gilded Age greatness, the Dodgers still evoked blue-collar perseverance through Depression indigence and daily leaps from inner-city danger across trolley tracks. Now they appeared more like Brooklyn's cowardly upper class, fleeing the city in loot-packed runaway cars. Moses had built the highways, but the name O'Malley became synonymous with their wreckage. An entire generation of New Yorkers would fantasize about cornering Hitler, Stalin, and O'Malley armed with a revolver and two bullets, and shooting O'Malley twice.[145]

Its eviction slated, the National League Town passed through the stages of grief.

There was denial: A radical cadre at Ebbets distributed the pamphlet "Dodger Fans of the World, Unite!" proposing that a boycott of the team and its advertisers would lower franchise value enough for fans to collectively purchase it.

There was bargaining: Former Giants manager Bill Terry offered to buy his old club outright, as did the team's wealthiest minority stockholder, Willie Mays devotee and lone vote against the move, Joan Whitney Payson. Dorothy Killam, the philanthropist wife of a wealthy Canadian banker, made a similar play for the Dodgers. But with the West Coast deals guaranteeing coast-to-coast broadcasting rights, massive new stadiums, and untapped oil beneath Chavez Ravine, speculated profits from the move were exponentially greater than the pocket change the bums and heiresses could ever collectively cobble together.

And there was certainly anger—it had already been simmering for years against the carpetbagging bourgeois who stripped the city for marginally higher profits elsewhere. But that boiling point had already hit in 1954. In January, one hundred workers seized the shuttering Brooklyn Permutit chemical factory to demand severance pay. The action inspired a larger occupation that fall to prevent American Safety Razor, an integrated eight-story Brooklyn factory roughly as old as the Dodgers, from moving to Virginia. When judges ruled the shop belonged to the owners, not the people, hundreds of unionists chained themselves to the gates, barricaded downtown Brooklyn's streets with cars and pickets, and faced down an approaching NYPD cavalry. In a barrage of truncheons, smashed windows, cut padlocks, and brutal arrests, the six-week occupation came to an end. "After seventy-six years," New York historian Andy Battle wrote, "ASR had fashioned its last razor blade in New York."[146]

Finally, there was sobered acceptance. New York's social and economic wounds had festered into an unmendable chasm, sucking both teams into the abyss. If their rallies had not saved the factories or stopped the Red Scare purges, how could mere fans expect a campaign around sports franchises to turn out any better? "Brooklynites did not feel empowered enough to affect the course of 'their' team's destiny because the surrounding culture dictated that sports were and should remain apolitical," American studies scholar Peter Marquis wrote. "[T]hey were cognizant that 'their' team, in fact, was not theirs as it belonged to a man whose private interests, in the end, trumped the community's."[147]

Only eleven thousand watched the last New York Giants game at the Polo Grounds. When it was over, the small crowd stormed the field, ripping out bases, grass, and outfield padding to shouts of *We want Willie!* The chant transformed into a final burst of anger as the crowd left the park for the last time: *We want Stoneham! We want to stone him! We want Stoneham—with a rope around his neck.*[148]

The final Dodgers game at Ebbets was comparatively somber. Fans grumbled and wept as they filed out to organist Gladys Goodding playing the perennial *wait 'til next year* anthem "Auld Lang Syne," now a funeral dirge. One Ebbets employee burst into tears. "This team has been my whole life. What is it now? Just a joke."[149]

In two years' time, a wrecking ball painted pale white with blood-red stitches would reduce Brooklyn's secular cathedral to the footprint for a new modernist slum. Thomson's shot had finally landed.

"What happened to all that energy generated by Dodger and Giant fans when the big split occurred and the electrons flew off into space?" Robert Moses wrote in a 1958 editorial for the *Herald Tribune*, recognizing the desertions had hit the city like a spiritual atomic bomb. "Did any of it stay around Ebbets Field or Coogan's Bluff as fallout or radiation? Is it subject to recapture or is my science hopelessly balled up?"[150]

Everyday life, of course, was little different than it had been in 1957. New York has always been a city either glorious or gutted—the landscaped green of a baseball field or the industrial wasteland beyond its fences. Now the verdant distraction of baseball was gone, taking all perennial hopes for next game and next year with it, leaving behind a permanent landscape of blight. Only the Yankees remained, another symbol of the city's mighty capitalists becoming richer as the poor lost everything.

The scapegoating of O'Malley would stave off their inevitable rage in the short term, but endless letters still flooding newspapers and City Hall with invective showed the legitimacy of Moses's plebiscitary milieu hung in the balance. With the last bastion of Tammany's politicians still clutching the city's purse on the bond-issuing Board of Estimate, Moses knew the promise of a National League restoration would crumble all opposition to funds needed to complete his reconstruction of New York. Adapting the same method Tammany had employed to deal with the malaise-induced rebellions of the 1870s—cohering the spreading and splintering metropolis around a new people's team—he concluded the column calling for the Willets Point stadium plan to move forward.

As soon as the 1957 season ended, Mayor Robert Wagner formed the Mayor's Committee to Bring a National League Team to New York. At its head was corporate lawyer William Shea, who had started his career in the Depression-era Tammany machine with O'Malley, and joined Moses's cadre of power brokers after World War II. His plainspoken charm, legal cunning, and connections in government, unions, business, intelligence agencies, and sports soon made him, as muckrakers Jack Newfield and Paul Du Brul wrote, the "clubhouse fund raiser and thinker" of New York's Moses-built "permanent government"—an "unelected consortium of bankers, brokers, and businessmen."[151]

The Committee's biggest challenge was to strong-arm organized baseball's para-state power to metropolitan will. Shea's team scored early when Commissioner Ford Frick defied the Yankees to designate New York as "open territory" in 1958. Any NL team was now free to move to Queens. Owners of the Phillies, Reds, Pirates, and Cubs entertained Shea's offer for a city-funded stadium and generous tax incentives, before politely declining to become the next O'Malley by betraying their hometown fans.

Shea's subsequent appeal for baseball's magnates to expand their ranks was also denied. They had privately determined that were they ever to add new teams, they should play in new markets out west, where rapid population growth had turned the Dodgers and Giants into baseball's most profitable franchises overnight. A third point of pressure came from Brooklyn congressman Emanuel Celler's hearings challenging baseball's monopoly in retribution for letting the Dodgers leave. Here, too, the westward orientation of organized baseball provided protection. Were Celler's crusade to gain any traction, the majors would absorb the Pacific Coast League, the only remaining minor circuit with a sufficient fan base to rival the majors. They could then buy off the votes of its teams' congressional representatives with promises they could cut the ribbon on a brand new major league park in Seattle, Sacramento, or San Diego.

Shea soon found a new line of attack to break the stalemate on the front page of the May 1958 issue of the *Sporting News*. "Third Major Must Come Soon" blared a headline below the photo of the man whose crusade to integrate baseball had brought the obstinate owners to heel before, Branch Rickey.

In the years since O'Malley's hostile takeover of the Dodgers, Rickey had moved on to semiretirement as the absentee minority owner of the Pittsburgh Pirates. He filled his time touring the country, accepting rewards, and giving public speeches about the bravery of Robinson, the absolute importance of baseball to a post-racial American dream, and the ever-present danger of international communism.

These speeches grew increasingly alarmed about baseball's bulwark against Soviet influence as the Cold War balanced. Team relocations, the contraction of the minor leagues from 217 teams in 1950 to just 38 in 1957, and ownership's resistance to expanding the majors had cost millions of Americans access to their once-beloved pastime.[152] TV broadcasts only further disconnected middle America as the more telegenic sport of football surged in popularity. With thousands of fans of the New York Giants switching to their gridiron sibling, he worried what would become of American society if this "brutish war-game" outran sophisticated baseball.

Shea's attempts to move a team to New York, he told the *Sporting News*, would only further harm baseball's standing. The Boston Braves had moved to Milwaukee in 1953, the Browns had left St. Louis for Baltimore in 1954, and the Dodgers' disappearance, he wrote, had been one of the most "egregious crimes" in American history. "A baseball club in any city in America is a quasi-public institution, and in Brooklyn the Dodgers were public without the quasi."[153] Another wrong could not make a right, nor would the sin of the government intervening to force the creation of a couple new franchises, whose initial weakness would further imbalance competitiveness to favor the increasingly dominant Dodgers, Braves, White Sox, and Yankees.

Rickey instead looked back to his mentor Ban Johnson's insurgency as a solution to the worst crisis the sport had seen since 1902. The upstart American League had reestablished teams cut across the Midwest and founded new ones, while its Yankee invasion ultimately made the business more popular, profitable, and patriotic than ever before. Rickey's proposed third major, with its premier franchise a combination of the lost teams of New York, would similarly nourish baseball-starved regions in the US and across its sphere of influence: "Havana, Toronto, Montreal, Vancouver . . . Miami, Houston, Dallas, Fort Worth, Atlanta, Minneapolis–St. Paul, Denver, and even San Diego, Oakland, and Seattle." From there, the major leagues could expand across the globe, serving as a propaganda arm for American democracy against the comparative coldness of Soviet calisthenics. Any attempt from organized baseball to block this necessary and inevitable rejuvenation of America's pastime through assertion of its monopolies on territory and labor, he warned, would "result in war."[154]

While the ambition of this plan was far beyond Shea's mission of bringing a single team to Queens, Rickey's combativeness, prestige, and proven capability made the two natural allies. By November, their conspiracy was hatched. As Shea continued pressuring organized baseball from the outside, Rickey worked from within by building his new renegade *Continental League* (CL).

Investors were so eager to break into America's most exclusive industry they ignored the radicalism of the combined utopian visions of Moses and Rickey. An entire baseball-based *new world order* was in the making, with Flushing Meadows its capital district. Millions of new fans would be won over with modern scoreboards, fireworks, postgame prizefights, and expanded roster spots for Black, Latino, and Japanese prospects. Disgruntled top-tier players and coaches from the AL and NL would be lured with reforms the owners had long refused, including pooled broadcast revenues to fund players' pensions and healthcare. Excess funds would subsidize free tickets and affiliated little leagues to ensure youth from Canada to the Caribbean would be well-versed in America's pastime for generations to come. By the time the Yankees notched another banal triumph over the Braves in the 1958 World Series, new franchises had been funded in Toronto, Denver, Houston, and Minneapolis–St. Paul, with other prospective investors eyeing Buffalo, Indianapolis, Miami, Seattle, Atlanta, Dallas, and San Juan.[155]

New Yorkers, however, treated the CL's announcement with trademark cynicism. Novelty could not match their nostalgia for Willie Mays and Gil Hodges, and the CL sounded more like a new minor circuit than a true heir to the bygone National League teams. This uncertainty threatened to scuttle the crucial element of the CL plan—construction of its Flushing fortress. When the proposal made its way to the Board of Estimate, its Tammanyites argued the CL was at best a boondoggle, and most likely a smokescreen covering Moses's ceaseless attempts to wrangle taxpayer funds for his pet project. And even if Rickey's wildest ambitions of major-league crowds were realized, Moses's neat estimation that the stadium's price would be rapidly repaid by rent was clearly based on fudged numbers that underestimated costs and overestimated future revenues.[156]

With public opinion mixed on the feud, letters between Rickey, Shea, and other city commissioners fretted about the "undercover work" of the Yankees in sabotaging the project.[157] Despite being the only game in town since 1957, attendance in the Bronx ominously dwindled each season, and they believed competition would only worsen the trend.[158] George Weiss lobbied politicians and press to put public funds toward new parking facilities for Yankee Stadium instead, as franchise owner Del Webb rallied organized baseball to treat the CL as an existential threat to their unchecked power.

To break the opposition, the CL's New York team would require an owner rich enough to bond beloved ballplayers from exile, fund the war through to its conclusion, and never sell-out the National League Town again. Their prime candidate was an heiress to one of the richest families in the world, former Giants board member Joan Whitney Payson. Payson's lineage intersected with Vanderbilts and Roosevelts; her husband ran a uranium refinery and chaired a company that built parts for submarine-launched ballistic missiles; her father sat on the board of the City Bank; and her brother—soon-to-be owner of the *Herald Tribune*—was a pioneer in a new investment strategy called venture capital. According to a 1957 issue of *Fortune,* she was worth up to $200 million—a multibillionaire by today's standards, and the richest woman in the world.[159]

While her aristocratic Mayflower lineage had always preferred the sport of kings—thoroughbred racing—baseball also ran in her blue blood. Her uncle, Harry Payne Whitney, had pioneered American polo with James Gordon Bennett Jr. at the pre-Mets Polo Grounds. A generation later, Payson matured in her family's Polo Grounds luxury box from socialite to mother of five. A midlife crisis came when the last of her children left for the Ivy League around 1950. Many of the other women in her dynasty were philanthropists, poets, art collectors, and publishers. They had established the Whitney Museum, the leftist *New Republic* magazine, and the progressive New School for Social Research. Payson had amassed her own modern art collection and invested in *Gone with the Wind* and *A Streetcar Named Desire*, but the most durable institution she had built until then was a Midtown children's bookstore.

"What would you do if you had my riches?" she asked her dinner-party guests one night. The most enticing response came from her surly stockbroker, M. Donald Grant: buy a baseball team, and run it.[160] Having grown weary of the prestige of rearing athletes at the family's Greentree Stables motivated only by the lash, with no real consciousness of winning, losing, or the adoration of the people, Payson instructed Grant to buy a share of the Giants.

The investment took her fandom to a new level. Play-by-plays were sent to her on tickers like stocks wherever she went, and the arrival of Willie Mays inspired her to buy in further until her 10 percent share put her on the team's corporate board. When the board met in 1957 to vote on the San Francisco plan, only Grant, via Payson, voted against the move. Days after the Giants played their final game, Mayor Wagner received a letter from Grant offering Payson's assistance in reestablishing the team.[161]

Rickey sized up Payson as a kindred spirit—a conservative believer in free markets, whose passion for baseball was greater than profit. But when the two finally met, Payson revealed herself among New York's pragmatic pessimists. She knew from her time among the baseball bourgeoisie that Rickey's promise of a "third major" was unlikely. For it to rise above minor-league status, the CL would need major leaguers to break their contracts, which could only happen through something neither of them wanted—federal intervention in organized baseball's monopoly. Maybe a few idealistic journeymen would defect absent government action, but if Rickey could not promise Mays, she told him, she had no interest in funding his fantasy league.

With Payson out, New York's Continental League team turned to lesser heirs. Dwight Davis Jr., son of the American tennis pioneer who founded the Davis Cup competition and served under Coolidge and Hoover as Secretary of War, and George Herbert Walker Jr., nephew of Senator Prescott Bush, both invested. So did Canadian banking heiress Dorothy Killam, who had made her own failed bid to save the Brooklyn Dodgers. But questions still lingered about how much of Killam's fortune—less than half of Payson's—could realistically cross the border to fund an American team.

With enemies merging and red tape tangling, Rickey flew to Payson's Florida estate promising a more candid conversation. This time, he revealed Shea's side of the conspiracy, admitting the most likely result of his war with the majors would be a CL defeat and armistice securing a new National League franchise for New York. It was what Payson had wanted to hear all along: the return of Willie Mays, if only in road uniform.[162] Moments after Rickey's departure, Payson rang Grant and ordered the transfer of $4 million to the CL. It was enough to buy out Davis and Killam for an 80 percent controlling interest. The infant team would be hers, and hers alone.[163]

With Payson's prestigious pocketbook secured, an emboldened Rickey officially announced the formation of the Continental League at an August 1959 press conference in Manhattan. He introduced himself as league president, promising a four-year plan in which major-league caliber play would start in two years, with a World Series contender ready in another two.[164] The journalists erupted in incredulous flurry—How would organized baseball react? How would they secure the rights to build stadiums outside New York? Where would they get the players? Rickey quieted the rabble with a few dramatic stomps of his cane. He would meet with baseball's magnates soon, he assured them. Deep down, they were good patriots who would do the right thing.

Commissioner Frick met with Rickey the next week with the peace offering Shea and Payson awaited. One or two expansion franchises, seeded from major-league roster scraps, were offered to avoid a prolonged battle over contracts and territory. But Rickey, backed by CL's non–New York investors, stood firm. He responded they could proceed the hard way, with player raids and political pressure to settle reserve-clause litigation in Congress, or the easy way: if the majors cooperated, the CL would build their rosters from scratch. Rickey's agrarian method of player development had pulled the Cardinals, Dodgers, and Pirates from the cellar in a short time span, he reminded them, and he had no doubt he could do the same for an entire league.

Frick emerged from the meeting feigning satisfaction. The "third major," he told the press, had organized baseball's support.

The announcement unleashed a wave of enthusiasm among millions of New Yorkers. As the CL farm system prepared for their first season in the South, letters filled local papers with suggestions for how a new New York team could properly combine the lost teams' traditions and fanbases, foster community roots, and socially benefit the city. Jonathan Lethem's 2013 novel *Dissident Gardens* depicted one semipro team of Queens socialists excitedly marching into Bill Shea's office with a proposal to brand the team the Proletarians.[165]

Wagner and Moses's time-tested strategy of unleashing popular support to bend bureaucracy crumbled all opposition at the Board of Estimate. Bonds were issued to start construction on the Flushing Municipal Stadium, a moment economist Roger Noll described as the beginning of a major shift in the sports business, "from a world in which teams owned and built their own stadiums to a world in which all stadiums were subsidized."[166]

But within organized baseball—the Yankees excepted—everything was going according to plan. Soon after the initial meeting with Frick,

Walter O'Malley, now the dominant figure among NL owners as millions filled the Los Angeles Coliseum to see the Dodgers, revealed in a letter to his old foe Rickey that they had only allowed the CL Trojan horse to pass its gates in order to steal its arsenal. They would press forward to absorb the New York team, Moses's stadium, and perhaps one other CL upstart into the majors.

The siege began. CL owners outside of New York received legal notices from nearby minor-league clubs demanding indemnities for breaching their territorial monopolies on professional baseball exhibitions. The figures were so intentionally exorbitant that the would-be magnates would have no choice but to initiate yearslong court processes that would prevent them from breaking ground on their new parks indefinitely.

Rickey returned to the *Sporting News* and other outlets to blast the maneuver, counterattacking with cash offers to major leaguers to jump sides. But after a year, the raids only claimed a single defector, CL farm rosters were staffed only by rejects from other circuits, and ground on most CL ballparks remained unbroken. Only one battleground remained: the US Senate.

"How come that sixteen men control a sport of 175 million people and confine the public exhibitions of the sport to 15 towns at the very time when 20 great additional cities wish to offer its people similar exhibitions?" Rickey bellowed in the Capitol at Senator Estes Kefauver's hearings to reintroduce legislation limiting baseball's monopoly in 1960. By fighting expansion, he continued, organized baseball was unintentionally committing suicide, like someone who "feels all right passing the 12th floor on a jump from the 20th."[167]

When a Senator asked why he had testified at previous hearings that the reserve clause and antitrust exemption were "harmless illegalit[ies]" that only a communist would oppose, he responded it was not he who changed, but his fellow magnates.[168] Far worse than bad business, their blackballing of the CL was an affront to the American intellect and way of life. With baseball's decline, and the rise of simplistic football and basketball as replacements, there would be an explosion of juvenile delinquency, and a reduction of America's stature on the global stage. If the CL were permitted to flourish, on the other hand, he promised baseball would assert itself as "the moral equivalent of war" that "may conceivably become a universal peacemaker among mankind."[169]

While Commissioner Frick's rebuttal was comparatively sheepish, organized baseball's victory was always assured. The public debate had all been a front for backroom horse-trading between senators protecting the monopoly of their allies in ownership and those angling for new teams in their states. The numbers were in organized baseball's favor, and the bill was sent back to committee for revision as a separate bill *defending* baseball's monopoly swiftly passed the chamber.

While it was a fatal blow for the CL, organized baseball was rattled by the vote's closeness. Over forty senators, including Texan Senate majority leader and soon-to-be vice presidential nominee Lyndon Johnson, and Richard Nixon, on track to win the Republican nomination for president, voted against the new antitrust exemption, proving that the CL's broad expansionist mission still had strong allies.

Players were CL-curious as well. While only one had defected to Rickey, his promises of pooled funds toward a better pension plan stood in stark contrast with their bosses' refusal to discuss pensions at all after they expanded the season by seven games to 162. If the CL somehow went forward, the owners worried their workers would demand commensurate benefits.

Shortly after the hearings, Frick called a peace conference in Chicago between the CL owners and O'Malley's expansion committee. Rickey attempted to rally his troops in a pre-meeting huddle, begging them to stand strong. But as the meeting ground to an early impasse, Braves owner Lou Perini floated a take-it-or-leave-it offer for the CL to dissolve in exchange for half of their franchises entering the majors within two years, and the other half at a later date.[170]

Rickey again urged his team to consider the lack of commitments in this proposal—Which teams and when? And by what mechanism would they fill their rosters? The CL owners, however, knew the Senate defeat left little other chance of salvaging their franchises. Perini's vague deal would relieve them of millions in liability from the minor-league lawsuits, and they jumped to accept it.

The long bluff finally called, Rickey threw his arms around Shea as they left the meeting. "I may never see you again," he told him, "but it was a great fight, a great fight."[171]

Organized baseball, Moses, Shea, Payson, the metropolis, and America were overjoyed. For the first time in half a century, baseball would expand—however slightly—and New York would be a National League town once again. It was an event no less momentous than the addition of two new US states the previous year, or the election of John F. Kennedy, who promised a new frontier in space, a few weeks later.

But most of the other CL owners and Rickey had lost. While New York, Houston, and Minneapolis investors would get their teams, the fourth expansion team eventually went to a new, non-CL franchise instead—country singer Gene Autry's Los Angeles Angels. After decades of waiting, five other CL cities would get their expansion teams under different ownerships, with Buffalo shot down entirely.

Over the next weeks, Rickey wrote the winning clubs with some parting advice, and more prophetic warnings of "trouble to come." The leagues, he wrote, would kneecap its newcomers by manipulating the expansion drafts to ensure they'd only get "crumbs from the table." With bottom-barrel players, they would be lucky to scrape out more than forty wins in their first seasons. To survive these lean years, he recommended they incorporate whatever they could of the novel and rebellious utopian spirit envisioned in the early days of CL planning. Moses's pretentiously modern new stadium in Queens should be craftily marketed to lure spurned Giants and Dodgers fans, and a new generation of youth, to loyally await the day when New York's colorful new people's team came of age for a destined showdown against their jealous big brother in the Bronx.

But even then, he cautioned, "the fantasy wears out rapidly with a disreputable club."[172] The new team would have to transition rapidly from novelty to genuine competitiveness, and he urged Payson to invest heavily in scouting, minor-league player production, and a full absorption of whatever talent remained in the dying Negro Leagues.[173] If they could make it to the World Series by around 1970, he wrote, the inherent wisdom of his project would be proven, and baseball and America could be saved yet.

Impressed by his unflagging vision, Payson offered Rickey a job running the team. Rickey said he would accept, under the condition she earmark $5 million in additional funding to make his vision a reality. Much of that sum would be used to continue test-piloting the CL concept of a communal farm system, with a central scouting bureau and draft-based system of promotion. Once the major-league owners saw the efficiency of this method, they would buy into the system designed to "establish equal opportunity for all clubs in the field of young talent."[174] Warren Corbett of the Society for American Baseball Research later noted the irony: "The goal was to level the financial playing field so there would be no Yankee dynasty and no charity case like the St. Louis

Browns. Branch Rickey, conservative Republican and fervent anti-communist, wrote a constitution for socialism in baseball."[175]

It was perhaps less the price tag than Rickey's apparent radicalism that led Payson to withdraw the job offer. She had entertained the egalitarian aspirations of the Continental League only as a lark, with her primary interest not in revolutionizing the game, but in nostalgia for Willie Mays, the Giants, and the once-lush arboretum of Flushing she had been chauffeured past as a girl on trips to the Polo Grounds. Her romantic vision dressed the team in pink and black, like the thoroughbreds of Greentree's stables, with a name referencing the silly little songbirds once ubiquitous in the pre-Moses verdancy—the Meadowlarks.

She handed off her designs and Rickey's more sensible suggestions to Grant, Shea, and their business partners. But they had already incorporated the team as the Metropolitan Baseball Club, a name that recalled the 1880 team while perfectly matching Moses's project of expanding New York's public square away from the Manhattan cosmopolis and toward an ever-expanding and powerful tristate suburban metropolis. In private, and among their journalist pals, the men exclusively referred to the new team as the Mets.

The name played perfectly to sportswriter enthusiasts of baseball history and abbreviation. Seemingly organic columns began calling them the Mets as well. But to appease Payson, a plebiscite was arranged in which the two names, alongside other suggestions submitted by mail, would be chosen by a twelve-person committee of sportswriters.[176] As hundreds of entries poured in, only Payson's fraternal *Herald Tribune* argued in favor of the Meadowlarks concept, and the ten finalists finally put to vote at a Greentree cocktail party were all decisively urban, including the Skyliners, Skyscrapers, Jets, and Mets. The Meadowlarks, and all other pastoral names, had been mercilessly mowed like Ardizzone's

Willets Point paradise a quarter-century prior. "I like this one," Payson said, showing the winning slip to the audience with resignation.[177]

Like the creation of the team, and the appropriation of public funds for their stadium, the result was an inevitability, manufactured behind the facade of a democratic relationship between the political machine and its constituents. Few minded this new incarnation of Tammany's honest graft. O'Malley and Stoneham had betrayed the people; Moses and Shea made them feel whole again.

The first woman to start a major sports franchise would continue to weigh in on the Mets' branding and personnel, but would generally be seen as little more than a doting matriarchal figurehead in her field box, showering gifts upon the players who lovingly called her "Ma Payson." Occasionally, in troubled times, fans would consult her, especially to rein in Grant as his megalomania expanded and he took fuller control of the franchise a decade later. "The men do it all," she'd sorrowfully admit to them, because "they're the ones who know."[178]

PART II

THE ANTI-TEAM (1962–1994)

Well, here we are at last. When the Emperor Titus opened the Colosseum in 80 AD, he could have felt no happier. . . .

This, my fine friends, is an event in literature, as well as sport. The folklore of baseball will climb like ivy over this stadium, encrust it with tradition, mellow it with the lurid colors of fiction, invest it with the visions of boyhood and the dreams of age, challenge the diet of the giants of Homer, . . . Mark Twain, and Dante, and put Paul Bunyan to shame.

When I think back over the dilemma of Walter O'Malley, torn between his love of Ebbets Field and the desire to be on the side of Los Angeles, I'm weak with the perspiration of dramatic suspense. At this threat of piracy, the entire nation stood aghast. More influences were brought to bear to hold the Dodgers in Brooklyn then to keep the French in Algiers.

Spare us your satire, shrieked the fans, you're speaking of the team we love. No, no, you can't take them away from us. Think of the rape of the Sabines. Remember Helen of Troy and the Face That Launched 1,000 Ships. A bum is a bum is a bum.

Strong men wept and little children cried in the streets, but it was all in vain—Walter O'Malley's rendering of Tosti's "Goodbye" made the first coronetist in Souza's band look like a National Guard bugler. . . .

From Walter O'Malley's angle there was to be sure no gold in them-thar Corona hills of ashes and refuse, celebrated by Scott Fitzgerald in The Great Gatsby, *and no oil or uranium in the off-scourings and leavings of Brooklyn, leveled to fill Flushing Meadow. This dubious real estate became a public park and is going to stay that way. How could we compete with an entire arroyo in California? This question, my fine friends, is rhetorical and calls for no answer. It is all, as the French say, of a great sadness. . . .*

Joy has returned to our favorite Flushing Meadow. The sun shines. Fans play. Children shout. And a great Macedonian cry arises from the crowd as another Casey, Casey Stengel, armed with his fractured English, comes to bat. . . . My faith in the ultimate triumph of the democratic process has been restored. I now believe there are absolutely no limits to what can be accomplished. At least in the field of sports. . . .

It's the old story. Those who won't admit defeat can't be beat.

—Extract from remarks by Robert Moses on October 28, 1961, breaking ground on William A. Shea Municipal Stadium

Moses appealed plaintively to us all: Am I not the man who blotted out the Valley of Ashes and gave mankind beauty in its place? It is true, and we owe him homage for it. And yet, he did not really wipe out the ashes, only moved them to another site. For the ashes are part of us . . .

—Marshall Berman, All That is Sold Melts Into Air

Chapter 5

THE NEW BREED

During the winter of 1961, a disturbingly operatic jingle hit New York's airwaves. It sang the story of an average New Yorker wandering the streets of a Manhattan now eerily desolate in daylight. He scans the sidewalks east to west, finding the butcher shops and bakeries shuttered, realizing in horror the city is totally empty.

Had everyone followed the runaway factories and middle class to the suburbs? Or had something far worse happened—like the postapocalyptic scenario of the 1959 film *The World, the Flesh, and the Devil,* in which Harry Belafonte's character finds himself New York's sole survivor of an atomic gas attack? *Where did they go?* an omniscient chorus begs in terror.

Then, the cheerful twist: *To MEET THE METS!*

The protagonist is suddenly transported to a sold-out ballpark, where the entirety of New York jumps and cheers manically in their seats. The players answer their enthusiasm by going on an offensive tear, socking homer after homer over the outfield wall. *So hurry up and come on down, 'cause we've got ourselves a ball club,* the song concludes, *the Mets of New York town!*

The song's writers, Ruth Roberts and Bill Katz of Long Island, had previously penned rocker Buddy Holly's soulful B-side "Mailman, Bring Me No More Blues," about a man expecting to be dumped by letter. Their contest entry for the new team's official song was the result of similar genre-bending: the commercial radio jingle, the choral stomp of a collegiate football fight song, and the 1894 vaudeville standard "The Sidewalks of New York."

Tammany populist Al Smith had revived the turn-of-the-century city sing-along "Sidewalks" to evoke nostalgia for New Yorkers drunkenly waltzing in the streets during his twenties political campaigns against Prohibition. After a few days singing the earworm to herself in strolls around her estate, Joan Payson believed "Meet the Mets" would perform a similar function—promising the return of civic mirth following the Dodgers' and Giants' departure, urban blight, and threats of nuclear annihilation.

She notified Roberts and Katz that the song was a winner, requesting just one addition. The anthem was completed with the line: *The fans are true to the orange and blue.*

The color scheme came from a submission for the team emblem by another contest winner, the cartoonist Ray Gotto, whose illustrations recalled the comic *Archie*. Gotto, too, imagined the abandoned city unified around the new National League team, inserting Brooklyn structures into Manhattan's imposing shadowed skyline, underlined by an illuminated Queensboro Bridge, and sewn together with orange baseball stitching.

The composition's dizzying spherical depth, vibrating with the complementary and contrasting tension of warm orange and cool blue, inked to comic-strip saturation, was finally stabilized by the Mets' buoyant uniform script, rising above the dark urban chaos like a neon-orange sun.

As an art collector, Payson recognized the populist avant-garde nature of comics and commercials. Pop art was the late-fifties fad in the downtown galleries, rebuking modern art's elitism by democratically merging low culture and socialist realism on grand canvases. Sticking with the aesthetic, Gotto's emblem became the basis of the Mets uniform, and political cartoonist Willard Mullin was hired to draw the cover of the team's inaugural yearbook.

The man who had anthropomorphized the Dodgers into the *Bum* was now given the reverse task: create a cartoon to guide the embryonic team's spiritual maturation. Mullin again chose a lowly caricature—a fidgeting, upright infant in a diaper and oversized Mets cap, his grimacing face on the verge of either a laughing fit or shrieking tantrum. Even if Payson's baby would be ridiculed in the sports section, the humble yearbook cover implied, it would at least be an endearing character for the funny pages.

When it came to baseball decisions, however, Payson installed a figure of grayscale severity—George Weiss, architect of the post-Ruth Yankee dynasty.

Hired to the Bronx in 1932, Weiss used the riches of Ruth and Gehrig to modernize Branch Rickey's Southern farm system, forging the conservative "Yankee mold" to produce immortals like Joe DiMaggio, Mickey Mantle, Whitey Ford, and Yogi Berra. When Weiss was promoted to general manager in 1947, the Yankees became even more imperial through baseball's New York–based golden era, winning ten pennants and seven world championships in twelve years.

Beneath Weiss during this stretch was his foil, hired as team manager in 1947, Casey Stengel. A veteran of the teens Dodgers and twenties Giants, Stengel looked like W. C. Fields with a sardonically soused wit to match. He had been known as baseball's clown prince since his sarcastic public feud with Charles Ebbets over pay in 1914, and an incident in his post-trade 1919 return to a booing Brooklyn crowd in which he doffed his Pirates cap to release a hidden sparrow into the stands.

After his playing career, an ill-timed managerial stint with the Depression-era "Daffy Dodgers" gave Stengel a reputation more clownish than clever. But Weiss perceived the brilliant mind buried beneath the cloddish facade, likened by Stengel's biographer Robert W. Creamer to a complex computer that discreetly analyzed decades of baseball knowledge before spitting out an inscrutable, but often prescient, conclusion.[179] Among Stengel's Yankee innovations were seminars for rookies during spring training—earning him the Brooklynese nickname *ol' perfessor*—and shifting players to different positions, like DiMaggio to first, Mantle to the outfield, and Berra to catcher. While ownership, DiMaggio, and other straitlaced Yankee standard-bearers never appreciated his eccentric screeds, schemes, and mannerisms, they learned to live with him as trophies piled up.

The latter half of Stengel's Bronx reign witnessed his once-charming habit of forgetting players' names getting worse, his monologues more incoherent, and mid-game catnaps more frequent. A loss in the 1960 World Series to the Rickey-integrated Pirates gave Yankees ownership an excuse to fire both the septuagenarian Stengel and the barely reformed segregationist Weiss. While Stengel's slipping dissuaded all but a couple teams from courting him, Weiss received calls from half of baseball, including Joan Payson. Wanting to stay in New York and get some revenge, Weiss signed on as the Mets' president, and talked Casey into reestablishing their odd couple as their manager shortly after.

Weiss would never get used to the team's comic branding, but Stengel immediately embraced it as a parody of Yankee sanctimony. After being fired, he had boasted to the press that the Yankees' long-term success and recent World Series losses were both results of them being too good for the American League.[180] Now returning home to his National League roots, he had the chance to definitively prove whether he was a senile clown, a genius, or some combination of the two.

At his introductory press conference, Stengel appeared the perfect fit as the first wearer of the Mets' new uniform. The home whites combined the bubbly cartoonishness of Gotto's emblem with nostalgic elements of his old teams—the blue pinstripes and cap of the Dodgers, on which the Giants' rusty insignia was polished to shine ostentatious orange. No one in the press pool was quite sure, however, whether it was cutting wit or the dullness of age when he opened with an allusion to the century-deceased amateur era: "It's a great honor for me to be joining the Knickerbockers."[181]

At their spring training opening presser in St. Petersburg a few months later, Stengel, the first man to *meet the Mets,* looked as though he *had* seen a ghost. When asked where they thought the team would finish the 1962 season, Weiss optimistically answered seventh place, while Stengel feigned a glance at their schedule and replied, "In Chicago."[182]

Rickey's prediction that organized baseball would attempt to smother their unwanted newborns in the cradle turned out half-true. In 1961, NL executives saw how the AL's new Washington Senators and Los Angeles Angels filled their rosters via an expansion draft generously offering all but a protected core of the league's players. When it came time for the Mets and Houston Colt .45s to choose players the next year, the NL increased draft protection to ten players per team, further narrowing options by allowing teams to conceal their best prospects in the minors beforehand. Baseball legend Rogers Hornsby, hired by Weiss to make the picks, remarked that what they expected to be a grab bag turned out to be a "garbage bag. . . . I mean, this is going to be really bad." The disarmed Colt .45s' GM Paul Richards concurred in his own post-draft press conference: "Gentlemen, we've just been fucked."[183]

To compensate for the slim pickings, Weiss spent $1.8 million of Payson's war chest on signing "as many old Dodgers and Giants as possible," George Vecsey wrote.[184] Although her top prize, Willie Mays, was not for sale at any price, a *Sporting News* comic praised the assemblage, illustrating Weiss painting the names of these fading greats as the new franchise face, with Billy Loes its left eye, Roger Craig its nose, Don Zimmer and Charlie Neal a broad smile. Completed under the shabby fedora of the Brooklyn Bum, with METS scrawled across the brim, cartoon Stengel remarks: "Reminds me of an ol' fren!"[185]

The old-timers of the team would attract nostalgic fans through the rough first Polo Grounds season—the first step to carry out the eight-year plan that Rickey had suggested to Payson. Step two sends the infant team toddling to a glorious new domed Municipal Stadium in Flushing in 1963. Fans would fill the space-age park's ample parking lots, glide up its escalators to the vast seating of quadruple decks, and marvel at the flashy lighting and "photorama" scoreboard displaying images of players, hopefully distracting from the still subpar spectacle on the field.

While the big-league plan proceeds, an army of scouts, led by Weiss's left-hand man, ex-Yankee and Manhattan Project manager Johnny Murphy, rebuilds the Yankees' dynastic farm system. In step three, tens of thousands of new fans cross the street from the 1964 World's Fair to see Murphy's debut crop—nicknamed the "Youth of America" by Stengel in reference to Kennedy's plan for a youth-led Peace Corps. The youngsters climb the NL standings in step four, allowing old Casey to gracefully pass the managerial torch to their thirty-eight-year-old expansion draftee first baseman, Gil Hodges. From there, the Dodger legend teaches the Youth of America to complete their journey: a sprint toward a world championship by 1970.

The plan was no less audacious than Kennedy's vow to step foot on the moon. News writers had a far easier angle with NASA, however, than their sports section counterparts did in selling the Mets' cosmic vision. Few of their youngsters appeared hype-able as they lost their first week of training games, and their veterans were so washed-up or humiliated that some planned to retire before Opening Day. A string of uninspiring columns sent team marketers scrambling for a new narrative to inspire faith through the launch failures and fatalities. They circled March 22 on the calendar—the date the Mets would host an exhibition game against the Yankees. If Americans believed that their far inferior space program could catch up with the evil might of the Soviets, perhaps the Mets, too, could earn adulation from an audacious rivalry.

Knowing the traditional sports pool was too rational to entertain the idea of a Subway World Series in the making, a raft of new invitations went out to New York feature writers. With the coming grudge match serving as its climax, spring training could be covered as the regrouping of the defeated forces of the National League Town. A half-century of genetic Giants and Dodgers hatred, revived through the bitterness of the spurned Weiss and Stengel, was returning, the marketers pitched, as a new type of baseball team—a *spite team*, dedicated to the revanchist populism of one day toppling the Yankee Empire.

The angle intrigued the editors, and a literary auxiliary went south. One was Robert Lipsyte, a twenty-four-year-old aspiring novelist and baseball neophyte from the *New York Times*. Sports was always the *Times*'s "version of the comics," he recalled. "They didn't care that I didn't know anything about sports because I could write."[186] Instead of the dismal games, he focused on funny and touching human interest stories at the camp. One followed Astoria college student John Pappas, who flew to St. Petersburg to demand a tryout. Murphy finally relented, watching him pitch for a few minutes before telling him to get back to class.

Teaming up with Lipsyte to cover the story was Stan Isaacs of *Newsday,* whose regular Out of Left Field column first described the Mets as "the people's team."[187] In the vulgar free-associative rants of Stengel, mostly tuned out by other sportswriters, the beatnik duo saw a fountain of jokes and koans reminiscent of Burroughs or Kerouac. When one writer asked Stengel if Don Zimmer was the "guts of the club," he responded: "Why, he's beyond that. He's much more. He's the perdotious quotient of the qualificatilus. He's the lower intestine."[188] Other rambles held political intrigue, like a throwaway comment about prohibiting the team from using their hotel pool. Lipsyte asked if this had anything to do with Florida's segregation, to which Stengel snapped: "None of them are allowed to swim, and I've also given them instructions that none of them are allowed to fuck. Now you put that in your *New York Times.*"[189]

Lipsyte's and Isaacs's absurdist accounts of the camp fascinated New York and the sports world, making the March 22 match-up the best covered in spring-training history. More writers were sent to cover the game, including *New Yorker* fiction editor Roger Angell—the first sporting event the future *poet laureate of baseball* would ever cover. "One sensed that this game was a crisis for the Mets," he wrote of the early innings, "their first chance to discover, against the all-conquerors, whether they were truly a ball team. A rout, a laugher, a comedy of ineptitude might destroy them before the season ever began."[190]

With Stengel's contempt for the disinterested Yankees B-squad growing palpable through the game, the motley crowd of 6,000 Dodgers, Giants, and even some Yankees supporters, stirred up by the young feature writers' portrayal of the doomed but plucky amateur squad, transformed into the first Mets fans. Unified by the vision of embarrassing the rich squares in a spring sneak attack, they cheered on Stengel's determination with an enthusiasm unseen at any other practice match. Improvised cheers, heckles, and chants grew with ironic fervor as the Mets took a lead in the sixth, blew it in the ninth, and then won on a walk-off single.

The excitement that swept through the crowd doubled back, the *Times*'s traditional sportswriter Arthur Daley wrote, "into that bastion of neutrality, the press box." The Mets had conceived of their personality, he continued, as a team with the "unexpected ability to pluck at heart strings. . . . There is an innate appeal to the spectacle of the have-nots giving a comeuppance to their betters."[191] Angell left the game with newfound appreciation for baseball, a game in which "every hometown fan, every doomed admirer of underdogs will have his afternoons of revenge and joy."[192]

Even then–Yankees beat writer George Vecsey concurred: "The sensitive front office of George M. Weiss was afraid this publicity would make the Mets look like amateurs, but the reaction could not have been better. Every shivering fan back in New York now realized that the Mets were the people's team."[193]

The marketing gambit had worked. Media hype from St. Pete jetted back to New York as the regular season began. After being blown out in St. Louis to start the season, the Mets were welcomed to New York for a parade to City Hall attended by 40,000 new fans won over by the colorful branding and viral press. At their Polo Grounds home opener the next day, Friday the 13th, Mayor Wagner threw out the first pitch of a rainy, muddy slog in a ballpark that had seen little maintenance during its five-year offseason. The luxury boxes flooded, leaving only 12,000 cheap-seat fans to cheer the 4–3 loss to the Pirates.

The Mets would lose the next game and the next. Then the next, the next, and the next. After losing their first nine games, they finally popped champagne in Pittsburgh to christen their maiden win. They then proceeded to lose three more, and seven of their next nine, for an impressively bad opening record of 3-16.

Many of these early losses, however, were kept close by thrilling late-game rallies that fell tantalizingly short. Something finally appeared to click in early May, when they won nine of twelve against the Braves, Cubs, and Phillies. Suddenly there was hope of a thrilling season-long race to stay out of the league cellar, making them, the *Post*'s Leonard Koppett wrote, "no worse than respectably bad."[194]

Then came a seventeen-game losing streak. New York had seen losing teams before, but they had never seen a *non-winning* team. The marketers, believing the well-established principle that losers could not draw, shifted all promotions toward the upcoming return of the Dodgers and Giants to the Polo Grounds.

And yet the spring hype continued to accumulate. After five years of banal writing on Yankee excellence, stringers began begging to jump into the Mets press pool. A new type of sports prose was evolving there, synthesizing the traditional comic street-beat style of Dick Young with beatnik prose and the class-conscious antiauthoritarianism of the emerging youth movement. Irked *Newsday* vet Jimmy Cannon derided these writers as "the chipmunks" after the shrill cartoon trio. Their preferred term, Jonathan Mahler wrote, was the "new breed of sportswriter."[195]

And the writers believed much of the Mets' roster were themselves part of their *new breed*—young workers creatively trying their best at a job for which they were not exactly qualified. Stengel encouraged this dynamic. He had never forgotten his battles over salary with Charles

Ebbets in the 1910s, and had subverted Senate hearings on baseball regulation by slyly mocking the owners' foot-dragging on expanding pensions and benefits.[196] Now among a Mets clubhouse of near-retirement vets and youngsters knowing their big-league stint was likely temporary, Stengel motivated players purely on the level of sticking it to the bosses—the better they did for themselves, the more bonus or holdout pay they could squeeze out of Weiss.

The Mets' first breakout star, Ron Hunt, for example, was an offseason teamster who jumped at Stengel's offer of fifty dollars or a new suit for each hit-by-pitch. "I didn't want to go to his tailor!" Hunt recalled. "I took the fifty bucks!"[197] During his time in the majors, he would be plunked more than any other player.

A third *new breed* of fans gestated on the commutes and in living rooms to the warm sights and sounds of Mets radio and TV broadcasts.

Endearing commentary from football sportscaster Lindsey Nelson, pro-union Pirates great Ralph Kiner, and the ever-optimistic Bob Murphy inspired a rising viewership enamored with the trio's smooth conversational dynamic. But WOR-TV's camera roaming the stands between plays in search of interesting personalities truly set the snowball in motion. A trickle of outer-borough youth began making the long pilgrimage to Harlem, seeking the camera's attention with colorful outfits and humorous homemade banners ironically extolling the pitiful players. Their family and friends tuned-in to see their few seconds of televised fame, inspiring an avalanche of new weirdos that completed the trifecta—a new sports counterculture of media, athletes, and fans collectively self-identified as the singular *New Breed.*[198]

Roger Angell, at first skeptical of the narrative as marketing hype, became a convert once he saw it in person during five games against the Dodgers and Giants at the end of May. "Even before we arrived at the park it was clear that neither the city subway system nor the Mets themselves had really believed we were coming," he wrote in the *New Yorker*.

> By game time, there were standees three-deep behind the lower-deck stands, sitting-standees peering through the rafters from the ramps behind the upper deck, and opportunist-standees perched on telephone booths and lining the runways behind the bleachers. . . . The shouts, the cheers, and the deep, steady roar made by 56,000-odd fans in excited conversation were comical and astonishing, and a cause for self-congratulation; just by coming out in such ridiculous numbers.[199]

Outdrawing even the golden-era Giants' World Series games, the May 30 Dodgers-Mets doubleheader crowd was the largest the Polo Grounds had seen since 1942. Loud applause and cheers came early for the refugee opponents as Sandy Koufax shut down the Mets through three and took a 10–0 lead by the fourth inning. In the bottom half, an explosive Hodges home run finally awoke the New Breed into a frenzy of dissonant jubilance. "Gil's homer pulled the cork," Angell wrote, "and now there arose from all over the park a full, furious, happy shout . . ."[200]

The first words of this coalescing chant were like a frustrated nudge called out to someone taking too long in the bathroom or driving too slow in traffic: *Let's go!*

The phrase first appeared in the English language as the last line of Shakespeare's *The Comedy of Errors*, ending the bickering between two twins about which was oldest by concluding: "And now let's go hand in hand, not one before another."[201] *Let's go* then popularly reappeared on 1942 recruitment posters reading, "Fight. Let's Go! Join the Navy,"[202] and was restored to its tragicomic tradition ten years later on a homemade banner at Ebbets Field that read LET'S GO BROOKLYN with the *Brooklyn Os* turned into faces—one smiling, one frowning.

As another decade passed, Angell heard annoyed whines of *Let's go!* accumulate against the Mets' lagging hitters. With Hodges's lightning bolt, the elements of frustration and adoration for the primordial team organically compounded—*Let's go! . . . Let's go, Mets! . . . Let's go Mets!*

Early Mets employee Dan Reilly claimed his friends had developed the chant through the same combination of cheer and jeer during the spring game against the Yankees. "It caught on almost immediately, and I vividly remember most of the fans in our section joining in. . . . It was the first time I recall ever hearing any baseball fans cheer their team on that way."[203] Perhaps Reilly and friends helped reintroduce the chant that afternoon, or perhaps this was merely parallel evolution; a twisted rally-cry emerging at the very moment the New Breed announced their break from their Dodgers-Giants lineage.

At the height of the chanting, one group of ex–Dodgers fans pulled the strings on a row of seven painted window shades to reveal O'MALLEY GO HOME!—repurposed from the anti-American slogan *Yankee Go Home* written on walls around the postwar US empire overseas. The cadre was chased away by security, but all the spiteful energy gave the forsaken team new life.[204] Just as the jingle foretold, the cheers of all New York translated to the Mets socking two more hits, and two more Hodges homers in game two, further amplifying the crowd's imposing roar. Fearing a riot, players of both teams exchanged nervous glances, and incredulous radio listeners called WABC to complain the euphoria must have been prerecorded to make the game sound more exciting.[205]

Koufax pitched out of trouble, and the Dodgers went on to sweep the doubleheader, but Angell concluded that he and LA had learned the same "odd lesson": "It is safe to assume the Mets are going to lose, but dangerous to assume they won't startle you in the process."[206]

Similarly astounded reports from the series spread the New Breed virus across the city and suburbs in what Koppett called *Mets syndrome*, and Lipsyte, *Metsomania*.

Among those to catch the bug was a kiddie contingent of New Breed adolescents, lured to the Polo Grounds by the carnival of color and noise. The front office was so swamped with inquiries from kids hoping to meet, or even play for the Mets, that the team hired extra operators.

Among the callers was future Mets broadcaster Howie Rose. Raised a Yankees fan, he had excitedly watched Roger Maris's record-breaking race to 61 home runs in 1961, only to immediately defect the next year. "I dropped my allegiance to the Yankees and became a Mets fan for the same reason so many kids of my age did at the time," he wrote, "the Mets were not our fathers' team, they were ours . . . I was narcissistic enough to believe that because I had become such a baseball fan in '61, that when this new team showed up the next year, it was created just for me: 'Here's your gift! You're a baseball fan? Here's a team of your own.'"[207]

Another young convert was my dad, Stuart Gittlitz. Before he had been bored on family outings to watch the Giants at the Polo Grounds, but, after seeing the radiant excitement of Mets games on TV went to a subsequent Sunday doubleheader and instantly became one of Angell's "Go! Shouters." "I was no longer just an observer," he recalled, astounded at how the energy reproduced itself based on an almost mystical belief that "our cheers were actually affecting the team's play. As the fans' noise level increased—without scoreboard prompting—it seemed the Mets would get a hit. . . . I had never felt that passion before."[208]

Most sportswriters similarly understood Metsomania as a rejection of the stuffy culture of Yankee Stadium. Lindsey Nelson wrote their games felt like visits to the Statue of Liberty or United Nations: "You couldn't bring pennants around, or noisemakers, or anything else that might draw attention away from the field and into the stands. The Yankees were remote, a proud, haughty team sufficient unto itself. The fans who watched them were expected to be spectators, not participants."[209] Angell added that the New Breed's enthusiasm in the face of near-certain defeat flew in the face of the transactional, capitalistic logic of the Yankees fans' expectations of perfection: "They coolly accept the late-inning rally, the winning homer, as only their due.... *They ought to damn well do better than this, considering what they're being paid!*" Asserting perfection as inhuman, the cheers for the struggling athletes of the Polo Grounds were truly "yells for ourselves," he concluded, coming from "a wry, half-understood recognition that there is more Met than Yankee in every one of us."[210]

The subtly anti-capitalist interpretation of the New Breed echoed throughout the metropolis, turning the Mets into a new vessel for the class resentment simmering since the evisceration of the workers' movement in the fifties. "This is a team for the cab driver who gets held up and the guy who loses out on a promotion because he didn't maneuver himself to lunch with the boss enough," the *Tribune*'s Jimmy Breslin wrote in his book about the 1962 Mets, *Can't Anybody Here Play This Game?* "It is the team for every guy who has to get out of bed in the morning and go to work for short money on a job he does not like. And it is the team for every woman who looks up ten years later and sees her husband eating dinner in a T-shirt and wonders how the hell she let this guy talk her into getting married."[211]

Marxist writer Peter St. Clair similarly recalled the emergence of the New Breed in a 2014 essay for the *Brooklyn Rail*. Born and raised in Midwood, Brooklyn, St. Clair had formed a gang of Dodgers hooligans in the fifties who subwayed to the Polo Grounds for away games, or to the Bronx to obnoxiously root for whoever was facing the Yankees, as a sort of political practice that replaced class with team colors: "with the Yankees in the capitalist role and the Brooklyn Dodgers as the workers." After five years absent their proletarian heroes, he noticed "all of Brooklyn [became] immediate Mets fans," and got the rascals back together to meet the Mets. "Jimmy and I and our friends Wimpy and Chipper roamed over the whole ancient structure during long summer doubleheaders (very long sometimes because although the Mets rarely won, they often battled their rivals into extra innings) . . . As a teenager harassed by my parents at home, teachers in school, and cops on the street[,] I identified with the underdog Mets."[212]

The blue-collar dives of National League Town, Breslin reported, were plastered with clipped newspaper photos of the team's antiheroes, especially the prodigiously erroneous infielders Marv Throneberry and Elio Chacón. First baseman Throneberry had been trained by the Yankees, traded to the Athletics for Roger Maris, and publicized as the Mets' Mantle after his early-season acquisition. Payson's praise for one of his early home runs earned him the nickname "Marvelous Marv," but the name became an endearing insult during his season of catastrophic strikeouts, bobbles, and baserunning boners.[213] And the worse he got, the larger and more demented his field-level fan club, who turned the bitterness of his bungles into a sweet jam of fruit-based puns on his name—CRANBERRY, STRAWBERRY, *WE LOVE THRONEBERRY!*

Venezuelan shortstop Chacón was a lesser cult figure. He briefly appeared on the NL champ Reds in 1961, and Payson shelled out over $75,000 to sign him after she saw him steal home against the Yankees in the World Series.[214] She regretted her choice by spring, when the light hitter and poor fielder fistfought Willie Mays in San Francisco after a hard slide into second. Only the letters praising Chacón's grit pouring into the front office from his dive bar fan clubs could save him from Payson's wrath.

Likely unknown to the Chacónists was the revolutionary road that brought him to New York. His professional career began with the Reds affiliate Sugar Kings of Havana. Among the finest minor-league clubs, with aspirations of going major in the Continental League, they managed to keep their schedule through the Revolution. After the guerillas' victory in 1959, the Reds attempted to move the team to the United States, only to have Fidel Castro order them to stay put.

The Sugar Kings played their final season amid the postrevolutionary euphoria. Armed fans routinely fired live rounds to celebrate the Kings as they fought their way to the Little World Series in 1959 against the Minneapolis Millers. After an on-field speech from Castro and disruptions by Santeria-practicing fans, Chacón led a rally in game seven that clinched the championship.

The scenes horrified the gringo players, but general manager Paul Miller insisted everything was "fine in Havana, baseball wise." The revolution had actually improved the team's situation, he claimed: "Our baseball fans have more money in their pockets than ever before. . . . Laborers have received substantial salary increases, rents have been lowered, and utility rates have been cut 30 percent."[215] But when a blast at a nearby power station the next season shook the stands, the league ordered the players off the island immediately. After a short stint playing as the Jersey City Jerseys, the Sugar Kings dissolved.

Castro was so infuriated at the expropriation he retaliated with his own—banning professional baseball in favor of amateur worker leagues, and seizing dozens of US-owned businesses.[216] When a subsequent CIA-backed invasion was thwarted, President Kennedy moved toward detente. He styled himself a new breed of politician—a generational break with the political establishment, appealing to the "Youth of America" ready to move on from Cold War confrontations in favor of peaceful coexistence. Seeing the parallels himself, the president went out of his way to meet with Stengel at the 1962 All-Star game. During a visit to West Germany the next year, a sign among the cheering throngs read, LET'S GO METS![217]

While the Mets and Kennedy had won much of white flight's children back to the American pastimes of baseball and electoral politics, much of New York's youth pined for the revolutionary fervor of Cuba, idolized the bravery of the Black-youth-led Freedom Rides and lunch-counter sit-ins, and gravitated toward leftist bohemia as an antidote to the banality of the suburbs. These were the feared marijuana-smoking juvenile delinquents, the first to be labeled "teenagers" as a consumer demographic in the fifties to sell hot rods, motorcycles, tickets to drive-in B-movies, records from the traditionally Black genres of bebop, rock, and blues, and the books of queer, neo-hobo beatniks. Now this vast population of baby boomers, better educated than any prior generation, were inheriting the United States and moving back to the city day by day with increased confidence that they could join with the have-nots to create a freer and more just America. The most famous of these middle-class suburban transplants, Bob Dylan, sang a Metsian curse: The slow ones, now picking up speed, will pass the present front-runners and sink the entire social order behind them like a stone.

One of their quasi-political gatherings foreshadowing the New Breed explosion was the 1961 "folk riot" in Washington Square Park. Communist Party–affiliated folkies called a "sing-in" that spring to protest the city's attempts to ban street musicians, leading to an unexpected influx of youth pouring from the West Fourth Street station. Kids with harps, guitars, and banjos in gingham, jeans, and wool sweaters marched in thick glasses, some waving tiny American flags or holding signs reading KEEP STRUMMING and PLAY HERE, NOT LONG ISLAND. A screaming match began with the cops attempting to block the park, and the exponentially swelling crowd soon overpowered them. The *New York Mirror*'s headline the next day blared: 3000 BEATNIKS RIOT IN VILLAGE.[218]

No longer able to counter the massive threat with blacklisting, bans, or brute force, New York's politicians shifted strategies after the riot. The ban was lifted, and the Village became a safe haven for the counterculture. Nonviolent songs, sit-ins, chants, and other previously taboo expressions of youthful exuberance like Metsomania would be tolerated as comparatively harmless next to the nihilistic riots of fifties rockers, let alone militant factory occupations, or the Marxist insurgencies spreading across America's overseas empire.

Some New Breed Mets made themselves at home in bohemia. Yale-educated reliever Ken MacKenzie, nicknamed "Mr. Peepers" for his scholarly thick-rimmed glasses, got an apartment in the Village where he frequently hosted teammates: "We'd walk around and see all the art shows, drop in to the coffee shops or just watch the people. We liked the people down there. Everybody was open-minded. That's the way we like to operate."[219]

Soon, the relative anonymity the players once enjoyed there was punctured as Metsomania spread downtown. Beatnik influencer, monologist, radio host, and flash-mob organizer Jean Shepherd began promoting the Mets on his show as "enlightening" after watching one of their pathetic losses to the Phillies: "You know, I think the thing that makes baseball the perfect thing that it is, is the fact that it is, it truly is, a kind of amalgam of all the human frustrations. . . . You see all the frailties, all the hopes, the desires, and the beautiful moments of instantaneous victory to be followed only by the inevitable."[220]

Geoffrey and Tatiana Hoover depicted the interplay between Metsomania and the downtown counterculture in dozens of interviews for their 1963 fan documentary *The New Breed.* Two brothers in matching Buddy Holly glasses exchange stories of the Mets' many bungles, as if recalling slapstick bits from *I Love Lucy.* A James Dean–esque greaser sullenly defends his pride in supporting the Mets. A grizzled New Frontier psychiatrist compares Mets fandom to sadomasochist sexuality. A young mother in cat-framed glasses introduces her Mets-cap-wearing newborn as Casey. A beatnik defends the team against the curmudgeonly slights of Dick Young: "These guys were playing, they just didn't know how to play baseball! . . . You see baseball is an art, and losing's an art. . . . As far as I'm concerned that makes them giants!" A skinny Black kid in a fedora adds: "The Mets as a team is supposed to be understood, you know. They are young, they are trying to make themselves understood to the fact that they lose, and they come from behind, and that's it. We're a good team and above all we got years ahead of us."[221]

With ticket sales soaring through the summer, one Polo Grounds beer vendor, who had worked Giants games for years, revealed the profitability of this carnivalesque scene: "You know, I don't think we've ever seen fans like these. They're loud, they're crude, they're obnoxious. They yell and scream. Yankees fans would've never taken any of that. . . . I never see a guy wear a tie to the ballpark. He's always worried about spilling something on it. The Mets fans—they don't worry about anything. They spill all over themselves, their neighbors, their wives, all over the stands. Great for business."[222]

As a young pro-am promoter in Connecticut, George Weiss had courted this sort of community enthusiasm as a way to sell tickets and concessions. "He hired clowns to entertain fans before the first pitch was thrown," biographer Burton Boxerman wrote, "and he encouraged organized rooting, urging fans to bring banners to the ballpark and wave them to help motivate the players."[223] But young Weiss had also been an "idealist . . . determined to build his team upon sportsmanship and sentiment, rather than upon a commercial basis."[224] After three decades with the Yankees, the entrenched traditionalist now loomed Grinch-like over the grounds in his office behind the center-field Rheingold Beer billboard, worrying the success of the New Breed could turn the young franchise into a hopeless haven of degeneracy.

Throughout 1962, he ordered security to go to war with the self-made placards in hope of restoring fifties placidity to the Polo Grounds. He justified the joy-kill by saying the signs blocked the view of other fans, but as Go! Shouters and Throneberry devotees filled the stands, Weiss and his goons were seen as villainous straight-men snobs to the New Breed's slobbish everyman. New Breed sportswriters reported these confrontations to add color to their columns, turning each bedsheet and placard into a hydra-head whose confiscation resulted in three more taking its place.

Even worse to Weiss than the wildness of the New Breed were the Mets' historically bad results. The man who had once chastised his wife "You're either first or you're nothing" when she celebrated her runner-up finish in a pillow-making contest, was tortured by *Long Island Press* writer Jack Lang's collection of the *neggies*—negative statistics and anecdotes celebrating record-breaking poor performances from the team. The pinnacle neggie came with their 118th loss in Chicago—the most of any team in the modern era.

With two more losses rounding the total to a Herculean 120 by the end of the 1962 season, Weiss came to accept the team was less his than Stengel's. The two had taken the job to spite the Yankees, and while he had failed to make them a competitive threat, Stengel succeeded spiritually by making his sarcastically dubbed *Amazin'* Mets far more fun. All further attempts by Weiss to enclose sweet Stengelian revenge with elegant Yankee lattice would only result in recurring slapstick scenarios in which the bums would steal his cooling pie to shove it in the old boss's face every time.

Weiss called off his goons and declared a day dedicated to the sign-makers in the 1963 season. Hundreds would parade the field with their banners alongside the team holding their own placards, assembled to read: TO THE METS FANS—WE LOVE YOU TOO! Stengel held the exclamation point.[225]

By then, many more crucial elements of Weiss's eight-year plan had deteriorated.

Fans expecting to open the next season at the domed coliseum in Flushing sang an auld-lang-syne farewell to the Polo Grounds at the final home game of 1962, unaware that progress on the new park was hopelessly behind schedule. A media blackout caused by a newspaper strike hid the truth through the offseason, and confusion spread as tickets for 1963 were sold as a set of two—one for the Municipal Stadium in Flushing, the other for a demolition-slated Polo Grounds.

When the strike ended shortly before the 1963 season, Lipsyte's visit to the construction site for the *Times* revealed the truth. Trade union work stoppages had been common through the harsh winter, several subcontractors had filed for bankruptcy on the far-over-budget project, and surveyors had ruled the marshland too soft for the heavy roof and expandable outfield seats. The space-age cradle of New Breed civilization, he reported, was little more than a toilet-shaped shell surrounding a muddy pit.[226]

Back at the Polo Grounds in 1963, franchise construction stalled as well. The remaining good knee of Stengel's planned replacement, Gil Hodges, gave out early in the year—and while Hodges would gladly have taken a promotion to manager then, Stengel's humor had made him the only truly irreplaceable Met. Hodges was traded to manage the Washington Senators instead.

In exchange, the Mets received another veteran in Jimmy Piersall. Widely admired for his public battle with bipolar disorder, he made his mark during the Mets' biggest victory of the year—a midseason exhibition against the Yankees.

An incredible fifty-two thousand tickets were sold for the "Mayor's Trophy" game at Yankee Stadium, a revived fifties tradition in which the Giants or Dodgers alternated against their hated rival to fundraise for amateur baseball leagues and claim citywide bragging rights. The vast majority of the crowd were Mets fans, Lindsey Nelson recalled, who cheered wildly as a Piersall swing sent his bat flying into the stands to hit an NYPD commissioner in the ribs.[227] New Breed jouissance grew from there as the Mets scored five in the third. Once the trophy was secured, Nelson witnessed "one of the great victory demonstrations in baseball history." Police guarded Mets fans from storming the field, sending them to the parking lot where a cacophony of tooting car horns joined congratulations shouted from windows above as the conquerors paraded to Manhattan. An improvised marching song for the occasion, to the tune of "John Brown's Body," went: *These eyes have seen the glory of the Yankees in defeat / They ain't even champions of 157th Street / Glory, glory, Casey Stengel / Our Mets go marching on.*[228]

Back at the Polo Grounds shortly after, Piersall was fired after running the bases facing backward in celebration of his hundredth career home run. "There's only room for one clown on this team," Stengel snapped.[229]

The Mets improved to over a million in attendance that year, outdrawing thirteen other teams and even approaching the pennant-winning Yankees' numbers. But a brief August winning streak following the Bronx victory prevented the Mets from topping the negative triumph of 1962. Disappointed by only 111 losses, a far-smaller crowd reprised "Auld Lang Syne" for another Polo Grounds farewell. Given the light attendance, and construction woes still stymieing construction in Queens,

Weiss worried they were singing for the franchise itself. Failure to secure the new stadium had already killed their sibling football club, the AFL Titans, and some wondered how long the irony-fueled Metsomania could last. "Even now," Lipsyte worried, "more and more ordinary people go to the Polo Grounds to watch a baseball game. As the Mets progress from incompetency to mediocrity, their psychological pull will be gone."[230]

The core of the New Breed, however, sang in blissful ignorance of all concerns economic or athletic. The year 1962 had not only been bizarre fun, but a revolutionary *year zero.* The crusty old Polo Grounds cauldron stirred old-timers, hipsters, pinkos, drunks, sugar-high kiddies, and newly empowered losers into a singular witches' brew that now poured through the city and toward Queens. In their bittersweet chants and flashy hats, an enchanting new way of life was forged by millions of cultists true to the orange and blue—spiritually ascetic for victory, and gluttonous for joy. Black and white, rich and poor, elder and adolescent, now greeted each other east side to west side with their absurd born-again slogan: *I've been a Mets fan my whole life.*

Chapter 6

ONE-DIMENSIONAL MASCOT

On April 17, 1964, the tribe of 50,000 New Breed faithful ascended the elevated train platforms and highways of Moses to peer upon their promised land for the first time.

At the tip of the vast valley rose brutalist Shea Stadium—a cream-toned concrete cage, decorated with a mid-century modernist diorama of steel orange and blue tiles. Through the open facade, steep elevators zagged up its triple decks. A staff of comely "usherettes" in orange blazers striped with blue, a costume inspired by airline stewardesses and the emancipated Gibson Girls who once cycled through Central Park to 1890s Giants games, waited at their summits to bring guests to their assigned orange, blue, or green seats. Above the field, a massive electronic scoreboard heralded the batting lineups, box score, and icon-like displays of players' faces. Far larger than Ebbets Field or the

Polo Grounds, the jet-age Colosseum made Yankee Stadium appear like a bronze-age ruin.

And to the south, across the elevated train tracks, rose another entire city of ceaseless entertainment and consumption—the Disney-designed 1964 World's Fair. Bars, restaurants, rides, modern art, an animatronic Abe Lincoln, and Michelangelo's *Pietà* boated from Rome were but a selection of the diversions to be found in its hundreds of pavilions built in the pop-art style of corporate modernism. This self-funding economic engine of Moses's vision would, after its decommission in 1965, leave behind New York's "true Central Park"—the largest urban green space of the world's grandest metropolis. As with hundreds of previous works, the benevolent bureaucrat had gifted the stadium's name to Bill Shea to secure the singular immortality he desired engraved on his Parks Department keystone—Robert Moses Park.

But once the cramped 7-train cars reached Willets Point station and gridlocked traffic gave way, the promised land's shortcomings became immediately clear. Shea reeked of fresh paint, and many found their ticketed seats yet uninstalled—the result of renewed labor strikes that plagued construction through its final-month race for Opening Day completion. "The phones didn't work," Matthew Silverman wrote in *Shea Stadium Remembered*, "the scoreboard message malfunctioned and misspelled names over and over due to faulty wiring, the field was soft, and the fence was still wet from being painted, among other complaints."[231]

Then there were the problems that could not be fixed—the icy breeze blowing in from Flushing Bay, the ceaseless roaring descent of LaGuardia's jets, and the genetic deformities of the toddler team itself. On the yearbook's cover, Willard Mullin's baby Met of 1962 had matured to a naughty infant, pulling a decoy home-plate welcome mat from beneath the cleats of a generic gray-uniformed NL opponent distracted by an idealized mock-up of Shea held by Stengel.[232] But the Pirates of Roberto Clemente, Willie Stargell, and Donn Clendenon were unfazed as they defeated the Mets for their first loss of 110 that season. "My park is lovelier than my team," Stengel sighed after the game.[233]

For all the flaws of Shea and its cartoonish tenant, their chaotic charm filled seats all year to remain the envy of the baseball business. Baltimore general manager Frank Cashen adapted their youth-oriented marketing to cartoonify the Orioles. The Colt .45s softened their image and chased the space-age trend by rebranding as The Astros. The Kansas City Athletics abbreviated the team's name to *The A's* in homage to the Mets' monosyllabic punch, and spent a fortune to get the Beatles to play at their Municipal Stadium after their historic August concert at Shea. Giants owner Horace Stoneham hired the usherettes' uniform designer to wardrobe workers at Candlestick Park in San Francisco. Even the ironclad Yankees, their attendance sinking since 1962, named their malapropism-spouting catcher Yogi Berra manager as an answer to Stengel, and ditched their long aversion to merchandising as shiny blue Mets caps became ubiquitous in public life. By the end of the season, Shea's 1,732,597 attendance was second to only the Dodgers, clobbering the Yankees by nearly half a million.

But concern still accumulated among the New Breed that the *a-changin'* times were outpacing *Amazin'* novelty. "The glorification of kookiness and ineptness just didn't sit so well in the suddenly darkened world," Koppett wrote, citing opposition to US foreign policy in Cuba and Vietnam, the explosion of far-left folk music and the libertine Beatlemania, and the mass emergence of the Civil Rights Movement (CRM) at the March on Washington as the most prominent distractions to baseball. "Signs could say other things than 'We Want Marv,' and the 'generation gap' was hardening into real conflict, and increasingly politicized young people were starting to find other outlets for sheer rebelliousness than rooting for the Mets."[234]

Mass identification with the Mets now appeared a singular early signifier of the more permanent cultural boom as the babies of the postwar fertility matured toward civic majority. Another had similarly announced itself in the spring of 1962, when a few dozen college kids calling themselves the Students for a Democratic Society (SDS) gathered at the United Auto Workers' summer camp in Michigan. In their "Port Huron Statement," SDS declared that their generation, the largest in US history, and with unprecedented access to higher education, would emerge as a new intelligentsia capable of breaking the conservative hegemony of upper-class whites. This second American Revolution would end the Cold War, seize the means of production for an autonomous working class, and break the politics of spectacle in favor of dynamic political communities on local levels. Inspired by the horizontally organized Black youth leadership of the Student Nonviolent Coordinating Committee (SNCC), their manifesto became widely considered the foundational document of America's political answer to the New Breed, the "New Left."

The SNCC likewise inspired young players in the Mets' farm system. Future center fielder Cleon Jones recalled in his memoir *Coming Home* playing for their International League affiliate Buffalo Bisons when they traveled south in 1964. That campaign placed nonwhite players on baseball's integrationist frontline, preparing Southern fans for the arrival of Hank Aaron's Braves in Atlanta two years later.

One night during a stand in Jacksonville, Florida, Bisons shortstop Elio Chacón, cut from the Mets after '62, was refused service at a restaurant. When the other Black players of the team heard the news, they decided to return for an impromptu sit-in modeled after the tactics of the SNCC. When police arrived, Jones informed them about the recently passed Civil Rights Act's ban on racial discrimination for employment and public accommodation. The players were promptly served.

When they returned the next night, the waitress again ignored them. Jones invoked federal law to management again, and she was fired on the spot. They returned again the next night to find the waitress rehired and apologetic. From then on, Jones wrote, it was their favorite place to eat in Jacksonville.[235]

The action-oriented and explicitly revolutionary posture of SDS spread through universities following the apocalyptic shock of the Cuban Missile Crisis, the Kennedy assassination, and Lyndon Johnson's Democratic Party shutting out the SNCC from their 1964 convention. Scores of radicalized New Breed fans would follow the Bisons that summer to the Deep South on a mission to register Black voters as part of the Congress of Racial Equality (CORE) and the SNCC's Freedom Summer strategy. Among them was Seymour Weiner, a war veteran whose movement work would be immortalized sixty years later at Citi Field's 2024 Opening Day, and the subsequent one-dollar hot-dog "everyone loves a wiener" promotion.[236] Two other New Breed activists, however, would not survive Freedom Summer to receive such prestigious accolades.

Mickey Schwerner had been a typical high school beatnik. He grew a goatee, traveled from suburban Pelham to Washington Square Park folk singalongs and the cafes of the West Village, and was so won over by the Mets in 1962 he moved to Queens with his wife Rita after college. Dedicated movement workers with CORE, the couple were among the first to volunteer to travel to Meridian, Mississippi, in January 1964 to set up a

"Freedom House"—a movement base—in an old office in the Black part of town.

A couple dozen local volunteers aided them in their effort, including James Chaney, a twenty-one-year-old college dropout. The trio bonded over politics, philosophy, and baseball to become so close that Chaney's mother described him and Mickey as brothers. One Meridian comrade said of Mickey: "More than any white person I have ever known he could put a colored person at ease."[237]

They were joined that spring by Andrew Goodman of Manhattan. A Dodgers fan since infancy, he invited Jackie Robinson to speak at his high school in 1960, later organizing fellow teens to participate in a sit-in at Woolworth's department store.[238] Such actions were far more dangerous in Mississippi, the locals constantly warned, where Klansmen and local sheriffs maintained a shadowy campaign of terror against integration.

In late June, Schwerner, Chaney, and Goodman went to investigate the burning of a Black church in Philadelphia, Mississippi. They spent a couple hours surveying the wreckage, interviewing locals, and passing out voter registration forms and leaflets for Freedom Schools. When their station wagon was trailed by a police vehicle on their way back to Meridian, Mickey hit the gas. He had outrun the law twice before, but this time Deputy Sheriff Cecil Price opened fire and hit their rear tire. The three were arrested—Chaney for speeding, and Schwerner and Goodman under feigned suspicion of having burned the church themselves.

They were held past nightfall. While it was a rule among movement workers to never venture out at night, the stranded trio had little choice but to risk making their way home on a spare tire. They were followed again, this time by a gang of Klansmen ordered to hunt for the "Jewboy with the beard and the bright blue New York Mets baseball cap."[239]

The trio was abducted outside of town and taken to the woods. Chaney was given the worst punishment—tied to a tree, castrated, beaten with chains, and executed. Schwerner and Goodman were forced to watch the torture of their Black comrade before being shot as well.

Their disappearance quickly made national news. Lyndon Johnson met with the parents of Goodman and Schwerner in Washington (Chaney's mother was not invited), and pledged an FBI investigation.[240] Navy sailors scoured the swamps of Mississippi, finding multiple victims of racist terror, including other CORE supporters and five unidentified Black men, before finally pulling the trio from the mud. An autopsy found red clay in Goodman's lungs, indicating he had been buried alive.

"My husband did not die in vain," Rita Schwerner said in mourning. "If he and Andrew Goodman had been Negro the world would have taken little note of their death. After all the slaying of a Negro in Mississippi is not news."[241]

The CRM's movement workers and activists had long known those fighting for freedom in the South were routinely stalked, attacked with bombs, kidnapped, mangled, and killed with police protection. Johnson's sudden interest appeared to them less a sign that the state would move forcefully against white supremacy than an indication of what the antiracist movement would fight next as the Klan and Dixiecrats were institutionally marginalized: the more covert institutional and economic racism of the North. As Malcolm X put it in a Detroit speech that year: "Stop talking about the South. Long as you south of the Canadian border, you're south."[242]

Over the past year, the young members of CORE's Brooklyn, Bronx, and Downtown chapters joined thousands picketing and blockading construction sites of hospitals in Harlem and Flatbush where only white workers had been employed. In early 1964, they helped organize a walkout against segregation in New York's public schools. Nearly half of all students walked out, many of them converging, arms linked, to blockade the Triborough Bridge. The press and CRM old guard denounced these actions for targeting their allies in the trade unions and city government. But the movement's youth saw the conflict as a necessary escalation; the pretensions of race-blindness among middle-class liberals were shielding the worsening conditions for Black and brown New Yorkers at work, schools, and public housing.

Their next target for disruption would be even more controversial—the trains and highways leading to Flushing Meadows. "Unless you formulate and begin to implement a comprehensive program, by April 20, which will end police brutality, abolish slum housing and provide integrated quality education for all," a CORE ultimatum telegraphed to Governor Rockefeller, Mayor Wagner, and Robert Moses read, "we will fully support and help organize a community-backed plan to immobilize all traffic leading to the World's Fair on its April 22 opening day."[243]

The "stall-in" tactic, as first suggested by Louis E. Lomax, was described by Joseph Tirella in his history of the Fair, *Tomorrow-Land*: "He called for five hundred drivers to make their way to the Fair in their automobiles and, by running out of gas or simply stopping on the way there, create a traffic jam of historical proportions. Moses's beloved network of newly renovated highways would be used as a roadblock, preventing tens of thousands from attending his Fair."[244]

All of New York was aghast at a threat akin to shutting down Disneyland. Walt Disney's engineer-corps of *imagineers* had built much of Tomorrowland, including the animatronic Lincoln looping abolitionist speeches in the Illinois pavilion, and the Pepsi pavilion's indoor boat ride cruising past hundreds of mechanical children of various nationalities singing an ode to a common humanity. However saccharine and commercial many found the message, what, New Yorkers wondered, did the antiracists have against the Fair? In the age of international commercial jet flight and the United Nations, it was *a small world,* after all, and the fair's slogan of *Peace Through Understanding* rhymed well with the Soviet Union's declared stance of ending the Cold War through "peaceful coexistence." Perhaps the hiring practices weren't perfect, they reasoned, but it was still, as another Disney-built carousel ride proclaimed, "progress."

Behind the cartoon facade, the activists argued, the Fair demonstrated New York's subtler version of Jim Crow. The National Urban League had complained about segregation of Fair staffing years prior, forcing Moses to hire two Black executives—UN diplomat Ralph Bunche and Jackie Robinson.[245] But with the fair's staff and builders remaining almost entirely white as it neared completion, CORE members protested at the UN with a banner reading *End Apartheid at the Fair and African Pavilions Built with Lily White Labor.*

Few other activists were willing to join the campaign as opening day approached. Not only was Moses still widely popular, he commanded a labor and political machine too big to challenge. Prominent Queens NAACP activist Roy Wilkins derided the stall-in and its rhetoric as "Brooklynese," issuing a statement with the SNCC's John Lewis and other CRM leaders calling it too disorderly, violent, and "revolutionary" to serve the interests of Black people.[246] CORE chairman James Farmer, similarly worried that the tactic would not end segregation but "might end CORE," met with the chapter demanding they call off the action. When they refused, the chapter was expelled.

From threat alone, the stall-in successfully revealed the factions in the movement who preferred compromise over confrontation. It also terrified a city already worried that the massive opening-day crowds would again clog traffic on a day the Mets were hosting the Phillies. When the morning came, Weiss announced the game would be postponed, supposedly due to drizzle.[247]

Moses, however, stuck to schedule. The NYPD mobilized an army of tow trucks, cruisers, and paddy wagons, overseen by several helicopters, determined to quickly identify and extract the stalwarts. But when only a small handful of motorists went through with the action, the cops discovered they were among the first victims of what would become a well-worn New Left tactic—*the prank*.

The successful diversion allowed the hardest members of CORE and their allies to gather within the Fair's gates. Janet Biehl recounted the action in her biography of CORE member Murray Bookchin: "[750 activists] fanned out to the various displays. Holding signs reading A WORLD'S FAIR IS A LUXURY BUT A FAIR WORLD IS A NECESSITY and SEE NEW YORK'S WORSE FAIR—SEGREGATED SCHOOLS FOR NEGROES, PUERTO RICANS AND RATS, some blocked the doors at the New York City pavilion; some climbed the Unisphere, a large structure donated by US Steel; some stood atop the Florida pavilion's giant orange; and some, at the Louisiana pavilion, demonstrated the use of cattle prods, wielded on Black prisoners in jails in New Orleans and Baton Rouge. First was a blockade of the Missouri pavilion, which immediately closed its doors when the protesters arrived."[248]

A climax of the afternoon came at the Singer Bowl, later converted to US Tennis's Louis Armstrong Stadium, where President Johnson arrived to deliver the opening's keynote address. It was one of his first public speeches since the assassination of Kennedy, Tirella wrote, an optimistic paean to the world of abundance, peace, and justice to come. But soon after he started, the protesters began to chant and charge the stage. "The demonstrators, held at bay by a throng of police, shouted 'Jim Crow Must Go!' and 'Freedom Now!' directly at the president, often drowning out his amplified voice. Three of the college activists sat on the shoulders of their peers and held up signs that were visible not only to Johnson, but for the entire crowd of politicians to see."[249]

The noisy detentions caused President Johnson to stumble in his speech. He began to address them directly, promising his "Great Society" programs would solve discrimination, a proposition to which the cuffed demonstrators could only laugh. At a picket of Schaefer Beer's pavilion for racist employment practices earlier that day, drinkers of the Brooklyn Dodgers' former sponsor taunted activists with racial slurs and jeers of "Ship 'em back to Africa" as the protestors were arrested.[250]

The disruption proved costliest to Moses. He had predicted 250,000 attendees that day, and yet just over 60,000 had braved the wet weather, protests, and police lines. With the veil of progressivism torn away, the Fair would never meet the 300,000 daily visitors needed to break even.

In the coming months, the shortfall revealed Moses had personally inflated attendance figures, projected and actual, to spend freely on the exaggerated anticipated revenue. This had been his method to secure the bonds to build Shea Stadium and countless other permanent and popular works. But with the two-year Fair cast into scandal, Moses's white lies, always defended as altruistic public interest, were now tarnished with an especially damaging revelation of self-dealing—he had taken a $100,000 annual salary for himself.[251]

Investors demanded what little returns remained after the Fair's closure. Despite his newfound infamy, Moses turned them down. The Fair, like the freeways, Shea, and the Mets, had all been ploys to build his dream park, and he told them the paltry remaining funds would still go toward that transition.[252]

And while those limited reserves meant the park would not be the neoclassical masterpiece Moses had envisioned, it indeed became a vital public sphere. During warm weekends it remains undoubtedly the liveliest in the city. Like the seats of the Polo Grounds and Shea in the sixties—diverse, defiant, and self-organized—it would have more in common with the integrated vision of CORE than the orderly, white respectability envisioned by Moses and Weiss. Speak to nearly anyone in any Latin American country and they will tell you of a relative in Queens who can likely be found playing soccer, eating street food from a stall, or dancing to a live band on a Saturday afternoon on its vast lawns amid a blue smattering of Mets caps. Instead of Robert Moses Park, it would be called Flushing Meadows Corona Park, as Moses's name, poisoned by the affair, became synonymous with corruption, destructive modernity, and racist urban planning.

Another revolt against New York's institutional racism emerged in Harlem that summer. The incident began when the superintendent of a white building in Yorkville yelled slurs and sprayed his garden hose on Black youth hanging out on the stoop after school. An off-duty officer, arriving after the kids chased the super away, fired a warning shot to disperse the group. When fifteen-year-old James Powell flinched at the sound, the officer imagined a knife in his hand and shot him dead. Witnesses to the slaying confronted the officer, with one shouting: "This is worse than Mississippi!"[253]

Two days later, CORE and the NAACP called a rally in Harlem. Such gatherings had traditionally calmed tensions, but the rage of Harlem's youth, and the deepening radicalism of CORE, turned the intended orderly vigil into a riot. The crowd advanced to the nearby police station and attempted to fight their way through. "I belong to a nonviolent organization," announced the chairman of Downtown CORE before the march, "but I'm not nonviolent. When a cop shoots me, I will shoot him back."[254]

When the crowd was repelled, the streets of Harlem were swarmed with chaotic street-fighting for hours. Among the thousands was Harlem native and high school basketball phenom Kareem Abdul-Jabbar. He wrote in his memoir, *Becoming Kareem*:

> I had never been so scared in my life, or so sure a stray bullet might punch through my back at any second. Even as I ran, adrenaline pumping my heart like a boxer's speed bag, I also felt a shared rage with the people running beside me. As much as I admired Dr. King, I, too, wanted to pick up a brick and throw it. Not just for James Powell but also for Emmett Till. . . . Some government suits would make a sympathetic speech, create a panel that would investigate the causes, dump some money on a couple of neighborhoods, plant a few trees here and there, and hope the dragon would go back to sleep for another ten years. Then it would be some other politician's problem.[255]

The rioting spread throughout the city's other Black neighborhoods, including the former environs of Ebbets Field. Jarrod Shanahan wrote in his history of New York City's expanding carceral system, *Captives*: "Nearly a week of looting, vandalism, and violent clashes with NYPD ensued in Harlem and the Brooklyn neighborhood of Bedford-Stuyvesant, with hundreds of arrests and injuries, one death, and upward of a million dollars in property damage. NYPD's response echoed the repression that had occasioned the rioting in the first place, including wanton beatings and 'warning' shots fired at crowds of black New Yorkers."[256]

Abdul-Jabbar, along with Bill Russell of the Boston Celtics, would remain an outspoken activist for the cause of Black people on and off the court, clearing the way for other basketball players to speak their mind as it surged in popularity.

Baseball, however, remained a refuge from politics in which its internal racial issues were imagined to be either resolved or resolving. Its players, however diverse, were discouraged from flamboyant celebration or speaking freely to keep up the perception they were little more than an infant automaton choir, repeating their functions endlessly for the gawkers floating by.

This sense that all of society, following the workers' movement's defeat in the fifties, was becoming a mechanized workplace devoid of revolutionary potential, became a central occupation for the New Left. The finest articulation of this critique was philosopher Herbert Marcuse's 1964 treatise on how the postwar order, represented by international capital alongside Moses, Stalin, and like-minded bureaucrats, had created an "industrialized civilization" to which no alternative appeared. To counteract the resulting malaise and keep the population producing and consuming, capitalism developed an all-conforming system of "false needs" through an endless proliferation of consumer goods, political rackets, and entertainment spectacles. These false needs, Marcuse wrote, corresponded to "the prevailing needs to relax, to have fun, to behave and consume per advertisements, to love and hate what others love and hate."[257] If workers get depressed in their marriage, they buy a washing machine or color TV. When they want justice, they go to the union representative, NAACP leadership, or a peace rally. When they want fun, they go to the World's Fair, Disneyland, or Shea Stadium.

And while the youth movements blooming in the sixties conceived of themselves as seeking true freedom and justice, Marcuse saw their calls for fairer representation, legislation, and wealth distribution opportunities for the machine to increase its efficiency. Disciplined by threats of foreign powers and nuclear war, and satiated by increasingly automated production of food, clothes, and shelter, the workers who once confronted capital by demanding control of the means of production became, even in their rebellion, functioning parts of the apparatus. Activists, too, had become like workers with a singular task, a spectator of a single team, an enthusiast of a single hobby or political issue. Marcuse referred to this postwar subject, stripped of his world-changing agency and infinite creative capacities, as the *One-Dimensional Man.*

An example of this deformed hybrid of man and spectacle can be gleaned from the story of Dan Reilly. He was one of the earliest New Breed brood—among the first chanters of *Let's Go Mets* at 1962 spring training, and a regular go-shouter at the unruly Polo Grounds. While buying tickets for the 1963 season, the Mets offered him a job in its expanding sales department. Dreaming of working his way up to influencing the trajectory of the franchise and sharing beers with the players at the World's Fair after work, he accepted.

He spent the next several months learning the manipulative secrets of ticket selling from veteran employees of the Giants and Dodgers. Big-time fans were told that seats closer to the field would allow the players to hear their chants of encouragement, improving the team's performance, while those wavering on their purchases were scolded for disloyalty—weren't they real fans? Didn't they want the Mets to win?

Taking to the task with New Breed enthusiasm, he soon caught the eye of Jim Thompson and Tom Meany in the Mets' promotions department. Early into the 1964 season, they called Reilly into their office for a meeting. On Thompson's desk, Reilly wrote, were "a ticket stub from a previous game, some Mets stationery, and several Mets souvenirs." *What did they have in common?* Thompson asked.[258]

Reilly, terrified he was being demoted to the merch shop, cautiously answered the obvious—each had the same cartoon of a Met player with a bulbous, smiling baseball for a head that first appeared as an illustration in their 1963 yearbook. Thompson nodded, adding that materials bearing the image of "Mr. Met" had been bestsellers among the growing population of younger fans. The reason for the meeting was then revealed. Thompson and Meany wanted him to *become* the cartoon.

Reilly was confused and humiliated. He had dreamed of a role in the front office, not the funny pages. As he considered how to answer, Thompson produced an enormous ball of papier-mâché painted white.

"'Try it on, Dan,' said Jim, with that big toothy grin of his," Reilly wrote. "Tom Meany stood off to the side of the room, holding back his laughter."[259] Reilly obliged, and before he knew it, the office door opened and he was pushed into a front-office howling in amusement.

The concept of a mascot had been mostly out of vogue in baseball since the nineteenth century, when clubs paraded African American little people, like Broadway actor Clarence Duval, as team pets. In the words of Robert B. Ross, these mascots provided "entertainment and a sense of superiority for white spectators and players."[260] There had been few replacements for the cruel practice since, with Walter O'Malley's clown resembling the Brooklyn Bum retired after two years in 1957, and the 1963 Mets' attempts to train a beagle named Homer to run the bases after home runs ending in failure when he wandered into the outfield after touching second base.[261] The living Mr. Met would be a new chapter in the evolution—something between Homer the dog and the Mickey Mouse characters that greeted Disneyland attendees.

Reilly was sworn to secrecy about his new job ahead of his debut between games of a doubleheader against the Giants on May 31. During the ninth inning of the first game, Shea's best-selling on record, he waited nervously in the Mets clubhouse, mask in hand. Seeing the outfit for the first time, players Rod Kanehl, Bill Wakefield, and Chris Cannizzaro demanded he put it on. "Well, I shrugged my shoulders and thought to myself, 'Why not? I've got to do this sooner or later.' So I placed that seam-laced baseball head squarely over my shoulders and into position. . . . They immediately laughed, good-naturedly, of course, and wished me luck."[262]

Reilly, now Mr. Met, proceeded to the area behind home plate. All he had been told to do was wander the field for the half-hour between games—he had no other plan or instruction. When the Mets lost, the gates swung open and the grounds crew rushed past him, winking and whistling. "I was now on my own, with nothing more than a sinking feeling in my stomach and an oversized baseball on my head."

He lurched onto the field, his breath pulsing in the humid helmet like an astronaut traversing his ship's portal for a spacewalk. One step onto the field and his already-limited senses were overcome by blaring sunlight and a roar of 57,000 yelps, horns, and cowbells exploding at the sight of him. Searching for safety, he instinctively drifted toward the Mets dugout, where fans immediately rushed toward the railing, shrieking with laughter and barraging him with questions—*Could he see? Who was he? What was he?*

Shocked, he stumbled back across home plate to the third-base side, only to meet an identical swarm. Knowing he had to stay on the field as long as possible, he continued his half-blind wander until the players returned for warm-ups. He exhaled in relief and made his way to the exit.

"But the ballplayers had other ideas," Reilly wrote.

> Seeing me for the first time, several of them began knocking my head playfully. As I turned around to see who was trying to get my attention, another player would jokingly tap my head from behind, causing me to turn again. This went on for several minutes, and the fans loved it. Other players decided to toss a few baseballs my way to test my vision. I held out my arms, hoping to catch a ball or two. But all I caught was a stream of baseballs hitting me squarely on the forehead. Once again, the fans howled with delight.

With the first pitch nearing, Reilly was finally permitted to escape to the clubhouse. Shaken by an ordeal reminiscent of Gregor Samsa's apple-pummeling in Kafka's *The Metamorphosis*, he chugged a can of Rheingold, disrobed, and made for the players' shower. "I must admit, that I felt a little odd," he recalled. "Somehow, I didn't feel like I belonged in there."[263]

He was soon summoned back to the front office, where his bosses greeted him with a mixture of laughter, applause, and jibes. The grounds crew, press, M. Donald Grant, and Joan Payson had all loved the spectacle. All that was left for Thompson and Meany to determine was how often he would appear. From then on, many of his coworkers referred to him *only* as Mr. Met.

Relieved of duty for the day, he sat and watched the rest of game two. No matter what the gig meant for him and his career, he thought to himself, it was good for the team and the fans. That was all that mattered.

The Mets trailed until the seventh, when they tied it 6–6 on a home run to center field that Willie Mays barely missed catching. The game stayed locked into extras. Inning after inning passed. Hour after hour. Gaylord Perry took the mound in the thirteenth. A slippery elm lozenge watering his mouth, his illicit spitball shut down the Mets with strikeout after strikeout.[264] At inning eighteen, still tied 6–6, three full games had been played that day—and there would be many more innings to come. Giants manager Alvin Dark was thrown out for arguing a check-swing strike. Willie Mays began using a Little League bat in protest. It began to rain. Stengel yelled for the grounds crew to call it. When they refused, fans started throwing debris on the field. Twenty innings passed, then twenty-one, and twenty-two made it the longest game in major league history. Although there was little doubt how it would end, Reilly must have wondered if it ever would.

Chapter 7

STORMING HEAVEN

"Oh my God! Not the *Mets*?" Betty Seaver cried.[265]

It was April 1966, and her son had just received a call that New York had won a special lottery for his contract after a dispute with the Braves. Many other major-league-ready young prospects might have had the same reaction at being selected for what was still easily the worst team in baseball. Somehow, Tom Seaver thought it might be the perfect fit.

Like tens of thousands of middle-class youth, he had not found his calling in the prescribed life of the US Marines, the Sigma Chi frat house at USC, or in working his way toward management at his parents' winery. "I was trying to find myself," he recalled. "I knew I didn't want to lift crates at $2.05 an hour for the rest of my life."[266]

Now he would follow the footsteps of tens of thousands before him into urban bohemia, where New Left iconoclasm and cheap rent in crowded crash pad communes birthed the sixties culture of public concerts, free meals, and free love. His beatnik older brother, Charles Seaver, had moved to Greenwich Village at the dawn of the decade to become a sculptor, social worker, and social justice activist. Charles inspired Tom's taste in rock, folk, and modern literature, and a nonconformist approach to his own artistic calling. The pitcher's mound, he said, was "one of the few places left where a person like myself can show his individuality."[267]

Since 1962, Stengel had prophesized that the Youth of America would transition the Mets to greatness, and Weiss's keen scouts clearly intuited generational genius in Seaver. His commanding fastball and crafty curveballs and sliders were all the more potent combined with his abnormally perfect recall for the idiosyncrasies of every hitter he faced, giving him the reputation of the sort of pitcher who could only be bested at first encounter.

Seaver chiseled 170 strikeouts during his debut 1967 season. With a 2.76 ERA, he won Rookie of the Year, establishing himself as the strongest pitcher of an artistic young rotation, alongside Jerry Koosman and Tug McGraw, to become the franchise's first homegrown star.

Seaver's arrival was the most promising development in a rejuvenation that began two years prior when Stengel fell outside a bar and broke his hip during the 1965 season. Finally with a pretext to retire the franchise's standard-bearing jester, Weiss installed floating coach Wes Westrum as the Mets' placeholder second manager.

Gil Hodges, Payson's top choice to run the team, was still under contract in Washington. Her second preference was Alvin Dark, the legendary New York Giants shortstop, then San Francisco's manager. But when Dark came to New York that summer, New Breed journalist Stan

Isaacs fouled the plan by printing Dark's remarks disparaging his Latino players. A clubhouse revolt of the Black and brown Giants followed, proving Dark an unsuitable candidate for the progressive Mets fan base.

Westrum stayed on in 1966 as an empty uniform while the Youth of America lurched from the NL cellar to second-to-last for the first time. But with neither the vision of a true major-league manager, nor the jocular gravitas of Stengel, the Mets plummeted to another dead-last finish in 1967. "I'm not comfortable with all this 'lovable losers' stuff everyone keeps talking about around here," Seaver told a teammate that year. "I've been on winning teams my entire life, going all the way back to Little League, and I don't intend to be part of a losing team now."[268]

Fed up with the hopeless team, George Weiss retired before the 1966 season. Payson's patience ran out, too. Recalling Branch Rickey's prediction that the team was forever doomed were they not to become champs by the end of the decade, she shelled out $250,000 to reacquire Hodges before the 1968 season.

The Brooklynite immediately embarked on the Long Island Railroad for a winter hearts-and-minds tour to win back suburban New Breeders. Joining him was twenty-three-year old outfielder Ron Swoboda, a burly and blithe slugging prospect anticipated to end up either the Mets' Mickey Mantle or the second coming of Marv Throneberry. The odd couple previewed the team's new dynamic: a roster of soft young recruits who Hodges, the muscular veteran of Robinson's Dodgers and the Pacific battles of Tinian and Okinawa, would transform into a disciplined military unit. "My name is Hodges," he said, firmly introducing himself to the motley spring-trainees in cowboy hats, Nehru jackets, mustaches, and sideburns. He announced a new order: strict curfews, no carousing in hotel bars, mandatory tips for maids, fines for farting in the clubhouse, and a decisively unhip dress code. "That's the way I do things. If that's a change, okay."[269]

Another ex-military man, Johnny Murphy, became the Mets' new general manager. He had left the Yankees' bullpen at the outbreak of World War II to serve in the seemingly less dramatic position of employment director at a nine-person military complex in Oak Ridge, Tennessee. The base rapidly grew to the size of a small city, its population of 75,000 researchers working at breakneck speed to produce the uranium to complete "Little Boy," the atomic bomb dropped on Hiroshima. His new role in the front office was a similar operation—enriching the raw potential of the Youth of America into an explosive force the likes of which the world had never seen.

When it came to America's new war in Vietnam, however, Hodges and Murphy worked to keep their troops far from the jungle meat grinder. What strings they pulled to protect their players from the draft remain a well-kept secret, but a 1968 scandal involving a National Guard corporal selling an Army Reserve spot to the Jets' backup quarterback for $200 was likely commonplace.[270] A large percentage of the Mets, including six pitchers, ended up reservists in 1968. And while their weekend army-base stints made managing the rotation a nightmare, it was a small price to pay to preserve the life and limbs of future weapons like flamethrower Nolan Ryan.

As the Communist guerrillas of North Vietnam continued their resilience against the US offensive, however, the once little-reported "police operation" turned into a scandalous war that increasingly came home to breach baseball's gates.

The previous July, Detroit police raided a speakeasy during an early-morning celebration for two recently returned Black veterans. Locals fought back, sparking a ferocious riot. During the Tigers' doubleheader against the Yankees later that day, management instructed their team and broadcasters to ignore the black plumes of smoke visible over the left-field fence. One Tiger summarized the directive as asserting: "Baseball must be a world of its own."[271]

The games were played without interruption, but once fans left the park they heard rumors that rioters were preparing an onslaught of Detroit's white districts. The Tigers moved their home games out of the city for the remainder of the riot—the largest in the US in over a century. Nearly 200,000 white Detroiters fled the city for good over the next two years, reducing the 1968 World Champs to a small-market franchise.

Similar riots broke out in Newark, Tampa, and 150 other cities that summer. A White House investigation found urban deindustrialization and white flight suburbanization were at the root of the unrest, which would only intensify the vicious cycle. Neither the piecemeal integration of the previous decades, nor Johnson's civil rights legislation, let alone Branch Rickey's vision of a baseball-based bourgeois integration, had been enough to defuse the time bomb of America's racial order.

The unrest returned days before the 1968 season. Martin Luther King Jr. was in Memphis that spring to support striking sanitation workers. Despite his religious and political commitment to nonviolence, he had been widely blamed for the riots, leading the FBI and white supremacists to constantly threaten his assassination should he continue his activism. On April 4, a sniper finally made good on the promise as he left his hotel.

Among the Mets, outfielder Cleon Jones was particularly heartbroken. He saw how Dr. King's dream of seeing Black and white kids playing together had desegregated the sandlots of his native Mobile, Alabama, where interracial games had been secretive and rare during his childhood. Now he feared his white teammates, if they cared at all, may have supported the slaying. A poll around that time revealed only 27 percent of the public approved of the pacifist's crusades against segregation, unchecked capitalism, and US imperialism.[272]

The early reaction from Commissioner William Eckert was not a positive sign. While President Johnson had declared a day of mourning, and virtually all sporting events, including hockey and golf, were canceled until King's funeral, baseball's owners declared Opening Day would be played on schedule.

The decision was about far more than gate receipts. Diverting riotous unrest between classes in the streets into passionate rivalries between teams in ballparks had been part of organized baseball's mission since the 1870s. The game's integration following antiracist boycotts and riots in Harlem served a continuation of that function, and King's pacifist movement patiently followed the path blazed, in part, by Rickey and Robinson. But now, Black Panther Party leader Eldridge Cleaver wrote, King's dream had been killed as white America's "final repudiation" of any nonviolent reconciliation: "The assassin's bullet which struck down Dr. King closed a door that to the majority of black people seemed closed long ago."[273]

As riots immediately spread to over a hundred cities over the next week, Dodgers GM Buzzie Bavasi explained baseball proved the door to equality was still open, and playing on schedule would help keep "people off the streets and to forget their anger."[274] Twenty years after Robinson, however, Black and Latino players were no longer interested in serving as symbolic diversion, nor did they fear risking their careers, or integration itself, by speaking out. They were now the game's biggest offensive stars, with only one white hitter, Rusty Staub, placing in the top ten of batting. In King's final speech, he had urged Black workers to use this indispensability to America's economy and culture as leverage to win equality: "Always anchor our external direct action with the power of economic withdrawal. That's power right there, if we know how to pool it."[275]

The first team to put King's words to action was its most diverse, the Pittsburgh Pirates. About half Black, three of their stars were personal acquaintances of Dr. King. Roberto Clemente had met him after advocating for desegregation within baseball clubhouses in the fifties, and had hosted King at his farm outside San Juan. Maury Wills met King briefly in Los Angeles while playing for the Dodgers, an encounter he described as more humbling than those with Hollywood stars and presidents. Donn Clendenon had been particularly close with King since his first semester as a teen prodigy at Morehouse College. Years later, Clendenon invited King to his offseason job at the Scripto pen factory to support a unionization drive of its mostly Black workforce.

When Clendenon heard the news of King's assassination before a preseason game in Richmond, he summoned the Black Pirates to his hotel room and suggested they refuse to play until after the funeral. They shared their plan with the Black players on the opposing Astros the next day. The white teammates on both teams joined next, some begrudgingly, others enthusiastically. White pitcher Dave Wickersham and Clemente announced the strike to the press, explaining: "We are doing this because we respect what Dr. King has done for mankind. Dr. King was not only concerned with Negro or whites but also poor people. We owe this gesture to his memory and his ideals."[276]

Most other teams held meetings following the Pirates' example. The Giants initially voted to play, only to reverse their decision once they learned their opponent Mets had voted to strike.

Ron Swoboda, a product of Baltimore's interracial sandlots, and outfielder Art Shamsky, were among the most supportive white voices in the clubhouse. "As a Jewish man, I think it was only natural that I fell into the more-sensitive camp," Shamsky recalled. "I didn't suffer any of the injustices that Hall of Fame slugger Hank Greenberg did . . . but I would occasionally hear some catcalls from the stands—particularly when I played minor-league ball in Macon, Georgia."[277] "There was so much sympathy and I knew they could feel what I was feeling," Jones said of the Mets' meeting. "If a team of baseball players could feel that way—brothers always—I felt that good progress could continue."[278]

Eckert conceded without a fight, making the Black-led action arguably the first successful industry-wide strike—and certainly the first mobilized around racial justice.

Play resumed on April 10, the day after King's funeral. The last of the riots, in which thousands were arrested, injured, and dozens killed, ended the next day. While there was little further discussion of the rebellion either way in a Mets clubhouse divided by liberals and conservatives in the aftermath of the strike, the unspoken political tension flared when the Mets left California three days later.

After being shutout 1–0 to Don Drysdale and the Dodgers, Ron Swoboda and another teammate chatted with two hippies outside Dodger Stadium. They left wearing love-bead necklaces, a symbol of the "Summer of Love" as recognizable as long hair and flared jeans.

Pitcher Don Cardwell, the losing pitcher that day, noticed the fashion statement a couple drinks deep on the flight home. "I didn't believe in the love beads nor the parades they were having," he recalled, "and two of our ballplayers were supporting this. That wasn't me. That just rubbed me the wrong way."[279]

Cardwell, renowned as the team's "ultraconservative," vented all frustration on his hippie teammate. "What are you doing with that shit on?" Swoboda recalled him saying. "The next thing I knew, Cardy went boom! and hit me in the jaw."[280]

Hodges stepped over the beads rolling through the aisle to break up the fight. For the past year, Swoboda had been among the most antiauthoritarian malcontents bristling at his demands for a clean-cut, disciplined team. But Hodges had been in Swoboda's cleats before—siding with Robinson against Dixie Walker's hate-strike in his rookie season with the Dodgers in 1947. If the Mets were ever to come together as a team, or the United States to pass through its accelerating racial and intergenerational conflicts, conservative veterans like Cardwell and progressive youth like Swoboda had to come to terms. In this case, a brief reminder of the dress code was all it took to settle the matter; Swoboda complied, stashing what remained of the necklace safely in his locker for luck.

The Mets were back in San Francisco that June when New York senator and presidential candidate Robert F. Kennedy was assassinated at a Los Angeles campaign stop.

Kennedy's antiwar stance, focus on poverty, and moving requiem for Dr. King had provided some optimism to the youth movement that racial and economic progress was still possible through the Democratic Party. The momentum of his campaign had even convinced the Youth International Party, the anarchistic *Yippies*, to scale back their plans to bring 500,000 youth to Chicago during the Democratic National Convention to burn draft cards, fight cops, and fuck in the parks. Now that another dreamer had met a mysterious and senseless death, the plan reverted to riot—Astros players would huff tear gas wafting into their Chicago hotel room from the battle between police, Yippies, Black Panthers, and other antiwar street fighters below.[281]

Eckert once again announced that all games, aside from those in New York and Washington, would be played on the date of his funeral on June 8—unless both teams agreed not to. Self-organized clubhouse meetings formed once again throughout baseball. The Giants again voted to play, and the Mets, *unanimously*, to boycott. "We felt like there wasn't any choice at all," Swoboda said. "This guy was probably going to be the next president."[282]

Giants owner Horace Stoneham was appalled. They had already lost revenue from Opening Day, and the second boycott threatened another sold-out sacred occasion—souvenir bat day. When he demanded the Mets either play or forfeit, National League president Warren Giles called Hodges to suggest a compromise. The Mets could have their boycott only if wages were docked to compensate the Giants' lost revenue. While most other teams who voted not to play were successfully pressured by similar threats, an unflinching Hodges sided with his players. The game was postponed without penalty.

The stance showed the baseball world the Mets had gone from bottom-dwelling joke into an assertively socially conscious force. The *Oakland Tribune*'s sports columnist praised the team for their "lofty principle," and Kennedy's press secretary sent a telegram thanking them for not putting "box-office receipts ahead of national mourning."[283]

By lending his support to the effort, Hodges showed his players that, beneath his hard-boiled affect, he had their back. The mutual trust closed the era of suffering Stengel and disobeying Westrum, and a winning streak began after Kennedy's funeral. By the end of the June, the Mets were in the middle of the NL standings with a .500 win percentage—easily the best position they had ever achieved midseason.

The New Breed fans who had drifted away post-Stengel—the pure baseball enthusiasts and the leftists alike—noticed the Mets' political transformation as well. In July, a group of young Mets fans stormed the offices of the *New York Post* demanding Jimmy Breslin retract a column that criticized the Communist Party as too conservative compared to the New Left. When *Post* editor James Wechsler confronted the group during their sit-in, he argued their support for a team run by the old-school Catholic Hodges proved Breslin's point. "Much to his dismay," Hodges biographer Mort Zachter wrote, "the communists strongly defended Hodges."[284]

By the end of 1968, attendance rebounded to the best numbers since Shea's opening year. Some 1.7 million turned out to get a glimpse of the reestablished people's team.

Radical politicization broke out across the sports world in 1968. Boxing great Muhammad Ali, a convert to the Nation of Islam, stoically faced jail time for his refusal to be drafted. In October, UCLA basketball player Kareem Abdul-Jabbar boycotted the Olympics in Mexico City, where US runners Tommie Smith and John Carlos accepted their gold and bronze medals shoeless in solidarity with the poor, their track jackets unzipped for blue-collar workers, and their fists raised high for Black liberation. Deeming their gestures "violent," the International Olympic Committee stripped them of their medals, and banned them from future Games.

While these actions paved the way for basketball players and boxers to vocally politicize their sports, the diamond saw little of equivalence following the funerals of King and Kennedy. The Black ballplayers who had emerged both baseball's top stars and its political vanguard rejected the revolutionary politics and interventionism of the New Left and Black nationalism. Curt Flood, Bob Gibson, Bill White, Willie Mays, and other players had all met with such groups only to come away preferring the Robinson path of interracial struggle in the workplace. "Sounds as if black power would be white power backwards," Gibson said. "That wouldn't be much improvement."[285]

In the long run, their choice protected baseball's "world apart" delusion, and its taboo on players publicly speaking their mind. But it had also protected the Black ballplayers from scandal—making it easier for them to push the radical labor politics of Dr. King in common struggle with their conservative white coworkers, ultimately giving baseball one of the strongest unions in the country.

Seeds of the new labor upsurge were planted on a monsoon-soaked Atlanta field earlier that May. Fearing injury, the Mets begged the umps for postponement. They complied when told to *shut up and play*, but after the game initiated the first arbitration process between the commissioner's office and the MLB Players Association (MLBPA) to reevaluate the decision-making process on safe working conditions.

From its establishment in 1953, the MLBPA had been little more than a "company union" that rarely demanded much more than fresh towels in the locker room. But in 1966, a year in which the Giants revolted against the racism of Alvin Dark, Hank Aaron denounced baseball's lingering racism, and Sandy Koufax and Drysdale held out against the Dodgers for higher salaries, players fed up with the greed of the owners elected a labor-movement leftist, Marvin Miller, to represent them as union president.

Compared to his predecessors, Charles Korr wrote, Miller "was like Lenin."[286] He grew up a New Deal and Brooklyn Dodgers devotee, studied economics at NYU, and became a chief economist for the United Steelworkers of America. He set his sights on baseball in 1965, theorizing that the players who came of age idolizing Robinson and Mays might share a similar cynicism toward the conservative style of workplace management to much of America's young working class.

In an early meeting with player representatives, Miller proposed restructuring the MLBPA as a more traditional industrial union, arguing that booming broadcast revenues ought to be shared toward their pension and healthcare. During his campaign for union presidency at 1966 spring training, Cubs manager Leo Durocher batted balls in his direction as he chatted up outfielders, and the owners warned their workers against electing a communistic "union boss" who would bring "goon squads" into the clubhouse. Miller ended up winning by a margin of 489–136.[287]

Miller immediately proved his value by forcing the Topps Chewing Gum corporation to compensate players for using their likenesses on baseball cards, and winning a small increase to minimum salaries in the 1968 collective bargaining agreement (CBA). Unaccustomed to dealing with union men, the owners were so relieved at Miller's seemingly humble raise request they overlooked the significance of another provision he had inserted into the CBA to send future labor disputes to professional arbitrators. The Mets' watershed protest in Atlanta provided the first test of this system that, in a decade's time, would finally overturn the century-old reserve clause.

When arbitrators ruled in the Mets' favor, Commissioner Eckert took the blame for missing Miller's Trojan horse. He was replaced with the hip but hard-line anti-labor lawyer Bowie Kuhn before the 1969 season. In an address to the players, Kuhn channeled the rhetoric of Miller and King to declare baseball an integrationist success story and a purveyor of social progress. But when Miller demanded a seat at the table at the owners' winter meetings at the Biltmore Hotel to discuss sharing broadcast revenues, Kuhn lifted the drawbridge and shut him out.

Miller called for a picket of the meetings, anticipating only a few team reps to interrupt their short winter break to attend. But a stunning 130 players appeared that afternoon, including Mets catcher Jerry Grote, Brooklynite Brave Joe Torre, and the Phillies' first Black star Dick Allen, donning a dashiki.[288] The strong turnout, along with the wildcat stoppages of 1968, signaled to Miller the time was right to call a formal strike before the 1969 season to bring Kuhn to the table.

Camps of the White Sox and Yankees, led by Mickey Mantle days before announcing his retirement, were ghost towns in February. But as the spring opened, some journeymen threatened with replacement reported to work. And despite Johnny Murphy promising no penalty for the holdouts, the Mets' reps defected from the plan entirely. Many on the roster viewed their franchise as a uniquely pro-worker "family operation." Players lovingly called their matronly owner "Ma Payson," and Johnny Murphy "Grandma." In defiance to Miller, Seaver and Grote organized their own spring conditioning camp off company grounds.

Even though Miller's "acid test" of player solidarity had proved less than euphoric, the owners' threat of replacement players rattled the broadcasters. NBC threatened suit, claiming fans would not tune-in to see minor-league scabs. Kuhn met Miller, and by March the two had reached a profit-sharing deal. It was far less than what he had hoped to win, but the owners' conciliation had been an admission that their workers, now organized across teams and leagues, were irreplaceable. From then on, Miller received standing ovations at union meetings.[289]

With the labor dispute resolved, and most of the Mets roster benefiting from their early start, Hodges arrived at spring training convinced the Mets' first winning season had arrived. His prediction of eighty-five wins met a murmur of snickers at his first press conference. Such preseason statements had always been treated as jokes—Mayor John Lindsay had recently quipped that there would be a Subway Series in 1969 *if only* the Yankees could manage a pennant, and Art Shamsky mused that he might break his Sabbath observance only for the World Series. But Hodges quieted the laughter with a stern reminder that he meant business: "Gentlemen, losing is no laughing matter."[290]

The mockery appeared at first warranted. Their woeful offense had put them at a second-to-last finish in 1968, Las Vegas oddsmakers gave the Mets 100–1 odds to win the pennant, and the *Washington Post*'s Computer Column, which claimed to be based on a supercomputer's detailed statistical analysis of each team, predicted the Pirates to top the NL, followed by the Cardinals and Cubs. The Mets then opened their season by dropping seven of their first ten.

Hodges, however, retained mysterious confidence. Unlike Stengel, he would not gab for hours about why he believed the Mets had a chance. His faith in the team was as private and spiritual as his Catholicism, and if he truly did know how they would pull it off, he kept it as close to his chest as his shirt-pocket pack of Chesterfields.

Everyone could see, at least, that Seaver was their biggest advantage. He led their novel five-man rotation to the fourth-best earned run average in the league in 1968, making the run differential in their losses closer than ever before. Aided by his early start, he won six straight games in early '69 to put the team at an even number of wins and losses. While some celebrated the accomplishment in the locker room, Seaver echoed Hodges's severity: "We didn't come here to play .500 ball this season. I'm tired of all the old jokes about Marv Throneberry and Rod Kanehl. We're here to win. You know when we'll celebrate? When we win the pennant."[291]

Seaver's determination rallied the team to charge forward in June into uncharted territory: a *winning record*. Inspired by the surge, Johnny Murphy relinquished five top prospects to acquire the type of slugger that had always eluded the franchise—Donn Clendenon.

Alongside his reliable .300 average and 100 RBIs, the veteran batter added intellectual leadership to the clubhouse's political dynamism.

Clendenon spent his youth playing baseball for the semipro Atlanta Black Crackers under the tutelage of Negro League stars Nish Williams and Satchel Paige. When he was accepted to Morehouse College on an academic scholarship at the age of sixteen, he dabbled in football and track but lost interest in a professional sports career, let alone one in baseball. Through his friendship with Dr. King, he was invited to a feast at a local Black civic club to be honored as Athlete of the Year, alongside Jackie Robinson as Man of the Year, with Branch Rickey delivering the keynote address. Rickey pled with Clendenon post-ceremony to follow in Jackie's footsteps and try out for his Pittsburgh Pirates.

Twelve years later, Clendenon regretted the choice. Not only was he yet to achieve his dream of playing in a World Series, the Pirates failed to protect him in the 1969 expansion draft. He was claimed by the upstart Montreal Expos, who then promptly traded him to the Astros for Rusty Staub. Clendenon announced he would rather retire from baseball to work at Scripto full-time than work under Astros manager Harry Walker, the brother of anti-Robinson hate-strike leader Dixie who had a similar reputation for racism. For perhaps the first time, a Black star answered the majors' "take it or leave it" offer with a firm *leave it.*

Montreal refused to reverse the deal. Burly ginger Staub, a future Met great, was already their inaugural star, marketed to Quebecers as *Le Grande Orange.* To settle the dispute, Kuhn summoned Clendenon and Scripto's president Arthur Harris to meet with both team owners to work out a solution. With Clendenon holding firm at the meeting, the Astros GM threatened to buy Scripto and clean house. "Harris began encouraging Clendenon to return to the game," Ed Hoyt summarized the affair for the Society for American Baseball Research. "The issue for management in the end didn't appear to be the money . . . but that a player had asserted his rights."[292]

Wanting to protect the company, and knowing his career was approaching its end anyway, Clendenon reluctantly agreed to play. Perhaps, he thought, some miracle could finally take him to October. The springtime trade to the stunningly second-place Mets at least gave him one last shot.

Ahead of the Mets were the odds-on favorite Chicago Cubs. They were led by the irrepressibly optimistic veteran Ernie Banks, who had broken the color line for the Cubs in 1953, and proceeded to become one of the best home-run hitters in baseball. Ron Santo, nearly as consistent, had won five Gold Gloves for defense, and displayed his enthusiasm for winning with a leaping heel-click after victories. Opposing players despised the arrogance of Banks and Santo, along with Wrigley Field's "Bleacher Bums," the traveling outfield hooligan army that had invented throwing back opposing teams' home run balls, alongside other projectiles and slurs. Equally reviled was their win-at-all-costs manager, Leo Durocher. Older New Yorkers remembered Leo "the Lip" from his transformation of the Dodgers into contenders in the forties, his steadfast support for Robinson and subsequent ban for consorting with gamblers in 1947, and his traitorous move to the Giants in 1948. Loved by the fans of the teams he managed, and hated by all others, he was a boisterous shit-talker, unapologetic about dirty play and cheating, and the perfect foil for the respectable Hodges.

In an early Wrigley series against the Mets that year, Durocher barked orders to take down Bud Harrelson with a hard slide and have Seaver intentionally drilled in the stomach. The Mets' outfielders were similarly targeted by the Bleacher Bums, who at one point threw a smoke bomb toward Cleon Jones.[293] "Sometimes it's better in baseball to let dying dogs die," Mets veteran Ed Kranepool said after the nightmarish sweep. "You need motivation on losing ball clubs. Why wake them up? Why motivate them? You always looked forward to beating managers like Durocher."[294]

The Cubs came to Shea in early July with a mere five-game lead on the still-streaking Mets. Fans filled the park to jeer their first true rivals, with a promotion allowing kids to enter free further swelling Shea past capacity with a delinquent partisanship most of the young team had never experienced before. A ceaseless roar that began with the anthem peaked in the bottom of the ninth. With the Mets trailing 3–1, the thunderous cheers surpassed even the descending planes, rattling the nerves of the Cubs' normally stellar defense into making two errors. Cleon Jones tied the game with a double, and Kranepool singled in the walk-off run.

"Maybe they'll take us seriously now!" Jones yelled during the clubhouse celebration. A grinning Hodges told the postgame press conference it was the most important win in team history. "That's what we're all here for, to make believers out of all you unbelievers."[295]

Clendenon observed the spiritual divergence between the two teams during a visit with an old teammate on the Cubs the next day. While the Mets' quarters rang with laughter and friendly card games between the players and their wives, Chicago was at each other's throats. Durocher chewed out his players, who muttered against their coach behind his back.

That night, with Seaver coming to the mound, more than sixty thousand pressed into Shea, with an overflow packing the 7-train platform. Drawing strength from the throngs, Seaver crafted his masterpiece. After eight perfect innings, only a harmless one-out single stood between him and perfection. The *Chicago Tribune* headline following the series read: A PORTENT OF DOOM?[296]

The insurgent series established the Mets as the latest New York franchise to embark on an unexpected run. Earlier that year, the Jets had their own miracle against the heavily-favored Baltimore Colts in Super

Bowl III, and the Knicks upset the Baltimore Bullets to advance to the Eastern Division NBA finals. Even as the Mets cooled off in July, their broadcasts became the de facto soundtrack of taxi rides, delis, and bars. "No one had seen that kind of midsummer fever in the city since the old Giants-Dodgers bloodlettings, fifteen or twenty years back," Roger Angell wrote.[297] The *New York Times* weighed the return of Metsomania against the *Apollo 11* moon mission. "A bartender was asked whether his customers were more interested in the Mets or the astronauts. 'The Mets, of course,' he said. 'Aren't you?'"[298]

After two summers of rage so arsonous that the political class, from City Hall to the Pentagon, had drawn up plans for widespread counterinsurgency, the *summer of '69* unfolded as an unlikely optimistic benchmark of the ending decade. There were race riots in York, Pennsylvania; tenant riots against evictions in Harlem; and the weekend-long queer riot outside the Stonewall Inn in Greenwich Village—but some credited the Mets with the failure of these revolts to spread as they had in previous years. "We calmed that damn town down," pitcher Gary Gentry claimed. "I remember getting all the 'Attaboys' and 'Thank-yous' from our city and state officials, as well as Governor Nelson Rockefeller and Mayor John Lindsay. You know, I don't think we knew what we were doing when we were doing it, but after it was over, I heard a lot about how we turned the town around."[299]

While it's difficult to believe the Mets created the quietude alone, they had certainly served their historic people's-team role. Just as the Tammany-minted 1880 Mets provided diversion for the unresolved class tensions of the Gilded Age, the 1969 Mets' run offered the New Left an off-ramp as it sank into a malaise following the election of Nixon and the prosecution of the Yippies and Panthers following the DNC riot in Chicago. They were revolutionary stand-ins for some, and for others a helpful topic of conversation when attempting to reach beyond the leftist subculture to working-class squares. "Politics should be as exciting as the New York Mets," Yippie founder Jerry Rubin wrote in his 1969 manifesto, *Do It!*. "People are always asking us, 'What's your program?' I hand them a Mets scorecard."[300]

Even those who attempted to stay with the *Movement* found it devolving into a performative blame-game between a proliferation of bizarre teams. That summer's SDS convention at the Chicago Coliseum took on the doomed atmosphere of Wrigley's locker room—its 1962 New Left manifesto now decisively lost in a snake pit of factional polemics. The SDS died at the convention's end with a volley of rival Stalinists chanting *Ho! Ho! Ho Chi Minh!* and *Mao! Mao! Mao Zedong!* at one another. The last SDSers left in disgust during the shouting match, as one New York Trotskyist cadre, the LaRouchites, seized the final word by answering them: *Let's! Let's! Let's Go Mets!*[301]

As political urgency receded, comforting symbols of mid-sixties optimism returned one by one. Bob Dylan released his first record since 1967, a crooning country album. The Beatles reemerged from hiatus to release a song denouncing revolution and play a surprise show on a Manhattan rooftop. In August, the half million who swarmed an upstate rock festival cooperated to overcome its disastrously poor planning by busting through the gates to create a free and self-managed autonomous zone dedicated to vague ideals of *peace and love*. Ellen Willis, rock critic and founder of the revolutionary feminist group Redstockings, described the Woodstock happening in the *Village Voice* as the moment rock 'n' roll revival reversed its dropout-culture consolidation in the radical milieu downtown, sending the once proudly proletarian bohemians back into the suburban mainstream. "A favorite pastime of Americans is rediscovering their origins—that's what the whole rock renaissance is about, after all. . . . Aren't the Mets contenders? Queens is where the working class calls itself the middle class."[302]

The editors of the *East Village Other*, the New York counterculture's paper of record, viewed the radical enthusiasm for the Mets with similar ambivalence. When Dean Latimer pitched a regular sports page devoted primarily to the Mets, his Yippie co-editors judged the request as something China's cultural revolutionaries called a right deviation—a temptation toward squareness. "Hippies are so Goddamn anti-American," he complained when they shot him down. "You mention baseball to them and you're liable to get belladonna dropped in your beer."[303]

But as their summer offensive continued, the countercultural nature of Mets fandom appeared undeniable. "Shea Stadium took on a carnival-like atmosphere," Shamsky wrote, with a proliferation of confetti, banners, and fireworks.[304] It was the new Haight-Ashbury or St. Marks Place; the latest cosmic center of the sixties' occult insurrection. Messianic signs, Afros, and puffs of marijuana smoke dotted the stands, with dropouts outside loitering like Deadheads begging for a free-ticket miracle.

The height of the frenzy arrived with the return of the Cubs in late August, their ten-game lead over New York now whittled to one. The stadium swelled far past capacity thanks to thousands of fans cashing in free tickets handed out as a promotion for a milk company before the season. In the top of the first, on-deck hitter Ron Santo noticed the massive energy in the crowd was even louder than it had been in July. "'Oh man, we're fucked now,'" Cubs batboy Jim Flood recalled him saying. "And that's when I saw the cat."[305]

Legend had it that dozens of Flushing's ferals had made Shea's netherworld their home since 1964, giving the locker rooms, reliever Skip Lockwood recalled, the "musty smell of a summer cottage."[306] Perhaps the noise had roused the feline from its lair, or perhaps he had been smuggled in and set loose as a Yippie or Stengelian prank. Either way, the black cat, an archetypal symbol of black magic and proletarian sabotage, now ran free through foul territory, fearlessly crossing Santo toward the dugout to glare directly at the Cubs' crashing manager. "Somebody get that fucking cat out of here!" Durocher yelled. Then, as if the symbolism had not been obvious enough, the cat ran directly across home plate and *into the Mets' clubhouse*, never to be seen again.

The hex played on the deepest fears of the Cubs and their fans. Their last world championship had been in 1908, when the Cubs avoided defeat by the Giants after a bizarre base-running error immortalized as "Merkle's Boner." New York fans rioted after the upset, and the Cubs proceeded to fail in each of their next seven World Series appearances.

The animalistic element of the curse first appeared in 1945. During the Cubs' pennant race, a local tavern owner brought his pet goat, Murphy, to Wrigley Field as a good-luck charm. When he and the goat were ejected, he angrily declared, "Them Cubs ain't gonna win no more." After the Cubs lost to the Tigers, desperate management invited Murphy back to no avail.

Some suspected the miserable play of the Mets in their first seasons was also evidence of a curse earned by roiling the game's traditional structure through forcing its expansion. Now, as the radicals, hippies, and beatniks of the New Breed riotously cheered their rebellious team toward first place, the curse reversed. The Cubs became the first victims of the Mets' demonic spite, a caprine revanchism against all baseball, still celebrated by some occultist fans in a satanic revision of their logo celebrating them as the goat-headed *Baphomets*.[307]

Pitching on two days' rest to stop the bleeding, Cubs ace Ferguson Jenkins turned into another sacrificial lamb. With the Mets up 7–1, their fans sang like a Greek chorus. "When they stood for the seventh inning stretch," Cubs infielder Nate Oliver recalled, "the lights went out and fifty thousand people stood up and started swinging these white handkerchiefs singing '*Bye bye Leo. Bye bye Leo. We hate to see you go.*'"

There was no stopping metropolitan momentum from there. Nearing divisional clinch on September 24 with a 6–0 lead in the ninth, future Mets broadcaster Howie Rose and two friends abandoned their penknife-engraved seats in the upper deck and made their way downstairs with plans to storm the field. When they reached field level, they were surprised to see every aisle filled with kids just like them. "We were three idiots that thought this was a great idea," Rose recalled, "that nobody else would think of such a thing and we'd be the only ones on the field. Wrong!"[308]

Field stormings, uncommon in baseball since Merkle's Boner at the Polo Grounds, now returned with sixties spontaneity. When Joe Torre grounded into a double play, Rose charged the field with approximately twenty thousand other militants believing a new age waited just beyond the barricades. The three hundred policemen had no prayer of quelling the mayhem.

As a few quick thieves dug out the bases, Howie and dozens more used their disc-shaped "Fan Appreciation Day" keychains as improvised sickles to reap chunks of turf for their growing household shrines of Mets memorabilia. Rose told his mom it was from center field, but she "was never quite convinced, thinking it was a different kind of grass."[309]

The "pennant locusts," as Roger Angell described them, continued the riot for most of an hour. Links of fence and slats of seat were ripped out, outfield fences were painted with graffiti, and the American flag was pulled from its pole. "They poured out of the stands like deranged lemmings, like the mob attacking the Bastille, like barbarians scaling the walls of ancient Rome, like maddened initiates in some Dionysian rite," Leonard Koppett wrote. "To call it vandalism was to slander the motivation; to call it souvenir hunting was to demean the age-old power of relic worship; to call it attention-seeking was to pronounce a petty, mean, insensitive judgment."[310]

"Our team finally caught up with the fans," said catcher Jerry Grote, describing the team spirit that had led them to the playoffs. Their champagne-soaked party, however, was nothing compared to the frenzy on the field. With the postgame party winding down in the Diamond Club, Seaver and Gentry snuck out to survey the damage. They thought it looked like the surface of the moon, or what America might look like after World War III, and yet it was a beautiful sight to see the social order of the baseball world turned on its head.

But there was still more damage to be done. Later that night, about a hundred fans returned to the stadium chanting *Shea belongs to the people!* They commandeered a pitching cart, turned hoses on one another, went to the broadcast booth and called an imaginary World Series, and tore through the clubhouses to ransack anything left.[311]

Groundskeeper Pete Flynn reported the locusts had stripped the grass, the outfield, the bases, and the team emblems. The normal four-hour cleanup shift extended to four days, with the extended crew of dozens working in happy reverence of the destruction. "We were all so young and excited," Flynn said. "We were true Mets fans."[312]

The Mets proceeded to the NL Championship Series against Atlanta. Hank Aaron was characteristically remarkable in game one, homering off Seaver to put the Braves up 5–4 in the seventh. Cleon Jones answered back in the eighth to begin a rally that won the game.

Aaron had felt the Braves' previous pennant misses were an injustice, but he couldn't help but admire the Mets as they proceeded to sweep the three-game series and win the NL pennant. A lifelong advocate for Black ballplayers, he was particularly proud of the heroic performances of fellow Mobile residents Cleon Jones and Tommie Agee. "Nothing was going to stop them," he wrote. "One of my teammates, Tony

González, said that we ought to send the Mets to Vietnam and let them win the war."[313]

It's possible the Cuban expat Brave made the remark knowing some on the Mets *did* want the war to end, as the rest of the country soon found out.

"I think it's perfectly ridiculous what we're doing about the Vietnam situation," Tom Seaver told United Press International the day before starting game one of the series. "If the Mets can win the World Series, then we can get out of Vietnam."[314] The *Times* republished the story the next day under the headline *Tom Seaver Says US Should Leave Vietnam.*

Such a public statement from any white athlete, let alone an ex-marine, active reservist, and baseball star on the eve of the World Series, was virtually unheard of—and the lack of outcry demonstrated how much heat antiwar Black athletes from Robeson to Abdul-Jabbar to Ali had absorbed. Seaver had made the remark to demonstrate precisely this point. It was now safe and normal to oppose America's empire.

The plan was suggested by the Vietnam Moratorium Day Committee. The left-liberal coalition planned a mass and mainstream nationwide march against the war on October 15 supported by "heartland" institutions like churches, small businesses, and moderate politicians. Some of the coalition were radicals disturbed by the growing backlash against the Yippie and Black Panther–dominated countercultural protests of previous years, including Moratorium's New York organizer, Charles Seaver. While the Seaver brothers may not have been totally politically aligned, the two agreed the war had to end—a possibility that once seemed about as likely as Seaver's start in game four of the World Series the same day.

Perhaps the lack of outcry came from the certainty that the Mets stood no chance. Bettors gave the 109-game-winning AL Champion Orioles, who sportswriters considered the best team since the 1961 Yankees, eight-to-five odds to take the series. Headlines in Baltimore promised

promised "Mets' Miracle Story Nearing End,"with star outfielder Frank Robinson charitably predicting the best-of-seven series would only last five.[315] "Bring on Ron Gaspar," he concluded. When someone corrected Robinson that the benchwarmer's name was *Rod, stupid!* he snapped back, "Okay, bring on the Mets and Rod Stupid."[316]

After the Mets lost the first game 4–1, Clendenon, one of the sole veterans of the youngest team in baseball, called a players-only meeting. "Gentlemen, trust me," he announced. "We are going to kick their asses for the rest of the series."[317]

He had seen in the sparse and dispassionate crowd at Baltimore Memorial Stadium that afternoon what their powerful opponents lacked—the Beach Boys' "good vibrations" or Jim Morrison's *mojo*—a confidence that everything will supernaturally go your way. All summer, umpire calls, bounces, weather, and nearly every other chance element of the game seemed to land in the Mets' favor, leading Seaver to declare in a fit of Aquarian mysticism during the Atlanta series that "God truly is a Met."[318]

But rationalist Clendenon asserted a less mystical path to victory. Since his acquisition and the early-July Cubs series, the people of New York and their team had worked as a singular unit at Shea. Their volume and energy inspired the team to put more balls in play, where what looked like "lucky breaks" were often the bobbles or missed calls of intimidated umpires and thrown-off opponents. If the Mets could win the next game in Baltimore, Clendenon promised, they could use that home-field advantage to clinch in New York.

Until then, the Mets would rely on what Roger Angell called the team's distinctly sixties' "guerrilla spirit." Early woes, injuries, slumps, and reserves duty had given their fluid journeymen roster a collectivity unlike any team in baseball history. Only Jones and Agee, for example, went to bat more than 400 times that season, while the Orioles had six players with over 500 at bats, as did the champion Tigers of 1968 and Cardinals of 1967. The result was every player felt closer to an equal part of the team's success in a way unparalleled to anything third baseman and poet Ed Charles had seen in his eighteen-year career: "Every one of us knew when it was time to pick the other guy up. The bottom of the order, a pinch-hitter, a man who'd just fanned three times—everybody figured, 'What the hell, what am I waiting for? Do it now, baby, because there's no big man going to do it for you.'"[319]

With battle plans drawn, the Mets' amorphous egalitarian platoons launched their ambush. They narrowly took game two 2–1 on a ninth-inning single by light-hitting Al Weis. Two days later at Shea, Agee led off the game with a home run against ace Jim Palmer, and would go on to save five runs with daring outfield catches. Winning 5–0, the Mets took the lead in their asymmetric war.

Then came game four and Moratorium Day. Reliever Tug McGraw arrived to the ballpark to see a young cadre fanned out around Shea distributing literature and holding signs. One read: BOMB THE ORIOLES—NOT THE PEASANTS!

He strolled over and grabbed their pamphlet titled *METS FANS for PEACE*. The playful zine, published by the beatnik Grove Press, included screeds against the war, a comparison of the World Series to the "Chicago 8" trial, a call to sing "Give Peace a Chance" after the national anthem, and a blank page for autographs. On its cover was Tom Seaver, squinting defiantly aside his antiwar quotes, wearing his batting helmet like a defiant soldier of Third World revolution.[320]

McGraw proceeded to the clubhouse and handed it to the ace with a smile. "You really say this?"[321]

But Seaver, already on edge ahead of his start, took a glance at the pamphlet and threw it out. Its return address revealed it had not originated from his brother's respectable Moratorium Day Committee, but the far more radical "Chicago Conspiracy"—the defendants, including Yippies Abbie Hoffman and Jerry Rubin, and Black Panther Bobby Seale, charged with orchestrating the riots against the Democrats in Chicago.

Feeling himself the latest victim of the Yippies' notorious pranks, Seaver regretted ever having made his comment about Vietnam. While he did end up buying a small ad in the New Year's Eve edition of the *Times* that year requesting a "prayer for peace," he rarely talked publicly about politics again.[322]

Antiwar Mayor Lindsay also got cold feet before the game. He had ordered all flags on city buildings, including Shea, flown at half-mast in recognition of Moratorium Day's mission. In response, the US Merchant Marine Academy band and war-wounded veterans scheduled to take the field for the anthem said they would boycott. When the police indicated they might strike as well, Kuhn called Lindsay. Worried an unprotected Shea could become the next Woodstock, Seaver took the field for the national anthem with the flag flying high, and a noticeable number of fans defiantly seated.[323]

With thousands marching through Manhattan, and a skywriter spelling out STOP WAR in smoke above Shea, Seaver threw the game of his career. He took a 1–0 shutout into the ninth when Dean Latimer, who had hidden subliminal *Let's Go Mets* throughout the *East Village Other*'s freaky layout after his sports section pitch was rejected, returned to the office to find the hippie editors now attentively huddled around the radio, "ears glued . . . like cops digging on a phone tap. . . ." he wrote. "They wanted to see how this guy could have a head like that and pitch decent baseball at the same time."[324]

They howled in agony as comrade Seaver gave up the tying run, returning to serious reverence when he heroically returned to the mound again in the tenth inning. In the moment they feared the Movement had peaked as a ghettoized counterculture that *real* America would never tolerate, a true square fought with two on, one out, and the rebel soldiers of the US and Vietnam in his heart. When Seaver battled through the tenth unscathed, the *Other* offices cheered alongside a citywide "rumbling crescendo," Koppett wrote, "in stands, in the streets, in offices, in homes, wherever a television set or radio could be tuned in."[325]

The happening continued to the Mets' side of the tenth, when Seaver's pinch hitter, some unknown soldier on the major-league baseball team openly aligned with the international anti-imperialist struggle, ambushed the Orioles with a bunt that forced a walk-off error. For a little while longer, the radicals believed the revolution was still underway. The Mets were up three games to one.

The whole city believed still when the Mets trailed 3–0 late into game five. In the bottom of the sixth, Dave McNally pitched a ball near Jones's cleat that scampered off catlike into the Mets' clubhouse. After a moment of confusion, Hodges emerged from the dugout with a ball scuffed by shoe polish, and the umpire motioned for Jones to take first on a hit-by-pitch. Weaver and McNally argued the obvious fraud be overturned. Keeping a scuffed ball in the dugout was an ancient ruse. Had Stengel tried it, the ump would have laughed him off the field. But Hodges was beyond suspicion, and New York's endless roar drowned out the protest.

Destiny resumed. Clendenon stepped to bat and smacked a home run. Al Weis hit another to tie the game the next inning, and Jones scored Swoboda on a double in the next to put the Mets up 4–3 going to the ninth.

Koosman walked Frank Robinson, then got outs on a grounder and fly ball. Davey Johnson came to plate as the O's' last hope, and swung for the fences. Off the bat, he and Koosman both were sure it was headed out. Jones ran back toward the track. A jet flew overhead, crossing the ball's path. Overtaken by the convergence as the plane passed and the ball began to drop, he froze, thinking back to the Go! Shouters: "our Mets fans who'd been with us since 1962, how faithful and trusting they'd been to us . . . to stick with losers."[326]

He reached out his glove, thinking, "We were finally going to give the fans justice. Not only that, we were going to be a winner for all New Yorkers. Be a winner for the underdogs. Be a winner for the country, and even the world."[327]

The ball landed in Jones's glove, crumbling him into a contemplative crouch. Time stopped. He imagined himself alone, the other players vanished, the crowd and jet quieted, allowing him to think back further, "to my ancestors, those who came from Africa just before the Civil War, enslaved people stolen from their homes by greedy, Godless people—heartless people guided only by profit and gain with no regard for humanity and the basic rights of all people."[328] This was for them, too.

At third, Ed Charles had similar thoughts—memories of listening to the pre-Robinson Dodgers on the radio in Daytona Beach, Florida, and praying that somehow, one day, he could play in a World Series. "And that's what I was thinking about as we celebrated and came off that field. It happened! The prayers I sent up before Jackie made it, praying that somehow I could play major-league baseball, play in the World Series, and win it—all of that stuff happened!"[329]

Shredded newspapers rained from the decks. Smoke bombs exploded on the field. Fans pushed away ushers blocking the dugout roof, swarming the team mid-celebration, and overpowering the grounds crew to steal the bases. Others leapt over outfield fences and descended the foul pole like firemen, resulting in at least one broken leg. "When I went down the steps," Koosman recalled, "fans were already piled three or four feet high—lying on top of each other—as they fell from on top of the dugout. I walked over the tops of bodies with my spikes. . . . It was nuts!"[330]

Payson cried with joy as she watched the mayhem from her infield box. Powerless against the crowd, her orange-blazered guards focused on breaking up scuffles and shoving away the peasants approaching her clutching tufts of grass like offerings.

As the fan riot continued, an all-star celebration soaked Shea's clubhouse in champagne. A drenched Swoboda dedicated the victory to "every loser in America," as the tough-on-crime New York Supreme Court Justice Samuel Leibowitz, sloshed nearby, issued a rare clemency: "I will even forgive Walter O'Malley for leaving Brooklyn."[331] NL president Warren Giles arrived to the fray to hand the championship trophy to Hodges. This was "the greatest thing to happen to baseball," the executive who had aggressively supported the Dodgers and Giants' flight from New York said, tearing up, "the greatest thing that's happened to the National League, and the greatest thing that's happened to me!"[332]

"They must have been lucky or good or something," Orioles infielder Don Buford mumbled in the stunned visitor locker room. "All we know about them is that they used to be funny. . . . We're not laughing at them now."[333]

In the course of seven months, the Mets transformed from baseball's historically worst embarrassment to its most venerated heroes since Robinson's Dodgers.

Banners of Agee and Jones hung throughout the Black districts of Alabama. Swinging parties raged in the bars and avenues of the "Body Exchange" district—described by *New York Magazine* as the straight equivalent of the swingin' scene around Stonewall, where Met Phil Linz owned a bar frequented by much of the team.[334] From there, the club went direct to *The Ed Sullivan Show* to drunkenly sing "You Gotta Have Heart"—a song from a musical about a hopeless squad of losers and a regular guy who sells his soul to Satan to beat the Yankees. After watching the act, Las Vegas promoters hired several of them as an offseason cabaret act, and bubblegum-pop label Buddha released an LP of their 10-song set. Another LP of the season's greatest broadcasted hits canonized the team with its enduring moniker: "The Miracle Mets."

The next day, half a million filled the Canyon of Heroes waving orange pennants and cheering the Mets as they had the returned moonwalkers two months prior. "It was like V-J Day in New York," William Ryczek wrote. "Confetti rained down from office windows. Strangers hugged each other on the street. Church bells rang . . . The Yankees had won 20 World Series titles, but not once had they been given a ticker tape parade."[335]

A newsreel captured the bedlam: all three mayoral candidates trailing the team's float in desperate search of a sliver of their spotlight. Every downtown street, the stock exchange, and Federal Hall draped white with reams of financial documents dumped from the windows of Wall Street, and shredded newspapers filled with stories about police shootings and hospital closures. Giddy youth, counterculture and square alike, frolicked through the bad news like freshly fallen snow. Some flashed peace signs to the camera, one hoisted on the shoulder of his two friends holding a sign contradicting Nietzsche's Zarathustra: "GOD ISN'T DEAD, HE'S PLAYING FOR THE METS."[336]

A mile uptown, Dean Latimer was finally granted the back page of the *East Village Other* for his sports section. In his first column, he contextualized the victory within all the bleak political turns of the last year as a sign there was still hope. If the election was held in 1969, he theorized, Nixon would have lost. The column ended with a telegram to Seaver before the World Series, cc'd to the *Other*:

> TOM SEAVER: WE WANT YOU TO KNOW OF OUR CONTINUED SUPPORT OF THE N.Y. METS IN THEIR

BATTLE WITH THE AGGRESSORS FROM THE AMERIKAN LEAGUE.

WE, MEMBERS OF THE CHICAGO CONSPIRACY, ALSO FIND OURSELVES LOCKED IN SERIOUS TROUBLE WITH A TEAM OF OUTSIDE AGITATORS KNOWN AS THE WASHINGTON KANGAROOS.

OUR TRIAL NOW TAKING PLACE IN THE CENTER COURT OF THE CHICAGO FEDERAL BUILDING HAS BEEN TERMED "THE WORLD SERIES OF INJUSTICE." IN THIS SERIES WE, LIKE YOU, ARE THE UNDERDOGS, AND TO ALL THE UNDERDOGS OF THE WORLD STRUGGLING AGAINST OPPRESSION WE OFFER OUR SUPPORT.

UP AGAINST THE CENTER FIELD WALL, BALTIMORE

POWER TO THE N.Y. METS![337]

Chapter 8

SHAME STADIUM

As hundreds of workers swept 2,000 tons of paper from the parade route, and the idealistic decade came to a close, editorials boasted the Mets' miracle had boosted "city morale."[338]

John Lindsay's reelection as mayor on November 4 was one direct result. His independent candidacy had previously been considered a long-shot after his antiwar and pro-civil-rights positions lost him the Republican primary. He was especially unpopular in the Democratic stronghold of Queens, where, due to a bungled blizzard cleanup earlier that year, his canvassers frequently had doors slammed in their face.

But as the Mets surged in the standings through the summer, Lindsay made himself a fixture in the clubhouse. The *Times, Daily News, Newsday, Long Island Press, Post,* and Channels 4 and 9 ran images of the mayor trading volleys of champagne after each celebration. His

1966 vision of turning Wagner's "city in crisis" into a tolerant and carefree "Fun City" had been vindicated by the lapse of riots in 1969, the surge of downtown party culture, and the thrilling championships of the Jets and Mets. "Don't Change Mayors Mets-Stream," became a campaign slogan, and Queens locals warmed up to his volunteers, Ron Swoboda and Ed Kranepool among them. One door-knocker reported: "Now they listen to you and say things. Other canvassers tell me they've had similar reactions in other parts of Flushing."[339] Lindsay emerged atop the divided field with 41.1 percent of the vote, winning Queens by just 4,000.

The previous night, President Nixon had addressed the nation in response to the massive and Mets-supported Moratorium Day protests for US withdrawal from Vietnam during the World Series. "I know it may not be fashionable to speak of patriotism or national destiny these days," he said, in a contradictory speech that pledged to "end the war" over the course of the next several months while preserving American dignity and global leadership. To do so, he called on "the silent majority" to mobilize in opposition to the antiwar movement.[340]

Swoboda joined Roger Craig, Ron Taylor, and Tug McGraw later that winter for a USO trip to Vietnam. Although they supported the fight against communism, after a few days drinking and smoking pot with the troops, everything they had heard about the war turning into a horrific quagmire was confirmed.

They even saw combat when the opening volleys of the "Mini-Tet" offensive hit their base outside An Khê. "The sun was going down as we got into our Jeep, and as we drove up this hill, and we looked back toward the front gate, and I could see something blow up," Swoboda recalled. "And then something blew up again! Boom!"[341]

As troops mobilized toward the gate, Viet Cong sappers infiltrated the base's helicopter pad to drop satchel charges. One US soldier died in the attack, and Swoboda returned from Vietnam convinced the war had to end as soon as possible. Not only was it "squandering our living capital and our living assets—young people," but also millions of Vietnamese: "We just decimated their culture. I feel a big guilt about that."[342]

The Mets' political commitments were first publicly tested on March 6, 1970, when they arrived to St. Petersburg for spring training.

The town, officially renamed "Metsville" for the day, held a parade to honor the champs followed by a feast hosted by Republican Governor Claude Kirk. Facing reelection, and seeing how the Mets had served Lindsay, Kirk toasted the Mets as "America the beautiful" in contrast to the antiwar protesters who he described as "hecklers in the uniform of the day, disheveled filth and long hair." Speaking next, Mets chairman M. Donald Grant agreed. The Mets were "real he-men," he said, compared to the effeminate hippies who "we must fight."[343]

The team was asked to stand following the speeches for a final round of applause. Unappreciative of Kirk and Grant's grandstanding, many did only with clear reluctance. Their conservative attire and short hair was the result of Hodges's dress code, not some political stance, Tug McGraw wrote. "As I received my award and everyone applauded, I turned around and faced Governor Kirk and gave him the peace sign."[344]

The disavowal of Southern conservatism, however polite, indicated the Mets still felt their championship was about far more than baseball—an affinity with the antiwar sentiments of much of their fan base that reflected a broader mobilization of athletes within the Movement that year.

Shortly after the 1970 season began, Nixon announced the war in Vietnam, far from winding down as he promised, had spread to Cambodia. For the first time, a significant number of college athletes took part in the renewed wave of occupations and strikes spreading across American universities. Berkeley sports sociologist Jack Scott wrote in *The Athletic Revolution* that many of the Columbia University jocks who organized right-wing squads to fight the 1968 occupations switched sides, with "eighty-five football players endors[ing] a petition supporting a nationwide student strike; and baseball, track, tennis, and golf athletes vot[ing] to cancel their competition." Radicalization of the sports world was the most promising sign yet the Movement of the sixties would be exceeded, Scott continued, causing one Nixon spokesperson to fret: "Once we heard that the athletes and pom-pom girls had joined the demonstrations, we knew we were in trouble."[345]

Psychology student and Mets fan Jeffrey Glenn Miller was among the 1,500 to participate in the May 4 strike at Kent State University in Ohio. He had spent the previous year cheering the Miracle Mets at Shea, attending the Woodstock Festival, and driving a taxi to save money for college. Now he lobbed stones at the National Guard troops sent in to disperse the students. When the troops responded with tear gas, Miller shouted "pig" and held a middle finger aloft as his group fell back into a parking lot. Some continued to push toward the frontline and cheered as their opponents appeared to retreat uphill. Once there, however, the troops raised their guns and fired.

"When the fusillade began," Paula Schleis later wrote for the *Akron Beacon Journal*, "a friend standing next to Jeff assumed the rounds were blanks, and turned to Jeff to tell him so. But Jeff was face down on the ground. He'd been dropped by a bullet that entered his mouth and shattered the base of his skull. He was 265 feet from the guardsman who shot him."[346]

The Mets played the Dodgers at Shea the next night under a flag returned to half-mast to mourn the dozens of students shot and four killed in the massacre, including Miller.

American sports had always been conceived of as a therapeutic distraction to politics. McGraw wrote that taking the mound had previously been his sole comfort, because it "takes people off my mind." But after Kent State, the dynamic reversed.

He was a soldier, a patriot, a celebrity, but he was also a worker and antiwar, and he identified broadly with the people—both those fighting and dying for peace, and the silent majority that supported the senseless war's expansion. He wrote in his diary that night: "I really don't know in which direction to head or what to do. Why? Because I'm a people and I'm screwed up."[347]

His teammates felt the same. "All the guys in the locker room were upset, and they talked it over and nobody had any answers," McGraw wrote.[348] "When we heard the news, there was no way to absorb it and still go on doing the usual routine. . . . I couldn't get myself to go to the ballpark and enjoy myself, for God's sake, playing a game of baseball."[349]

The most popular team in New York, if not all of sports, now discussed boycotting the game. "Listen, I was in the service, too," Hodges told McGraw as they weighed the protest. "It was a different situation, a lot more clear-cut. . . . But the thing that stays is your commitment to what's right. . . . If you let the worst in us ruin the best in us, you'll never find the answer. We'll look for it together."[350]

The Mets' firm answer after the assassinations of King and Kennedy in 1968 had been to strike. Two years later, Hodges convinced them it was to suit up, shut up, and play the Dodgers.

A Gallup poll after the massacre showed 58 percent of Americans blamed the students for the violence. Nixon's foretold "silent majority" was on the move, and the morning of May 8, four days after the massacre, it would roar through the streets of New York.

A vigil of over one thousand students, hippies, radicals, and workers assembled at Wall Street that morning to mourn for the dead of Kent State and demand an end to the wars and repression. Nearby, thousands of Manhattan building-trades workers, many from the World Trade Center construction site, attended a pro-war rally organized by conservative AFL-CIO leader Peter J. Brennan. Cops cheered them as they marched toward the vigil, scattering the peaceniks before besieging City Hall and returning the American flag to full mast. Proceeding to nearby Pace University, they beat students and professors unconscious, along with a few police and medics that tried to intervene.

A sleeper-hit film that summer named *Joe* served as another symbol of the growing cultural fracture between the workers and radical youth who had harmonized at Shea the previous year. Its titular protagonist was a blue-collar New Yorker who, after too many drinks at the local sports bar, teamed up with an upper-class Republican for a hippie-murdering rampage through crash pads and communes. The story was a clear criticism of how the silent majority sublimated their envy of the righteous, libertine youth in its desire to see the Movement put down by force. The film's marketers, however, sold it as a pornographic revenge fantasy against the left.

Faced with the eruption of murderous reaction, the protests receded as most of the Movement, like the Mets, retreated to the safety of apolitical counterculture. Revolutionary feminist and rock critic Ellen Willis reflected that Shea, Woodstock, and other communal ruptures of 1969 represented "a very real enactment of a moment of mass freedom"—the sort of irruptive events her Redstockings and their sibling Yippies hoped would transform spectators of rock and baseball into political actors. But they had only come about "through a marketing scheme that got out of control and succeeded through the sheer will of the crowd."[351] Once the mud-orgies ended, all utopianism was hosed off, and the sanitized sixties was repackaged as a consumer-friendly product.

Woodstock's follow-up, for example, was held at Shea Stadium in August, 1970. Janis Joplin, Miles Davis, Dionne Warwick, Creedence Clearwater Revival, and Richie Havens performed with none of the self-organized chaos of the prior year. The "Festival for Peace" became the model of rock fests to come—safe and well organized, with a portion of the proceeds theoretically making its way to some good cause.

There was little hope for the Mets to buck the trend. They were no longer underdogs, after all. Joan Payson predicted the Mets would continue winning championships through the mid-seventies, and Ted Williams declared the team a dynasty in the making due to their farm system's dual championships in 1969.[352] Locked in a pennant race with the Pirates through the summer, ticket sales rivaled the Dodgers' all-time 1962 record. But the New Breed fans and sportswriters who once loved the team *win or lose* now scorned poor performance. Swoboda slumped, Nolan Ryan was wild, and there were no Marvelous Marv–esque adoring nicknames or fan club for new third-baseman Joe Foy, who often arrived to the park too stoned to field his position.

A still "screwed up" McGraw was the first to succumb to the pressure during a summer game in San Francisco. Sent in to get out of a bases-loaded jam in the eighth, he called a mound meeting with the infield to set up a trick pickoff—the type of creative play for which the Mets were beloved in 1969. Hodges immediately stormed the field to break up the plot with uncharacteristic fury. "He said if we didn't win this game, it would be my ass," McGraw wrote. He dutifully pitched out of trouble before collapsing in the clubhouse in a nervous breakdown. "You couldn't tell if I was laughing or crying."[353]

The rest of the team went on to crumble as well. A late-August first-place tie faded in the final weeks of September, when the Mets lost six of seven tragically close games against Pittsburgh. The same team that had shocked everyone by even earning a winning season the previous year were now cursed by the wrathful city for finishing third.

While Nixon had reversed on his pledge to end the war, he fulfilled his promise to expand repression at home. Antiwar radicals and revolutionaries were systematically harassed and framed on drug charges, prosecuted in conspiracy trials, and assassinated—like Black Panthers leader Fred Hampton, killed by police as he slept in his Chicago apartment on December 4, 1969.

Faced with widespread violent backlash, antiwar protests dramatically subsided. Most radicals were no longer able to believe that change was possible, and retreated to the quiet pursuit of their individual well-being and careers. Others retreated to underground cells, hoping to reignite the revolution through covert militant actions.

Among them was Robin Palmer's cell of the Weather Underground, a former SDS faction dedicating itself to armed struggle after its collapse. As he assembled a team to bomb state and corporate institutions in Manhattan on the one-year anniversary of Hampton's murder, he began to suspect that one recruit, Steve Weiner, might be a police informant.

One night in early 1970, the cadre fed Weiner drugs until he was incredibly stoned, and subjected him to a lengthy interrogation. When Weiner answered their questions to the group's satisfaction, Palmer apologized for the grilling. Weiner said he understood, and suggested the cadre reconcile by going to a Mets game. Palmer convinced himself this was definitive proof his comrade was on the level, later telling sixties radicalism scholar Jeremy Varon he believed: "No Mets fan would be so unsportsmanlike as to infiltrate a group."

But in the early morning of December 4, 1970, police awaited the group as they assembled in the Upper East Side carrying material to firebomb the First National Bank. After a brief scuffle, the six were arrested and charged with attempted arson. While it remains unknown if Steve Weiner truly supported the Mets, he *was* an FBI informant.[354]

A year after the miracle, New Breed sportswriter Leonard Koppett wrote, the ecstasy had passed, leaving behind "bleak residue: life in the city had not improved." Crime and fear of it was on the rise. Hip nightclubs and restaurants began to close. Strikes, white flight, and ethnic tension continued into a third decade. "When the realization sank in that the moment of unity and joy provided by a championship team really didn't produce any lasting after-effect, the mood of disillusionment was even stronger than it had been before the 'miracles' occurred."[355]

Even with their countercultural bona fides in question, the Mets remained the best team in New York, and, on paper, the team to beat in the NL in 1971. And yet the results were the same—a third-place finish, with an identical record.

Some roster improvements for 1972 were made during the offseason, including trading wild Nolan Ryan to the Angels for All-Star shortstop Jim Fregosi. But by the final week of spring training, the team noticed Gil Hodges taking on a frail pallor. The pressure of returning to the playoffs in his contract's last year had driven him back to the chain-smoking habit prohibited by his doctor after his first heart attack.[356] Adding to the stress was a renewed labor conflict threatening the regular season.

The owners were determined to halt the gains from 1968 and 1969. Those years of labor militancy had inspired the unionization of players in Mexico, Puerto Rico, and the umpires of both leagues. When union head Marvin Miller demanded a greater portion of baseball's booming revenue from league expansion and broadcasting be set aside for players' healthcare and pensions, the magnates coldly refused. Miller was nervous about their prospects in the era of leftist retreat. The players, however, were so indignant after watching sixteen of their twenty-four representatives traded or cut from rosters over the previous three seasons they voted 663–10 to strike if no deal was reached by the end of training. The deadline passed, and the final exhibition games were canceled.

On Easter Sunday, Hodges tried to take his mind off the drama at the golf course. After twenty-seven holes, he collapsed with a fatal heart attack.

The baseball world, especially the remaining golden-era Dodgers, were devastated. Roger Kahn's book *The Boys of Summer*, released the previous month, revealed many of Hodges's former teammates struggling through low-wage jobs in their retirement, unable to make ends meet on the paltry pre-Miller pensions. Forty-seven-year-old Gil was the last among them still on a major-league payroll.

The death of Hodges marked a prelude to a forthcoming dark chapter in Mets history, foreseen on one of "Sign Man" Karl Ehrhardt's placards displayed, and swiftly confiscated, six years prior at Shea: WELCOME TO GRANT'S TOMB.

Ehrhardt had been among those in the New Breed who, since 1962, identified team chairman and Payson's stockbroker M. Donald Grant as the source of the franchise's worst instincts. Payson, Johnny Murphy, and Gil Hodges had always checked the influence over day-to-day operations he always desired, but Murphy's death shortly after the 1969 World Series marked the beginning of the end of the clubhouse's familial spirit. Now Hodges, protector of team democracy, was gone as well.

With greater control, Grant's vision for running the Mets was a preview of the neoliberal era of chauvinistic financial tyranny. He was well known for bringing franchise stockholders to the clubhouse to degrade the athletes as "boys," Rob Edelman wrote for the Society for American Baseball Research. Players were expected to "smile on cue, accept whatever deals management offered them, sign their contracts, and play ball. Their salaries, he believed, should be comparable to that of the average American working person, rather than similar to the remuneration of a stockbroker or CEO."[357]

Hodges's funeral was scheduled for April 6, Opening Day of the 1972 season. Even were the strike to end, the Yankees announced their game that day would be delayed in his honor. Grant refused any such concession, telling the press the Mets would play as scheduled. Bud Harrelson issued a statement on behalf of the mourning team that they would be at the funeral, even if it meant forfeiting the game.

With trepidation setting in as the strike extended into the regular season, Miller held a pep rally in New York. The most convincing speech came from Giants union representative Willie Mays. If he could put his six-figure salary on the line, he said, they should too.[358]

The strike continued. So, too, did Grant's callousness. Hodges's apparent managerial heir was Whitey Herzog, a coach widely beloved by the press and respected by players, who had succeeded Murphy to keep the Mets' impressive farm system on track. But Herzog also saw Grant for what he was: "a stockbroker, a guy who didn't know beans about baseball but thought he did."[359] Grant told Herzog he was giving the job to the more-submissive Yankee great Yogi Berra. Worried Herzog would leak the news to the press, Grant instructed him to keep away from his friend's funeral.

Moments after Hodges entered the ground, Grant convened a press conference at Shea. He announced Berra as the new manager, and revealed that he had traded three top prospects for power-hitting Rusty Staub. Under different circumstances the press may have praised the moves. But on the day of Hodges's burial, they were appalled by Grant's celebratory tone.

Understanding the franchise was no longer the labor-friendly operation it had been in 1969, the Mets held strong as the strike went another week. After a cumulative eighty-six canceled games, representing about $5 million in losses, the owners met Miller's demands.

The strike had been far costlier to the owners than the players, whose $600,000 in lost salary was offset by substantial boosts in pension and healthcare contributions. "It was a lesson the owners had hoped the Players Association would never learn," Robert Burk wrote. "Ironically, because they had forced the showdown in their effort to break the union, only to be the ones to cave when the going got tough, the magnates had been the most responsible of all in teaching their players the value of solidarity."[360]

Miller now saw a way forward to taking down the century-old cornerstone of the owners' dominance—the reserve clause. Two years prior, Cardinals star Curt Flood, inspired by the bravery of Black Power athletes like Muhammad Ali, Kareem Abdul-Jabbar, and Arthur Ashe, had sued major-league baseball to become a free agent, arguing the clause violated his Thirteenth Amendment rights as a form of involuntary servitude. At the heart of the matter was his 1969 trade to the Phillies, a team Flood believed to have a particularly racist fan base. Miller was skeptical the argument would work, but as a proponent of championing the grievances of Black and Latino players, the union agreed to fund his cause.

Even with once-steadfast defender of the reserve clause Jackie Robinson testifying on his behalf, the Supreme Court ruled 5–3 against Flood. After the defeat, Miller told players of a new tactic for winning free agency through the arbitration process won in the 1968 CBA and first tested by the Mets in rainy Atlanta. Dozens, perhaps hundreds, of unsigned or unpaid players would hold out for a full season and challenge their reserves with labor arbitrators. Miller knew this was asking for a major sacrifice, but after seeing how well players managed the threat of missed games during the strike, he confidently moved forward with the plan.

The Mets opened the 1972 season with similar confidence, and Berra at the helm. It was their best start ever, winning twenty-five of their first thirty-two games to take first place in the division.

Although Berra's quotable Yogi-isms and unorthodox managerial style reminded many of Stengel, his wit and strategy were often more the result of malapropisms and bizarre luck than ancient baseball wisdom. Sportscaster Gary Cohen likened Berra to the nearsighted cartoon character Mr. Magoo, who comically stumbled through life, serendipitously avoiding the dangers surrounding him.[361]

Soon enough, Berra and the Mets' luck began to run out. Without the military discipline of Hodges, injuries mounted, and the Mets began to sink in the standings. With Staub out for months, the clubhouse needed a new leader. Payson had only one name in mind—Willie.

While Grant had no interest in acquiring a union-militant superstar long past his prime, it was well known Payson had always wanted to make Mays a Met. In 1966, hippy-dippy comedian George Carlin joked she would trade the entire team for Mays, throwing in half a million and a kangaroo on top. For his part, Mays had wanted to stay a Giant for life, requesting a ten-year $750,000 contract that would see him transition from the field to management. He was crushed when Horace Stoneham only committed to the aging legend for five years. Then, in early May, when the Giants were in New York, he was traded to the Mets for a single prospect in a salary dump.

More than 35,000 turned out to a rainy game at Shea to see Mays's first game in orange and blue. Pete Hamill wrote in *Sport* magazine about his messianic debut hit: "With the count full and the rain falling harder, Mays lined the pitch over the left field wall. It may have been his most dramatic swing ever. Willie Mays ran the bases, carrying all those summers on the forty-one-year-old shoulders, jogging in silence, while people in the stands pumped their arms at the skies and hugged each other and even, here and there, cried."

The Giants playfully tried to block Mays as he ran. When he reached home plate to find his former teammates standing outside the dugout clapping with the rest of Shea, he made a slight wrong turn toward the visitors' side before realizing he was once again at home in New York. "[It was] some peculiar sign that we might be able to erase what happened," Hamill continued, "eliminate the sense of cynicism that flooded the city in 1958. . . . Some forgotten promise had been kept."[362]

Despite moments of brilliance like these, his play deteriorated with his aging joints each game. Knowing his best years were long behind him, he attempted to be New York's baseball savior off the field. In a time of social fracture, he wore symbols of Christianity, Judaism, and Islam around his neck. When a Black Nationalist group called on him to support racial separatism, he abruptly ended the meeting. He returned to his fifties' hobby of surprising kids playing stickball around the city, largely finding working-class neighborhoods in terrible disrepair. Many housing projects, even those on the site of the former Polo Grounds, prohibited baseball altogether.

He found a field to play that August on a visit to Rikers Island. The recently opened city jail, designed to be a model for progressive incarceration, had opened to severe budget cuts and a correctional officer union determined to make life for its overcrowded, almost entirely Black and brown population a living hell. Addressing five hundred inmates in attendance that day, Mays said, "I don't think my coming here is going to change anything for you and that things will be any different when I leave, but I want you to know that I'm very happy to be here just the same. I understand what's happening here."[363]

For the third consecutive year, the Mets finished in third place with eighty-three wins. Lindsay's "Fun City" decisively came to an end when the Mets-branded mayor announced he was giving up City Hall to run for president against Nixon as a progressive Democrat. Nixon won the general election decisively, hammering another nail into the sixties' coffin.

Political and economic malaise deepening, Tug McGraw returned to his depressive spiral. By the summer of 1973, his ERA was above six, and the injury-riddled Mets were in last place. Without the steady guidance of Hodges, the game that had previously given McGraw's life meaning and consolation from the world's cruelties now appeared to him a factory in which he had become a second-rate mechanic.

In July, after the Mets had lost six of their last seven, he sought advice from Hodges's insurance-salesman friend Joe Badamo. Like many in his field, Badamo had improved the confidence of his sales pitches by dabbling in psychologist Abraham Maslow's theories of self-actualization. The method could be applied easily to the mound, he told McGraw: Envision the result of the pitch, and then make it happen. The key to self-actualization was not what he felt, not what he knew, and certainly not reality, but what he *believed*.

"That's it, I guess," McGraw responded. "You gotta believe." He left the session knowing he had no other choice than to turn himself over to the saccharine conceit. When a group of fans heckled him on his way into Shea, he told them: "There's nothing wrong with the Mets. You gotta believe!"

An hour later, the inspired fans shouted the slogan at the confused team during warm-ups. "The next thing you know we had a group of pitchers in the outfield and I was giving a big sermon on how you gotta believe," McGraw wrote. "It was a joke, you know. We were all laughing about it."[364]

After batting practice, the team was summoned to meet with Grant. The players knew he was at the center of a crisis of leadership in the franchise, widely compared in the press to Nixon's scandal-wrought White House after Watergate. Like Nixon, Grant blamed everyone but himself. He accused general manager Bob Scheffing of talking him into the Nolan Ryan trade. He blamed Payson for hiring the deadweight of Mays. He blamed Berra for the team's lack of discipline. When he demanded Scheffing fire Berra for not whipping the team into shape, Scheffing suggested Grant do it himself, knowing he didn't have the courage.

Grant's speech, Jerry Koosman recalled, was equally awkward and noncommittal: "He raised one finger and said, 'Number one, you have to have heart. Number two, you have to have—'" Already pepped, McGraw leapt from his stool to interrupt with a guttural scream Koosman likened to Hulk Hogan's: *YA GOTTA BELIEVE!*[365]

One by one, the Mets began to laugh at what they believed to be McGraw taking their widely despised boss down a peg. Grant sulked away as McGraw continued to manically repeat his new mantra. "I started running around the clubhouse to each locker hollering at guys,

'Do you believe?' . . . grabbing guys by the hair and pulling their heads up and yelling, 'You gotta believe.'' And everybody thought I was crazy."[366]

Chairman Grant may never have forgiven the slight, but he was powerless to be rid of McGraw as he rebounded to his former excellence that summer.

Nor could he dispel the derisive catchphrase as it became the idiotic idiom of the downtrodden Mets fan, shouted at players and one another, printed on placards, and scrawled on homemade shirts. It was the revival of the sixties' spirit of ironic hope in the face of hopelessness, updated for a decade in which yoga, self-help, and parapsychology grifts like the Rajneeshees, EST, and Scientology rapidly seized the terrain abandoned by the revolutionary movement.

The supplication was all-the-more necessary as New York teetered on the edge of social and economic collapse. Manufacturing continued to vanish, white-flight tax base erosion was near the point of washout, and the movement fighting for power to the people was now secluded in academies, the Democratic Party, underground micro-sects, prisons, or tombs.

Politicians and bureaucrats turned themselves over to the power of positive thinking as well, fudging numbers to hide immense budget shortfalls in hopes of some miracle. Such things were possible, after all. The Mets had proven it in 1969.

Soon they would do it again. Team veterans had returned to health, McGraw was looking like the best closer in baseball, and struggles from the rest of the Eastern teams put the last-place Mets only seven games out of first with a month to play.

It was an improbable gap to leap, but faith was now mandatory. Massive crowds cheered the Mets home and away throughout September as fans flocked to see Willie Mays, who had announced his retirement earlier that year, in uniform for the last time. Enthusiasm for Mays and

McGraw's mantra propelled the Mets in the standings game after game. By the time of Mays's farewell ceremony at Shea on September 25, they were tied for first. The Mets won that night, and continued to win, finishing the month with a record of 20–8. On October 1, the Mets clinched the division in Chicago with McGraw on the mound.

They entered the playoffs with a record of 82–79, and nearly the worst offensive stats in the league. Their opponents, the Cincinnati Reds, had won ninety-nine games with a relentless offense, featuring Joe Morgan, Tony Pérez, Johnny Bench, and Pete Rose, still remembered as one of the greatest in baseball history. After splitting the first two games of the asymmetric series in Cincinnati, the Reds arrived to a riotous Shea crowd determined to smash the *Big Red Machine*.

The first night, the Mets led 9–2 in the fifth when Rose, already widely hated among players for his dirty play and complaints about missed wages from the strike, slid hard into Bud Harrelson at second. The two brawled, benches cleared, and fans pelted beer cans toward the melee. Once separated from Harrelson, Rose chucked cans back at the seats. The moment play continued, an empty whiskey bottle flew a few feet from Rose's head, and the Reds ran for safety.

The Shea PA pled for fans to calm down lest the umpires declare a Mets forfeit. When this failed, Willie Mays, yet to appear in the series, emerged from the dugout like Casey in Mudville, holding his fingers in a peace sign and yelling, "Look at the scoreboard! We're ahead! Let 'em play the game."[367] With the rising tumult quelled, the game went on, and the Mets won.

Two days later, at the decisive game back at Shea, Mays appeared in his first at bat of the postseason and chopped an infield single to put the Mets up 4–2.

The Mets went on to clinch the pennant. A *Sporting News* column described the fans turning into a "Maniac Mob," throwing trash at the

Reds' wives in the stands, pushing past the 340 officers on the field, and chasing Pete Rose into the dugout, where his teammates wielded their bats against the rioters sacking Shea.[368]

The Mets' World Series opponents would be their far superior imitators, the Oakland Athletics. Owner Charles Finley had continued to rebrand his team as the East Bay's answer to the New Breed Mets and stodgy Giants since chasing the counterculture by moving the team from Kansas City to Oakland in 1968. He styled them as the *Swingin' A's* in unique green and gold uniforms, doling out bonuses to his talent for adapting hip facial hair and nicknames like Rollie, Blue Moon, and Catfish. After their 1972 championship, Finley made an even more blatant robbery by marketing the team as the *Amazin' A's*.

Beneath the facsimile, the Athletics were less a West Coast mirror of the Mets than their spiritual foil. Their hipness was derived not from underdog spirit, but from the individualist professionalism so obsessively pursued in what Tom Wolfe dubbed the *"Me" Decade*. "The old alchemical dream" of sixties collectivism, Wolfe wrote, had changed from dreams of the communal synthesis to the self-interest of the capacious individual, a new alchemical process of turning "base metals into gold."[369]

In his 1981 essay "The Amazing Mets and Structuralist Activity," literary theorist Jerry Herron gleaned that chemical process completed in the A's elite assemblage and gold jerseys, and the 1973 World Series a final battle for the identity of America in the seventies. "Professionals are never amazing," Herron wrote, "only amateurs are, because when they succeed, it's a surprise, a wonder, a true gift. Professionals do what they're supposed to do, every time, on cue; their craft consists in the elimination of chance, the displacement of the amateur." The Mets, on the other hand, had retained traces of sixties spirit. "They were amazing because people wanted to be amazed: we were looking for shared happenings, not private performance."[370]

While the A's had stolen their sixties' valor, the Mets' mediocrity following 1969 and bizarre run to the pennant in 1973 were a speed-run re-creation of their decadal hero's journey from worst to first. Now, on the verge of another optimism-manifested miracle, they could prove it had been no fluke. All tragic stretches would only be preludes to come-from-behind glory, embryonic in their origins as the restoration of New York's great people's teams. They had vindicated the Brooklyn Dodgers with Hodges at the helm in 1969, and would now do the same for the New York Giants with Mays, reestablishing themselves as a new breed of dynasty to replace the fading, Berra-abandoned Yankees. It would be colorful as the Summer of Love, antiauthoritarian as a student protest, and progressively patriotic like the administration of Mayor John Lindsay. All season, Berra had summarized this comeback narrative of the Mets as the city's and the sixties' comeback saviors with his oft-repeated catchphrase: *It ain't over 'til it's over.*

Even the A's faithful filling the Oakland Coliseum for game one seemed to grasp this narrative force by giving the loudest ovation for any player to Willie Mays. He became a one-man Mets throughout the early series—simultaneously representing their nostalgia for a golden era of New York baseball, their irrepressible drive against the odds, and their ultimate frailty. He stroked a hit in the first inning of game one. In game two, he fell on the basepaths and later missed a fly ball in the ninth, allowing the A's to score twice to tie. In the twelfth, Mays struck a Rollie Fingers fastball to center field for a game-winning RBI that tied up the series.

In the decisive seventh game back in Oakland, a Reggie Jackson home run put the A's up 5–1, but miracle stirred in the top of the ninth. The

Mets took a run back on an error. With two on base, the tying run came to plate as second baseman Wayne Garrett. He had two home runs in the series, and had been the best hitter in the Mets' late-season run, but had been cold in the postseason, batting .087 against the Reds, and, aside from the two long-shots, remained hitless with eleven strikeouts during the championship.

Mays sat in the dugout, bat in hand. Since witnessing Bobby Thomson's *shot heard 'round the world* in his rookie season, he had always dreamed of scoring a similarly heroic blast. "But Berra never looked his way," Hirsch wrote. "He had clearly lost confidence in him after the second game, and Mays was forgotten the rest of the way."[371] Garrett swung mightily under the ball, lofting it gently out of the infield and into a waiting gold glove.

With belief dead in the dugout, the underdogs were put to sleep. Yogi's catchphrase was now in-utterable, and few could even summon the optimism for a nostalgic *wait 'til next year.* "The time for general-admission amazements had passed," Herron concluded, "things had changed, and the formerly amazing Mets lost. And that's when the sixties ended."[372]

"I don't feel nothin'," the dejected Say Hey Kid told reporters before rushing out of the locker room, abandoning his uniform and equipment behind him. At his September retirement speech at Shea, when there was still hope, he had said with tears in his eyes, "I see how these kids are fighting for a pennant," before ominously concluding, "and to me it says one thing: Willie, say good-bye to America."[373]

New York City defaulted on its debt the next year. The federal government refused to provide a bailout, believing they had spent too much and taxed too little. Bankers and corporate executives stepped into the void, forming an Emergency Financial Control Board (EFCB) to supplant the city's elected officials.

It was the beginning of what is now known as the "neoliberal" era. In the months and years to come, what remained of La Guardia and Wagner's *Little New Deal* for New York was decimated. Welfare, housing, and school budgets were cut. Hospital, fire, and police budgets were slashed in poor neighborhoods. Although people of color represented 33 percent of the city, their public sector jobs amounted to 44 percent of the cuts.[374] From 1969 to 1977, nearly a third of manufacturing jobs left New York. White flight went into overdrive, and the city's population decreased by nearly a million in the decade. Queens' white population, once 85 percent of the borough, dropped to 65 percent by 1980.[375]

Police, angered by budget cuts, dutifully spread a morbid narrative in tracts distributed to tourists arriving at LaGuardia with a grim reaper on its cover beneath the words WELCOME TO FEAR CITY. The area around Yankee Stadium, relatively untouched during the fifties' white-flight wave, collapsed into a poverty that would make the Bronx world-famous as a symbol of urban decay. The 1979 movie *The Warriors,* and the genre of *Bronxsploitation* films that followed, portrayed a postapocalyptic city, choked with the black smoke of buildings burned by landlords for insurance money, its streets run by nihilistic gangs denuded of any sixties revolutionary pretense. One of these *Clockwork Orange*–esque squads in *The Warriors* was the Yankees-pin-striped "Baseball Furies" of Riverside Park, a barely exaggerated version of the real-life uptown "Second Base" gang.

New York was merely the first urban center to fail, allowing the disaster-capitalist model to replicate across the country as a stopgap to the spirals of blight. Progressive optimism was gone, replaced with a return to the nineteenth-century governing philosophy of keeping the rich happy, and letting the poor fend for themselves. Across the country, prices of essential commodities like gas skyrocketed as wages remained stagnant. President Carter, elected in a last-ditch effort to preserve the patriotic visions of solidarity and social movements, acknowledged America had entered into hopeless malaise.

Those radicals who refused to join Carter's coalition continued to drift toward the margins of grassroots networks of activist social movements, union factions, micro-sects, communes, cults, and mafias. Jack Scott, the Berkeley sports sociologist central to the collegiate "Jock Liberation" movement that rattled the Nixon administration four years prior, was ousted from running Oberlin's athletics department. Scott's philosophy of democratic teams claimed brief improvement until the athletes revolted en masse against his heavy-handed idealism. He subsequently became an accomplice of the Symbionese Liberation Army, an armed cadre that considered the Weathermen too soft. In 1974, they kidnapped billionaire heiress Patty Hearst, sexually abusing and torturing her until she agreed to become a spokeswoman for their hopes of sparking an improvised guerrilla war nationwide. When the small cadre was killed or scattered by police, Scott drifted away from politics altogether.

The New Left had sought to change the world without taking power. The classical Bolshevik and anarchist vision of proletarian dictatorships and juntas that seize power in order to smash the state and replace it with workers' councils was replaced by the New Leftist vision of molecular, horizontalist revolution. But without mass working-class support, it didn't really matter what the leftists wanted. They would be remembered as dogs who briefly had their day, before returning to their permanent status as, at best, lovable losers.

Countercultural icons no more, the Mets sank deeper into Grant's Tomb after the 1973 near miracle, becoming a decisively unlovable team tortured by the deformed sixties spirit.

In a 1974 decision supported by anti-feminists and some women's liberationists alike, the New York Human Rights Commission declared Shea's Ladies' Day, which offered free and discounted tickets for women, illegal.[376]

The Mets' progressive racial legacy was the next domino to fall. During 1975 spring training, Cleon Jones was arrested for indecent exposure in St. Petersburg after police found him in a car with a white woman. The charges were dropped, but Grant cited "family values" to fine Jones a team-record $2,000, and force his public apology at a press conference.

Early in the season, Shea held a pregame tribute to the US Army. Cannons were fired at the climax of the ceremony that blew a hole through the right-field wall, as if to avenge the Mets' antiwar stance six weeks after the victory of the Vietnamese people.[377]

The worst result of sixties militancy for the Mets would ironically come as a result of the players' climactic triumph over the reserve clause in 1975. Miller's arbitration strategy paid off when Athletics closer Catfish Hunter successfully won free agency after Charles Finley refused to pay his $100,000 salary. A bidding war ensued in which the Yankees' new Midwestern shipping-magnate owner George Steinbrenner, who had used the Bronx's ill-repute to fleece the city for a $160 million rebuild of Yankee Stadium, came out on top with an offer of $3.75 million for five years—over seven times Hunter's previous salary.

When another former Mets World Series antagonist, Orioles' pitcher Dave McNally, won free agency later that year, the union had the opportunity to destroy the reserve clause once and for all. A faction of players and owners influenced by the right-libertarian ideology of laissez-faire capitalism pushed this line. But recognizing this would flood the market and decrease salaries across the board, Miller worked out a deal to reduce player reservation to six years, alongside a clause barring owners from colluding to reduce free agent offers.

A free-agent feeding frenzy would come, nonetheless, thanks to Finley's fire sale of his once mighty A's. In the four years after Hunter's victory, the mean major-league salary doubled. The Yankees topped the market, with an average salary of $200,000 for starters, including $600,000 for Reggie Jackson. As early adapter of New York's new financial dictatorship, the Yankees returned to glory with a pennant in 1976, and championships in 1977 and 1978.

Grant, on the other hand, was among the delusional few who believed baseball's artificially low labor costs could be sustained by ignoring that players had ever won free agency. His sole justification was the players' traditional loyalty, to the familial franchise a fading sentiment that finally died with Joan Payson in 1975. As dissent accumulated, he fired Berra and Scheffing, cut Mays's advisory position, and traded Tug McGraw after misdiagnosing a harmless cyst on his shoulder as a career-ending injury. McGraw proceeded to play a central role in the Phillies' NL East dominance and 1980 championship.

In 1976, frustration boiled over. Seaver and Dave Kingman were underpaid, and Grant refused to spend for a reliable hitter. Seaver negotiated directly with Payson's daughter, Lorinda de Roulet, only to have the deal sabotaged by Grant leaking a story to the *Post*. The formally progressive New Breed paper of record, recently purchased by far-right media magnate Rupert Murdoch, reported that Nancy Seaver's envy for Nolan Ryan's $1 million contract fueled his greedy demands. Knowing the story came from Grant, Seaver refused to report to work, and was immediately traded to the Reds.

The same day, Kingman was dealt for light-hitting Bobby Valentine. Jerry Grote, Jon Matlack, and Jerry Koosman followed into exile for speaking out. Even Mr. Met was fired, replaced by a mascot paid in outfield grass—"Mettle the Mule."

The press dubbed Grant's answer to Nixon's purges the Midnight Massacre. The remaining Mets played in shame following Grant's gutting of the team's spiritual core. Most fans boycotted, with season ticket holders arriving with signs reading SEAVER LIVES and WHERE IS TOM? as they watched the Mets fall back to last place for the first time in a decade. Just as the EFCB had looted New York's public goods, Grant had slashed and burned its people's team.

A month after Grant's massacre, on July 13, 1977, the Mets hosted the Cubs for a night game. In the sixth inning, Lenny Randle stepped in to bat for the Mets, down 2–1. As he awaited the throw, Shea went pitch-black. For a moment, Randle believed he had died.

The blackout was citywide. When an emergency generator restored the lights to the exits from the stadium, the crowd refused to leave. Two Mets players rushed to their cars and drove them onto the field with headlights blaring, allowing a crew of Mets including Bobby Valentine, Bob Apodaca, and an injured Bud Harrelson to simulate a sandlot game as others signed autographs to keep the fans entertained until the game was officially postponed.[378]

While the fans left satisfied with the impromptu spectacle, chaos erupted around the city. New York's working poor, their futures robbed by the financial regime that took control of New York in 1975, now had the opportunity to loot back. Widespread rioting continued even after power was restored, leading the city to concede to the FEAR CITY messaging by shifting its dwindling funds toward police and prisons.

But a garden of counterculture bloomed in the blighted zones of decay. Abandoned buildings became collective working-class homesteads or canvases for street art; turntables and mixers stolen during the 1977 blackout blended the beats that backdropped hip-hop; and cheap downtown real estate turned into experimental venues for the emerging neo-beatnik movement of punk. The Payson heirs had a chance to revive the impoverished team in conjunction with this underworld renaissance after stripping Grant's power for the 1979 season. Knowing even less about baseball than Grant, however, Charles Shipman Payson, Joan's widowed husband, focused on selling the franchise, while his daughters drained its coffers, fantasized about rinsing and reusing foul balls to save money, and dated the indifferent players.

With attendance plummeting to record lows each year, Shea became like Ebbets Field during the Depression—a miserable few bums huddled around the thin stew of a team. The dust-bowl atmosphere was heightened by the buggy-pulling mule corralled behind home plate, and relievers growing corn and tomatoes in the bullpen for sustenance. Hopes were so dismal that a New Jersey paper promoted a contest for fans to predict when the Mets would be eliminated from playoff contention, with its grand prize September tickets to "Shame Stadium."[379] Even the notoriously disrespected comic Rodney Dangerfield could punch down: "The Mets have been in the cellar so long they're thinking of decorating."[380]

Chapter 9

THE ROBO METS

In 1980, a former union leader and Cubs announcer promised an optimistic national renewal modeled after big capital's takeover of New York City. The red tape of New Deal and Great Society bureaucracy would be slashed. Government funds would pour into police, prisons, and the armed forces for renewed Cold War saber-rattling. His outsider campaign, widely mocked in the media, triumphed in a landslide. It was, Ronald Reagan proclaimed, "Morning in America."

A corporatist new dawn broke for the Mets as well. After the shameful previous seasons, a group of investors purchased the team for a record $21 million, more than twice what George Steinbrenner had paid for the Yankees in 1973.

The new majority owner was Nelson Doubleday Jr., a childhood Brooklyn Dodgers fan and heir to one of the world's largest publishing empires.

Doubleday's riches poured in to refurbish Shea after years of municipal neglect. Plastic seats replaced the old wood, luxury boxes were installed, and the facade's rusting tile dioramas were scrapped in favor of neon-light ballplayers glowing over a fresh sheen of blue paint. "They changed the whole look of it," Howie Rose recalled. "It's almost as though they played in two different ballparks."[381]

Additional supernatural talismans completed the exorcism of *Grant's Tomb.* A banner hanging outside the revived stadium read *The Magic is back*, and a kinetic sculpture of a massive Red Delicious apple in an inverted magician's cap appeared in the outfield batter's eye. With each home run, the misshapen avatar of metropolitan greatness would defiantly emerge from the void, just like New York from its decade of doom.

For Doubleday, the nostalgic mission ran deeper than sixties sentimentality. Although it was well known by then that his great-great-grand-uncle had nothing to do with creating the sport, surviving in family history was the myth's origins in Abner Doubleday's role in the establishment of the occultist Theosophical Society. Their prophetess, Madame Blavatsky, had foretold the American melting pot was brewing a savior race, a message that resonated with the man who fired the first shot at the Confederacy in Fort Sumter, commanded ten thousand Union soldiers at Gettysburg, and ordered that fleeing slaves be welcomed into Union lines as "persons, not chattels."[382] Long after the well-known American hero's death, devout Theosophist Albert Spalding spun the apocryphal anecdote as a patriotic denial of the game's international origins, while also venerating his faith as it fell into infamy as a child-abusing coven of millenarian witches.

Nelson Doubleday may have known an even more esoteric angle of the lore. After resigning as president of Theosophy, Abner presided over New York's chapter of the socialist Nationalist Club, comrades of the ex-Mets on the "We Are the People" Giants who founded the Players' League. The cartoon infant of the 1962 yearbook had marked the rebirth of the original Mets after Spalding killed their league in battle, and Doubleday's 1980 yearbook summoned the star-child back again as a more realistically illustrated adolescent Mets fan, smiling mischievously in untied Converse All-Stars, under a headline reading: THE NEW NEW YORK METS . . . THE PEOPLE'S TEAM.[383]

Each element of the Mets' history was thus presented in the marketing offensive—cosmic forces, the underdog enmity of middle-class youth, and populism.

Behind these promises, however, was the magical thinking of neoliberalism—the Reaganite new world order that believed consolidated financial wealth trickles down to bootstrap-pulling workers. And beneath that economic voodoo was the nihilism of corporatist cybernetics, and wide-scale reaction to the social progress of the sixties—two factors that would eventually send the reincarnated people's team spiraling toward antisocial chaos.

A Steinbrenner-esque spending spree on players and ballpark experience gained speed through the early decade. Rehired Seaver and Kingman lured back post-Payson apostates. The retired Ebbets organ's replacement sound system blasted rock hits between innings. Fireworks nights, concerts by the Clash and the Who, and a pregame Playboy Bunny softball match attracted younger and edgier elements. Attendance rebounded past the million mark, with many returning home in flashy Mets merch distributed free at the gates.

By 1984, the Mets boasted rookie speedster Mookie Wilson, reliable reliever Jesse Orosco, chain-smoking field marshal Keith Hernandez, and George Foster, known as the "black bat" in Cincinnati for leading the National League in home runs using a hickory-stained Louisville Slugger that he joked had "integrated the bat rack."[384]

Three top prospects were elevated as well: Darryl Strawberry, the first-round-pick slugger from South Central LA whose signing bonus was a major-league record; Ron Darling, the half-Hawaiian, half-Quebecois carpenter's son; and shy nineteen-year-old Dwight "Doc" Gooden, soon to earn the nickname *Doctor K* for leading the league in strikeouts in 1984 and 1985. To raise their profile, these players were encouraged to take sponsorship deals for sneakers, car dealerships, beer, soda, and hair dye, synergistically boosting the team's profile during commercial breaks.

As the Mets went from worst to first between 1984 and 1986, the DIY spirit of the sixties returned to Shea's seats. Trademark chants developed for certain players: a boo-like *Moook* for Wilson, and a groaning *Darr-rull* for Strawberry. Homemade banners returned with the force of a Soviet May Day parade. Hawaiian-shirt-wearing fans of Darling and Gooden taped *K*'s for each strikeout near the left-field foul pole, a territory claimed forever as the "K Korner." In another innovation, soon to generalize through sports fandom for generations, fans imitated the Mets' superstitious ritual of turning their caps inside out to mystically summon come-from-behind rallies.

By outdrawing the Yankees for the first time in a decade in 1984, the Mets decisively reclaimed the city's heart. In contrast to the booming payroll of Steinbrenner perennially failing to buy pennants, they appeared to New Yorkers a gritty and diverse collective of hard-hats, sweating and fighting through their workday in the Shea pit, before drinking and snorting away their wages at seedy nightclubs each night. And like Frank Sinatra's drunken multicultural Rat Pack, the Mets were star entertainers, projected an approachable everyman-ness alongside tough-guy personas as they fought to make it to the *top of the heap*—something Shea celebrated by blasting Sinatra's "New York, New York" after wins.

Later appropriated by the Yankees, the song told the story of a metropolitan transplant proving his worth by conquering the greatest city in the world. No other team in the eighties (except for the Chicano-coded *Fernandomania* Dodgers) brought together these two seemingly contradictory elements of the countercultural working class—the "real" New Yorkers who had survived the arsonous decay and depopulation of the seventies, and white flight's returning children. This latter group, like the beatniks and New Breed bohemians of the sixties, earnestly rejected the quiet safety of the suburbs in favor of urban edge, finding in the Mets a perfect compromise between the downtown avant-garde scenes of art, hip hop, poetry, and punk, and the traditional conventions of working-class life.

But lurking within Doubleday's rainbow coalition was a new cohort derided by both conformist and hipster elements as the *Yuppies*. The slur, spray-painted threateningly on the walls of downtown wine bars and luxury condos, satirized the sixties generation's maturation from the internationalist youth-revolutionary Yippies to *young urban professionals*. This was a generation, theorist Jean Baudrillard wrote, that had rid themselves of all nostalgia for the "wildness" of the previous decades, and "refocused upon themselves, in love with businesses not so much for profit or prestige as for its being a sort of performance, a technical feat. . . . The yuppies are not defectors from revolt, they are a new race, assured, amnestied, exculpated, moving with ease in the world of performance, mentally indifferent to any object other than that of change and advertising."[385]

These foot soldiers transforming New York into a cybernetically financialized playground for the rich were mostly attracted to the

Yankees' corporate brutality. But despite their party-punk aesthetic, the Mets were wired into the same circuit board, and the yuppies had few friends better than the team's largest minority owner, and overseer of its baseball operations since 1980—nouveau-riche real-estate mogul Fred Wilpon.

Wilpon grew up a Dodgers diehard who played alongside Sandy Koufax at his Brooklyn high school. After an injury ended his pitching aspirations, the New Breed convert started the development firm Sterling Equities with his wife Judy, a former secretary of Branch Rickey, and brother-in-law Saul Katz. "Great time to start a business," Katz recalled of how the trio struck it rich building Westchester condos during the seventies. "Economy falling apart, then the oil embargo. . . . Because we had built condos, the money we were making was taxed as ordinary income, so, in order to protect against paying the tax, we started traveling all over the country buying what we thought were tax shelters. . . . The 'tax shelters' turned into cash cows."[386]

As the Mets languished in Grant's Tomb, Wilpon's wealth bought him access to batting practice at Shea, where his old Brooklyn acquaintance, Joe Torre, tipped him off that the team was for sale. Wilpon brought the news to his rich neighbors in tony Nassau County, Doubleday among them.

As the more vocal partner, Wilpon diligently brokered his status in Shea's executive suites to become a central player in Manhattan's financial-tower construction boom. Sterling soon broke ground on the stylish Lipstick Building, which upon completion in 1986 would headquarter the vanguard financial, communications, and computer companies of the eighties—Telecom Plus, Citigroup, and Bernie L. Madoff Investment Securities. Rising upon the corner immortalized as an open-air sex market for young male prostitutes by the 1976 Ramones song "53rd & Third," the colorful postmodern skyscraper planted Wall

Street's flag in Midtown, reclaiming seedy Manhattan for the *greed-is-good* era.

Among Wilpon's first hires was Frank Cashen as general manager. The bow-tied Southern dandy had worked in the advertising department of the Baltimore brewery that produced Colt .45 and National Bohemian before rebranding another of the business's products in 1964, the Baltimore Orioles. Using the Amazin' Mets' commercial success as reference, Cashen cartoonified the team's brand as he experimented with applying automated beer production to baseball. In 1968, top scout Lou Gorman and second baseman Davey Johnson were given access to the brewery's state-of-the-art IBM 360 computer system. As Gorman sought to evaluate talent with the emerging art of sabermetrics—computer-generated baseball statistics—Johnson began simulating ballgames by the hundreds in an effort to convince his manager to give him the coveted second spot in the batting order.[387]

Johnson believed his computer printouts steered the Orioles' effortless glide to the 1969 World Series, where bookies, sportswriters, and the IBM 360 alike assured easy victory. But when Johnson made the last out at Shea against a team data-designated as "horseshit," faith in the cybernetic revolution was shaken.[388]

Wondering if the Miracle Mets represented something more than statistical anomaly, the sabermetric pioneers (at a firm run by a coder who had previously analyzed guerrilla warfare for the Pentagon) cataloged all 310,000 plays of 1969. According to Alan Schwarz in his history of baseball statistics, *The Numbers Game*, a conclusion was reached that "smaller player contributions [had been] hidden forever . . . a reliever coming in with the bases loaded getting a clutch fly out . . . a batter's groundout that moved a runner from second to third before a game-winning sacrifice fly. . . . No way existed to meaningfully measure these concepts."[389]

One result of the study would be the Wins Above Replacement stat (WAR), a measure of how one player's successes translated to the rest of the team's ability to actually win games. Despite its recapitulation of individual player value that left the guerrilla synergy of the Mets elusive, WAR would eventually become an official MLB metric, and a guiding strategy for Gorman and Johnson once rehired by Cashen to the Mets' farm system in 1983.

The duo hired a techie Mets fan named Lou Oddo to turn the small and powerful IBM XT personal computer into a portable team-builder for the Mets' minor-league Tidewater Tides affiliate. With computer-generated lineups, the team immediately went on a winning streak.[390] Oddo went on to develop software for military drones, and Johnson was promoted to manage the Mets.[391]

The team's 1984 media guide showed Johnson seated at a computer screen predicting further glory for Hernandez, Orosco, and Strawberry.[392] "He was always putzing around with his stupid computer," Strawberry recalled, voicing the annoyance of many who suddenly found themselves oddly placed in the lineup, or relegated to the minors during a hot streak. "He'd come walking in with these complex stats relating at-bats to the times he was stranded on second base to the number of hangnails he'd pulled off himself."[393]

But the results were undeniable. For the first time since 1969, the Mets won ninety games in 1984, a year, Strawberry admitted, the magic truly returned: "Our pitching staff would jell, our hitting would become consistent, and our defense would begin to play as a team instead of like a bunch of guys playing pickup schoolyard stickball."[394]

The improvement continued the next year when the Mets won an all-time-high ninety-eight games and shattered their single-season record with 2.7 million attendees. In their climactic final game, a sold-out crowd poured confetti and cheered endlessly for curtain calls from the New York heroes. Even though their loss that night cost them the division title, the players emerged one by one, acknowledging their reestablished emotional link by tossing their inverted rally caps to the fans.

"What a great feeling to know that you're part of a team that's got the makings of a league champion," Strawberry wrote of that bittersweet evening. "But maybe that's where the seeds of discontent also started to sprout."[395]

The PC/XT's impeccable evaluation of on-field performance had developed a new division of baseball labor. The computer produced the lineup, Johnson made in-game decisions, and the clubhouse was left free to manage its own culture. The dynamic suited perfectly Johnson's disinterest in replicating the style of the "old dictator managers."[396] So long as the roster lived up to their stats, he could in turn ignore whatever they were doing before and after games.

As Johnson and the more professional-minded Mets—represented by born-again Christian catcher Gary Carter—napped or read in their hotel rooms or the front rows of team flights, a faction known as the *Scum Bunch* radically redefined team culture. The hard-partying group began with bullpen stalwarts Doug Sisk and Jesse Orosco, who beelined to the nearest strip club after games, littered the plane's back rows with beer cans, and powered though game-day hangovers with black coffee and amphetamines. In time, more and more of the bench was bunched into this *Animal House*–inspired fraternity—a ceaseless fuck-fest that would grow in size and degeneracy for nearly a decade.

At the center of the divide between upstanding citizens and hedonists was first baseman, and soon-to-be team captain, Keith Hernandez. As a Cardinal, the on-field perfectionist and Civil War history buff had been central to a scandal in which dozens of players through the league were revealed to have scored cocaine from Pittsburgh's mascot, the Pirate Parrot. Although Hernandez swore abstinence from then on, he also defended his actions as common—40 percent of all major leaguers had used the drug, and he claimed to have done so only in healthy moderation.[397] He nearly quit baseball rather than accept his trade to the Mets following the scandal in 1983, but soon grew to love the New York fans who had a similarly ambivalent attitude to a drug ubiquitous among stock-traders and shelf-stockers alike.

As the Mets entered 1986 the statistically predicted team to beat, the intoxication of success expanded the Scum Bunch's hegemony. "I fell into this group partly because I felt that they had kind of a license to be bad," Strawberry recalled. "If the Scum Bunch said throw that hamburger out the window or spit beer on someone, then I'd do it with a vengeance because I wanted to belong."[398]

Such belonging had eluded Strawberry his entire life. He and his two older brothers had played baseball in college as a path out of poverty for the large family supported by their mother, who worked for a telephone company. Strawberry was just twenty-one when he arrived to the majors with comparisons to Willie Mays—in fact, the media made him out to be potentially more significant than Mays, because he would be the first Black star to begin his career in New York, instead of the Negro Leagues or another MLB franchise. "I wasn't prepared for the hype," Strawberry wrote in his memoir *Darryl*.

> No one told me how the media game was supposed to be played and what I was supposed to do. . . . Was I supposed to walk across the East River next? Actually that would have been easier than reading every day in the papers about the miracles I was expected to perform any minute now. At nights I would

> lie in bed as sirens blared beneath my window and planes roared overhead as they circled the city and say, "Mother, get me out of here." I was absolutely paralyzed with fear![399]

The unmeasurable pressure of the press, fans, and business of baseball on the young players overwhelmed any chance of coping healthily with their premature arrival to stardom. But the inner alienation of Strawberry, and fellow prospect phenom Dwight Gooden, was incalculable to the PC/XT as the 1986 Mets appeared just as dominant as its simulations foretold. Nor could Johnson see any harm in the sex, drugs, and interpersonal affection shared freely in the orgiastic back seats as they jetted toward an easy pennant.

"Part of what binds a winning team together is its closeness, and in 1986 few teams were knit quite so tightly," Peter Golenbock wrote. "Mets players hugged and celebrated and shook hands and high-fived at every opportunity. Opposing teams hated the Mets for their shows of affection."[400] "Play together, our team's real tight," Strawberry rapped on the team's "Get Metsmerized!" hip-hop track released that year, "Don't mess with us, we're dynamite!"[401]

As the season progressed on program, the party rockers turned into frontline pugilists against antagonists jealous of their physical warmth, their loud fans, the cockiness of Hernandez and Carter, the hard play of Ray Knight and Lenny Dykstra, and their joyful curtain calls. On-field fistfights broke out at four games that season—with the Mets fighting for each other with a passion equaling their drunken postgame celebrations. "A team on the march to the championship that develops this attitude is no longer a team," Strawberry wrote, "it's more like a gang. You hang together, you chill together, you go to war together."[402]

During a July road trip, second baseman Tim Teufel ignored the protests of a Wild West–themed Houston bar's bouncer when he walked out with a glass of tequila. A fight ensued between several members of the team and the bouncers, who they later learned were off-duty cops. Despite the subsequent arrests and media blowup, manager Davey Johnson took the side of his players in their revanchist war of New York versus rural America. "We all had targets on our backs," he wrote. "There were people out there who didn't like us because, first, we were from New York and, second, we were in first place."

While the cop-loving media was horrified, the fight only deepened the team's legitimacy as proud champions of New York's returned supremacy. In mid-September, with the Mets a game away from clinching the division, thousands of fans traveled to Veterans Stadium in Philadelphia to storm the field in celebration. They smashed up seats after the meaningless loss as a preview of the destruction to come when they subsequently clinched at home.[403] Six thousand poured across the Shea barricades to rush players, rob equipment, and rip out turf.[404]

While field-stormings were a long-running tradition in baseball, especially at Shea, what were once considered harmless extensions of the "Summer of Love" were now deemed inexcusable by sportswriters. A *Times* editorial decried the Mets' clubhouse culture of "macho, fist-waving, curtain-calling style" as an extension of the inner-city crime still hindering the city's march toward economic stability.[405] Comparing the fans to muggers, they called for an NYPD roundup.[406]

The scolding had no effect on the red-hot team. Victory in Houston against the likely cheating Astros in the NL Championship Series resulted in their most vindictive and hedonistic night yet. Destruction of the visitors' clubhouse proceeded aboard their United Airlines charter, where beer and champagne progressed to liquor and cocaine. Fistfuls of cake flew as three rows of seats were ripped out to create a communal mattress, amorously shared between players and their significant others.

The fans awaiting them at Kennedy cheered as their heroes emerged post festum, in various stages of undress, soaked in frosting, fluids, and vomit.

Frank Cashen, deeply disturbed by the Scum Bunch's tumorous spread throughout the team and fan base, passed United's $7,500 bill for damages to the players as a warning against future blowouts. When the penalty was delivered at a clubhouse meeting before game one, Johnson promptly negated it. "I think in the next four games, you guys are gonna put a shitload of money in this team's pocket, more than enough to cover this bill," Gooden recalled him saying. "So fuck this bullshit."[407] He ripped up the bill, tossing it into the air as the team erupted in defiant epithets for their boss, and all others futilely attempting to control them.

The Mets entered a World Series as heavy favorites for the first time. Despite their opponent's spirited 3–1 comeback to take the pennant, the PC/XT rated the Red Sox's chances slim. All that was left unforeseen was how widespread and destructive the inevitable victory riot would be.

Ed Koch found himself in a similar quandary to Cashen—equally needing to stave off an orgiastic citywide sports riot while appearing a John Lindsay–like partner in their inevitable victory. The sweating mayor, notorious for his ignorance of sports, glad-handed in the dugout before the game in a blue Mets cap and NYPD shirt. "I'm learning to love baseball," he told reporters as his calvary of riot cops surrounded the stadium and confiscated beer from tailgaters outside. "I like the crowds and the cheering."[408]

Still hungover, the Mets were blanked 1–0 in game one. Lethargy continued the next day, when what should have been another pitchers' duel between Gooden and Roger Clemens ended in a 9–3 rout to put the Sox up 2–0 for their Fenway return.

The Mets' bats finally awoke to answer the ceaseless volley of assaults and slurs from Boston's notoriously combative fan base. Their lopsided wins in games 3 and 4 appeared a return-to-form. But when Gooden struggled again in game 5, and the Mets' late-inning rally fell short, the Sox left their home stand one game away from an odds-defying upset.

Boston appeared to have turned the tables, out-Metsing New York as if cosmic punishment for their big-budget corporatization and Yankee-like confidence. With the nearly unbeatable ace Clemens returning to the mound, their first championship since Ruth's 1918 World Series wildcat strike was in sight. But during game six at Shea—unanimously considered among the most glorious in baseball history—the again underdog team proved themselves worthy of their miraculous lineage.

They did so with tremendous help from the people. If the early-series certainty of victory, riot-shaming, and Prohibition-style policing had contained fan exuberance for the opening games, the specter of returned humiliation reawakened the New Breed's defiant spirit. At Shea's gates, Koch's occupying army redoubled confiscations after liquor bottles were discovered smuggled in banners and props. Seconds before Ron Darling's first pitch, all barriers were revealed futile when Cessna-dropped soap opera actor Michael Sergio parachuted onto the field waving a *Go Mets* flag. As cops led him to jail through the Mets' dugout, Darling gave him a high five, and the players arranged to fund his legal representation.[409]

An early two-run Sox lead and top-form Clemens' inside heat couldn't cool the frenzy. Veteran broadcaster Vin Scully repeatedly expressed his awe at the crowd's ceaseless volume. Rattled Sox defenders bobbled, and the Mets kept battling up the pitch count. North of a hundred pitches in the seventh, Clemens begged for the bench. The Mets eked out a 3–3 tie in his absence, taking the game to extras.

A volley of blasts in the top of the tenth put the Sox again up two, finally quieting Shea to sickly silence. Backman swung for the fences, as did Hernandez. But the big apple, dormant all series, remained in slumber. One out remained to prove whether Johnson's computer had crashed again, or if Doubleday's magic hat had been empty all along.

Then, deep in Shea's control room, came a fortuitous malfunction, a three-word curse. Above the impotent apple, the Diamond Vision scoreboard prematurely displayed: CONGRATULATIONS RED SOX!

Hysterical hubris returned to Shea at first sight of the potent jinx. Carter, then Kevin Mitchell struck singles. Fans cried, ripped their banners, and prayed to their occult talismans as Knight drove in Carter, bringing Wilson to the plate. Boos for the Sox pitching change shifted to chants of "*Moo-kie*". Wilson, batting just .184 in the postseason, wore Bob Stanley down with fouls until he threw wildly inside. Mookie went flying, quickly recovering to wave in Mitchell as the ball skittered to the backstop. The game was now tied 5-5, with Knight galloped to scoring position as the potential winning run.

The epochal at bat continued. Toilet paper streamed into Stanley's sight as Mookie stroked the eighth and the ninth pitches foul. "Can you believe this ballgame at Shea?" Vin Scully said on the NBC broadcast in the moment before the tenth pitch was finally batted into play. "A little roller up along first…" he said, anticipating aging and ailing Bill Buckner's tortured footrace with Wilson to the base before gasping, "Behind the bag! It gets through Buckner! Here comes Knight and the Mets win it!"

Scully remained speechless for three minutes as NBC cameras panned the celebration. Frat boys, curly-haired burnouts, preppies, old-timer Brooklyn fans in flatcaps, and one ghoul in a menacing rubber Halloween mask hugged, clapped, and danced in the seats. Police patted the hugging Mets nervously as they formed a line to prevent a stampede. The stunned Sox watched in silence, their champagne rapidly wheeling out from their visitor clubhouse like a Broadway scene change. "If one picture is worth a thousand words," Scully finally said, "you have seen about a million words. But more than that, you have seen an absolutely bizarre finish to Game 6 of the 1986 World Series."[410]

The apple finally emerged below the scoreboard, its prior error corrected to WE WIN!! and the idealistic slogan of '86: BASEBALL LIKE IT OUGHTA BE!!!

An effortless win two nights later gave the Mets their second world championship. The celebration started before Orosco could even make the final out with a flare tossed into the outfield. Once he dispatched the final star-crossed Sock, the NYPD cavalry galloped through the orange haze onto the field as the players dogpiled in safety.

Although contained at Shea, raucous celebrations spontaneously spread throughout the metropolis. The football Giants halted play due to the rowdiness arriving with the news to the Meadowlands. New Yorkers took to parks and courtyards with fireworks and booze throughout the inner city. Inside one Long Island housing project, Doc Gooden downed shots and lines at a victory party hosted by his dealer.

While the seasoned substance abusers of the team managed to pull themselves from bed for the celebration parade the next day, a too-hungover Gooden watched on TV. Years later, he recorded his few sparse memories: "I heard Davey talk and politicians get booed. I saw a kid with a hand-lettered sign."[411]

After the brawls, fan riots, plane-trashing, and MIA Dr. K, Cashen finally recognized the seeds of discontent budding toxic fruit.

One root was Johnson's techno-optimist style that reduced all expectations on management and players to mere performance of individual stats. Combined with the union victory of liberalizing baseball's labor market through free agency, the players collectively had more autonomy than ever. This was a nightmare for Cashen and other executives, in which cybernetic certainty, free-agency-motivated individualism, and sport-wide worker solidarity combined to supplant the very concept of the team unit. This was perhaps most evident on Johnson's Mets, where some socialized solely through hard partying, and others put on headphones and punched *play* on their Walkman to kill time until their contract was up.

The owners took inspiration from Reagan to claw back their authority on both fronts. Just as he had launched a ruthless war on organized labor with his evisceration of the air traffic controllers' union in 1981, they secretly colluded through the decade to nullify the union's prior gains by restricting their free agency and arbitration offers. And to reassert control over the players' personal lives, the rhetoric of Reagan's widely popular War on Drugs was adapted with the demand for random testing in the aftermath of the Pirate Parrot scandal.

The union countered both offensives and eventually won. The noticeable drop in contract value led to collusion charges confirmed by labor arbitrators after the 1987 season. Some $10.5 million were rewarded to the players in lost wages, with strict measures installed to prevent the practice's continuance. When it came to drug testing, the union firmly refused any pretense short of a player's conviction in court. But with the collusion still unproven in 1986, Cashen suggested Gooden could improve his salary arbitration's outcome by submitting to drug tests voluntarily. Hoping the deal would give him some extra cash, and an impetus to sober up, he agreed.

That offseason, Cashen clipped two other notorious bad apples by offering a lowball contract to Ray Knight and trading Kevin Mitchell. The moves, clean-cut Mookie Wilson wrote, did little to slow the Scum Bunch's rampage, while ripping the "heart and soul" from the clubhouse.[412]

Mitchell's scapegoating was particularly offensive to the team's Black players. George Foster had alleged racism during the 1986 season after being benched during a prolonged slump: "I think the Mets would rather promote a Gary Carter or a Keith Hernandez to the fans so parents who want to can point to them as role models for their children, rather than a Darryl Strawberry or a Dwight Gooden or a George Foster."[413]

When the comments ignited widespread indignation and mockery in the press—characteristic of the era's pretentious "race blind" backlash against the gains of the Civil Rights Movement—Foster apologized and attempted to clarify his point. He understood that he had been benched for Kevin Mitchell and Mookie Wilson, both Black, and acknowledged that Strawberry and Gooden had become widely promoted stars. He wasn't calling Johnson or the Mets specifically racist, but wanted to voice how pervasive racist stereotypes translated to relative impatience for Black players during slumps or personal crises. "What George said about race prejudice generally does not seem so far-fetched to me," Brooklynite Yankees second baseman and future Met Willie Randolph told the *Times*.[414] Nonetheless, the "shut up and play" attitude that had always dogged ballplayers, especially non-white ones, won out. Foster was immediately cut from the Mets and widely denounced for playing the "race card."

Cashen was correct to worry about Doc and Darryl's future, but it was not only the influence of the Scum Bunch that would terminally interrupt their careers. Their struggles with anger and abuse were rooted, like Foster's, in a racial order that kept Black America chaotically impoverished. In his memoir *Darryl*, Strawberry traced his alcoholism and anger back to the sudden outbursts of his addict father, the poverty his family was forced to survive once his mother broke away from the abuse, and the lack of understanding whites had for these common struggles.

Gooden also grew up surrounded by violence and substance abuse. Much of his family was involved in Tampa's criminal underworld, and he witnessed his mom shoot and injure his father after young Doc accidentally revealed his dad's infidelity. While some white Mets, like Lenny Dykstra, had similar pasts, it proved far more difficult for African

American players to break from these cycles of violence due to a refusal to acknowledge that a star athlete could still suffer from racism.

Shy Gooden nonetheless never joined the Scum Bunch, and claimed to have kept away from the hard stuff until pressure mounted in 1985. "The K Korner was restless. The fans wanted strikeouts—more strikeouts," he wrote of the fervor surrounding him that season. "I hated seeing sports page headlines that read 'METS WIN, BUT GOODEN ONLY FANS FIVE.'"[415] When he took his anxiety back home, some friends at his cousin's brothel cut him a line to see if it would take the edge off. The jolt of confidence from that single first sniff pointed the way to coping with his newfound celebrity.

Ready to put the crutch behind him after the championship, Gooden sobered up after missing the Canyon of Heroes, and was one of the few Mets who accepted an invitation to the White House on November 12. After Reagan joked that he had intended to parachute into the ceremony, Gary Carter, who had recently visited Honduras along with Nolan Ryan on a State-sponsored trip to provide support to the newly elected anticommunist regime, presented Reagan with a personalized Mets jacket.[416]

Gooden would experience the brutality of Reagan's war on crime firsthand back in Tampa the next month. He and some friends, including Brewers prospect Gary Sheffield, angered a cop dining at the next table at the local Chili's after a charity softball game by laughing when he asked them to keep it down. When the group was pulled over after leaving the restaurant, Gooden demanded an explanation. "This nigger has a smart mouth," one officer reportedly said before ordering them out of the vehicle.[417]

"They proceeded to beat all of us unmercifully," wrote Sheffield, "until we were black, blue and swollen."[418] One officer twisted Gooden's arm, proving he knew who the player was when he threatened to break it and "end his career." Already in a chokehold and covered in blood from a forehead wound, Gooden pretended to lose consciousness and went limp.

Only when a white couple passed the scene did the officers finally relent. Gooden and Sheffield were transferred to the custody of Black officers nearby. When a search for drugs came up empty, they were processed on charges of resisting arrest and battery on a police officer.

After their release that night, Gooden's enraged entourage proposed evening the score. "The idea was that we would get our revenge by driving around Tampa at a high rate of speed. Then, when a cop pulled us over—*any* cop—*bang*! We were going to blast him."[419]

After driving only a block, Doc wisely backed out. Retribution, he decided, was better left to his lawyer and the Tampa NAACP. Once the arrest and lawsuit were made public, the civil rights organization reported a deluge of supportive calls from hundreds of Mets fans, and Gooden eventually won his case thanks to the white couple's testimony.

Riots hit Tampa later that winter after the police murdered a young local named Melvin Hair with the same chokehold they had used on Gooden. The *Times*' George Vecsey, however, sided with the assailants. In one column, he cited an illegally leaked blood-alcohol report to chastise New Yorkers who thought Tampa police were anything like those of the Jim Crow South.[420] "The police have too many reasons to be edgy these days," he wrote in another, "too many addicts and lunatics and Rambos and Dukes of Hazzard on the loose. The thing to do with an armed police officer is say 'yes, sir.'"[421]

Black New Yorkers knew well that neither racist police brutality nor lynchings were bygone Southern phenomena. Around the same time of Gooden's beating, a bat-wielding white mob's murder of twenty-three-year-old Trinidadian immigrant Michael Griffith, whose car had broken down near the white enclave of Howard Beach, Queens, was the latest lynching to show how the city's economic recovery had only exacerbated its racial divisions. As hospitals closed and rents soared, Koch's all-white administration echoed Reagan in blaming addiction and homelessness for all racial strife, and proposed more police violence and incarceration as its only solution.

Gooden found himself in police custody again during his return to New York before spring training. JFK airport police had found a gun on his girlfriend, detaining him on suspicion that he had put her up to it. Although never charged, another round of media scolding awaited him in St. Petersburg. Days later, Cashen ordered the drug test, and Doc started the season in rehab.

Gooden's absence proved costly in 1987. The Mets ended the year in second, just three games short of a return to the playoffs. Knight and Mitchell were deeply missed on the team as well. While their replacements, Howard Johnson and Kevin McReynolds, were both statistically better, Mookie wrote, "Talent isn't everything. . . . They lacked the killer instinct."[422]

More clubhouse sanitization came in the offseason. Senior Scum Bunchers Sisk and Orosco were traded to the Orioles and Dodgers. Doc's drug-free return in 1988 healed the prior season's depression, catapulting them back to first with 18 of their 100 wins. The return to form, however, came with a reinfection of 1986's scummy swagger. Unreformed team vets and newcomers alike gleefully replicated the triumphant pranking and partying tradition for which the Mets had become so notorious that the film *Rookie of the Year* portrayed its sluggers like the Alpha Beta frat boy antagonists in *Revenge of the Nerds.*

Even in LA exile, Orosco inspired a season-long grudge match with his old team by lathering the hat of new teammate Kirk Gibson with shoe polish during spring training. As Gibson became a clubhouse leader on the Western Division champion Dodgers, he made it clear he had no interest in replicating the decadence of their hated New York rivals. "Basically, I don't want to be a part of their fun and comedy act," he told the *Los Angeles Times* after forcing Orosco to apologize for the prank. "I'm not a radical guy."[423]

The Mets were heavily favored to beat the Dodgers in the NL Championship Series. LA had only beaten them once all year, and the Mets took the first game by scoring three off Dodgers closer Jay Howell in the ninth to take the first game of the series.

While many fans saw the thrilling come-from-behind victory as a return to mystical form, pitcher David Cone betrayed the team's overconfidence in a *Daily News* column, printed before game two, titled "It Was Justice—Not Luck." Cone's screed derided Howell as a "high school pitcher" and insulted the Dodgers as the lucky ones for even coming close to beating their frontrunner betters.[424]

With the clipping pinned in their clubhouse, the Dodgers scorched Cone to even the series. They battled ferociously from then on, clinching the pennant in game seven with an Orel Hershiser shutout. The Mets would not see another postseason for over a decade. Cone's cocky column, Roger Angell wrote, cost the Mets not only a 1988 championship, but perhaps "two after that, because they were so strong."[425]

Gibson, on the other hand, was so worn out from his desperate desire to punish the Mets that he watched his team win the World Series from the bench—appearing only once as pinch hitter to swat a heroic walk-off home run.

With the Mets' proprietary magic gone west, the mystical bonds between teammates unchained. "Golden boy" prospect Gregg Jefferies was despised as the clubhouse Yuppie. Sick of platooning, Mookie Wilson begged to be traded. Gary Carter resented Keith Hernandez for being made co-captain, and Hernandez's lobbying against Strawberry's "star attitude" cost him the NL MVP. The two started bickering immediately when they saw each other at spring photo day, where snaps of their brawl moments into the shoot provided a perfect image for the 1989 team.

Davey Johnson once claimed to love "selfish players," telling them: "Worry about yourself and I'll worry about everyone else."[426] But with their unifying gang-mentality gone, the Mets plummeted to their lowest record in seven years. During his career-worst season, Hernandez felt for the first time since his reluctant arrival to the Mets six years prior that "we don't deserve to win."[427] Strawberry concurred as his batting average sunk to .225: "Suddenly the baseball season and our pennant race didn't seem fun anymore. It seemed like just another job. Just another day at the office, a shift on the assembly line."[428]

Even when Strawberry's numbers rebounded in his final year before free agency in 1990, he told the press he was ready to return home and become a Dodger, no longer wanting to be an automaton of the soulless franchise he now called the *Robo Mets.*

Reagan's *morning in America* darkened in the eighties' twilight—the collective impulses of the sixties vanishing from a now stridently individualist cultural horizon. Veterans of the Black Panthers, Yippies, and Weathermen became stockbrokers, CEOs, and politicians. The Vietnam-era taboo against America's vicious military-policing of the world ended with a widely supported war on Iraq. The expansion of the nascent internet to newly affordable personal computers gave rise to boutique communities offering refuge from social-political chaos. The Soviet Union collapsed, its aging Marxist bureaucrats turned into organ dealers scrapping the worker state's deformed corpse for cash.

Attempting to keep their own empire alive, Wilpon ordered a spending spree. Vince Coleman, Eddie Murray, and Bobby Bonilla joined the team, inflating the payroll to the highest in the MLB by 1992. None would ever come close to replacing the power, media appeal, dynamism, and solidarity of the bad boys they replaced.

When the Mets plummeted to fifth in 1991, the populist pluck of Mets fans dissolved, too. To the extent the Mets still remained the people's team, they now reflected a working class disintegrating from petty resentment and nihilism for a better future. This process had been underway in 1986 as well, but watching 162 miserable Mets games after work could now no longer numb the hopeless boredom of awaiting their turn in the middle class.

Conservatives swept to power in New York through the early decade. Their law-and-order rhetoric blamed crime and homelessness on the progressive policies installed during decades of Democratic rule in New York. Calls to sports radio station WFAN began to sound identical to those on conservative talk stations, with aggrieved fans blaming the team's ills on the greed of lazy Bronxite Bonilla or coddled Yuppie Gregg Jefferies with the same bile spewed by Rush Limbaugh's ditto-heads against welfare queens or politically correct leftist students.

Wilpon replicated the GOP too with his attempted rebrand of the franchise around Christian "family values." The team's spring training camp was moved from party capital St. Petersburg to isolated Port St. Lucie, and the born again evangelical ex-Yankee Jeff Torborg replaced Davey Johnson as manager in 1990. He banned alcohol from flights, formed a Bible study group, and encouraged players to inform each other's wives of infidelity. In *The Worst Team Money Could Buy*, Bob Klapisch and John Harper wrote of this era: "Operating in the largest, most liberal city in the country the Mets had somehow managed to become one of baseball's most conservative organizations."[429]

Neither the personnel changes, nor lonesome Port St. Lucie, nor Christly Torborg could prevent a new bunch sprouting from 1986's scummy soil. Players smuggled liquor in soda bottles on team flights and erected walls of silence around the Bible-thumpers. In 1991, Strawberry ended up in the same rehab as Gooden after assaulting his girlfriend in a drunken rampage.

Like Gooden, he found the facility refreshing. Unlike the nihilistic partying of their teammates, blind-eye-turning of Johnson, and unforgiving media, their fellow addicts treated them as real people with real problems instead of robotic role models. More relief came when Strawberry arrived home in a Dodgers uniform the next year. While Cashen had told the press the Mets would be better off without his streaky performance and unprofessional attitude, Dodgers manager Tommy Lasorda put Strawberry at ease, telling him that baseball should not feel "like punching a time clock. . . . You have to treat it like a game and you'll excel at it. Treat it like working the night shift someplace and it'll become a chore."[430]

The purge of the team's 1986 core accelerated with Strawberry's departure. Cashen had fired Davey Johnson; then Wilpon fired Cashen in 1991. Lee Mazzilli, Wilson, Dykstra, Sid Fernandez, Hernandez, and Carter were let go in rapid succession. Carter's replacement as catcher and team leader, Rick Cerone, was released after one year for being "too political." The unrest only worsened in a clubhouse divided between white conservatives praying in one corner and Black players rolling Cee-lo in another. At least Cashen's replacement Al Harazin provided some unity. Whenever the GM ventured among the players, the discordant clubhouse joined together in a cruel chorus of hisses and meows. Blamed for the franchise's bad luck, the players called him the "black cat"—the defining symbol of sixties Mets magic now invoked only as insult.[431]

The next-generation Scum Bunch may have been more covert with their substance abuse, but their unrestrained libidos put their notorious predecessors to shame. Never before had a team been so publicly chauvinistic about their nightly prowls: "You can get sex every night. On the road, at home, it doesn't matter," shortstop Kevin Elster boasted to *Sports Illustrated* in a 1991 interview. "If you're talking about the number of guys who get a little head in the back of the bullpen during the course of the season," David Cone told Klapisch and Harper, "you're talking about a pretty large number."[432]

The sexual binges became a sport overshadowing baseball during the dismal 1991 season, complete with its own lecherous lexicon. Flirty women in the seats were identified as *gamers*, who they aimed to either *crush* or *beat up*. The first inevitable scandal broke toward the end of the season when three supposed *gamers* sued the franchise and Cone, who had allegedly invited them past a hidden partition in the bullpen where they said he exposed himself and violently threatened them for refusing his advances. Less than two weeks later, news broke that another young woman told police Cone had raped her in his Philadelphia hotel room.

Denying the headlines, he was permitted to pitch against the Phillies. "I spent the whole day with one eye on the hitter and one eye on the tunnel," he told the *Daily News*' Mike Lupica, "wondering if the police could actually show up in the middle of a game and arrest me."[433]

The heat never came. The Mets settled the bullpen incident out of court, and no charges for either incident would ever be filed. "One lieutenant told me, 'I think you're immature,'" the anonymous Philadelphia woman told the *Post*, "that I shouldn't be out by myself, and that I brought the whole thing on myself."[434] The Philadelphia police tasked with investigating sex crimes, who called themselves the "Lying Bitches Unit," were soon found to have dismissed an improbably high number of similar claims. Little better were the sportswriters, who portrayed all accusations against beloved athletes as gold-digging exaggerations. Many cheered Cone for overcoming adversity that night as he proceeded to pitch one of the greatest games of his life.

Shortly after the Mets finished in fifth place in 1991, lawyer Anita Hill testified about the sexual abuse she endured while working for Supreme Court nominee Clarence Thomas. The hearings inspired widespread discussion in the media, workplaces, and homes about the prevalence of sexual harassment, date rape, and misogyny in American culture. Another Mets scandal opening the 1992 season showed how little the sports world had been affected.

During spring training, a woman filed a complaint with Port St. Lucie police claiming Dwight Gooden, Vince Coleman, and Daryl Boston had trapped her in Gooden's room and raped her. Fearing the typical accusations of looking for a payout, she refrained from filing civil charges. But with backlash underway against feminism's popular reemergence, media figures like Howard Stern, Katie Roiphe, and *Post* writers either fabricated reasons why one might lie about date rape, or otherwise blamed her for the assault because she had gone to Gooden's house willingly, and gave goodbye kisses when she was finally permitted to leave. The police concurred, declining to file charges.[435]

While the team was shaken by these scandals, it's unclear they learned any lesson other than to be more suspicious of press, management, and fans. Believing gossip columnists were following them to bars, pitcher John Franco organized a media boycott, and Bonilla, whose perpetual slump inspired such a boom of boos at Shea he began wearing earplugs, threatened to beat up Bob Klapisch during a postgame interview. Coleman showed how little respect the team had for Torborg's preaching the next year by shoving him during an early-season game. When Coleman refused to apologize, *Torborg* was fired.

More explosions came as the Mets sunk to dead last during the summer of 1993. Pitcher Bret Saberhagen threw bleach and firecrackers at reporters in two separate July incidents, and Coleman and Bonilla tossed M-100s at hecklers as they exited Dodger Stadium shortly after. Among the three fans injured in LA were an eleven-year-old boy and a one-year-old girl.

An unignorable line finally crossed, Coleman took the blame. He was suspended, then traded away in what Wilpon promised would be the beginning of renewed deep-cleaning. Even this had been a hard decision, he told the press. Coleman was one of the best players on the team, but he had finally learned an important lesson: "Being a baseball player goes beyond stats."[436]

I was seven when my dad took me to Shea for the first time the next season to meet the Mets. They were terrible, he told me, and they probably would be for a long time. Nonetheless, I could sense in his admiration for them that, sometime before I was born, they were great.

My main memory was the half-hearted Nickelodeon Extreme Baseball parking-lot amusement park, commissioned by Wilpon to promote a family-friendly atmosphere. As for the game itself, two vivid incidents remain.

One was seeing Darryl Strawberry come to bat for the Giants to now-sincere boo-like heckles of *Darr-ul . . . Darr-ul* punishing him for having left the Mets. When I later saw this treatment bringing him to tears in the *Simpsons* episode "Homer at the Bat," I became deeply ashamed of having joined the jeering.

The second incident was a little skit between innings late in the game. Barney the Dinosaur emerged from the stands on the first-base side, toddling around and dancing along the base line to a chorus of boos. Barney was a kindly and innocent, albeit corny, children's programming mascot who was, for some reason, violently despised by men and young boys for his message of equality and love. As the venomous response to Barney's appearance turned to middle fingers and swearing, Mr. Met, revived that year from Grant's Tomb, strolled toward him.

A Wilpon-era re-creation, his head had been rebuilt gargantuan, perhaps three times the size of the 1964 prototype, complete with internal levers to contort his eye, eyebrows, mouth, and prosthetic tongue into various uncanny grimaces and sneers. He approached Barney holding what appeared to be a real bat, stopping a few feet short from his apparent foe to size him up before viciously beating him to a roar of applause.[437]

PART III

WAITING TO EXPLODE (1994–2025)

Why do people live in New York? There is no relationship between them. Except for the inner electricity which results from the simple fact of their being crowded together. A magical sensation of contiguity and attraction for an artificial centrality. This is what makes it a self-attractive universe, which there is no reason to leave. There is no human reason to be here, except for the sheer ecstasy of being crowded together.

—*Jean Baudrillard, America*

A crowded stadium was an obvious target. There were reports that a man had been found sitting in his car with ominously highlighted maps of the area surrounding Shea and LaGuardia Airport. And yet, they came. They came to say they weren't afraid. They came to support and celebrate New York City. That's what the Mets stood for, whether we wanted to or not . . .

—*Mike Piazza, Long Shot*

Chapter 10

CITY OF SHADOWS

During the 1993 offseason a massive trade was finalized—hundreds of thousands of blue-collar jobs to Mexico in exchange for cash considerations.

Like its ballplayers, American workers had become too privileged, the Clinton administration economists behind the North American Free Trade Agreement (NAFTA) argued. Outsourcing industrial jobs was a tough-but-necessary measure to stay competitive in a globalizing market. It was a fatal blow to an organized labor movement already in perilous decline—a clear transfer of wealth from the working class to their bosses that decades of business-minded demobilization left them incapable of refusing through argument or force.

Similar concessions were made in the sports world that year. The football players' union followed their basketball brethren in accepting a salary cap, relinquishing the unlimited expansion of free-agent salaries for theoretical parity between big- and small-market franchises that, the owners insisted, would expand profits overall.

But in their own 1994 CBA negotiations, the baseball union firmly rejected the scheme. Unlimited free-agent signing was the players' greatest victory of their century-long struggle for an equitable profit share since the creation of the National League. The average salary rose from $19,000 to $241,000 in sixteen years of Marvin Miller's union presidency, and continued to rise at pace with overall revenue under his protégé, Donald Fehr. If profits were unevenly shared or spent among the owners, Fehr argued, that was their own problem.[438]

Seeing some logic to Fehr's suggestion of revenue sharing, Mets owner Fred Wilpon joined the Orioles' Peter Angelos, uniquely pro-worker from his years representing unions, to seek conciliation in the talks. The two had helped avert a lockout the previous year, pointing out that missed games hurt small-market teams worst, and that all past work stoppages only increased the players' solidarity while impeding the profits earned through cooperation.

One result of a lockout attempt in 1990, for example, was a win for the union's demands for new expansion teams. The Colorado Rockies and Florida Marlins turned out to be a massive windfall of new fans and broadcasting revenue, with attendance reaching seventy million for the first time—a fifteen-million increase from the previous year. Would it not be better, Wilpon's faction argued, to ditch the salary cap for the "luxury tax" suggested by President Bill Clinton's Labor Department? It was a limitation on free-agent spending the union could accept, in which owners could still spend freely, with an incentive to avoid a certain threshold past which they would be forced to compensate smaller-market teams.

But such self-restraint was unthinkable to the hard-liners around Jerry Reinsdorf, owner of the Bulls and White Sox. He asserted to his colleagues that the inability of baseball owners to reap the higher profit margins of their NBA counterparts was an unacceptable indignity to their class. Following the example of his Chicago magnate forefather Albert Spalding, he assured satisfaction could only be won by baiting the players into a war of attrition. "You do it by taking a position and telling them we're not going to play unless we make a deal," he said, "and being prepared not to play one or two years if you have to."[439]

As negotiations continued into the 1994 season, Reinsdorf won the majority of his fellow magnates to the warpath. The strike began in mid-August, and the remainder of the season was canceled in September.

No matter their class sympathies, baseball fans' ultimate partisanship is only for their uninterrupted consumption, and their disappointment in the first year without a World Series since 1904 turned to anger that there were no signs of thaw as spring training approached. Seizing upon the frustration, the owners announced that the 1995 season *would* be played—if not by its entitled stars, then by a deserving group of replacements.

While the union held firm to their certainty that major-league fans wanted major-league talent, the press promoted the fill-ins with inspirational profiles of working-class youngsters. Among them was Honolulu native Benny Agbayani, tapped from Hawaii winter league obscurity to become a Met. "My career wasn't going anywhere," Agbayani recalled. "I was never a top prospect, one of those players people talk about eventually being in New York."[440]

Only Angelos refused to take part in the drive that was far uglier than the puff pieces suggested. The Blue Jays shifted their schedule to Florida to evade Canada's labor laws against strike-breaking, and coaches like the Yankees' Buck Showalter and Tigers' Sparky Anderson lost their jobs for voicing reluctance to field scabs. Most would-be replacements, too, had to be threatened across the picket line. Pitcher Rick Reed was told by the Reds' Nazi-sympathizing owner Marge Schott to suit up or be blacklisted. "Reed's mother was sick," Tim Kurkjian wrote for ESPN, "he was paying her medical bills, and he couldn't stop working. So he played."[441]

While an MLBPA statement promised only to sanction the replacement's agents, the Mets' New Yorker union reps took a harder position. "Our negotiations are not any different than any negotiations in a labor situation," Bobby Bonilla said. "Try to cross a Teamsters line, and you'd end up in the East River."[442] When closer John Franco, the reputedly mob-connected son of a worker who belonged to New York's persuasive sanitation union, was asked if this could mean retaliation against replacement batters on the field once the strike ended, he responded, "I don't throw balls. I throw fists."[443]

Fearing hard pickets at major-league parks on Opening Day, the National Labor Relations Board intervened on the union's side on March 22. Another ruling from district court judge Sonia Sotomayor restored the prior bargaining agreement, uncapped. Reinsdorf's planned yearslong siege broken, the owners reluctantly accepted the luxury tax compromise, and their triumphant workers reported to training for a season that would begin only a month late.

But when Opening Day arrived, players everywhere found their home fields far from faithful. Cubs fans threw their giveaway magnetic schedules on the field. Players Association president Donald Fehr was booed out of Yankee Stadium. A sign in Philadelphia read: "WE FORGIVE YOU PHILS NOT! BRING BACK REPLACEMENTS."[444] A plane flew over the Reds' home opener with a sign reading: "OWNERS AND PLAYERS, TO HELL WITH ALL OF YOU." Joe Girardi, previously a fan favorite, was booed in his first plate appearance of the season at Coors Field in Denver. At Shea, three fans in Sharpie-scrawled shirts reading GREED bribed an usher to let them on the field, where they paid twisted homage to the Yippies by sprinkling dollar bills at the feet of the players before raising their white fists in imitation of the 1968 Olympics Black Power salute to a standing ovation from the small crowd.[445]

What one player dubbed "Fan Upheaval Day" proved Reinsdorf's plot had not been entirely in vain. The fans had bought into the owners' narrative that the union's refusal to accept a pay cut indicated they cared more about personal enrichment than the game's integrity or hometown loyalty. The sex, drug, and gambling scandals that rocked the Mets' and other clubhouses were similarly amplified in discussions of the strike, inspiring more resentment against the average ballplayer who made forty-seven times the average American salary, while refusing otherwise-commonplace humiliations like randomized drug testing. Even blame going to both sides was another win for the owners, recasting the labor struggle as a mere squabble between millionaires.

Not since the 1919 Black Sox scandal had ballplayers been so artfully scapegoated—an indication of how decades of attacks on industrial unionism proceeding the NAFTA coup de grâce had rolled class consciousness back to pre-Depression oblivion. Perhaps if the strike had been won through Franco and Bonilla's proposed hard pickets, and not intervention from Clinton and the courts, fans would have been forced to choose which side they were really on. The militant athletes instead encountered the anti-worker sentiment described in Jerry Seinfeld's cynical joke about fans rooting not for the player, but the uniform: "If he goes to another team, they boo him. This is the same human being in a different shirt. They hate him now. *'Boo! Different shirt. Booooo.'*"[446]

With resolve chilled on both sides of baseball's class struggle, a period of relative cooperation opened that eventually led fans to forget the strike had ever occurred. In the 1996 CBA, players conceded to the owners' scheme of establishing new divisions, an additional divisional playoff series, and a wildcard slot for the top runner-up. While this meant additional games for the players, it gave several more teams each year a chance to make and compete in the playoffs. The codification of the luxury tax, while ultimately reducing salary expansion in the long run, similarly encouraged competitive balance by deterring would-be Steinbrenners from buying free-agent super teams.

Another thrilling concession was regular-season interleague play. Since the shock of the first MLBPA strike in 1969, ownership factions of the two autonomous leagues had slowly unified into a singular anti-union front called Major League Baseball. Historic distinctions between AL and NL gradually faded from there, and the concept of a singular, annual climactic championship series between their top teams ceased making sense from a business perspective. The players had always opposed the interleague scheme that would complicate their schedule and increase travel times, but the windfall of revenue from fans flocking to see another league's stars and enjoy annual curated confrontations between regional rivals like the White Sox and Cubs, Dodgers and Angels, and Mets and Yankees, soon proved worth the trouble. The once-epochal "Subway Series" would soon happen at least twice a year, with each game guaranteed to sell out.

Attendance finally rebounded to surpass pre-strike levels in 1998, pumped both by these reforms, and the players' inflating muscles. Management now happily deferred to union insistence for privacy as use of creatine, human growth hormone, and other illicit performance enhancers became common. The fastballs of mad flamethrowers Roger Clemens and Randy Johnson began to regularly top 100 mph, as strongmen Mark McGwire, Sammy Sosa, and Barry Bonds smashed past the home-run records of Ruth and Aaron. The game that had so recently appeared as exciting as a contract negotiation now exploded in nightly fireworks displays of heat and dingers.

In this feel-good era of surplus and substance, the wounds of the strike healed between players as well. When Rick Reed joined the Reds in 1995, a clubhouse revolt against the would-be scab convinced owners to trade him to New York, where the Mets likewise threatened to burn his uniform. A merciful intervention from Franco permitted Reed his wardrobe, but banished him from team meetings, and his locker to Shea's defunct Jets locker room.

Reed accepted his isolation with contrition and earned the nickname "Poor Man's Greg Maddux" as he stoically led the team to their first winning season of the decade in 1997 with a 2.89 ERA. Franco welcomed him back to the clubhouse, upgrading his status to provisional observer of team meetings in 1998. "I really didn't know much about what the union meant," Reed told the *Daily News* that season. "But when you spend a whole year and see what the union does, it kind of makes you feel like crap. They really help players."[447]

Heckles of *scab* still came from opponents, but as Reed won sixteen games and the Mets entered the wildcard race, Franco shot back with 1986 combativeness: "Everyone in the clubhouse supports him. I'd go to war with him."[448]

The post-strike balance put the playoffs in reach for Mets, but the spiritual return-to-form that would bring them back to October was the result of a rebellious new organizational "look and philosophy" introduced by their eccentric new manager, Bobby Valentine.

"I was a radical," Bobby Valentine wrote in his autobiography to sum up his youthful progression from a pompadoured greaser hooligan in suburban Stamford, Connecticut, to the long-haired Dodger that Latino fans cheered as *El Loco.* He spent the seventies learning scrappy play from Tommy Lasorda and the politics of Black liberation from Dick Allen, with offseasons spent trading joints and meditations on Buddhism with the hitchhikers he met on freewheeling road trips.

After his playing career was cut short by injury, he coached under the laissez-faire Davey Johnson with the Mets in the eighties, then transformed from California hippy to Texas maverick with George W. Bush's Texas Rangers. Notorious in the early nineties as baseball's "most ejected" manager, trouble finding a job after Texas sent Valentine to Japan in 1995. For one year, he studied the "samurai mentality" of the Chiba Lotte Marines' "Iron Shogun" Hirooka-san, until a call came from New York asking him to put down the blade.

After years of mismatches, Valentine quickly proved a perfect fit for the Mets. His Stengelian wit combined with the "team-as-community" ethic he had learned from Gil Hodges's Brooklyn Dodgers teammate Lasorda, and the sabermetric system he had developed under Johnson. From his permanent perch on the top step of the dugout, the unrepentant heckler replicated the brilliance of the golden age's great manager Leo Durocher, vexing opponents and umps with a mixture of trash talk, innovative small ball, and rule-bending. "Every time I got a player from another team," he told the *New Yorker*, "after I asked him his wife's name, his kids' names, and if he had a place to stay yet, I would say, 'Hey, while they're fresh on your mind, can you give me the signs you were using with your last team?'"[449]

The long war on scum also finally reached armistice with Valentine's arrival. The offseason restaurateur understood workplace recalcitrance, whether from busboys or ballplayers, only hardens in reaction to prohibitionism. Just as George Orwell's Parisian boss had "allowed us two liters of wine a day each, knowing that if a *plongeur* is not given two litres he will steal three,"[450] Valentine evoked city ordinance and front-office pressure to ban liquor-guzzling and chain-smoking in the locker room, before winkingly offering Shea's laundromat as an anything-goes break room.

With fresh air in the clubhouse and a winning spring in Valentine's debut 1997 season, the front office's second top priority for its new coach approached in June, when the Mets went to the Bronx for their first non-exhibition games against the Yankees.

The 1996 world champs boasted a roster as formidable as any team in the past half-century, and the Yankees caps and Jeter shirts ubiquitous throughout the metropolis proved their reemergence as the city's premier franchise after a Mets-dominated eighties. Even with nearly identical records at the time of their first match-up, the better or more popular team was never in doubt. But the results on the field mattered less to Wilpon than play in the press, he told Valentine, because "the Yankees own the back pages."[451]

Head-to-head, the clear contrast between the two franchises throughout the three-game series indeed revived the press-friendly historic Mets narrative as the *anti-Yankees.* Visiting fans accustomed to Shea's chintzy family fun were shocked by the Bronx's barbarism—a product of the imperious corporate style George Steinbrenner learned from his favorite book, *Leadership Secrets of Attila the Hun.*[452] In homage to the man they lovingly called *the Boss*, the Stadium crowd once perceived as button-up conservatives in the sixties had mutated into the *Bleacher Creatures*—a beer-chugging pinstriped army, renowned for demanding player acknowledgment through ritualistic "roll calls," and ceaseless attacks on visiting fans. An especially crude example arrived in the seventh inning, when the Stadium's traditional singalong to the Village People's gay anthem "YMCA" transformed into a deeply homophobic parody aimed at anyone in a Mets hat: *Why Are You Gay?*, the Creatures sang, *I saw you sucking that D-I-C-K.*[453]

Another clear stylistic foil between the teams developed from the broadcast's dugout shots of the Mets' animated manager and his cross-armed counterpart, Joe Torre. The former union-militant Met had landed the job after Steinbrenner fired Buck Showalter for supporting the 1994 strike. Derided in the press as "Steinbrenner's muppet," Torre hid his brilliance behind a depressive demeanor that suggested the superstar assemblage could succeed on autopilot.[454] When journeyman Dave Mlicki shut out the Yankees in game one, the underdog victory conversely appeared the product of Valentine's wily grin.

After a respectable 6–3 loss the next day, the Mets came from behind to bring the rubber game to extras, only to lose in the tenth. The narrow defeat had been a spiritual victory for Valentine, however, with Wilpon's directive fulfilled in weeks of debates about the series and the teams' dueling identities raging in tabloids and sports radio.

Thirty-five years of politely trading center stage was over—the Mets had emerged from the wings to steal their share of the spotlight. And in the new era of expanded playoffs, the annual interleague games became a tease of an increasingly probable fulfillment of Mets Messianism—a Subway World Series. "If we had to write a perfect season," Valentine said, "I think everyone in the organization would have the opponent be from the Bronx."[455]

With a third-place finish in 1997, Valentine's vibe shift had revived an enthusiasm sufficient for the trauma of the early-1990s *Worst Team Money Could Buy* narrative to fade. Franchise purse strings finally loosened, leading to some tepid trades and signings that fielded an undoubtedly stronger team in 1998. Still clearly lacking, however, was a true star slugger. Midseason, they would get one by trading for Mike Piazza.

Born in the batting cage, Piazza represented a new type of American ballplayer that had eluded the Mets since the blue-collar Scum Bunch ran preppy prospect Gregg Jefferies from the clubhouse. His used-car-tycoon father had spared no expense on equipment and personal trainings to make him a pro, with additional assists coming from family friend Tommy Lasorda. After Piazza's years of Dodger batboy stints, Lasorda talked the team into using their final 1989 draft pick on him and urged their patience as the mediocre catcher struggled in the minors.

While his defensive skills would never impress, his offensive power became so formidable in the early steroids era that he landed a starter position with the Dodgers in 1993. Years of nepotism finally paid off with 35 home runs in his rookie-of-the-year season; the silver spoons of his youth smelted into the first of ten consecutive Silver Slugger awards.

He remained a top star of the homer-happy decade as his free agency approached in 1998. Piazza desperately wanted to stay in the Dodgers family, but the O'Malley heirs had sold the team the previous year to Rupert Murdoch. The Australian Fox media mogul proceeded to bleed out every last blue drop of Dodgers traditionalism, telling his shareholders he had acquired the team only as "a battering ram and a lead offering in all our pay television operations."[456]

Murdoch's baseball agents offered Piazza a contract extension millions below his worth, an appraisal certified by a press corps portraying his refusal to sign as avarice. Dodgers fans largely embraced the *diva* narrative, with one denouncing history's greatest hitting catcher in the *Los Angeles Times* as the "poster child for the Generation-X ballplayer," whose demanded market-value millions would be better spent by Murdoch "on a sequel to the Spice Girls."[457]

The manufactured backlash succeeded, and Piazza was traded midseason to the Marlins for Gary Sheffield. After a week of moping in Miami, he was traded again to the Mets for Preston Wilson, son of Mookie. Neither the family betrayal, the slight to the Mets' own powerhouse catcher Todd Hundley (exiled to left field and traded to LA after the season), nor the *Post*-owning Murdoch's propaganda had apparently phased Flushing fans. Piazza arrived at LaGuardia to cheering swarms, and proceeded to the clubhouse welcoming party where John Franco rewarded him with his uniform number. An hour after landing, number 31 took the field to a permanently doubled Shea crowd.

The trade was a rare fruit of Nelson Doubleday intervention. The increasingly silent owner's nostalgia for Strawberry had been aroused by the maligned slugger—his bat Viagra for the Home Run Apple, and his everyman style wavering between macho swagger and tortured fragility. Also like Strawberry, an initial struggle to adjust resulted in a prolonged slump that abruptly ended the honeymoon in a chorus of *boos*. But once his potency was restored after a few weeks, Piazza recognized the sympathy of Shea's scorn. The fans, sharing Doubleday's fantasy, were urging him to force his partner Wilpon to give him whatever amount the Dodgers had denied. They *boo*ed, he came to understand, because they *wanted* him to get paid.

Piazza ended the 1998 season with 32 homers, and a .348 average since his arrival in Queens. A month later, he signed a seven-year, $91 million contract—the largest in baseball history. He bought a place in Tribeca, began dropping into Eddie Trunk's late-night metal show on shock-jock WNEW, and frequently appeared in gossip columns dedicated to New York's most-eligible bachelors.

At last, the Mets had a star rivaling the Bronx constellation. He shined especially during the teams' annual interleague competitions, powering the Mets to take the seasonal Subway Series for the first time in 1999, and appearing to be New York's more authentic star as he bested the Yankees' rageaholic Texan ace Roger Clemens again and again.

Now recognizing themselves as the vanguard force against the universally despised dynasty, Mets fans began echoing Shea's stairwells after each game with the new war cry popular throughout all baseball: *Yankees Suck.*

The chauvinistic slogan was the product of Boston, where Yankee hatred was a way of life. Earlier that year, Boston jock-hardcore band Ten Yard Fight printed a *Yankees Suck* shirt that sold out so quickly at their final show, they reprinted it without their logo for a crew of punks to hawk outside every Fenway game. The DIY business boomed into a national operation, with variations becoming the alternate uniform of every baseball fan with sadistic fantasies of bringing the Yankees to their knees.

Shea had debuted their own subtle anti-Yankees merch the previous year—their black alternate uniform. What began as a search to close the merchandising gap turned into a noir rebrand for the cartoonishly colored team now overshadowed by the Yankees' navy cloud. "My thought was this," uniform designer Bob Halfacre recalled to Paul Lukas at ESPN, "I've only been to New York three or four times in my life, but what I remember is shadows. You have all these skyscrapers, so everything has shadows . . . city of shadows. One side of the street is sunny and warm, the other side is in shadow and cold."[458]

The team's aesthetic darkened still with their choice of "LA Woman" as the rally anthem of their wildcard thrust. Adapted from *City of Night*, John Rechy's 1963 novel drawn from his life as a streetwalking bisexual beatnik in Manhattan, the noir tune fashioned Doors frontman Jim Morrison as a down-and-out prowler in Hollywood, its closing dirge of

"Mojo risin'" an anagrammatic reference to the warped confidence he received by achieving nightly orgasm.

Third baseman Robin Ventura has never fully explained why he chose the early-seventies anthem of bohemian hedonism, but it clearly resonated with his teammates. After each come-from-behind push, everyone on the club, "from the salsa aficionados and hip-hop fans to the country-western boys and metalheads," Bob Klapisch wrote, "becomes an instant Classic rock devotee, if only for the loud refrain."[459]

The possibility of the Mets' first title in over a decade was all the more seductive for marking their first postseason penetration simultaneous to the Yankees.

Jim Mutrie and John Day had conceived the original Mets as avatars of New York's underworld against the elite Gothams, with the merger of the two into the black-clad Giants setting the stage for their 1890 revolt against the capitalist system. Rivalry with the Yankees, and everything they represented, was the team's historic purpose.

Yankees fans understood the subversive nature of the Mets' challenge as well. No matter how much their payroll soared or record improved, they would always be degenerates in comparison, representing everything despicable to the Manhattan and suburban elites—weakness, poorness, unruliness, and, as rumors of Piazza's homosexuality accumulated, fruitiness.

Yankee Stadium's bleacher culture bled into the halls of my Westchester middle-school, where *Mets suck* and other slurs were shouted at me in my black Piazza tee from the navy sea of Jeter shirts. One of only a handful of Mets fans in my district, my fandom placed me firmly among the mall-goths, weebs, juggalos, and *Magic: The Gathering* players in black Hot Topic tees sporting nu-metal album covers or non-sequitur rebellious slogans like *Normal people scare me.*

I could strut my Mets gear in pride for a few weeks until the run died in Atlanta, where the team suffered the same impotence as the unfrozen swingin' sixties agent from the 1999 hit *Austin Powers: The Spy Who Shagged Me*—they lost their mojo.

While the rivalry with Ted Turner's powerhouse had been overshadowed by that with the Yankees, the humbling defeat in the NLCS established the Braves as a new explicitly political foe. The ex-Confederacy's favorite team had finished first every year for a decade, its fans celebrating each victory with a chant mocking the Cherokee warriors expelled from Georgia in the Trail of Tears.

These signifiers had all seemed trivially distasteful until Braves closer John Rocker's *Sports Illustrated* interview shortly after their loss to the Yankees in the 1999 World Series. Pictured holding a rifle in real-tree camouflage, he disparaged Valentine, the Mets, their fans, other beloved New York athletes, and nearly every subgroup of New York's diverse population. When interviewer Jeff Pearlman asked if he would ever play for the Mets, he snarled that he could never imagine riding the 7 train alongside "some kid with purple hair next to some queer with AIDS right next to some dude who just got out of jail for the fourth time right next to some 20-year-old mom with four kids."[460] Mets fans, even those who may have shared some of these bigoted sentiments, could only proudly retort, *Yes, that's us!*

As the Mets prepared to march into the new millennium, a Union army against the tomahawk-chopping rednecks and diamond-crusted conservatives beloved by Mayor Rudy Giuliani, the winter's riots against the World Trade Organization summit in Seattle recalled their black garb's revolutionary connotations. From within a protest coalition of labor and direct-action activists decrying the WTO as executors of NAFTA-like policies hostile to the rights of workers, indigenous populations, and the earth's ecosystem, a mysterious thousands-strong faction appeared. Dressed head-to-toe in black, they set fire to trash cans, rushed police lines, and hurled bricks and hammers through downtown financial district windows.

The *black bloc* was a militant tactic imported from German antifascists by radicals seeking to restore the street militancy that had vanished in the US after 1968. While the diverse backgrounds and political ideas of the signless street-trashers were hidden by their uniforms, their anarchistic and anti-capitalist graffiti sprayed on smashed-up corporate storefronts inspired millennials like myself to believe Giuliani's law-and-order policing, and the Yankees' financial might, could be fought head-on. Their anonymizing chic added to the intrigue by implying that doing so could be done in style, and without fear of arrest.

Even if few other fans besides myself appreciated this aesthetic convergence, the Mets' lawless manager had himself employed the black-bloc tactic earlier that year. In the twelfth inning of a tense game against the Blue Jays at Shea, Valentine was tossed for protesting a catcher's interference call against Piazza. Forgoing his normal dramatics, he quietly skulked to the clubhouse, where he disguised himself in a black Mets shirt, black cap, sunglasses, and eyeblack pasted under his nose as a false mustache, before returning to the dugout to manage the team toward a fourteenth-inning walk-off victory.

League officials had difficulty punishing the incognito coach, identified by adoring fans and broadcasters only as "Roberto Valentino." Even their eventual wrist-slap of a two-game suspension, to be served at Valentine's leisure, betrayed a universal admiration for the hilarious crime that would become as iconic to the Mets' anarchic spirit as the black cat incident of 1969.

Less remembered, however, was the anti-imperialist spectacle that opened the game. Venezuela's new socialist president Hugo Chávez, in town for a UN visit, had thrown the ceremonial first pitch in a personalized Mets jersey gifted by several of the team's Latino players. Years later, when Chávez nationalized oil wealth and defied a US-backed coup with a Valentino-esque return to power, agent Peter Greenberg warned his Venezuelan clients, including Mets Edgardo Alfonzo and Roger Cedeño, that he could become the next Castro. "'Don't worry,' they told him.'He loves baseball. He won't mess with the baseball players.' Then I remind them that Fidel loves baseball, too."[461, 462]

The resumed struggle to topple the Yankees' empire began at Shea's 2000 Opening Day with a fervent chorus of *boos* for Rudy Giuliani's appearance on Diamond Vision. The Yankees-loving mayor had always received a smattering of playful jeers at Shea, but this was different, Matthew Callan wrote: "The boos at Shea have an edge to them, for Giuliani's popularity is at its lowest ebb."[463]

As the mayor approached the end of his second term, the once-revered law-and-order Republican had accumulated working-class ire for his crusades against municipal unions, censorship of transgressive art, and steadfast defense of the most egregious incidents of NYPD brutality. Most infamously, he stood behind the department in three shocking incidents against unarmed Black immigrants—the 1997 torture of Abner Louima, the killing of Amadou Diallo in a hail of forty-one bullets the previous winter, and the murder of Patrick Dorismond only days prior.

The Mets kept within striking distance of the Braves through the spring, and embarrassed Giuliani again by taking the regular-season Subway Series opener 12–2 in the Bronx. Piazza bested Clemens once more in the laugher. In his twelve at bats against the ace, Piazza had stroked seven hits (including three homers) and nine RBIs, with his third-inning grand slam that night so disturbing to the Yankee faithful that many, Steinbrenner included, made an early exit from the park.

Bloody revenge came in July. The rainout in the previous series was rescheduled as a Subway doubleheader played in both stadiums. A few hours after the now-Yankee Doc Gooden triumphed in his old park, Clemens took the mound in the Bronx determined to avenge his June humiliation. He pitched hard and inside to put the Mets down in order in the first, setting up his chief antagonist Piazza to lead off the second. Taking no chances, the rageaholic Rocket fired a 92-mph pitch directly at his head.

"The sharp crack of ball connecting with his batting helmet resounds throughout the stadium," Callan wrote. "Piazza crumples in a heap and stares into the stadium lights."[464]

Clemens paced, his smug anger turning to obligatory concern as trainers slowly walked a concussed Piazza to the dugout. He proceeded to dominate the stunned and Piazza-less Mets that afternoon before claiming in the post-win press conference that the pitch was an accident.

To Piazza and the Mets, this was a lie of legalistic necessity. Had Piazza not ducked, the two-seamer would have hit his eye, blinding or killing him.[465] More postgame remarks from Yankee top brass did little to dispel this narrative. "The bottom line, not to disrespect anybody, is the fact that he won," Torre said. Bench coach Don Zimmer, whose two-week coma after being similarly struck in the head during a 1953 Dodgers minor-league game had led to the mandatory wearing of batting helmets, said Piazza had acted like a "little man" for denouncing Clemens. "I feel sorry for them," Steinbrenner added. "They had to take the focus off the fact that they got their fannies handed to them."[466]

The rivalry was now a blood feud. Mets GM Steve Phillips barred the Yankees from the weight room and demanded Torre keep the two teams apart the next day. The Mets salvaged the final game to put the 2000 Subway Series score at Yankees 4, Mets 2. With the Mets far behind the Braves and clinging to a narrow wildcard lead, the smug front-runners hoped the matter was settled there.

But Piazza returned from his near-death experience a few days later determined to even the score in October. "I had gotten into the spirit of New York on the social level," he recalled, as chants of *MVP* greeted his every appearance with the unleashed Mets surging through the summer, ending August tied for first with the Braves.[467]

The feral rampage found a new anthem in the Baha Men's "Who Let the Dogs Out"—a Caribbean Junkanoo earworm about the unleashed sexual energy of men partying together. When the Mets clinched the wildcard slot just a game behind the Braves in September, the Baha Men re-recorded the track as "Who Let the Mets Out," including a vow to *Beat John Rocker!*[468]

That climactic confrontation with Rocker never came, however. Police escorts and guards had protected his every appearance at Shea that year, and an NLCS rematch was prevented when the Cardinals swept the Braves in the first playoff round.

The Mets, powered by recently called-up youngster dark horses Timo Pérez and Benny Agbayani (his scabbing also long forgiven), then dispatched Mark McGwire's Cardinals with similar ease to Barry Bonds' Giants in the first round. Pérez leaped joyfully after making the final out in the surprisingly easy five-game upset, Shea thundering so loudly for the first pennant since 1986 that Gary Cohen worried it would collapse.[469] Giuliani's army occupied the field to block a revanchist return of the field-storming tradition; the contained crowd proceeding to thunder the staircases with the booming war cry against the big boss to come: *Yankees suck! Yankees suck! Yankees suck!*

"We cannot afford to lose to the Mets," Steinbrenner told Torre before the first game of the first Subway World Series since 1956. "There's just too much at stake here for us."

While Steinbrenner hated the Mets so much that he pressured the team to beat them handily even in exhibition games, his fear was now about far more than a loss of bragging rights. Billions in funding for premium cable channels, a new stadium, and the political future of New York were on the line.

Giuliani's sweetheart deal to rebuild Yankee Stadium seemed inevitable until 1998, when the perilous collapse of a section of the old park before a ballgame reminded taxpayers how badly Steinbrenner had fleeced the city for a $160 million rebuild in the seventies. And with Giuliani's popularity still plummeting, it was likely a more progressive, less Yankee-boosting mayoral administration would be elected during the last year of Steinbrenner's lease on the ballpark in 2001. A third consecutive Yankee championship would cement the team's institutional power in New York, while a humiliating defeat by the Mets, he warned, could send the team following the Jets and football Giants to Jersey exile.

The Mets, on the other hand, entered the series relatively carefree. Their owners, too, hoped a championship could help secure funding for a TV network and Shea rebuild, but had always pledged to do so on their own dime. In the break leading up to the series, the players made lighthearted rounds on morning and late-night shows, while the Yankees initiated a total media blackout as they prepared for the match-up Torre called his "worst nightmare."

"It doesn't seem like you're enjoying this, Joe," Valentine told his counterpart, as they exchanged lineup cards before the first game in the Bronx.

"What the fuck is there to enjoy?" Torre replied.[470]

After Billy Joel sang the national anthem, Al Leiter dueled David Cone in a hard-fought game that seemed to preview a close and lengthy series. The Mets took a lead into the bottom of the ninth, Armando Benítez's blown save sending the game to extras. Over five hours after the Piano Man's performance, the longest World Series game in history ended with a twelfth-inning Yankees walk-off hit.

Game two centered on the first rematch of Piazza and Clemens since July's assassination attempt. "Clemens treated every one of his starts as preparing for Armageddon, none with more emotion than Game 2 of the 2000 World Series," Tom Verducci wrote.[471]

After striking out Pérez and Alfonzo, Clemens sniffed, spit, and grunted as Piazza stepped to the plate. Piazza looked nervous in his black-and-blue helmet, breathing into his hands and wincing as the first two inside fastballs landed for strikes. He made weak contact on the fourth pitch, shattering his bat and sending the ball dribbling foul down the first-base line. A noise of shocked exasperation emerged from the crowd as Clemens fielded the broken barrel, lifted it over his head, and fired it in the direction of Piazza's perfunctory trot.

Stunned by the bizarre act of aggression, Piazza turned to his rival on the mound and began a slow approach. Regardless of Clemens' intentions, he and the Yankees had alpha-dogged the Mets for years, their jock fans treating wimps like me much the same in lunchrooms across suburbs. But broken out of their kennel, the rivalry's archetypal structure neared its confrontational apex. Pitcher and hitter were now two men with a very serious problem between them, sizing one another up for a pivotal showdown that everyone knew would prove more decisive than any recordable play.

"What's your problem?" Piazza barked. He had been dreaming of this exact confrontation for months, even working with a karate instructor on a plan to approach, parry Clemens' first punch, and then rock him in the face. With both teams converging to the field, Clemens meekly avoided eye contact, shrugging toward the umpire with a smug excuse, “I thought it was the ball.”

Piazza froze, desperately searching Clemens’ face for any signs of belligerence. “I was yelling back at a voice, pushing my way toward a closer, clearer confrontation. The fans were howling. There was so much ambiguous energy buzzing around, I couldn’t process it all.”[472]

The moment passed; he obeyed the umpires and returned to position. Revenge now could only come from a big hit, but the fight-averse indecision recurred as he checked his swing, sending the ball harmlessly to second for an inning-ending groundout.

Although only one game and one half inning had been played in the series, it felt over from then on. Clemens remained nearly unhittable as the Yankees chipped their way to a 6–0 lead going into the ninth. Piazza finally connected to homer off his reliever to make it 6–2. He sparked a rally that continued against Mariano Rivera with Jay Payton’s three-run shot. The lunge at a miracle ended there, restrained like Piazza in the first, a run away from evening the score.

An on-field performance by the Baha Men before game three pledged the leash would truly come off at wild Shea. Sadly, the Mets’ front office had neutralized much of the home-field advantage by waiting until the Yankees had clinched the AL pennant to sell tickets at a higher price for the increased demand. Packs of Bleacher Creatures ended up snatching tens of thousands, claiming far more territory than the Mets’ crowd had in the Bronx. With battles raging in the seats, Rick Reed’s strong start and Benny Agbayani’s streaky bat squeaked out a 4–2 win to put the series at two games to one.

The ticketing accommodation had not been enough for Steinbrenner. Deep within Shea, he raged at the visiting clubhouse’s municipal decor with trademark snobbery: "I can't have my players sitting on these little wooden stools," he complained. "I want them to feel they're at home. Hell, they are at home. Just in the wrong ballpark. This place is a dump!"[473]

Once the win confirmed a third game would be played at Shea, Steinbrenner ordered leather furniture trucked to Queens for his players. An answer to the insult seemed to come in the eighth inning of game four, when, the official story goes, the dousing of a trash-can fire set somewhere in the stadium caused an overloaded water pipe to burst in Steinbrenner's royal lounge, soaking him and ruining his Chesterfield sofas. "There were accusations that maybe I had done it," Valentine wrote. "Maybe I did. I can't remember."

Whether or not Roberto Valentino had turned arsonist to cause the karmic flood, little justice would be found on the field. Novelist Rick Moody sketched the grim perspective of Mets fans throughout a game frozen at 3–2 Yankees from the fourth: "Benitez, with a bad knee, is like a bruise on the heart every time he emerges from the bullpen; Edgardo Alfonzo and Timo Perez, so commanding in the playoffs, are about as useful at the plate as the banners waving above the center-field fence; most valuable free agent, Mike Hampton, cannot handle the northeastern chill, blows grimly upon his palms."[474]

Rivera closed out the eighth and ninth, restoring Yankee command. Facing elimination down 4–2 in the ninth the next night, Piazza came to the plate with the chance to keep the fight alive with a homer. "It was the story of the series," Piazza wrote of his fly-out. "I couldn't deliver a punch."[475]

The Yankees had their *three-peat.*

"There isn't always justice," Bobby Valentine wrote when reflecting on the series years later. "I suppose the Yankees were supposed to win it. I don't know."[476]

That was certainly how I felt attempting to get out of bed the next morning knowing the middle-school mocking that awaited me. It turned out to not be so bad—I received far fewer *Mets suck* jeers than conciliatory *you guys had a great run.*

Their brief moment of insecurity past, Yankees fans seemed generally more polite from then on. Mets magic had been revealed to be just another millenarian fantasy, like the Y2K bug, Christian rapture, or a black-bloc insurrection against international capitalism. Anarchy's ridiculous mojo-apple had risen only to meekly retreat back into the shadows.

It was the story of the decade: history culminating in this eternal social order. A quote from an iconic slacker film ran through my head during the endless offseason: *Your revolution is over, Mr. Lebowski. Condolences. The bums lost. The bums will always lose.*

Chapter 11

FULL AUTONOMY

The Subway Series loss, crushing as it was, did nothing to change the Mets' status as the people's team. Losing, with the narrow sliver of hope that they might one day beat the odds and win, had always made them relatable. This was and remains the dream of the vast majority of New York's population—to rise above their station, even for a moment, despite their deepest doubts that such a thing will ever happen.

But despite its common usage among leftists, "the people" has never been synonymous with the left or the working class. The 1888 Giants' version of "the people" referred to Manhattan society as a whole—the carriage class, bohemians, and workers alike. Marx critiqued the international emergence of this sort of "populism" as a counterattack on the workers' movement, adapting its resentment of the elite while ignoring "the interests and positions of different classes."[477] Populist invocation of "the people" became a unifying political vehicle of vulgar socialists, the progressive bourgeoisie, anti-immigrant nativists, and the Ku Klux Klan alike. A century later, the concept of "the people" remains dangerously incoherent. So too does the concept of the "people's team."

Until the corporatization of the eighties, the Mets were unquestionably a team branded toward the cultural left. They were civil-rights–supporting peaceniks and subcultural working-class outsiders compared to the conservative major-league establishment. A poll conducted in 2020 confirmed some of the spirit of the sixties remained—the Mets had the highest percentage of Democrat-identified fans in the MLB at 42 percent, and the second-lowest number of Republicans at 28 percent.[478] Our history would be incomplete, however, if we wrote off that lowly quarter's view of the Mets—especially in light of the team's disastrous right-wing trajectory in the early aughts.

Strident conservatives were franchise founders—Branch Rickey the Hooverite, Joan Payson the Rockefeller Republican, the Skull and Bones Yale set around George Herbert Walker Jr. and George Weiss, and their steadfast supporter Richard Nixon. New Breed muckrakers Jimmy Breslin and Jack Newfield both drifted from left to right populism through sixties, and Wilpon's family-values rebrand in the nineties continued to influence the franchise into the new millennium.

Nixonite columnist and Mets diehard Peggy Noonan entered the contested terrain of the people's team's significance during the 2000 Subway Series. Spinning the contest between the populist right and liberal elite, she wrote the Mets were the team of "square, flat Long Island and the striving unchic boroughs—the team of the middle and working class. . . . The Mets are the team of the nobodies. They are the team of those lacking in status, the ones with no special claims, the people who'll never be in style."

The Bronx Subway Series triumph to her typified Republican hopelessness at the end of the Bill Clinton's second term, with the Yankees, she wrote, representing the Democrats' traditional Tammany coalition of "Wall Street greedheads and deputy mayors and union chiefs and the kind of people who used to be called Broadway swells. And of course immigrants and working people."[479]

Al Gore, Hillary Clinton, and progressive mayoral candidate Mark Green all led the polls following the Yankee triumph. But in November, Noonan's underdog party pulled off the miracle the Mets could not. The right-wing-majority Supreme Court halted a Florida recount that Gore was likely to win, coronating Texas Rangers owner George W. Bush on some inscrutable technicality.

Still, the ignoramus's ascension appeared a momentary fluke. Hundreds of black-bloc anarchists threw eggs at his limo before his sparsely attended inauguration, and Bobby Valentine had to fight his way through protesters to visit his old boss on a White House trip to celebrate the 2000 NL champions.

Then came the attacks of September 11, 2001—an event Noonan described as a Metsian disaster in which we collectively "lost the national luxury of assuming nice things will happen."[480]

Liberalism's bounce-back after Reagan and Bush Sr. sprang from the illusion that a conflictual history had ended with the Cold War, thus restoring an inevitable arc toward indefinite economic and social progress. The morning of terror sent that trajectory chaotically astray through the legs of the Harvard-educated rules-based international order. In a single morning, all widely held antiwar, antiracist, and antiauthoritarian principles of American politics were wiped away, replaced by millions of American flags, making the entire country look like any street in Long Island's whitest enclaves. The popular rebirth of bloodthirsty patriotism following the attacks would infect every aspect of American society—including, finally, her beloved *Metties*.

The team was in Pittsburgh that morning, hopelessly behind the Braves at the tail end of their NL championship hangover season. They emerged from their hotel rooms as news of the first impact spread, gathering in the lobby to watch together as the towers burned and collapsed on live TV. "At that moment," Piazza wrote, "we realized, as most Americans did, that life in the world's greatest country had suddenly, tragically, changed."[481]

Moments later, their road manager received a call warning the danger was getting closer. Another plane hit the Pentagon, and yet another mysteriously crashed *outside of Pittsburgh*. Fearing they could be a target, the team bused back to New York. As they crossed the George Washington Bridge, they saw downtown Manhattan still enveloped in the concrete death cloud of ash.

For the first time not related to labor action, the baseball season was postponed indefinitely, and the team arrived at Shea hoping to get home to their families as soon as possible. But because all flights were grounded as well, Valentine instructed them to report the next morning for workouts, just in case.

As the manager drove home, he received a call that the city was moving its search-and-rescue operation base to Shea Stadium. He immediately turned the car around.

The team returned the next day to find Shea transformed into a bustling staging hub for first responders preparing to enter the tangled pit of Ground Zero—their manager in the thick of it, manically barking orders to position them at different work stations to sort supplies, run errands, and serve at the volunteers' kitchen. Valentine had several friends missing in the implosions. He believed his managerial expertise and creativity could help save them.

The team quickly proved their worth in the effort, even visiting Ground Zero to greet the ashen volunteers and pass out Mets caps. The first responders returned the favor the next day at Shea, gifting the Mets hats from FDNY, EMS, and NYPD.

But after days of digging, not a single survivor was found. Valentine's mania turned to despair, then anger. Just as he was about the pick up the phone to ask Bush about enlisting, the White House called first. Valentine would not be needed for the war on terror abroad, the message went, but for the war at home instead.

The now-unanimously-supported president told the country we had been attacked not because of America's Middle East foreign policy (as Osama Bin Laden stated), but because the terrorists "hate our freedom." The economic paralysis in the days after the attack thus appeared al-Qaeda's *true* victory, and the American people could fight back by courageously spending money at bars, restaurants, theaters, and malls. To support the effort, the Mets were to resume their schedule for a September 21 game against the Braves at Shea—the first mass gathering in New York since the attacks.

With relief staging moved back to Ground Zero, Shea reopened with patriotic pageantry. A red-white-and-blue ribbon replaced the Twin Towers in the center-field skyline logo above both teams lined up in their NYC first-responder caps. They removed them solemnly for the national anthem, and rushed forward to hug their Southern rivals with a crowd of over forty thousand powerfully chanting *USA! USA! USA!* When Mayor Giuliani was given special welcome at the end of the ceremony, the traditionally booed Yankee partisan received a prolonged ovation.

The game was tight and tense through the mid-seventh. Between innings, Liza Minnelli's punchy rendition of "New York, New York" woke up the city that doesn't sleep with its rally cry to "make a brand new start of it." After the Braves took a one-run lead the next inning, Piazza came to the plate with a runner on and finally hit back.

The network had instructed the broadcasters not to make "any references within the baseball vernacular to bombs and explosions and things like that," announcer Howie Rose recalled.[482] As the shot drifted toward the seats, Rose cautiously said, "This one has a chance . . ." Once the ball landed, Fran Healy lost all restraint: "This place exploded! This place has been waiting to explode all night!"[483]

Reporter Mike Puma wrote the game would go down as forever "linked to the healing that began for New York after 9/11." Howie Rose added that the homer "enabled us to see the significance of baseball in the lexicon of what America is." Valentine imagined Piazza's bomb traveling so far it would "land in Baghdad."[484]

Far from playoff contention, it hardly mattered that the Mets won that night or that every other team would perform the same nationalistic gestures in the days to come. Their Subway Series loss had proven they were not the best team in the city, but their relief efforts and taking the field on September 21 had made them the most *patriotic*. "I was glad it was us and not the Yankees," Al Leiter proudly recalled.[485]

"New York, New York" was soon replaced at Shea by Irving Berlin's "God Bless America." Written on the eve of World War I, the song that became the anthem for mobilization to Europe and Vietnam became baseball's seventh-inning standard as America prepared for war in the Middle East.

Two weeks later, the bloodshed of Operation Enduring Freedom began. Missiles rained on Afghanistan. Nearly 200,000 would die there by the time of the United States' retreat twenty years later. Even peacenik politicians and pundits gave Bush a blank check for endless war and domestic surveillance at home, as did the once antiwar Mets. Their unflinching support helped reassure an entire generation *this won't be Vietnam.*

The war underway, a massive ovation greeted George W. Bush's first pitch at the World Series in the Bronx. "Standing on the mound at Yankee Stadium was by far the most nervous moment of my presidency," he told ESPN. "A bounce would kind of reduce the defiance—the act of defiance toward the enemy."[486]

Fans and players continued to dutifully rise and salute the flag the next season as the US Army became bogged down in their doomed decades-long war against Taliban guerillas. They continued to pledge allegiance as Bush pressed on for an invasion of Iraq that was completely unrelated to the 9/11 attacks. The majority continued to bless America's new war, nonetheless, figuring it was in the same ballpark.

A few teams finally dropped "God Bless America" in 2003 when Bush prematurely declared the war in Iraq over. A year later, a civil war and brutal counterinsurgency still raged, and images of US soldiers gleefully torturing Iraqi detainees leaked in 2004. Finally, one all-star first baseman declared he would no longer stand for it.

"I don't rise for "God Bless America" because I don't believe it's right," Blue Jay Carlos Delgado told the *Toronto Star.* He had been an outspoken opponent of US militarism from his youth in Puerto Rico, where the US Navy had used the island of Vieques to test munitions since the seventies, terrorizing locals, poisoning the land and water, and wrecking its natural beauty. "I don't believe in the war. . . . I think it's the stupidest war ever. . . . Who are you fighting against? . . . We have more people dead now, after the war, than during the war. You've been looking for weapons of mass destruction. Where are they at?"[487]

Shea still reveled in its post-9/11 glory, continuing the "God Bless America" ritual each game. Like the war on terror, however, the patriotic

Mets found themselves in a quagmire of defeat. They had finished last the previous two seasons. As their nineties stars declined, offseason appeals to Latino free agents like Delgado who could revitalize the team were met with reluctance.

The baseball world now considered the Mets to be a thoroughly conservative operation. The team's franchise core of aspiring Republican politician Al Leiter, allegedly mob-connected union-militant John Franco, and newly devout Catholic Mike Piazza were all reputed to have unusual sway over the team's management and clubhouse culture. Leiter had banned hip-hop from the clubhouse, and Piazza firmly placed himself on the right wing of baseball's cultural divide by consistently opposing full revenue-shares for postseason games, and by his poor handling of allegations concerning his sexuality.[488]

These rumors began in 2001 when an editor at *Out* magazine asserted he was dating a closeted star ballplayer from a "major-league East Coast franchise."[489] A year later, Page Six interpreted a recent comment by Bobby Valentine that the majors were "probably ready for an openly gay player" to be a "preemptory strike" in advance of Piazza's admission that the *Out* letter was about him.[490] A subsequent *Gawker* blind item asserted he was not only dating weatherman Sam Champion, but that the two were building a beach house together.[491] While none of this was ever substantiated, many found the sensitive, intensely conflicted, and stylish catcher, who showed up to Shea one day with his hair sassily bleached blonde, a convincing closet case. For every fan who hoped it was all lie, many more prayed it was true, and that the happy couple would soon be seen proudly frolicking in Fire Island's elite gay enclaves without shame.

"First off, I'm not gay," Piazza said bluntly in a 2002 press conference putting the story to bed. "I'm heterosexual and I date women. That's it.

End of story."[492] While he did not condemn homosexuality, he also failed to cosign Valentine's call for tolerance with a Seinfeldian *not that there's anything wrong with that.*

What really dissuaded Latinos from joining Piazza's team, however, was his well-known hostility toward their demands. Since his time in Los Angeles, he had argued that foreign-born players were overly privileged because they received training in Caribbean academies. In 2003, Piazza opposed Mets second baseman Roberto Alomar's request for management to hire a translator so Spanish-speaking players could better express themselves at team meetings and to the press. "When they arrive on US soil," Piazza later wrote, "it's on the Latin players to learn English." When conflicts inevitably emerged due to these attitudes, he believed himself the victim of a "secret brotherhood, a Latin mafia type of thing that had it in for me."[493]

Further suspicions of anti-Latino bias in the Mets organization came from a history of disregarding Latino stars. Closer Armando Benítez, like Bobby Bonilla before him, was a frequent scapegoat for the team's failures since 1999. Melvin Mora and Edgardo Alfonzo were dumped at first sign of a slump, despite their postseason heroics. Bear-tooth-necklaced reliever Turk Wendell once told Vladimir Guerrero to "go frickin' back to the Dominican" after intentionally hitting him with a pitch.[494] How was it that the team playing within the largest Hispanic population center in the country had never fostered and promoted Latino talent to the same level as the Astros or Dodgers? It looked as though the team and front office had abandoned their neighbors in favor of Noonan's vision of a white suburbanite fan base, more likely to bring Latinos home to mow their lawn than for a barbecue.

Concerns about the organizational bias only deepened as post-9/11 Islamophobic hysteria turned against immigrant workers. Foreign-born Latinos then represented over a quarter of major-league rosters, a number comparable to the Hispanic percentage in service and manufacturing sectors of the US labor force as a whole. While most immigrant ballplayers, like their non-athlete counterparts, had to keep their head down and accept discipline and poverty as they worked toward a secure contract, their top stars were beloved in the US and in their home countries, where logos of their teams were proudly worn and painted in bodegas. The Mets emblem, however, was nowhere to be found. If given the choice between them and another team, what Puerto Rican, Venezuelan, or Dominican teen prospect or star free agent would sign to a club where they'd be treated as second-class players?

After another losing and low-attended 2004 season imperiled financing for a new stadium and cable network, Fred Wilpon finally understood the poor fit of the Mets' Uncle Sam mask. With full authority after buying out Nelson Doubleday (who had wanted to preserve Shea), he installed his neophyte son, Jeff, as chief operating officer to oversee a cultural shift; and fired Valentine for speaking out against the move. "The way things were going, who was going to want to watch our new network?" Jeff Wilpon worried. "Who cared about the Mets?"[495]

The facelift began as soon as the season ended with the hire of Omar Minaya as general manager. The Dominican-born, Queens-raised, lifelong Mets fan had already made his mark on baseball as a pioneer scout in the Caribbean in the nineties, where he had spotted and trained the likes of Sammy Sosa and Ivan "Pudge" Rodriguez. He became the Mets' assistant GM in the late nineties, a period in which he constantly pressed ownership to make the team more Latino-friendly. He gave up after 2001 and took a job in Montreal to become the MLB's first Latino general manager with the Expos. With Wilpon now admitting the error he had made by ignoring him and letting him walk, Minaya agreed to come back so long as he was given "full autonomy." This meant no interference in baseball matters from the Wilpons, let alone their clubhouse conservatives.

The request was granted and well publicized. Leiter and Franco left the team. Minaya hired Tony Bernazard as VP of player development, widely respected by Latino players for his central role in the MLBPA. Willie Randolph, the Brownsville native and New Breed Mets fan previously considered to coach the Mets and Yankees only as a "token candidate," became the first Black manager of any major New York sports team.[496]

The rapid restructuring sent a message throughout the free-agent market that the Mets had reversed their gaze from Long Island to the Black and brown inner city in a clear prelude to a spending spree. As Minaya set to work going after Delgado and Carlos Beltrán, his phone rang. On the other end was the star pitcher of the recent world champion Boston Red Sox, Pedro Martínez, inviting the new GM to his home in Santo Domingo.

Martínez was considered by many then, and many still today, as the greatest righty in the history of the game. It was widely believed that Martínez's rural Dominican magic, including carrying around little-person actor Nelson de la Rosa as a good-luck charm, had broken the Curse of the Bambino the previous year. But Pedro did not believe in curses, nor sabermetrics, as Red Sox GM Theo Epstein learned when he showed Martínez his declining statistics during early 2004 offseason contract negotiations. "You know what?" Martínez told him. "Why don't you take that computer and stick it up your ass, young buck—I'm out of here."[497]

The Mets' analysts had seen the same numbers as Epstein. After his 2001 rotator-cuff injury, he began walking more hitters, striking out fewer, and giving up homers at an above-average rate. But in Santo

Domingo, Minaya told him he didn't care about the numbers. Every game Martínez pitched ran on Dominican television, and even Dominican Yankees fans hung Pedro's photos in their uptown bars and turned out to root for him when he took the mound in the Bronx for the hated Red Sox. That popularity, Minaya admitted, would help rebrand the Mets to attract Latino prospects who, in turn, would help "build up their TV network."[498]

From there, the two spoke of the Mets' historic character. "Pedro's very spiritual," Minaya recalled of the meeting. "We talked about the underdog spirit."[499] He would do for the Mets what he had done for the Red Sox—restore team identity while banishing the dual superstitions of curses and statistics. All that was left to discuss was cash. After a short bidding war with the Red Sox, they agreed on a four-year, $53 million contract.

"Now that you have Pedro, I'm interested," Carlos Beltrán told the Mets shortly after Minaya closed the deal.[500] Wilpon had already sold Beltrán on his *New York-is-the-greatest-stage-in-the-world* sales pitch earlier that winter, convincing him to pursue a deal with the Yankees, instead. When they turned him down to avoid a luxury tax penalty, he called back, inking a seven-year $119 million contract days later.

Next Minaya went after the top prize—Carlos Delgado. He and Beltrán were such close friends, he assumed one Carlos guaranteed the other. But after years of having *USA! USA! USA!* grunted at him with each appearance in New York, Delgado suspected the Mets' newfound progressivism was only a cynical ploy to "play the race card." He demeaned Bernazard as "the highest-paid translator on the planet" during their meeting, and characterized his answer to Minaya afterward to the press: "I'm not doing you any favors, you're not doing me any favors because we're speaking in Spanish. I'm a man first."[501] Shortly after, Delgado signed with the Marlins for less than the Mets' opening offer.

To prove the rebrand was more than skin-deep, Minaya began appearing regularly on WADO, the Mets' Spanish-language radio station, and on WFAN's new *Latin Beat* sports talk show. Sponsorship deals with Puerto Rico's Banco Popular were arranged, which included free tickets and shuttle buses from the tri-state area's Hispanic neighborhoods to Shea. The sales department began hawking tickets with Beltrán's nickname for the team, the *New Mets,* translated by its newly hired Spanish-speaking operators to the new moniker ubiquitous in *El Diario* and in TV ads starring Colombian American actor John Leguizamo: *Los Mets.*

An additional campaign titled *Next Year Is Now* alluded to a 1947 Brooklyn Dodgers–like rebirth on citywide billboards reading: "Next Year Is a Crowded 7 Train" and "Next Year Is Pedro and Piazza Speaking the Same Language."[502] The line alluded both to Piazza's notorious distaste for the Spanish language, and a longstanding family feud with his new teammate. Pedro's brother Ramón had hurled complaints about Piazza's catching skills in LA, and Piazza errantly fired back comments calling Pedro's Red Sox contract an overpay. When the two faced each other in 1998, Pedro drilled Piazza with a pitch in revenge. "It shows you all that money can't buy you class," an injured Piazza said after the game. "He wants to talk about class?" Martínez responded. "He was a millionaire since he was a kid."[503]

A Flushing truce was declared that held throughout the 2005 season. Piazza transitioned to first base, allowing Martínez to throw to backup catcher Ramón Castro. The rest of the team jelled around Martínez's cheerleading positivity and Metsian sense of humor. During the first inning of one of his starts against the Diamondbacks, Shea's sprinklers came on just as Martínez took the mound. Instead of storming off the field, Martínez smiled, grabbed a towel, and frolicked in the chaos. "Only with the Mets," he wrote of the incident, "they have that wild, sometimes messy side to them, and this was another instance of it. If a sprinkler delay had happened at Yankee Stadium, heads would have rolled. I also reveled in it. Water and rain have always been a blessing to me."[504]

Attendance returned to 2000 levels, which Michael O'Keeffe of the *Daily News* attributed to Martínez, now the most popular player in New York according to a poll of sportswriters, and the thousands of new fans who came to each of his home starts: "His presence has turned Shea Stadium—which had the pizzazz of a morgue last year—into a funhouse this season. As he won 15 games with a 2.82 ERA, Pedro's energy and humor rejuvenated the Mets, turning the team from unlovable losers to exciting contenders."[505] They finished the season third in the division, ending the winning-season drought that began in 2001.

Minaya found more missing pieces for 2006, including Yankees ace Orlando "El Duque" Hernández, closer Billy Wagner, veteran shortstop José Valentín, forty-seven-year-old veteran Julio Franco, starter Óliver Pérez, and, at last, Carlos Delgado.

The inferior contract Delgado had signed with the Marlins the previous year lacked the no-trade clause the Mets had offered, allowing them to bring him to Shea in exchange for a slew of prospects. Delgado was happy to join Beltrán on a better team, he insisted to the press—but would he happily join him to *bless America* during the seventh inning stretch?

Even though the vast majority of the country now saw the war on terror as a pointless quagmire, and most other ballparks had ditched the jingoist relic, the Wilpons insisted the farce continue at Shea. "The Mets have a policy that everybody should stand for 'God Bless America,'" Jeff Wilpon said at Delgado's introductory press conference. "He's going to have his own personal views, which he's going to keep to himself."

Speaking next, Delgado reluctantly conceded to the mandate, adding: "Just call me Employee Number 21."[506]

The passive-aggressive remark referred to the uniform number Delgado had chosen as homage to Roberto Clemente. The fellow Puerto Rican slugger had supported the Civil Rights Movement, initiated the 1968 clubhouse revolt against playing before MLK's funeral (instrumental to the Mets' late-sixties reversal), and perished when a plane he had chartered to smuggle humanitarian aid past the US-backed far-right Nicaraguan government crashed in a storm. Understanding the strength of Delgado's convictions, Minaya had assured him after the trade he would be free to stand or sit as he pleased. But the bitter press conference confirmed his suspicions—the "full autonomy" of *Los Mets* was all a facade.

Fred and Jeff Wilpon were the shadow GMs, baseball insiders knew, with Minaya merely their chief advisor and spokesperson. Delgado arrived to a clubhouse with fewer Latino players than the major-league average, yet still riven by its notorious racial resentment. Adam Rubin anonymously quoted one Met sneering that year the team would soon be "up-and-coming third baseman David Wright and twenty-four Hispanic players."[507]

Pedro Martínez credited another cruel Wilpon intervention the previous summer for costing him the majority of the season. Randolph had agreed to give him extra time off to recover from a toe injury, only to be overruled by Jeff: "While I'm the boss here, you're going to have to do what I say."[508] Pedro's toe got worse after the start, and he spent most of 2006 on the bench as a cheerleader.

It was nonetheless their best season in decades. Beltrán and Delgado combined to hit 79 homers and 230 RBIs, José Reyes stole 64 bases, and Wright established early stardom by batting .311. They handily won the

NL East and swept the Dodgers in the division series, proceeding to a match-up against streaky St. Louis for the pennant.

The back-and-forth National League Championship Series is today solely remembered by Mets fans for two moments in its climactic seventh-game finale: Endy Chávez soaring over the left-field wall to rob a home run in the sixth to keep the game tied, and Beltrán's at bat in the bottom of the ninth.

New York was down two runs with two outs and the bases loaded. A hit would tie and bring Delgado to bat, and an extra-base hit would clinch the pennant. The count 0–2, Beltrán watched the rookie Adam Wainwright throw a curveball, letting it pass without even a Casey-like whiff. Behind him, real-estate mogul turned reality TV star Donald Trump ominously leered with an umpire-like glare as strike three was called, and the Mets' season ended.

The two moments took on the character of America's view of Latin workers as a whole. On one hand there was Chávez, a Venezuelan journeyman loudly cheered with *Endy sí, Chávez no!* by some expats in protest of their homeland's socialist president. His defensive heroics were characteristic of the "self-made" mythos around Caribbean players. Crusoe-like on their destitute islands, they were thought to have learned the game, sportswriter Dave Zirin wrote, "without shoes, using cut-out milk cartons for gloves, rolled-up cloth for balls, and sticks and branches for bats." Training on these uneven playing fields had made Edgardo Alfonzo and Rey Ordóñez the centerpieces of the greatest defensive infield in baseball history for the Mets in the late nineties, and now Chávez had become the latest *Horacio Alger* to leap above his station.

Carlos Beltrán, on the other hand, was expected to be nothing short of Señor Octubre since hitting eight home runs and batting .435 for the Astros in their 2004 postseason. Despite Beltrán batting nearly .300 with 3 home runs in the NLCS, David Wright wrote in 2020 he still frequently hears the caught-looking that closed the series singled-out for the entirety of the team's failure. Wright responds to the scapegoating that the Mets had never faced the rookie Wainwright before, who in years to come would establish himself as an elite closer. "So, no, I don't blame Beltrán one bit. I don't think anyone should. We never would have gotten to where we did that year without him."[509]

The xenophobic cognitive dissonance of *Endy sí, Beltrán no!* fueled to a fever pitch for the remainder of the *Los Mets* era. WFAN callers and cable news pundits alike painted Hispanic immigrants, America's economic backbone, as lazy, privileged, and selfishly working in the world's biggest market for the big bucks, alone. Early-nineties gripes about overpaid free agents and *welfare queens* combined with the recent paranoia of Third-World invasion. Legislation advanced to treat the US-Mexico border as the new front in the War on Terror, and the Department of Homeland Security, created by Bush under the pretense of preventing another terrorist attack, spawned the gestapo-like Immigration and Customs Enforcement (ICE). Now, every petty caught-looking would be treated as a nothing short of a crime against America.

The rise of baseball's Latino stars was a century in the making, beginning with America's imperial expansion into Spanish Caribbean territory at the dawn of the twentieth century. Plantation workers in Cuba, Venezuela, and Puerto Rico were taught the game as a way to both discipline and indoctrinate them into the superior ways of their new American overseers. Two generations later, a handful of white and mestizo players made it to the majors, long before Blacks were permitted in the game.

The largest influx of Latin American ballplayers came in the nineties following the passage of NAFTA as major-league teams combined Branch Rickey's farm system with the offshoring techniques of US manufacturers by setting up low-overhead academies in Venezuela, Puerto Rico, the Dominican Republic, and South Korea to train thousands of prospects from an early age.[510] In *Welcome to the Terrordome*, Zirin compared these offshore academies to sweatshops, arguing that MLB has a responsibility "to provide them with a real education," and wages "commensurate with what US players are making." Knowing the owners would never do this voluntarily, he called on stars like Martínez and Delgado to pressure their union to "demand that baseball not merely strip-mine the DR of its baseball talent and ambition, but give something back to those who can't turn on a 96 mph fastball. That is what is called globalization from below: accept the new global commercial realities, but also demand that social justice and human rights accompany those realities."[511]

Zirin's proposal reflected the vision of the internationalist *alter-globalization* movement that sprung from Seattle's anti-WTO riots in 1999—demands for fair compensation, safe conditions, and workplace autonomy for the lowest rungs of an increasingly globally intertwined working class. While the MLB supplies the best of its offshore output with the necessary visas to work legally, the same can't be said for those working in the slaughterhouses that make ballpark franks, the farm workers harvesting potatoes for fries and milking cows for little batting helmets of soft-serve, and the domestic workers who care for the front office's homes and families. Every aspect of MLB's backend, like the American economy in general, reaps its profits from the heavy exploitation of Latin American and other immigrant and offshore labor—from the cooks, cleaners, and tailors in ballparks, to the production of merchandise and equipment in free-trade zone factories throughout the Caribbean, Latin America, Bangladesh, and Indonesia.

The standard major-league baseball, for example, is itself painstakingly hand-sewn by hundreds of workers at a Rawlings sweatshop in

Costa Rica. A worker there told the *Times* in 2004 that after working in temperatures that exceed ninety degrees for thirteen years, he made under $3,000 a year. "The balls have to be exactly alike, totally perfect," he said, "and for this work people are paid $50 or $60 a week. A machine can't make them—it has to be done by hand. But they demand the precision and speed of a machine." One workers' rights advocate monitoring the factory told the *Times*: "If the players would actually stand up, it would have enormous consequences."[512]

Activist pressure campaigns against third-world sweatshops succeeded in forcing transnationals like Nike to alter its policies, and inspired American Apparel to market its living wages and legal advocacy for immigrant workers in its ads. The MLB and MLBPA, however, responded to the protests with feigned ignorance of the low-wage, high-intensity production process injurious to the vast majority of ballmakers. The Latin-friendly promotions of Los Mets and other teams likewise only responded to pressure from workers and consumers to confront anti-Latino sentiment publicly, while turning a blind eye to all off-field exploitation.

As the global war on terror turned against US immigrants in 2006, grassroots organizing on shop floors and online culminated in the millions-strong May 1 Day Without an Immigrant general strike—the largest in the history of the United States. "Restaurants were shuttered, meat processing plants were idled, ripe fruit laid waiting to be picked, and the nation's largest port stood at a near standstill," Adam Welch wrote in the *Industrial Worker*. "Classrooms were empty in some cities as well, as students, often joined by teachers and staff, skipped school in support."[513]

The mass work stoppage shook the US economy. Draconian anti-immigrant legislation that would criminalize undocumented workers was stopped in its tracks. Still, there was no sign of Zirin's suggested support for the movement from baseball's Latino stars. Gary Sheffield speculated that these players now found themselves in a role similar to the Black integrators of the 1950s—a new phase of the owners' strategy of filling rosters with players in positions more precarious, and thus more obedient, than those who came before. "They have more to lose than we do. You can send them back across the island. You can't send us back. We're already here."[514]

While these comments drew quick condemnation from sportswriters claiming Sheffield was pitting players against one another, his Venezuelan Tiger teammate, Carlos Guillén, told the *Detroit Free Press*: "I'm glad somebody spoke up. . . . In my first at-bat, I hit a double, and I missed first base. I was out, and they screamed at me. I didn't know what to say. If I had said anything, they would have sent me home. . . . That happens to every Latin player. They are afraid to talk."[515]

What would it have meant for the Mets if players like Delgado had not been so publicly intimidated into silence? The case of Martínez being forced to play injured indicated the team could have at least avoided the epidemic of injuries that persisted through the rest of the Wilpons' reign. In a similar incident the previous year, Jeff Wilpon forced newly signed Japanese star Kazuo Matsui to play a televised spring-training game with a broken finger to "build excitement" for a season in which he would spend thirty-eight games on the disabled list.[516] In 2008, an unnamed Mets executive called Billy Wagner a "wimp" for mentioning a pain in his elbow, which soon required season-ending Tommy John surgery.[517]

Aside from the health benefits, encouraging players to openly express themselves often deepens identification with fans. Freethinkers like Pedro Martínez were beloved for having more to say about the Mets' struggles than the generic *we played hard out there* pablum, just as Donn

Clendenon, Cleon Jones, Tom Seaver, and Tug McGraw won back the New Breed by signaling their support for the Civil Rights Movement and opposition to the Vietnam War. Were they permitted to do so, Los Mets could have given voice to the widespread exhaustion with post-9/11 saber-rattling, or led the baseball front in the movement against the racist scapegoating of Latin American workers. They could have done so without even straying from the sport's middle-class idealism—immigrants, through their tireless work of accepting low wages to keep the American economy strong, deserve *at least* the narrow security, opportunity, and autonomy of native-born workers.

The Mets had, in fact, found success through embracing some form of meaningful partisanship in every prior decade. In the early aughts, however, the team could only mirror New York's broader retreat from leftist politics: class-neutral, profit-motivated, uncritically patriotic, and apolitically diverse. And just as the alter-globalization and antiwar movements fizzled in Bush's lame-duck term, the Mets became synonymous with catastrophic late-season chokes.

The first historic collapse came in the final weeks of the 2007 season. As a seven-game lead in the NL East disappeared in their 5–12 closing stretch that cost them a return to the playoffs, a *Late Night With Conan O'Brien* sketch showed Mr. Met attempting to put his too-large head in an oven, then through a noose, and chug pills that would not enter his false mouth.

This time, Willie Randolph caught much of the blame for their failure to advance. When struggles carried over into the 2008 season, he told *The Bergen Record* that the heat he and others took appeared motivated, in part, by racism.[518] He apologized for the comments after a media backlash, but a month later, as the team climbed toward a winning record on a California road trip, Randolph was fired.[519]

While the sections at Shea who chanted *Fire Willie!* were satiated, the cruel timing reminded others of Grant's midnight massacre or

Steinbrennerian vindictiveness.[520] A Black coworker of mine said he tossed his Mets caps in the trash when he heard the news, vowing to never support the team again.

The Los Mets campaign officially ended with the firing of Bernazard and Minaya soon after. Moving forward, the team's identity would be based not around Carlos Beltrán, José Reyes, or Johan Santana, but third baseman and future team captain David Wright. The straitlaced son of a Norfolk Police Department chief was a law-and-order opponent of drugs and cheating, a clutch hitter, and an enthusiastic ambassador to fans. But to many in the fan base, like *So Many Ways to Lose* author Devin Gordon, Wright lacked the unique Mets spirit identified by Minaya and Martínez: "[He] looked like Captain America, so he got to be the anointed one."[521]

Gary Sheffield, who briefly became a Met in 2009, put Gordon's sentiment another way: "The plain fact is that white owners want white franchise players. White men want white sons."[522]

However superficial the pretenses of the Los Mets experiment had been, its corporate goals were achieved. The attendance boom won increased authority for Jeff Wilpon, a deal for the team-owned Sports New York (SNY) premium cable station to rival the Yankees' YES Network, and $616 million in public funds to build an $850 million new park to replace Shea.

The giveaway, along with a Yankee Stadium replica built in the Bronx, found further pretense as part of New York's bid to host the 2012 Olympics Games. London won, but taxpayers footed the bills anyway. Shea Stadium had been the result of a similar cash grab, only this time the new ballparks would belong to the teams, not the city.

Blueprints for the new park displayed Fred Wilpon's singular nostalgia for the Brooklyn Dodgers. His designs for Jackie Robinson Field honored Ebbets' brick-dominant design and arching main entrance. Inside the modernist-retro facade, however, would be a cookie-cutter ballpark, improving on many of Shea's quirky flaws, with no added character.

A $400 million ad buy from the Wilpons' banking partner sacrificed another element of the vision. Although images and quotes from outspoken Robinson would hang in the rotunda, the new park's name would perfectly reflect New York City's transformation after decades of selling its identity to finance capital—*Citi* Field.

Days before the greatest financial crisis since the Great Depression, with Citi's shell rising ominously on the horizon, the Mets played their final scheduled game at Shea on September 28, 2008. They were in the midst of another impressive late-season choke, having led the division most of the month until collapsing again with six losses in nine games. Still, a win in that final game against the Marlins could give them a wild-card slot, and a dignified death for Shea.

After a quiet first few innings, Beltrán, the lonely hero of the suddenly anemic batting order, homered to tie the game 2–2 in the sixth. The Marlins answered with two homers in the eighth, and the Mets "went down without a whimper" from there, Keith Hernandez wrote in *Shea Good-Bye*: "And suddenly reality set in for their fans everywhere: the Mets have done it again. . . . [SNY] Director Bill Webb panned his cameras through the stands at Shea, focusing on individual shots of a bevy of distraught Mets fans. It was a montage of despair—some fans were crying, others were speechless, with gaping mouths and hands on top of their heads."[523]

It was the dark version of Fred Wilpon's perennial mission of playing "meaningful games in September." When he made this remark in 2004, he evoked an underdog team battling for a playoff spot. Now they were a wealthy team struggling against another historic collapse—an inside job his son Jeff openly fantasized about hastening by driving a bobcat through Shea as soon as the season ended.[524]

In a postgame ceremony, a procession of Mets heroes, including Ed Charles, Cleon Jones, Ron Swoboda, and Willie Mays, touched home plate for the final time and shuffled into the dugout darkness. Seaver closed the ceremony with a last pitch to Piazza. The two walked off the field as Oyster Bay bard Billy Joel performed "New York State of Mind," a funerary alternative to "New York, New York," traditionally played after Met losses.

Chapter 12

ATROCITI FIELD

During Shea Stadium's final games, Christopher Nolan's record-breaking blockbuster *The Dark Knight* portrayed New York City as the neo-noir Gotham. Besieged by an underworld network of gangsters, politicians, and financial elites, antisocial violence spins out of control. The anonymous vigilante Batman reemerges as the city's last hope to oppose the ringleader—a nihilist bank robbing clown named Joker. During the chase, Joker threatens to unmask Gotham's people's hero as the millionaire Bruce Wayne—the product of the same corporate-criminal web he claimed to be fighting. Wrestling with the contradiction, Batman fakes his own death, telling Commissioner Gordon that "you either die a hero, or you live long enough to see yourself become a villain."[525]

The Mets found themselves in a similar position as they prepared to open their luxurious new home. Their reputation as the people's team had worn thin after three decades of top salaries, and a franchise valuation that jumped from $21 million in 1980 to nearly a billion with the construction of Citi Field.[526] Still, in the shadow of the far richer and aesthetically evil Yankees, that vast wealth could always be overlooked by fans who presumed the Mets were eternal underdogs generally on the side of *good*.

But as Shea came tumbling down alongside the global economy, their dark secret was revealed. The exponentially expanding fortune behind the team had never been the product of gate receipts or Wilpon's wise investments, as devoted fans presumed. The Mets were instead funded by golden eggs, laid by a Penguin-like banker who was among the greatest villains of the coming Great Recession.

Fred Wilpon first encountered Bernie Madoff, like he had Nelson Doubleday, at the dawn of the eighties through their kids' wealthy Roslyn school district. Madoff was then an ambitious salesman, working his way up from the grifty penny-stock trade to pioneer computerized trading. Along the way, he opened a private wealth-management business that delivered its small circle of clients annual returns of 18 to 20 percent with astounding regularity.

While top investment companies like Goldman Sachs and Merrill Lynch refused to touch what most presumed to be an unregistered hedge fund, Wilpon saw those firms as Yankee-like compared to the scrappy ingenuity of Madoff. By the end of the decade, nearly every penny of Wilpon's real estate and sports holdings corporation Sterling Equities was invested with Madoff, who had made his headquarters in Wilpon's Midtown Lipstick Building.

From Wilpon's prestigious perch, Madoff appeared a figure comparatively trustworthy to the notorious Wall Street rogues downtown.

He chaired the Nasdaq in 1990, later serving as advisor to the Securities and Exchange Commission, where he was considered for chairman. With the increased credibility came billions more in investments from a growing list of clients, including America's wealthiest financiers, European banks, philanthropic organizations, and in-the-know upper-middle-class retirees.

The enormous returns allowed the Mets to operate nearly at cost as a loss leader for Sterling's portfolio. Wilpon directed all team profit to a payroll only surpassed only by Steinbrenner's Yankees, knowing if the Mets stayed relevant, blue-chip prospective clients would eventually become his captive audience at Shea's luxury boxes. It seemed a perfect system, where interest on cash created interest in baseball, which in turn provided more cash investment from the select clientele of Gotham's baseball-loving elite.

When Steinbrenner sold his shipping company in the nineties, Wilpon believed himself poised to eclipse his wealth and elevate the Mets back to their premier mid-eighties status. And yet, no amount of money or business ingenuity seemed to deliver the consistent pennants and championships that could bring Sterling's stature to the next dynastic level. Where, Wilpon must have wondered, was his baseball Madoff?

In the early aughts, the publication of Michael Lewis's *Moneyball: The Art of Winning an Unfair Game* kicked off an algorithmic arms race. The book described how Athletics general manager Billy Beane used sabermetric methods (learned, in part, as a Met under Davey Johnson) to turn a team with $33 million into a postseason competitor with the $111 million Yankees in 2001. Through mathematical ingenuity, small-market teams could build affordable journeyman rosters, combining overlooked individual talents to synergize more wins. Fred and Jeff Wilpon counted themselves among the book's fervent devotees, believing the miracle alchemy of 1969 had finally been decoded, and the combination of moneyball and Madoff-made millions would revive Mets magic.

The strategy, already counterintuitive to most field-level managers, was implemented at Shea with chaotic top-down shifts in strategy, personnel, and budget. By the 2006 playoff race, fortunes spent on big contracts for players and analysts alike had left day-to-day operations threadbare. But when Wilpon asked Madoff to withdraw $54 million to buy out his previous broadcasting contract to launch SNY, Madoff responded the money was tied up, offering an interest-free loan instead.

The next year, the team's financial officers realized they would again run out of operational expenses without a playoff berth. When the Mets choked, their solution, Howard Megdal wrote in *Wilpon's Folly*, was to again attempt to "scrap[e] the last bit from all of the Madoff accounts."[527]

The bubble burst shortly after. Citigroup, the Mets' largest corporate sponsor, reported massive losses in late 2007 from their exposure to the failure of millions of subprime mortgages, pushed aggressively to lower-working-class clients who had demonstrated no ability to pay them. When the news revealed investment in the predatory and fraudulent debt was widespread among major financial institutions, the markets entered a winter free fall. Bank stocks dropped up to 40 percent. Lehman Brothers filed for the largest bankruptcy in US history. Citibank and Bear Stearns, Sterling and Madoff's major trading partner, neared collapse. Wilpon's knocks on the door of Madoff's Lipstick lair were now joined by thousands of others, desperate to secure their share of the $17.3 billion fund before it was gone.

The money wasn't there, they soon learned—and never had been. Instead of investing the money, Madoff had taken it for himself, using the remainder of new investments to pay out his previous clients' annual returns. A few new suckers were found to float the decades-long scam, but he was broke by fall. With nowhere left to run, he took one last limo ride from the Lipstick Building to Wall Street, where he turned himself in to the FBI.

After news of the largest Ponzi scheme in history broke in December 2008, Jeff Wilpon confirmed the reports linking his father to Madoff. He insisted, however, that they had no knowledge of the scheme, that only Sterling's partners had been affected, and that the team itself was self-sufficient.[528] This was a blatant lie, Megdal wrote, because the team's "primary source of working capital no longer existed."[529]

The truth came out when Madoff's middle-class victims began searching for compensation from his biggest profiteers. They found Sterling and the Mets were far more heavily invested in the scam than they were letting on, holding a stunning 483 accounts with Madoff.[530] Wilpon branded himself a savvy investor, yet his full purchase of the team from Doubleday in 2002, and exorbitant player spending in deferred payments—most notoriously, the buyout of Bobby Bonilla's $5 million contract for five times its value, paid in annual installments over twenty-five years—indicated a strange faith that the enormous returns would always keep coming. Even when he allegedly sensed trouble in the early aughts and began diversifying funds away from Madoff, one investment went to the smaller "Bayou Superfund" Ponzi scheme, exposed in 2005.

Whether or not fans believed Wilpon's defense that he was only an unwitting chump, animosity accumulated against him and the rest of the financial elite as the Great Recession's effects hit. Hundreds of thousands of jobs were lost in the city, doubling the unemployment rate, increasing food stamp enrollment by 50 percent, and homelessness by about 25 percent.[531,532,533] Billionaire Mayor Michael Bloomberg announced a new round of severe budget cuts to public agencies and social services, further exacerbating the crisis's effects on the working class.

With his golden goose in the pen, Wilpon followed suit by slashing payroll for players, analytics, and even the team medical department—a likely contributor to the astounding rash of player injuries that cost the Mets more wins than any team in the National League through 2016.[534] A disdainful fan base dropped attendance by almost a million in the inaugural season of the Citigroup-branded ballpark, with another million disappearing over the next three miserable years. Even after the cuts, the falling revenue, the millions owed in deferred payments, and the costs of fighting the $1 billion suit Madoff's victims brought against Wilpon, spiraled annual losses toward $70 million by 2011. Far from a consolatory people's team during these dark times, the Mets appeared more like the next crooked financial institution headed toward a deserved doom.

At the tail end of their third consecutive losing season in 2011, the Mets finally showed some life with a 12–2 win in Atlanta. Statistically eliminated after handily losing six straight at home prior, they had appeared "devoid of purpose" and "drifting aimlessly through the final weeks," Andrew Keh wrote in the *Times,* until the offensive burst that the players attributed to wanting to play spoiler to their longtime rivals. "They are playing for something," outfielder Angel Pagan told Keh. "We want to prevent them from getting it."[535] The Mets went on to win the series, and the Braves ended up missing the wildcard by a single game.

A day after the blowout, thousands of demonstrators found similar purpose by turning their Recession despair into combat against society's front-runners. After a rowdy march through Wall Street, they set up camp a stone's throw from the *Charging Bull* statue in Zuccotti Park. Combining the colorful and disruptive street tactics of the Yippies and alter-globalization with inspiration from anti-austerity square occupations in Europe and the Middle East, the Occupy movement spread its encampments to over seventy cities nationwide and nearly a thousand internationally, vowing to stay put until Barack Obama bailed out the 99 percent of people who had lost savings, jobs, and homes in the crisis, instead of the 1 percent whose greed had caused it.

Howard Megdal proposed a similar solution as he covered the 2011 lawsuit alleging Wilpon was a "willfully blind" accomplice to Madoff. Instead of fighting the charges to the end in an attempt to preserve the Mets as a starving cash cow for replenishing his ill-gotten fortune, Wilpon could settle the suit by transferring ownership to the middle-class clients burned by Madoff. The Mets would "suddenly represent both the fan-owned excitement of the NFL's [publicly-owned] Green Bay Packers . . . and helping people who lost everything due to a heinous criminal. . . . Imagine the ads! 'Take your family to the ballpark—and help this family get back on their feet.'"[536]

Megdal's redistributive idea gained little traction, and neither did Occupy's. Despite Obama's promises of *hope and change*, the Bulls and White Sox fanatic was as chauvinistic in his defense of the elite as those teams' anti-worker owner, Jerry Reinsdorf. In the late fall, Obama made his politics clear by coordinating police nationwide to evict the squares and crush all attempts at reoccupation. When a general strike called for May Day 2012 never materialized, Obama and Wall Street considered the threat safely passed. Days before Wilpon's trial was set to begin that spring, the $1 billion suit was settled for $162 million.

With Madoff sentenced to 150 years as scapegoat for the rest of the corporate crooks who enabled him and created the broader crisis, business was free to slowly return to Bush-era hubris. "Stock markets recovered, banks cut their losses and consolidated," Marxist writer Loren Goldner observed in the aftermath of Obama's bailouts and suppression of Occupy, "the top 1% of the population continued to take an ever-greater percentage of 'income growth,' while in the US, the 'real economy' stagnated or declined."[537] Hundreds of thousands who had lost homes and jobs, many of them African Americans making their first foray into the middle class, got nothing.

In an episode of *Family Guy* during this bleak era, Stewie Griffin sits at Citi Field. "Opening day, and here's the first pitch," the broadcaster says, immediately followed by a mighty crack. "And the season's over." Stewie throws down his Mets cap in disgust.[538]

The same joke about the Mets' chronic hopelessness had been employed by reference comics for decades interchangeably with the cursed Cubs, Bill Clinton's libido, and Donald Trump's ridiculous hairdo. Even with their brief playoff runs, new stadium, TV network, and the beloved captain David Wright, the Mets always managed to revert comfortably back to this punchline mean—less Billy Beane than Mr. Bean.

But the Madoff affair supplemented the familiar feeling of inadequacy with the new existential peril of economic free fall. Fans had little confidence that the *Wilponzis,* as they now called them, could scheme their way to safety through a moneyball-style recreation of Madoff in the aggregate. He had assembled a rogues' gallery of investors, including Trump colleague Anthony Scaramucci, racist comedian Bill Maher, alleged 1-800-Flowers fraudster James McCann, and insider-trading billionaire Steve Cohen.[539] Even the notorious pyramid scheme Amway got in on the action, opening its sole storefront—a juice bar—at Citi Field. When Megdal visited hoping to buy a juice, or any other physical product, he found the shop didn't actually sell anything at all.[540]

Commissioner Bud Selig intervened by installing Sandy Alderson as austerity-minded general manager for the 2011 season. The Vietnam-era CIA agent turned corporate lawyer had run the Athletics in their early moneyball years, earning a reputation, A's outfielder Dusty Baker said, as the first GM "from the business side."[541] He was promoted from there to MLB operations, where he impressed brass by crushing an umpire strike in 1999, and providing PR for the scandal-ridden Dominican training camps in the aughts. Ten years later, the Mets became the latest disgrace that needed his corporate-minded crisis management.

With more autonomy than Minaya ever had, square Alderson smoothed Wilponian eccentricity. He defied fan protests at Citi to let beloved speedster José Reyes sign elsewhere to keep Wright. Beltrán was traded to the Giants for prospect Zack Wheeler. Bobby Valentine look-alike Terry Collins became manager, proving nowhere near as memorable during his competent seven-season stint. "The fun is long gone," George Vecsey wrote in the *Times*. "Alderson is coming in after the party is over and he's had to kind of open the windows and hose it down."[542]

"Just keep doing your job, guys," is how pitcher R. A. Dickey summarized Alderson's *Don't think* philosophy. It was a mandate to accept the austerity regime without question: "We're deep in our diamond-shaped cocoon. . . . Maybe we'll be staying at Motel 6s on the road this year."[543]

A knuckleballer salvaged by Minaya from baseball's scrap heap in 2010, Dickey became the surprise winner of the Cy Young Award of the season in 2012, which served as a lone bright spot of the rebuild year. In his memoir *Wherever I Wind Up*, Dickey tells a story of overcoming a tortured past of disability, sexual abuse, sleeping in abandoned buildings, biking to games, and the poverty of minor-league life to make it to the Mets. In contrast to the on-paper perfection of Wright, Dickey reminded fans of Tug McGraw, Turk Wendell, and so many other idiosyncratic dark horses the team seemed to welcome with open arms.

Screwball reliever Daniel Herrera was excited about his 2011 trade to New York from Milwaukee. He appreciated escaping previous teams' strict dress codes—nobody cared about his long hair or baggy jersey on the

Mets. The uncompetitive clubhouse's atmosphere was lighthearted, with teammates sometimes sharing joints after games. "It was just a place that most everyone wanted to play," he said, "where people knew they could be themselves and have their personality kind of come out as well."[544]

The everyman identity of players like these kept the Mets' traditional countercultural fan base alive. Mets hats were as ubiquitous at Occupy Wall Street as they had been in mass movements since the sixties, a sign that the returning millennial children of white flight settling in hip enclaves along the L train stilll embraced the brand, even after the financial crisis they had helped kick off mortgaged their futures.

The hipster love, reclaimed from the sixties in the aughts, can be traced to the twee Mr. Met shirts made in the nineties by indie rock band Yo La Tengo—named for 1962 shortstop Elio Chacón's Spanish-language call of *I got it!* misheard by his gringo teammates as "yellow tango." Another twee band, indie-pop Glaswegians Belle and Sebastian, released a beautiful ode to Mike Piazza in 2003, in which two eloping lovers escape their dreary work lives to watch a Mets game and fantasize about his rumored homosexuality."[545]

Shoutouts came too from hip-hop legends like the Beastie Boys, Pharoahe Monch, Action Bronson, A Tribe Called Quest, and, most frequently, Nas. Unlike braggadocious Yankees references by Jay-Z, Cam'ron, and Ghostface Killah, the Mets were mentioned as an offbeat icon of city life, referencing the emcees' working-class Queens origins and quotidian heartbreaks. New York's hardcore and punk scenes similarly repped the Mets as signifiers of the DIY underground. "When I go to a gig and I see punks with Yankees hats on," Herrera said, "I'm intrigued how that fits into their ethos. The majority of punks I see at shows and hardcore fests, it's lots of Mets hats."[546]

Advertised as an inferior yet legit urban brand, suburban transplants embraced the Mets to ease their gentrification anxiety while straddling the line between authenticity and irony. Since moving to Williamsburg in 2006, I gravitated toward this hipster stereotype of fashionable nonchalance. While I occasionally wore vintage Mets caps scored from free boxes or thrift shops, I mostly stopped following the team as I became an anarchopunk following the Subway Series and the Mets' embracing post-9/11 chauvinism. An anti-corporate Occupier a decade later, I rolled my eyes when punks or comrades told me the Mets were somehow still the people's team.

Evidence for my cynicism came when Dickey was traded to Toronto after his Cy Young season. In return, the Mets got flamethrowing prospect Noah Syndergaard. For his Norwegian heritage and Viking locks, he earned the nickname "Thor," after the god of the Norse pantheon appropriated by Marvel as a superhero. He joined Captain America Wright, and a rotation headed by Matt Harvey, nicknamed the "Dark Knight of Gotham" by *Sports Illustrated* for his Batman-esque gloomy stoicism and fondness for New York's noir nightlife.

Harvey's moniker arrived with the final installment of Nolan's Batman trilogy, *The Dark Knight Rises*. The blockbuster cynically depicted Occupy Wall Street as useful idiots, their protests against the financial elite serving as cover for the pseudo-populist strongman Bane to attack the stock exchange, empty the prisons, and finally seize the entire city. "We take Gotham from the corrupt! The rich!" he announces. "The oppressors of generations who have kept you down with myths of opportunity, and we give it back to you, the people!"[547] As mobs drag the wealthy into the streets, Bane bankrupts Wayne Enterprises, forcing a broke Batman to return from self-exile to stop him from blowing up Gotham to avenge crimes of Western civilization, and to restore his family's wealth.

Alderson's austerity-era superhero rebrand followed this conceit. The Mets were no longer the adorable antiheroes of the funny pages or Adam

West's Batman from the zany sixties' series, but hulking vigilantes from the grittified Marvel and DC comic universes. Their mission was to save the Mets, and thus the city itself, from a Great Recession malaise only worsened by the anarchistic anger of Occupy and the emerging Movement for Black Lives. That Bruce Wayne, like the Mets, was a scion of the criminal elites whose greed created and fostered their underworld counterparts no longer mattered—Harvey's Dark Knight signal shone in the night sky as a lonely beacon of hope that social peace would be restored.

But dark-horse heroes still surrounded the Justice League core. There was union leader and "nicest guy in baseball" Curtis Granderson; Wilmer Flores, the middle-position soul of the team after his on-field tears reversed an announced trade mid-game; and Jacob deGrom, a self-branded "simple man" drafted in the 272nd round as a shortstop and retrained into an elite pitcher.[548] "These young guys really took the brunt of that [low] payroll," Herrera said, referring to how the young players were cruelly optioned between the majors and minors to keep costs and service time low. Even as they stayed nearly the worst-paid team in baseball in 2014, the Mets' historic formula of stellar pitching to compensate for lackluster offense elevated them to second place in the NL East.

And yet attendance, which had sunk throughout sports in the Great Recession, stayed nearly worst in the NL that year. Citi Field sorely missed the DIY enthusiasm that one fan said felt "buried behind with the rubble of blue Shea."[549] And even to the extent that some wanted to buy into the superhero branding, Wilpon's crooked front office culture appeared alive and well. Clubhouse manager and Wilpon loyalist Charlie Samuels was busted stealing millions in game-used memorabilia, and Jeff Wilpon cost the team another big settlement after allegations of harassing and firing of an employee for becoming pregnant out of wedlock.[550]

A protest of fans fed up with the Wilponzis opened the 2015 season. A crowdfunded billboard campaign outside Citi featured Mr. Met grimacing alongside the words: *FRED, JEFF, SAUL . . . SELL THE TEAM.* Another, playing on the 1973 slogan, read: YA GOTTA LEAVE![551]

The front office responded to the discontent in an open letter to fans. Cosigned by many of the team's historic greats, it argued the Mets' struggles were not a result of mismanagement and low payroll, but the lack of faith in Fred and Jeff to right the ship. "The victory you earn is sweeter than the victory you're given," it venomously opened, concluding with an order to show their "Mets pride" by signing what sportswriters called a "loyalty oath" to Alderson's *Don't Think* strategy.[552] When the unprecedented passive aggression from ownership received swift backlash, several of the players rescinded their signatures.

The Wilpons faced further protests that year against their Lex Luthor–like plans to seize and destroy the approximately 250 metalworks, demolition yards, and auto body shops ringing Citi Field. This unsightly "Iron Triangle" zone had been considered an eyesore since the dawn of the automobile age in the 1920s, when Robert Moses began converting the area into parkland. But even after the completion of Flushing Meadows Corona Park, the US Tennis center, Shea Stadium, and Citi Field, a misshapen shard of the ad-hoc industrial park remained. Their original Italian and Greek immigrant owners had gradually turned over the shops to their Hispanic employees, who maintained them as an anachronistic remnant of an earlier mode of production—a cooperative ecosystem that shared skills and parts to offer quick and inexpensive service for motorists.

Wilpon and other developers, including Donald Trump, followed in Moses's footsteps with plan after plan for the city to force out the shops by seizing the land through eminent domain. Hundreds of workers would be displaced, and the city's motorists would be left at the mercy of chains like AutoZone and Pep Boys in exchange for a shopping mall, casino, condos, amusement park, or, most popularly, another athletic facility.

The financial collapse had put the project on hold until around 2013, when a modified blueprint allowed the city to finally seize most of the Iron Triangle for a soccer stadium and adjoining luxury housing. With evictions looming, the shop owners and workers organized protests outside City Hall and Citi Field, recalling those that had targeted the World's Fair fifty year prior. Their signs linked Wilpon, Madoff, Bloomberg, Queens Borough President Claire Shulman, and the NYPD in a racist and corrupt web working to benefit real estate magnates instead of Queens' working class. Some targeted the Mets directly—their NY insignia aside the words KICKING ME OUT and DISCRIMINATORY DEVELOPMENT PROJECT.

After a year of more protests and city board meetings, the coalition was forced to compromise. Most of the shops would close in exchange for the city paying for their relocation to a remote area of south Bronx. Perhaps the dual movements to save Willets Point from Wilpon would have achieved better results had the billboard-buying fans overlapped with the workers. But the square of highways Moses had built specifically to separate the recreation zone from its surrounding barrios are rarely crossed for anything other than free street parking or a postgame Szechuan feast. Fan discontent with the Wilpons' villainy, it seemed, could only be expressed to the extent it negatively affected the Mets' results.

The Recession-era Occupy and BLM movements likewise fizzled in 2015 from an inability to penetrate the workplace, and thus the economic foundations that reproduced a society of racialized class inequality. All attempts to move toward broader working-class activity, like Occupy's proposed general strike, had gone nowhere. Only tepid liberal incrementalism seemed possible—body cameras on cops, a new healthcare "marketplace," and empty promises to relocate the

Iron Triangle. This was the political small ball typical of the Obama era: "[You] avoid errors," he said on the 2012 election trail, "you hit singles; you hit doubles. Every once in a while, we may be able to hit a home run."[553]

As most of the punks and hipsters around me decamped from radical politics to apolitical irony, I wondered if he was right. Their mass mobilizations swung for the fences, sometimes resulting in thrilling rallies cheered by millions. But by failing to even the score against the 1% before their third out, the unsatisfied crowd made for an early exit. Beginning to believe the radical activists and black bloc-ers perhaps did not have a winning strategy, I followed the 99% to Citi Field.

The Mets had been on the brink of another gutting after a bad spring in 2015. But when a July surge put the team a game behind the Washington Nationals in the East, Alderson reversed course, acquiring Yoenis Céspedes at the trade deadline. The Cuban refugee lived the American dream: blasting homers by day, and returning home in a different SUV each night. Second baseman Daniel Murphy turned into a star slugger through devotion to God. Matt Harvey, the bat signal engraved on his gear, finally appeared a deserved hero. "Time after time," Tom Verducci wrote in *SI*, "New Yorkers walking in the opposite direction would stop in their tracks and process this tall, dark knight who looked . . . familiar . . . yes, it was the phenom . . . the city's great hope."[554]

Although I preferred the *alt-comix* of Chris Ware and Daniel Clowes to the superhero stuff, I went to my first game at Citi Field in September to see the caped crusaders myself. The Mets had clinched the Eastern Division days before. Maybe they, like Bruce Wayne and Steve Rogers, would use the superpowers they had been given through the nefarious machinations of capitalism to somehow save America from itself in October.

I admired the sincerity of the Jackie Robinson rotunda, the original misshapen Mr. Met costume in the museum, the ten-dollar promenade seats and open access to the field level (a stub was required at Shea), and vegan food options, including an Occupy-themed pizza slice.[555] But mostly, it felt like any other new stadium anywhere in the country. There was a Coca-Cola corner, outfield pedestrian bridge, and gate-kept premium bars and food courts at every turn. At least Shea's most bizarre feature, the Home Run Apple, was back by popular demand. Although it now appeared to be a genetically modified variety, regrown with perfect roundness and red sheen, residing no longer in a magician's cap, but a tombstone-shaped void.

As I watched Max Scherzer no-hit them that frigid night, my hopes for their postseason diminished. The game was the low point of a dismal final week, culminating in a 90–72 record that was the worst among the NL's playoff contenders, and costing the Mets home-field advantage to the heavily favored Dodgers. There was no team-of-destiny narrative, no unifying slogan or "Who Let the Dogs Out" anthem, and no Rocker, Clemens, Nixon, or Giuliani supervillains for the underdogs to vanquish.

Even Harvey signaled skepticism for 2015's prowess, telling the press that summer he was considering sitting out the postseason altogether to protect his arm's longevity. When he no-showed a scheduled workout before the Dodgers series, the unexplained desertion left many wondering if the Batman comparisons had set the young ace up for failure. Keith Hernandez, who had likely heard the rumors of Harvey's struggles with drug abuse and depression, recalled telling the pitcher's agent the character "would come back to bite Harvey. . . . He built himself up to be something unreal."[556,557]

After deGrom outpitched Clayton Kershaw to take the first game in LA, a heroic origin story finally appeared in game two. The Mets led 2–1 in the seventh when Chase Utley—already known as a "Met killer"—slid hard into rookie Rubén Tejada at second base to prevent an unlikely double play. The dirty slide broke Tejada's leg, an injury from which his career would never recover. The Dodgers took the lead that inning, going on to win the game and even the series.

While Utley defended the play as good ol'-fashioned hardball, the Mets were appalled. "He has injured people. This isn't something new," Wright told reporters after the game.[558] At last, the Mets understood themselves not as the doomed loss-leader scion of an evil real-estate empire, but as avengers of Tejada and every journeyman whose career had been ruined by the selfish violence of cold-blooded psychos like Utley.

Hobbled Tejada took to the field before game three back in Gotham on crutches, holding up a closed fist to massive applause from the largest crowd Citi Field had ever seen. The cheers transitioned to a vicious chant of *We want Ut-ley! We want Ut-ley!* The team's bane wisely spent the game on the bench as the tortured Dark Knight took the mound. "It's like an opera or a good novel," poet Frank Messina told the *Times*, "the plot is thickening."[559]

After a rocky first inning, Harvey settled in, and the Mets began to hit with a vengeance. A new hero emerged in previously underappreciated Daniel Murphy. He hit three home runs and batted .333 in the five-game victory over LA, earning the moniker "GOAT" for his arguably *greatest-of-all-time* performance in the coming NL Championship Series against Chicago. A central plot point of *Back to the Future Part II* had been the Cubs claiming their first world championship in over a century in 2015. But Murphy's .521 batting average and four homers restored the timeline, cursing the Cubs anew with an embarrassingly easy sweep.

The *Times* credited the Mets earning their fourth pennant after six losing years to Alderson's application of moneyball, but the fans showed their preferred narrative with a proliferation of Captain America, Thor,

GOAT, and Batman iconography throughout the postseason.[560] Harvey got the ball for game one of the World Series against the defending AL champs, the Kansas City Royals. In a stark omen, Alcides Escobar drove his first pitch to center, where Céspedes misplayed and then booted the ball as Escobar rounded the bases for the first World Series inside-the-park home run since 1929. The game went back and forth from there, proceeding deep into extra innings. In the fourteenth, Wright made a throwing error, and the Mets lost.

I watched these games, pauper-like, looking in through windows of bars. The Recession economy had returned me to the same job I had before college—delivering fried chicken from a trendy Williamsburg restaurant on my Met-blue Peugeot fixed-gear. The gig afforded little downtime to sit and watch the series, let alone buy a $500 standing room ticket for the Mets' Citi Field return.[561] Nonetheless, the heroic run rekindled some flicker of my devotion for the 2000 team I had taken for redeemers of all New York's underdogs. I even found myself wondering where I might be, and what the world could have been like, had they won.

More traumatic memories of the Subway Series returned when the Royals handily took game two against a suddenly struggling deGrom. Syndergaard opened game three at Citi by throwing a pitch above Escobar's head, an act of intimidation aimed to chill the hard-hitting leadoff man. Thor went on to win the game and keep the fantasy alive, but the Mets went back to looking like cosplayers during Halloween's game four. Murphy butted a ball in the eighth, costing the Mets the lead. Closer Jeurys Familia proceeded to blow his second save of the series.

Fogging sports bar windows again on frigid November 1, I watched the Dark Knight rise to blank the Royals through eight innings, then courageously cast aside his regular-season health concerns to demand the ball for the ninth. A walk, a double, and another Wright misplay evaporated the narrow lead. By the time tearful Wilmer Flores struck out looking to end the World Series in the twelfth, I was counting my paltry tips, concerned more with bundling up for my shift the next day than the shame of defeat.

The Mets had played moneyball with money in the aughts, and moneyball without money in the tens. Both decades produced the same result: stretches of mediocrity and mismanagement punctuated by odds-defying yet doomed dashes toward championship. There was no secret algorithmic weapon capable of changing their choking ways, let alone saving the city from its corrupt overlords.[562] The 2015 Mets had punched above their weight during a thrilling streak before reverting to the mean. They were neither heroes nor villains, but comic-strip punchlines—Charlie Brown somersaulting helplessly after kicking air.

Twelve months later I again peered through bar windows during my shift—this time watching the Democrats' Midwestern "Blue Wall" crumble to bloody red. By quitting time it was clear another New York real-estate criminal, Donald Trump, had triumphed.

When the Cubs had fulfilled their prophecy a year late days prior, it felt as though the progressive cosmic order initiated by the Mets' black cat 1969 magic had collapsed with Shea. The piggish basis of *Back to the Future*'s villainous bully Biff Tannen had made a reality-defying comeback. The mood I experienced biking through Manhattan the next day could only be compared to the shock after 9/11, although lacking any of its unifying optimism.

The Mets had choked again in their wildcard qualifier game against the Giants a month prior. As he watched Citi Field emptying from the 7 train after the game, Julian Casablancas, frontman of the Strokes, a moody garage-punk band that had inspired me and countless thousands of others to move to Williamsburg in the mid-aughts, began to hum a melancholic tune. In the months to come, he developed it into an indie-rock eulogy mourning the Mets' loss, Occupy candidate Bernie Sanders' defeat in the spring primaries, the generation of Trumpist doom coming as a result, and his overall failure as a rock star to use the culture industry to change the world for the better: "I was just bored playin' the guitar. Learned all your tricks, wasn't too hard. It's the last one now, I can promise you that. . . . The only thing that's left is us, so pardon the silence that you're hearing is turning into a deafening, painful, shameful roar."[563] The song would be called "Ode to the Mets," appearing on *The New Abnormal*, the Strokes' final album, as its closing track.

Shortly after the election, a fire at a queer DIY venue in Oakland called the Ghost Ship killed thirty-six. Emboldened Nazi Trump supporters on 4chan organized a "Right Wing Safety Squad" campaign of calling fire code inspections to shutter dozens more leftist DIY spaces nationwide. Among them was a venue in Williamsburg called Shea Stadium in hipster homage to the fallen municipal field. The city had "lost its second Shea Stadium to bureaucracy," Matthew Trammell wrote in the *New Yorker*. "Like its namesake, the club housed a few local stars and the occasional hit."[564]

In January, the rehabilitated reality-TV star became president. Swearing to deport all undocumented immigrants, ban Muslims from the country, slash taxes on the rich, crush unions, ban abortion, and roll back any hope of preventing climate catastrophe, he buttressed the vastly unpopular platform with pseudo-populist promises to protect American workers from the foreign conflicts and stagnating wages caused by deals like NAFTA. After eight years of Obama's timidity, the feeble campaigns from the declining Bush and Clinton dynasties behind the forever wars and deindustrialization deals were no match for Trump's promises of vengeance against their establishment. In his inaugural address, Trump quoted Bane, promising to take Washington DC's power and "give it back to you, the people."[565]

It was a lie, of course, but the Democrats had made little counteroffer to the working class in terms of material promises or entertainment. In one night, the central myth of American liberalism that had persisted from Branch Rickey's integration of baseball, to the uprisings of the sixties, to the small ball of the Obama era, was decisively smashed. The long arc of history did *not* bend toward justice. No one was coming to save us.

Chapter 13

BACK IN BLACK

In the late fifties, a juvenile delinquent terrorized the affluent ball-fields of Jamaica Estates, Queens. He sported a capacious pompadour, slicked into an imposing plateau, earning him the street name "Flat Top Donny." A power-hitting catcher imitating Yogi Berra, he stepped to the plate surly, with pursed lips, swinging for the fences each time. Opposing pitchers learned to appease him with gentle lobs, fearing his typical post-strikeout routine of slamming down his bat and taking out his rage on the nearest teammate.[566]

Donny's baseball career continued at an upstate military academy after he was caught terrorizing Central Park pedestrians with a switch-blade. He claimed to have been a two-way prospect, who hit like Ted Williams and threw fastballs topping 80 mph. But when Red Sox and Phillies scouts showed up contract in hand, he turned them away like dogs. Baseball stars weren't making enough then, he recalled, so he went into the family slumlord business instead.[567]

After a few years shaking down his father's tenants, Donny earned the massive loan that turned him into the mafia-inspired real estate playboy known as *the Don.* He built an empire of the biggest, greatest, most luxuriously-branded chintzy apartment buildings, hotels, casinos, and golf resorts the world had ever seen. Setting his sights on sports in the mid-eighties, he drew up deals for a "Trump Stadium" for the Jets next to Shea, a purchase of the Buffalo Bills, and a new baseball league to rival the crooked MLB during the 1994 strike.[568] These ventures went nowhere. For all his bravado, Trump's petty criminality and business ineptitude were well known among New York's elites.

When his closest sports ally, the likeminded George Steinbrenner, passed away in 2010, Donald Trump reinvented himself as a populist politician. Like the nineties Yanks, he promised to make America dynastic again with a philosophy cribbed equally from the late greats Roy Cohn and Steinbrenner: *Win so much you get tired of winning.* Stadiums nationwide filled with bleacher creatures in his campaign's red ballcap, embracing the revanchist triumphalism by chanting *lock them up!* against all opponents.

These campaign promises fell by the wayside after the election. His narcissism surpassing all politics, Trump had few bigger goals during his first hundred days than throwing out the ceremonial Opening Day first pitch at Yankee Stadium. But despite maintaining a close relationship with Yankees GM Randy Levine, the tradition that began with William Taft in 1910 ended with Trump in 2017. Once again, polite society and sports alike shut its gates to the vulgarian.

The rejection was a result of the massive protests countering Trump since inauguration. Activists blockaded entrances to his ceremony, and a reappeared black bloc fought riot cops on K Street into the evening beneath the black fumes of burning limos spray-painted with the slogan *We the People.* Millions of feminists marched the next day against his anti-abortion agenda, and international airport terminals coast to coast were occupied in response to his "Muslim ban" the next week. As the Mets sold away their 2015 journeymen core that offseason, my attention shifted decisively back to the politics of this *Resistance* coalition—specifically the antifascist squads assembled to defeat Trump's alt-right street movement.

In their propaganda, one New York City antifascist group adapted the union worker tradition of combining their local's name with sports logos for hard-hat stickers. "Antifa" was placed in a darkened Mets emblem in one, and Mr. Met became a street-fighting hooligan wielding a nail-driven bat in another. "I immediately thought of the [1986] Mets' scrappy yet violent image," the stickers' designer, eighties Mets devotee J. Ratsky recalled, "that for me captured a part of the essence of NYC in a moment of trying to stand up and defend our neighborhoods, our scenes."[569]

After months of tit-for-tat street brawls, an all-star showdown between Antifa cadres and the alt-right met that August in Charlottesville, Virginia. Dozens were injured during the bloody hours-long melee, culminating in the death of antifascist Heather Heyer when one Nazi rammed his car through a crowd celebrating the alt-right's early retreat.

Despite Trump defending the Nazis as "good people," the core of his fascist brawlers fractured after the violence. The Resistance likewise dulled as much of Trump's agenda was stymied in the courts. The Democrats abandoned their flirtations with the activist *Abolish ICE* blockades soon after, moving instead toward negotiations for more humane detention centers and a "smarter" border wall. With the cruelty of ICE Trump's biggest political liability as the 2020 elections approached, he pointed out that deportations had actually been *higher* under Obama.

Even though most of the country wanted *anyone but Trump*, much of the Democrats' voting base knew another Clintonesque candidate, incapable of speaking to the issues of workers, citizen and immigrant alike, risked repeating 2016. All hope for an effective left-populist opposition, then, steered toward another New Yorker who had been radicalized by New York's golden age of baseball.

Bernie Sanders grew up a progressive Brooklyn Dodgers devotee. A talented high school athlete and student leader, he countered Ebbets' war celebrations with a high school campaign to fund scholarships for Korean war orphans.[570] When the Dodgers left for California, O'Malley's greed turned Sanders into a committed socialist. "I don't want to tell you that was the sole reason that I've developed the politics that I've developed," he told the *Times*. "But as a kid, I did see in that case about the greed of one particular company. And that impacted me."[571]

From there, he became a civil rights activist, moved to a Vermont commune in the late sixties, and worked his way up the political ladder from Socialist Workers Party elector to mayor of Burlington, Congress, then the Senate. Never losing his social-democratic Dodgers orthodoxy in the process, he advocated for the players and fans whenever he could. During 2005 PED hearings, he sneered that Congress was wasting its time grilling athletes about steroids instead of addressing childhood poverty. He fought legislation permitting the MLB to underpay their minor leaguers a decade later. The owners claimed the bill was vital to maintain small-town teams, only to announce they would cut forty-two of them in 2020 after its passage. By then, Sanders was leading the Democratic primaries and all head-to-head polls against Trump. He told MLB Commissioner Rob Manfred to check the billionaires' greed, save the teams, and pay minor leaguers a living wage, or face renewed hearings on baseball's antitrust exemption.[572]

I gathered with twenty-six thousand other Bernie supporters across from Nas's childhood projects in Queensbridge Park that October. It was a scene far more diverse than the protests I had been to over the past decade—New Yorkers of all ages, backgrounds, and sports-team loyalties, energized not only to defeat Trump, ICE, and the remnants of his fascist foot soldiers, but also the inept and conservative Democratic Party establishment, and the millionaires and billionaires they worked for.

Sanders seemed destined to win the nomination after surging in the polls through the winter and placing first in Iowa, New Hampshire, and Nevada. But ahead of the February 9 primaries, Barack Obama returned from retirement to call on his remaining competitors to drop out and unite behind the candidacy of his former vice president, Joe Biden. The lifelong conservative Democrat, whose sundowning speeches boldly promised that "nothing would fundamentally change" were he to outpace Trump, instantly went from the weakest candidate of the crowded field to front-runner.[573] With the right wing of the Democratic Party ascendant, and Sanders fading from the picture, the MLB went through with its threatened cut of dozens of minor-league teams.

As the electoral tragedy played out, COVID-19 rampaged across the world through airports, freighters, and cruise ships. The entire government, from Trump down to blue-state Democrats, imagined the United States so invulnerable to the world's problems that testing was virtually nonexistent. Only when players of the Utah Jazz independently confirmed their infections in March, and the NBA suspended its season, was the reality finally acknowledged—the deadly disease was here, and had been for many months.

Nonessential businesses were abruptly closed, with millions laid off en masse. This included thirty thousand workers at baseball parks, spring training facilities, and all minor-league rosters. When the MLB extended a $300 weekly stipend to those players, Nationals closer Sean Doolittle, an outspoken Bernie supporter and member of the Democratic Socialists of America, rallied his teammates to raise funds to support their minor-league brethren. When the campaign spread throughout the sport, the ashamed MLB restored the meager stipend at $400.[574]

Meanwhile, the virus feasted on the "essential" workers required to report as normal. New York City was hit first and hardest as the disease spread through jails, logistics centers, and kitchens. These workers, lifelong recipients of substandard healthcare, took the disease home with them to their families and neighbors. Hospitals were soon inundated with gasping patients, and the city considered digging mass graves in public parks as morgues filled far past capacity.[575] By summer's end, the disparities of race and class in the pandemic measures, and American healthcare in general, would be revealed by a death rate for African Americans fully doubling that of whites.[576]

The grim lockdown stretched on quietly the next two months until the end of May, when a horrifying video emerged of Minneapolis police murdering George Floyd, a forty-six-year-old Black man, infected with COVID and accused of passing a counterfeit bill at a grocery store. The resonant example of the daily systematic disregard for the lives of the Black and poor in policing, prisons, and public health sparked mass outrage, beginning with an intense, multiracial demonstration on May 27 in Floyd's Minneapolis neighborhood. Big-box stores were systematically looted, their parking lots repurposed into free distribution centers for the liberated goods. Growing crowds besieged the police station where Floyd's killers worked the next night, and burned it to the ground.

The revolt, like the video that inspired it, went viral. A mob stormed CNN headquarters in Atlanta and the police union's AFL-CIO headquarters in DC. Another crowd swarmed and breached the White House gates, forcing Trump to cower in a subterranean bunker. Eleven thousand similar protests and riots spread through three thousand cities and towns in all fifty states over the next month.[577] The *Times* reported up to twenty-six million participated, making the George Floyd uprising likely the largest mass movement in US history.[578]

I witnessed the unrest in the streets of New York. For a full week, dozens of spontaneous marches emerged from nearly every neighborhood in the city, crossing all major bridges toward downtown Manhattan at sunset. There, the rage turned to a festival of reappropriation—nearly every luxury storefront between SoHo and Central Park was emptied, with iPhones, Gucci bags, vintage champagne, and cash distributed freely amongst the rebels.[579]

Even when the most intense phase of the rioting died down, the lockdown nostalgia for sports, brunch, work, the election, and other pre-pandemic banalities faded away. Early warnings from faux-ally politicians that the marches would be Trump-emboldening superspreaders were proven false—COVID rates only dropped in the fresh air, and every attempt to crush the movement with federal troops expanded its ranks. Mass assemblies met daily at an encampment outside City Hall Park through July to strategize on returning billions spent on the NYPD to the impoverished communities they terrorized. These "partisans of a new way of living rejected the atomization of the pandemic," city historian Andy Battle wrote. "The normal seemed to have been punctured."[580]

With these radical demands reaching unprecedented popularity, the terrified forces of normality launched their counterattack. Floyd's murderer, Derek Chauvin, was indicted in late May. A week later, politicians in both parties promised a new round of tepid police reform that would ban chokeholds and no-knock raids, and require body cameras. Knowing neither concession would curb the power of police to determine who lives and dies with impunity, these gestures had little effect. A far more formidable plan emerged later that month—the NBA, NHL, and MLB would resume play.

Just as the disappearance of professional sports indicated arrival of the crisis, televised games in empty stadium "bubbles" sought to show the end was in sight. At their July Opening Day ceremonies, ballplayers lined up before the national anthem with Black Lives Matter patches on their sleeves for a pre-recorded speech asking fans to quietly "acknowledge the pain of the Black community." Some players on the Yankees, Nationals, Dodgers, and Giants invoked 49ers quarterback Colin Kaepernick's 2016 silent protest against the police murders of Philandro Castile, Freddie Gray, and countless others, by kneeling through the anthem and speech. The Mets did not.[581]

"For me, taking a knee just isn't enough,"[582] Dominic Smith, the lone African American on the Mets' 2020 roster, explained after the game. While Kaepernick was cut from his team in retribution at the end of the year, as was Athletics catcher Bruce Maxwell for adapting the gesture in solidarity the next season, kneeling became an effective form of crowd control during the uprising. An outmaneuvered NYPD had knelt with protesters several times in a media-friendly sign of solidarity, only to "beat the living shit out of us one hour after," one protester reported.[583] Departments around the country adapted the tactic, as did politicians when they returned to Congress draped in kente cloth. "The Democrats kneeled in silence for eight minutes and forty-six seconds, exactly the length of time Chauvin's knee dug into Floyd's neck," Black struggle scholar Tobi Haslett wrote. "Their gesture echoes Colin Kaepernick, but given the details of Floyd's passing amounts to a pantomime of his murder."[584]

Smith had experienced anti-blackness, both personal and structural, his entire life. Growing up amidst the poverty and terror of the Los Angeles County Sheriff's Department's officer gangs in South Central, he received a scholarship for training at the Compton Urban Youth Academy—one of the MLB's few player-production facilities oriented toward African Americans due to their high cost compared to Caribbean equivalents. Once drafted, Smith visited similar private academies throughout the country on road trips, recognizing in the disparity between training camps for white upper-middle-class youth and his own the reason why less than 8 percent of major-league rosters were African American in 2020, with three teams fielding none at all.[585] In 2017, the year Smith joined the Mets, he co-founded the BaseballGenerations nonprofit to reverse the trend of baseball training becoming "a privilege only available to higher income families."[586]

But even for Black youth lucky enough to get contracts, he found the hostility that confronted players since Jackie Robinson's first seasons remained common. Fans in the Southern minors heckled his "nappy hair" or called him "Fat Albert." During spring training in 2020, Smith reported being denied service at a Port St. Lucie restaurant for being Black. In another incident, a road-rager yelled: "You probably stole that car, you nigger."[587]

Smith credited the camaraderie of teammates Pete Alonso, Jeff McNeil, Michael Conforto, and J. D. Davis for supporting him through these incidents. After years in Polar Bear Pete's star shadow as his first base backup, he finally landed a starting role as designated hitter when play resumed in 2020. The position first arrived in the NL that year after the players' union successfully pushed the league to adopt the DH against owner concerns that it would inflate payrolls. He went on to have a career-best season, batting .316 and leading the team in RBIs.

Despite his breakout success, normality returned outside the athletic bubble, and the mandated isolation between games turned into an endless doomscroll of social-media consumption of the brutality returning with it. BLM patches and END RACISM slogans painted in football end zones could not stop the violence, and Smith became convinced that most of his fellow athletes didn't truly care about the unceasing degradation of Black lives. The depression was deepened by his inability to socialize with his teammates off-field: "I didn't know how to feel the feeling that I was feeling."[588]

In late August, a video circulated of officers in Wisconsin shooting Jacob Blake twenty-nine times in the back during a traffic stop. A new round of riots broke out in Kenosha, including the arson of a Department of Corrections building. With Trump back on the campaign trail, an emboldened right-wing militia arrived on the third night. One of the semiautomatic-wielding vigilantes opened fire on protesters when they attempted to disarm him, shooting three and killing two. Horrified, the Milwaukee Bucks voted moments before their first NBA playoff game to refuse to take the court. The playoffs were postponed entirely once the Lakers and Clippers joined the wildcat strike.

Smith started a group chat with other Black ballplayers in hopes of organizing something similar for baseball. On August 26, the day after the shooting, he surprised his teammates by kneeling during the national anthem at Citi Field. "They were pretty upset," he said after the game, although not for the reason he feared. "They wanted to be there by me while I did it and to show their support out there on the field."[589]

Mets manager Luis Rojas called a clubhouse meeting the next day. The team voted to take action, as did their opponent Marlins. Jeff Wilpon and the MLB caught wind of the plan, telling players only a one-hour walkout would be permitted. Instead, the teams took the field on time, held a forty-two-second moment of silence to honor Jackie Robinson's number, covered home plate with a Black Lives Matter shirt, and jogged off the field, refusing to return. "It's not about Black versus white," Smith told the press after the walkout. "It's not about police versus minorities. It's about power over the powerless."[590]

With fourteen other baseball teams boycotting their games that day in similar fashion, and the wildcat strike spreading to the WNBA, MLS, and even the NHL, sports' renewed cessation threatened to return the spring unrest in far more dangerous form. In their analysis of the George Floyd Uprising, the abolitionist group Spirit of May 28 argued the inability of its proletarian participants to move the struggle from the streets to their jobs had served its major limit: "The link between police murdering Black people and workplace struggles remained a sizable chasm with no clear bridge."[591] Now the actions of Black athletes like Smith provided the first high-profile crossover between the streets and workplaces—an example that could be immediately replicated nationwide.

But after three days of the strike Barack Obama once again picked up the phone. Hoping to stop its momentum as he had Sanders', he called its widely perceived leader, and the most famous athlete in the country, Lakers forward LeBron James. An election was coming, Obama reminded him, and if the players really wanted to fight racism they should focus all effort on turning out votes against Donald Trump. The NBA and the basketball players' union reached a deal later that night. In exchange for taking the court, the unused arenas would be converted to voter-registration and ballot-receiving sites.[592]

The strike ended; sports and election seasons returned to schedule. The Lakers beat the Heat to take the NBA championship as the Mets, three games short of a wildcard slot after the walkout, crumbled in September. Chants of *LeBron James sucks* rang out at MAGA rallies, but Trump's support from Wayne Gretzky, Mariano Rivera, and Mike Piazza were no match for basketball's GOAT—LeBron's assist set Biden up for a narrow November buzzer beater.[593]

That winter, hundreds of thousands of New Yorkers lined up at the city's largest vaccination site, Citi Field. Hospitalization and death rates dropped dramatically afterward. What little remained of the lockdown was lifted once Biden came to power, alongside pandemic subsidies for unemployment and healthcare. As ballparks filled for the 2021 season in the days before the anniversary of Floyd's death, the police murder of Daunte Wright just outside of Minneapolis failed to spark a new cycle of struggle.

While sports and the election had quieted the streets, reverberations of the crisis year continued to echo throughout the reopening economy.

Labor organizer Sarah Ahn of the Flushing Workers Center called the pandemic an "eye-opener" among the workers surrounding Citi Field. "We see the callousness from bosses who don't really care about their employees. They're just driven to make the most money possible."[594]

Union drives emerged everywhere post-pandemic, including, for the first time, in the minor leagues. "Beyond just the typical working conditions and low pay and all that," pitching prospect turned labor lawyer Harry Marino recalled in an interview with the *Tipping Pitches* podcast, "they really realized, 'Wow . . . We have no say over this at all. We're missing an entire season here, we don't even know what's happening.' . . . I think that feeling of powerlessness really resonated with guys."[595]

Marino had co-founded Advocates for Minor Leaguers (AML) for this effort after Bernie's failure to prevent the poverty-wage legislation of 2016. Operating as a third party, AML won some quiet clubhouse support by successfully suing the MLB for spring-training pay. But their traction was limited due to a fear described by MLBPA patriarch Marvin Miller to *Slate* in 2012: "The notion that these very young, inexperienced people were going to defy the owners, when they had stars in their eyes about making it to the major leagues, it's just not going to happen."[596]

AML organizer and former Mets catcher Josh Thole described to *SI*'s Emma Baccellieri how a post-pandemic whisper campaign carefully navigated that fear after their pandemic humiliations. "You build trust with two guys in the clubhouse. They tell three guys, and then those three guys tell two more guys, and next thing you know, you have half a clubhouse on board." Mets pitching prospect Trevor Hildenberger added he'd evangelize the campaign to his teammates "loud enough where other players can hear, but not so loud that it was like a team meeting and it was raising ears in terms of team personnel."[597]

The racial reckoning of 2020 was another impetus for the renewed push. AML co-organizer Bill Fletcher Jr., a scholar of Black workers' struggles, lifelong Mets fan, and self-described "patron saint of lost causes," told me he believed living wages for prospects could help reverse the shrinking number of African Americans in the game. "It's not just about interesting Black youth in baseball, it's the price of admission into baseball. Little League on up, the price parents have to pay to get kids involved becomes prohibitive. . . . So this is another class and race issue."[598]

Another catalyst for the nationwide boom in union organizing was a labor market tightened post-lockdown. Millions had vanished from the US workforce, including the million dead from the virus by the end of 2022, and the unknown millions more temporarily or chronically disabled by long COVID. Many of those fortunate enough to remain able-bodied declined to return to their jobs, either to evade the risk of infection, or because the lockdown had given them time to pursue other forms of happiness.

Some of these ex-workers joined post-Uprising shoplifting rings, started Instagram-based artisanal small businesses, or became amateur Wall Street sharks. The Reddit forum *r/WallStreetBets* became a platform for coordinating massive market manipulation, turning pandemic checks into small fortunes while punishing the hedge funds short-selling brick-and-mortar businesses, like GameStop and AMC Theaters, that they predicted would not recover from the lockdown. Among the targets of this grassroots movement was one of the richest men in the world, and new owner of the Mets, Steve Cohen.

Mets fans were jubilant when the news of Cohen's record $2.4 billion purchase of the team broke during the 2020 Subway Series following Smith's walkout. While Reddit's Robin Hoods saw him as the piggish villain depicted in the 2023 film about the GameStop affair, *Dumb Money,* we preferred his depiction as financial rock star Bobby Axelrod from the Showtime series *Billions*—always one step ahead of rival magnates and the Feds, and generously showering his illicit gains on his fratty clubhouse of Wall Street wolves. It mattered little that Cohen became the greatest Recession-era crook after Madoff in 2013, narrowly avoiding prison time by paying $1.8 billion—the highest SEC fine to date—for a pattern of trading on unreleased internal reports from medical and tech companies. Nor did we mind that social-democratic Mayor Bill de Blasio and other city progressives had desperately tried to block his purchase of the Mets on grounds of "moral turpitude."[599] Just as Biden would bring stability and sanity to the United States, so too would "Uncle Steve" rescue the Mets from years of the grifting Wilpons' eccentric mismanagement. And if another hustler had to run the team, at least he was no small-time crook.

There was also relief that he had outbid the Bronx combination of ex-Yankee Alex Rodriguez and then-fiancée Jennifer Lopez. Cohen branded himself a New Breed '68er, raised in the same Gatsbyesque Long Island enclave as the Wilpons, with photos of Ed Kranepool taped to his wall and afternoons spent sneaking past ushers to Shea's field level.[600] Myth or not, he promised to spare no expense to turn the Mets into perennial contenders, like the Dodgers or Yankees, as an act of partisan philanthropy. "I don't care about the cost side," he told CNBC. "If I can make millions of people happy, how cool is that? And so I actually view it as a civic responsibility."[601]

The oligarch demonstrated his benevolent disregard for Wilponian book-balancing from the jump. All-star shortstop Francisco Lindor, acquired in a winter trade, was given a record ten-year, $341 million contract extension before ever taking the field. Under a mushroom-cut of seapunk turquoise curls, the new franchise face had earned the reputation of a consistently clutch hitter, a flashy fielder, and the most charismatic player in the game. The MLPBA player rep's natural leadership abilities carried over to the clubhouse of other lovable stars: the gentle power-hitting Polar Bear Pete Alonso; shy perfectionist Cy Young winner Jacob deGrom; and fitful flamethrower, suddenly the best closer in the game, Edwin Díaz. Crowds filled every other seat of socially-distanced Citi in 2021 to cheer on the seemingly unstoppable juggernaut whose payroll neared the league lead at $200 million.

Cohen supplemented the free-spending with homages to Mets history correcting the apparent shame Wilpon harbored for the team's seditious and scummy past. A list of franchise players, including Darryl Strawberry, Doc Gooden, and Willie Mays, had their numbers slated for retirement. The beloved Old Timers' Day game for retired Mets was scheduled for the first time in nearly twenty years. A statue of Tom Seaver, recently deceased from COVID, was erected in monumental bronze astride Shea's retired apple outside the 7 train. The Jackie Robinson Rotunda's Mets Museum was expanded with exhibits celebrating the 1969 black cat game, the brashness of the 1986 bad boys, and Dom Smith's 2020 walkout.

Perhaps the most significant restoration for millennial fans like myself was the black uniform. The alternate's quiet retirement during post-Madoff austerity seemed a white flag in the team's historic battle to topple the Yankees, leaving the Subway World Series humiliation unhealed. In the "Back in Black" hype video for the rebellious wardrobe's return, a montage of calendars and clocks running backward were intercut with images of the 2000 Mets celebrating their pennant beneath a resolute emcee voiceover: "There was a time we feasted like none other. It's back again, as we rep our pastime. Yeah, you heard right. It's *black* again, for a brand new time!"[602]

As the Mets decisively topped the East at the All-Star break, even guillotine-sharpening leftists began hailing "Uncle Steve" as a populist savior. He engaged with fans on social media and in person on strolls around Citi, and appeared an iconoclast among his fellow magnates by putting the team above market pressures and profit. In Marxist terms, he had stepped in the role of a *Bonapartist* ruler—a populist strongman from the elite's ranks who emerges during crisis to provide restabilization and relegitimization through completion of stalled revolutionary projects. By borrowing battle slogans and costumes of the past, fans believed Cohen had decisively swept Wilpon's apocryphal goal to achieve meaning only in September playoff races into the dustbin of history. Cohen promised a World Series *within five years* of his purchase, and with the trade-deadline acquisition of Cubs hero Javy Báez, it looked as though it might be achieved in just one. The guerrilla insurgents were now a mighty Napoleonic army in revanchist advance against the crumbling conservative empires of the MLB.

But a July slump following the trade revealed that the expectations of a fan base who had once found familiar comfort in failure suddenly raised to Yankee hubris. As the team slipped out of first in August, hateful *boos* filled Citi for slumping Lindor and Báez. The players responded with a shocking counterattack of a *thumbs down* toward the scornful crowd after hits. Not since the 1995 post-strike "Fan Upheaval Day" had the bond between the

Mets and their fans been so badly torn—the spiteful gesture of black-clad players now turning to grip the fans by their jeering throats.

The resulting choke was historic. The Braves took the lead in the East, and the Mets sunk away from the wildcard, ending the season the first team to ever finish with a losing record after leading a division for one hundred consecutive days. The common millennial anxiety of "imposter syndrome" had proven correct—Mets heroism, more than money and wardrobe, required a journey traversing the edge of tragedy. In that sense, 2021 had at least served a fitting opening act.

As the mighty Mets biblically crumbled in Queens, the lowliest underlings of their corporate structure notched an epochal triumph at Maimonides Park in Coney Island.

At their game on September 11, 2021, several members of the Mets' single-A Brooklyn Cyclones and their Jersey Shore BlueClaws opponents emerged from their dugouts wearing a blue wristband reading *#FairBall*. The hashtag campaign, organized by Advocates for Minor Leaguers and the clubhouse network of union organizers, led to stories about what it was like to struggle through the high demands and low wages of minor-league life. Even after the post-pandemic pay increase, they earned poverty-level wages of $12,000 to $16,800 a season, forcing players to subsist on fast food and sleep four in a room on air mattresses, if not homeless in their cars. Few fans may have noticed the illicit wristlet, but by joining Doolittle, Lindor, and Báez's gestures toward shattering the taboo of ballplayers publicly stating dissatisfaction, it became a tourniquet to stop the bleeding.

Confronting their nervousness of how a minor league union might reshuffle the deck in their contract negotiations with the MLB, several major leaguers immediately voiced their support, including Mets manager Luis Rojas: "These are guys that are choosing baseball as their career," he told the *Daily News*. "They want some impact when it comes down to their economic choice."[603] Three days after the game, the rattled owners conceded free, furnished housing for minor leaguers. Unsatisfied, AML redoubled efforts in 2022 after winning the vocal support of Lindor and $1 million from the MLBPA to continue organizing.

The fraternal bonds carried over to the MLBPA's CBA negotiations that winter. When the big leaguers stood strong against demands for a salary cap, the owners ended three decades of labor peace by initiating a ninety-nine-day lockout. With Opening Day already delayed when talks resumed, Cohen's extravagance emerged as the central issue. "Our sport feels broken now," one executive said, referring to the Mets payroll boom to $283 million with a new round of spending that included a record $43.33 million annual salary for future Hall of Fame ace Max Scherzer.[604] In place of a salary cap, the owners now demanded a "Cohen Tax" of 80 percent of expenditures past $290 million to be redistributed to other teams. Seeing the demand as a de-facto cap, Lindor, along with fellow bargaining committee members Scherzer and Brandon Nimmo, voted against the proposal. But in a general vote, the large majority of the players voted for the compromise, ending the lockout.[605]

The MLBPA nonetheless appeared more militant than ever that year. A post-pandemic Gallup poll found that 68 percent of Americans approved of labor unions—the highest figure since 1965—and a poll of baseball fans found 45 percent blamed the owners for the lockout, and only 21 percent the players.[606] When Dodger Stadium workers organized with Unite Here threatened to strike during the 2022 All-Star Game, the MLBPA announced they would refuse to cross their picket line, and the labor dispute was resolved shortly after. Then, in September, the MLBPA sent the minor leaguers union digital authorization cards. Within a week, a majority of the 5,500 prospects signed up on the online platform, cleared for use by the NLRB during the pandemic, expanding MLBPA ranks roughly fivefold in one of the swiftest unionization campaigns in American labor history.

What happened next was an even bigger shock. Perhaps due to the high levels of player solidarity and public support, or perhaps believing minor leaguers would be more amenable to limitations on top-star salaries, the MLB voluntarily recognized the union. "I figured it would be a couple of years, and at that point, ideally I'd be either out of baseball or I'd be a big leaguer," Mets prospect Tom Hackimer told *SI*. "There was a collective excitement, collective celebration," teammate Josh Hejka recalled of the minor-league clubhouse celebrations that surpassed any prior on-field victory. "It felt like it overcame the individuality of pro ball."[607]

Armed with the spirit of solidarity, and led by a new pro-labor manager in Buck Showalter, the Mets marched through the 2022 season with a militant confidence unseen in decades. Pete Alonso slugged 40 homers, Edwin Díaz was near-perfect with a 1.31 ERA, Jeff McNeil took the NL batting title with a .326 average, and the Mets won 101 games for their best record since 1986.

But once the division title came into sight, imposter syndrome returned. The black uniform had been taken out of mothballs specifically to defeat the blood-rival Braves and Yankees—and Mets indeed defeated both in July laughers. Tragedy returned in late August and September, however, when they lost *eight of nine* to those teams, including a final sweep in Atlanta that knocked them back to the plebeian wildcard. There, another CBA-negotiations loss appeared as a new hurdle: the new three-game wildcard series playoff against the second-seed Padres at Citi Field.

Cohen's imperial army reached their Waterloo. Homer after homer sailed over "Mad Max" Scherzer's head in game one; his heterochromatic orange and blue eyes, now stripped of their famed postapocalyptic-warrior intensity, glanced apologetically at the sold-out crowd collectively groaning, *$43 million for this!?* Down 7–0 in the fifth, meta-referential existentialist comedian Nathan Fielder captured the soul of every Mets fan as he stared in unflinching despair at his frazzled image projected for a curiously long span on Cohen's comically oversized center-field videoboard, the largest in professional sports.

I biked to Citi the next night, optimistic only for my chances to score a cheap paper standing-room ticket at the box office. The last time I had gone to a postseason Mets game was the 2000 pennant-clincher against the Cardinals with my dad. Cherished stubs from that game mildewed in a shoebox of middle-school mementos, recalling the scrappy Mets clearing the bench to battle some minor Cardinals aggression, and sending the black-clad Shea rabble home triumphantly chanting *Yankees Suck.*

I easily scored the ticket and paced the field level through the first innings. Brief crests of enthusiasm washed through the conspicuously unsold-out crowd as Lindor homered in the first, and deGrom's struggles in each early inning resulted in just one run. When Nimmo stroked an RBI single in the fourth, my solitary chant of *Let's Go Brandon*—an ironic anti-Biden slogan I believed popular among the left and right alike—was only echoed by a small group of sinister Trumpists. Even after the Padres' bullpen collapse, only a few sporadic *Let's Go Mets* cheers erupted among the crowd leaving Citi. The game had felt far too uphill, leading many to instead mournfully murmur the season would end the next night, and they had likely seen free-agency-eligible deGrom's final win as a Met.

Down 4–0 in the middle game three, social-media fandom desperately coped that the Mets' offensive no-show was the result of illicit sheens lacquered on each of Padre starter Joe Musgrove's earlobes. The conspiracy theory broke Twitter containment and made its way to

Showalter, who smugly marched to the field demanding an investigation of the sticky stuff. The umps found it was all *fake news*; the auricle slicks were merely the same painkilling menthol rub slathered over historic postseason Mets antagonists from Buckner to Clemens. Showalter shrugged and walked back to the dugout, the orthodoxy that the best-funded campaign always wins as dead in baseball as presidential elections.

Steve Cohen had learned to conquer the stock market less from his professors at Wharton business school than at the frat house poker table between classes. In the game that nearly perfectly balances luck and skill, he found his edge by gathering as much information as he could on his opponents, forming a plan, and coldly sticking to it until his chip stack was so high no one could stop him.

After two disappointing seasons, fans cheered Cohen as he rearranged his chips for a new round of big bets on future Hall of Fame pitcher Justin Verlander, Japanese sinkerball phenomenon Kodai Senga, and hefty contract extensions for fan favorites Brandon Nimmo, Jeff McNeil, and Edwin Díaz. His "fuck you money" blasted past the Cohen tax by $50 million for an Opening Day payroll of $330 million—making the 2023 Mets by far the highest-paid American sports team of all time.

Yet 2022's spiritual slump continued unabated. Díaz disappeared for the season after celebrating a win for Puerto Rico during the World Baseball Classic. Forty-one-year-old Verlander likewise missed the early season with an achy elbow, returning to a team struggling to keep their footing as its slumping hitters became targets of a record number of hit-by-pitches. Even if Citi's Jacobins believed it noble for billionaires to spend their absurd fortunes on premium entertainment for fans that raised player salaries overall, opposing pitchers apparently saw Cohen's team much like his Redditor nemeses—entitled fat cats to be taken down a peg.

Such assaults had rallied the Mets in years past. No such fight appeared in 2023. "Out of all the teams I played on," veteran outfielder Tommy Pham told Lindor, "this is the least-hardest working group of position players I've ever played with."[608] The team collapsed in May, and stayed down as they the beanings continued through the summer.

Cohen finally cashed out midseason. The entirety of the blue-chip roster stack was put on the block, with Scherzer, Verlander, and other vets exchanged for young, controllable prospects years away from the bigs. Fans finally began to doubt Cohen's desperate tilting as the Mets sunk from the wildcard race after waving the white flag. Desertion spread among the players who had survived the sell-off, as well. Alonso changed his walk-up song from the Queensbridge house standard "Shook Ones, Part II" by Mobb Deep to "It's a Great Day to Be Alive"—conservative country star Travis Tritt's anthem of divorced men. Another Met gone country, Jacob deGrom, went on to win a World Series ring in Texas that year, alongside the deadline-acquired Scherzer.

The immense misery of 2020 had provided a glimpse of optimism that enough was finally enough. Workers who had been abused by police, bosses, politicians, and corporations appeared finally ready to rise up in massive numbers to reshape American politics. The temporary flurry of stimulus checks, reformist feints, and reopening of the leisure economy proved an effective diversion allowing the political and billionaire class to temporarily restore their legitimacy.

Steve Cohen's bailout of the Mets could be seen as another element of the recuperative strategy. But betting chips at the poker table and financial commodities on the market is a very different game than running New York's people's team—whose success had always come through forging a strong alliance between the downtrodden and disgruntled Metsian elements of society and a team conscious of their symbolic role to redeem them where the rest of the capitalist superstructure had failed. Even if Cohen's rebrand of the team into a dynastic powerhouse like the Yankees or Dodgers was a success, that link would be severed. The franchise's identity would be transformed beyond recognition, like a gritty *Peanuts* reboot in which Charlie Brown reappears as a star-punting varsity jock.

With expectations lowered as the Mets sank from wildcard contention late in the 2023 season, enjoyment returned to the carefree mode that dominated the majority of their sixty years. A steady attendance of about 33,000 each night came out to root for the "baby Met" prospects Brett Baty, Francisco Álvarez, and Ronny Mauricio. Weekend hip-hop and EDM DJs turned games into an East Williamsburg nightclub, and security became increasingly permeable to outside food, THC vapes, and hidden booze pouches. Fans cheered every Ruthian Shohei Ohtani blast when he visited with the Angels, and even playfully *boo*ed when the Mets pitched around him. By the time the team ended their year with their worst record since 2017, we remembered that winning was never really the point.

One loss that year did bother me, however. I came to Citi Field for the first time that season to cheer on the Nationals' new starting first baseman, Dominic Smith. Before the game I went to snap a photo of the display celebrating his walkout in the museum, only to find it had been removed. A little later, a pregame tribute video for Dom received only lukewarm applause. Taking this as a measure both of the extinguished fires of 2020, and of how well the last quarter-century of ownership had purged the New Breed spirit from the franchise's historic narrative, I began to write.

EPILOGUE

The Gay Grimace Mets

MARCH 29

As in 1969 and 2006, the season opened amidst spreading wars and social reaction. The proxy conflict in Ukraine had become an endless meat grinder, and the Israeli Defense Forces were progressing toward a promised genocidal clearing of the Gaza Strip. More horrors were on the horizon, with war hawks saber-rattling against China and Iran, and the climate crisis accelerating at such an alarming pace that each month broke all prior heat records. A domestic war on women and queers threatened reproductive rights and gender autonomy. What, if anything, would the 2024 Mets and their fans have to say about this bleak juncture?

At nine in the morning, I put on my Dom Smith jersey-tee beneath a jacket and layers of sweaters, and biked through the early spring chill to the marina parking lot outside Citi Field. I arrived on a bench facing Flushing Bay, the frigid winds whipping my face on a promenade renamed for Malcolm X shortly after the 2020 uprising.

Behind me, members of the 7 Line Army (T7LA) set up their grills, coolers, and cornhole boards. Soon, hip-hop, cock rock, and country music filled the air from Bluetooth speakers as the frigid winds stiffened flags attached to their SUV tailgates: T7LA, the United States, the Mets, and the "thin blue line" of police between order and anarchy.

I pulled myself out of doomer paralysis and mingled at the center of the action. Generals passed out Coronas, 50/50 raffle tickets, and customized orange uniforms to their troops. While a handful were cagey when I requested interviews, expressing a vague disdain for journalists reminiscent of leftists at protests, most were happy to tell me their virtually identical stories of joining the group.

Prior to enlisting, they attended games only with their family, with their couple of friends also interested in baseball, or alone. Many had struggled with cancer, addiction, or abusive relationships, worsened by social isolation to the point of total hopelessness. They had found solidarity and community in the fan club, consisting largely of suburban Queens and Long Island residents, that began in 2012 as a merger between the soccer-hooligan-styled "Citi Field Sheas" and DIY Mets merchandiser Darren Meenan in an effort to bring energy to the new stadium. As it grew into the thousands, T7LA became renowned for supporting one another both emotionally and financially, believing that being a Mets fan means maintaining loyalty through the bad times and the good—a credo that extended to the relationships built in their outfield section, tailgates, and riotous away-game marches.

As for the 2024 season, they admitted hopes were not high. When I asked if that really mattered, their answers were also identical: "not really."

The previous seasons' collapses had embarrassed the team's image enough to ward off the top free agents—the Dodger dynasty won top prizes Shohei Ohtani and Yoshinobu Yamamoto over comparable offers from Cohen. The big names adverse, the Mets' most significant acquisition came in the front office, with the signing of David Stearns in the new role of president of baseball operations. The Manhattanite millennial maven had rejuvenated the Astros and Brewers, and now returned home to begin fixing the team he had loved since Valentine. He signed an overlooked slew, including unproven Samoan American pitcher Sean Manaea, unwanted DH mercenary J. D. Martinez, and Yankee castaways

Luis Severino, Harrison Bader, and manager Carlos Mendoza. Stearns's new data analysts and cutting-edge "pitching lab" would mature "baby Mets" Francisco Álvarez, Mark Vientos, Brett Baty, and the midrange roster in the rebuilding year. The modest goal was to eke out a winning season as the Cohen Tax penalty subsided, repairing the franchise's finances and reputation enough that the Yankees' rental Juan Soto could be lured in a 2025 spending spree.

An hour before game time, T7LA troops assembled in formation beneath their flag to march the Shea Road toward Citi. At a 2016 away outing in San Diego, hundreds of them had chanted and pushed away police barricades on their way to Petco Park, where beloved pitcher and hapless hitter Bartolo Colon rewarded them by slugging his first career home run right to their section. "I see how riots start," conservative comedian and T7LA member Jim Breuer, said of the day. "We march out in the street and the feeling of taking over a city is exhilarating."[609]

Few subsequent marches had matched that hooliganry, I was warned, and I indeed found myself diverting from the buzzed noontime saunter for a peripheral loop of Willets Point. Astride construction fences surrounding the massive plots for new condos and stadia, mechanics outside the few remaining garages smoked and stared into the deep mud puddles of New York's worst-maintained street, indifferent to the giddy Opening Day throngs entering the ballpark.

I met my friend Margeaux Marks at the apple. Seven years ago, she fulfilled her lifelong dream of moving to New York, and fell in love with the Mets after attending Tylor Megill's 2022 combined no-hitter, closed by Edwin Díaz. "We crammed eight people in a five-seat SUV and drove home with the windows down, listening to 'Narco' on repeat," Margeaux told me as we entered and rode the escalators to our seats in the last row of the promenade.[610]

Flashy attractions like Díaz's viral "Narco" entrance were the Mets marketers' plan to break even in the lean year. A gauntlet of LCD screens lined every available Citi surface, alternating between advertisements and "digital baseball cards" of the starting lineup. A DJ crew spun upbeat tunes in the ersatz nightclub Coca-Cola corner. Capering atop the clubhouse was the most controversial new attraction, the Queens Crew dance team. The announcement of the non-sexualized cheerleaders, a promotion clearly geared toward New York's youth, drew attacks on social media and call-in shows as a pitiful replacement for the Japanese stars—often by the same older cohort that drools over each of Citi's grotesque new culinary roll-outs: like the French onion soup burger, cheesesteak hot dog, and rainbow cookie egg roll.

When the game against the Brewers began, Margeaux and I covertly blew THC vapor into our jackets, searching through binoculars for the team's human element. Aside from Lindor and Alonso, the team boasted no true stars, no playboy sex icons or outspoken iconoclasts. We scraped together theories of their characters from squints of interaction with fans and other players, their "Drip Report" fashion profiles on Citi Vision, and the contextual clues of their chosen walk-up music. Pete Alonso's first-inning entrance to Rage Against the Machine's anti-police anthem "Killing in the Name," for instance, suggested with its refrain of "Fuck you I won't do what you tell me" a subtle protest to the offseason calls for him to loyally extend his contract with the Mets in his walk year before free agency.

But the thermal-shrouded Mets showed little character or offense through the ceaseless windchill. Lukewarmth finally arrived in the eighth. Down 3–1, benches cleared after notorious "Met-killer" Rhys Hoskins slid Utley-like to take out Jeff McNeil at second. When the slide was ruled legal, the bully Brewers rubbed their eyes in the international gesture of *crybaby* for McNeil's anger about the senseless aggression, and proceeded to put the tired team to bed.

APRIL 4

The opening home stand continued the malaise stretching back to 2022. The Brewers swept, and the Tigers took the first two of the next series. No-hit late into the final game, Gary Cohen sighed on the broadcast: "Nobody in the ballpark. 0–5. Hitless through seven. Feels like rock bottom."

SNY's auteur director John DeMarsico panned the sparse crowd to find comedian Max Wiener, his curly locks draping a purple fur jacket, dancing without concern. Seconds later, Alonso slapped a home run to tie the game. When the Mets went on to win, fans online memed the "Rally Pimp" as the season's first viral savior.

APRIL 12

The Mets returned to Citi Field after a 6–2 road trip. A slumping Lindor was greeted with a standing ovation, the result of Steve Cohen's campaign to support the player after his wife Katia received violent and sexist threats online. "I'm usually all for triggering male fragile egos and find it borderline comical when I get cowardly social media hate," she shot back on Twitter, "but when lowlifes like this bring my husband and kids to the conversation, whew, that really crosses a boundary."[611]

Neither the MLB, which profiteers from sports-book partnerships, nor Cohen, actively lobbying to build a casino in the Citi Field parking lot, admitted the explosion of such anger emanates from the fools separated from their money by the sports gambling business. A heartened Lindor, however, hit a single in the win, raising his average to .111.

APRIL 14

Dwight Gooden's number was retired in a pregame ceremony—part of Cohen's campaign to rehabilitate the notorious eighties bad boys erased by the Wilpons.

I asked Allison McCague, host of the feminist Mets podcast *A Pod of Their Own,* how she felt about the celebrations for Gooden and Strawberry that omitted their reported histories of violence against women. "We consistently joke—though it isn't even really a joke—that we wish this team had more championships to celebrate so we can perhaps stop talking about the 1986 Mets entirely," she responded. "And maybe someday that will happen. But until then, those players will unfortunately continue to be idolized."[612]

In a short speech, Gooden expressed his regret at having ever left the team, and recalled the years spent pleading with the front office to allow him to finish his career in Queens. After thanking Steinbrenner for offering him refuge with the Yankees, fans began to boo. Doc raised his hands defensively. "I'm not saying nothing. I'm always a Met!"[613]

APRIL 22

At the end of the 2023 season, some teams opened games with a moment of silence for the Israeli victims of October 7, and a number of Jewish players throughout the MLB, including Alex Bregman and Dean Kremer, denounced Hamas's incursion and antisemitism in general.[614]

There was no subsequent mention in baseball of the eliminationist war of revenge that followed, in which unknown thousands of Gazans were killed, and millions starved and permanently displaced. Breaking the silence, a group of activists on the Subway platform outside Yankee Stadium dropped leaflets and a banner reading: MLB & RANDY LEVINE, GENOCIDE IS NOT A GAME! THE BRONX LOVES PALESTINE![615]

The group's statement attacked the staunch Zionism of the Yankees ownership and several of its players, calling for other New York fans to protest their teams' Israeli ties as well. After some brief searching, I found little ground for a similar protest against the Mets. While the Wilpons had hosted an event at Citi supporting illegal West Bank settlements, Cohen's investments in Israeli firms appeared marginal in his massive portfolio.[616] The Bronx banner drop turned out to be the last pro-Palestinian protest in baseball all year.

On the team itself, only Harrison Bader had commented on the war at all. The selectee for Israel's World Baseball Classic team wore a Star of David on his belt to honor the hostages taken by Hamas, pledging to wear it until their release. With all ceasefire negotiations refused by Israel and the US, it remained there the entire season.

APRIL 27

The Mets hit a skid, losing their fifth out of six games in their melancholic new "City Connect" alternate—a uniform concept borrowed from the NBA that allowed franchises to market a wholly distinct brand for their teams connected to "the personality of the city."[617]

Aside from the dying Athletics and traditionalist Yankees, the Mets held out against the gimmick longer than any other team. Their uniforms had already incorporated metropolitan aesthetics since their inception, with their "city of shadows" black uniform concept predating the City Connects by over two decades.

But with merch sales lagging and attendance low, the team cashed in. The Mets' dark gray design invoked the grit and dreariness of New York's concrete subways and streets, with pinstripes composed of tiny MTA tokens, and 7-train purple lining the sleeves and Nike swoosh. Fan response was generally positive, aside from two complaints on color. While they identified with the gloom, the grimy backdrop and *New York* lettering gave it the appearance of a gray road uniform, making the players appear like strangers in their own home, dressed like a sidewalk that the Cardinals walked all over.

The joyous purple, on the other hand, was far too sparse. The fans demanded more—and soon got it.

APRIL 30

Attendance had been startlingly low through the first month—a 20 percent drop representing a 150,000-fan deficit from 2023. Only the Athletics saw a starker decline.[618]

Half of Citi's concessions were closed during the week, with the few open catering to a near-equal proportion of road-team fans. Meanwhile, the Phillies and Yankees surged. Even drizzly weeknight games in the Bronx outdrew Doc Gooden's number retirement ceremony.

In another desperate attempt to fill Citi Field, the Mets held a one-dollar hot dog night inspired by the viral sensation of Opening Day's veteran of the game, Seymour Weiner—whose laudable record of fighting in World War II and the Civil Rights Movement was overshadowed by a name punny enough to be paged at Moe's Tavern. The Mets went on to win, improving their record to 15–14 as a drunken food fight broke out in the stands.

MAY 1

After a week of brutal NYPD raids on pro-Palestinian encampments at campuses including NYU, Columbia, the New School, and City College of New York, New York's annual May Day protest called to expand the movement to the broader working class.

In the late sixties, images of devastated Vietnamese villages, children charred with napalm, and senseless police brutality against student protesters mobilized the mass, militant movement championed by Mets fans and players. Now, dozens of similar images appeared daily on social media, and polls showed Israel's rampage was widely unpopular. But the movement gained little traction against the repression, justified by smears of antisemitism despite having been organized cooperatively by Jewish and Muslim students. The May Day protests were small and uneventful, leaving the antiwar sentiment unthreateningly cordoned away from workplaces, electoral politics, and sports.

MAY 13

Before a game against the Phillies, I stopped by Citi's shuttered pin-trading booth to meet Joe, a member of T7LA. He and wife Kaitlyn make punk-inspired bootleg Mets pins and stickers under the moniker of their DIY mascot, *Mets Jr.* "We came up with this idea. . . . What if Mr. and Mrs. Met had a kid and then that kid was a little shithead? Like a Dennis the Menace or Bart Simpson type. . . . Felt really fun, tapped into the subversiveness we were going for."

The Mets Jr. Instagram account tells followers when and where to meet to get the merch. "It's kind of like a secret club," he said, handing me a sticker of Met Jr. holding the Social Justice Pride flag. "I think with how things are right now, it's more important than ever to be visible in your support of our LGBTQ+ friends. I always wanted what we did to be mischievous and antagonistic to big corporations (bootlegging their IP), but I also wanted it to be known that we support and love all Mets fans."[619]

Things had been looking up for the mascot couple since the previous year, when Mrs. Met became a sports sex icon after a curve-flattering photo of her went viral. But as I took my seat in a largely empty section near the right-field foul pole before the first inning, I scanned the ballpark and spotted only her husband. Her Twitter account had been mysteriously deleted earlier that month as job postings appeared online for a replacement actor to fill the uniform.

I wondered if the Mets' woes had put their relationship on the rocks. Boyish Brett Baty played like a Little Leaguer. Ringer J. D. Martinez was having the worst season of his career. Trying to find his inner sunshine through the gloom, a still foggy Lindor began walking to the plate to the Temptations' "My Girl."

As the close game reached late innings, an IPA-chugging Phillies sadist covered in hipster tattoos began to heckle our nebbishy section. "Have another beer!" someone eventually shouted back. He agreed and returned with twenty-four more ounces of belligerence. Finally quieted when the Mets took a 4–2 lead to the ninth, our counsel shouted: "Now go drive home!"

The lights at Citi Field went dark to the sound effect of a power shutdown. The beats and trumpets of *Narco* heralded Díaz's gallop to a field illuminated with flashing red and blue lights (nicknamed "bisexual lighting" by contemporary cinematographers). The viral entrance did not inspire the faith it had during Díaz's near-perfect 2022 season. His velocity, control, and confidence had reduced post-injury. After giving up a home run, he walked the bases loaded and hit Alec Bohm to blow the save. As our record fell to 19–21, the Philadelphia ogre returned at the last minute to call us all fags.

MAY 18

As the Mets kept losing, I kept watching, trying to recall the historic fun in watching the *#LOLMets* find *new ways to lose.*

Few others were so patient. Baty was exiled to the minors in exchange for a swaggy lifelong Mets fan from Connecticut, Mark Vientos. For the first time in years, Lindor, batting .190, was placed in the leadoff spot against the Marlins. He was hit by a pitch in the first and scored. When Díaz blew a 9–5 lead in the ninth on a grand slam, Mets fans declared the season over by spreading memes of a smiling Lindor under the word ELIMINATED.

Blogger Mack Ade wrote a column suggesting Cohen again "blow up" the team by trading anyone over the age of thirty for prospects. In what was apparently meant to be a private direct message on Twitter, Cohen publicly responded to the post: "All in the future, not much we can do until the trade deadline."[620]

MAY 29

The Mets clubhouse has always acted out their historic comic/tragic role with either the ironic confidence of *Ya Gotta Believe*, or the wall-punching frustration of post-choke Mike Piazza. During a lifeless sweep by the Dodgers at Citi on May 29, dropping their record to 22–33, the mood in the clubhouse swung decisively toward the latter.

At the peak of the catastrophe, reliever Jorge López was ejected for arguing a meaningless call. As he left the mound, the humiliation of being the "worst teammate" on "the worst team in the whole fucking league" overcame him, he told reporters after the game.[621] Several of his bullpen-mates had been cut for similar poor showings, and he decided to save Stearns the trouble by tossing his glove to the sparsely populated seats in disgust. A Yankees fan, front row for some *#LOLMets* comic relief, caught it.

MAY 30

Morale hardly improved when López was immediately fired for acknowledging the team-wide frustration. Over the now two-season-long slump, hundreds of similar gestures had expressed the same feeling: Alonso's sullen head shakes, McNeil's bat-slamming shouts of *FUCK* (audible through the ballpark and on the broadcasters' mics), and tearful Díaz's fetal-position posture on the bench after blown saves.

Finally acknowledging the crisis, Lindor called a players-only clubhouse meeting. "My instincts were telling me it was the right time to get everybody out," he said. "The players, we don't really get an opportunity to talk like that. . . . When everyone's in meetings like this and we look at each other eye to eye and you say something and you say 'yeah, you mean that, I got you,' it goes a long way."[622]

I was surprised to learn meetings like these are rare. Teamwork is now forged in pregame drills, not hangouts, as players often put in earbuds and go their separate ways after games. The situation had gotten particularly bad on a team where, Lindor later admitted, most everyone was "fed up with each other."[623]

But in the closed meeting, the private insecurities and resentments were finally aired. Disputes turned to mutual recognition of team-wide problems that, if they could not solve themselves, management would solve for them with more cuts and trades.

Lindor's sunshine smile steered the bleak mood toward a sunnier horizon—the third wildcard slot was not yet out of reach. If the players held one another accountable, they could at least appear to be a team that *cared* in the face of fan alienation and trade-deadline demolition. J. D. Martinez described it as a resolution to ignore the critics and contracts, and play just for the enjoyment of the fans, or failing that, their own. "You know what, they say we suck, we suck. Let's suck!" he summed up the attitude of the team after the meeting. "Let's go suck together. Let's go have fun sucking."[624]

MAY 31

Following López's cut, Jose Iglesias was called up from the minors as a backup infielder. The affable thirty-four-year-old Cuban defector was an all-star, with flashy fielding and a high career batting average. But he had spent 2023 at home after failing to win a major-league contract. Worrying his career was over, he penned a song confronting his depression.

In the voice of his Latin-pop alter-ego Candelita, he croons of finding happiness, despite having nothing, by staying in pursuit of his dreams. Everything bad that gets in his way will be pushed away in the process.

Dropping his insistence on a major-league contract shortly after recording the track, he signed a minor-league deal with the Mets. Celebrating his return to the bigs, he played "OMG" for some of his teammates. Part *Ya Gotta Believe* self-affirmation against the seemingly insurmountable cruelties of the baseball labor market, and part secular prayer, it fit perfectly with the recent clubhouse resolution. "We just give everything we got, every pitch, every bat," Iglesias said. "And then usually the god of baseball—he helps you when you go with the right energy and the right attitude."[625]

JUNE 1

On the day of Darryl Strawberry's number retirement ceremony, the home run apple was painted with hundreds of seeds to resemble his saccharine namesake. The sobered slugger, now a traveling pastor spreading hope and faith to fellow addicts, spent much of his speech preaching directly to dugout.

"These are the greatest fans you will ever play in front of," Strawberry said to a team watching in reverence. "They will stand on their feet for you and cheer you on. They will let you know when you suck. Don't worry about it, guys. It's part of it. But push through, because you guys have it. You have the talent. Believe in each other. Care for each other. . . . The best is yet to come for you guys."[626]

The Mets went on to lose 10–5 to the Diamondbacks, dropping their record to 24–34. Iglesias recorded his first RBI.

JUNE 3

The Mets' social media imagery switched to a trans-inclusive Pride Month color scheme, and their first Pride Month post of "Baseball is for everyone!" attracted a barrage of homophobic hate in dozens of comments attacking the Mets as a "degenerate organization."[627,628] Most other MLB teams have pride nights; few embrace their LGBTQ+ fans more than the Mets. Citi celebrates the entire month, while others, like the Yankees, go gay only for a day.[629]

In his second start that night, Jose Iglesias recorded three hits, an RBI, and scored twice in a thrilling win over the Nationals. After the game, J. D. Martinez urged Iglesias to play "OMG" for the rest of the team in the clubhouse. "Bro, this is a good song. We gotta play this. We gotta ride this out. We gotta use it."[630]

JUNE 12

Post-meeting optimism began to find footing. Francisco Álvarez returned from injury. Candelita's clutch hits and spirited defense improved confidence. But the Citi crowd was not yet faithful after another blown save from Díaz against the lowly Marlins on June 11.

All the prior marketing memes had worked to build some hype in isolation—the jouissance of Seymour Weiner, the campy Rally Pimp, the DIY community around T7LA and Met Jr., and the proliferation of purple-piped gray jerseys in the stands. Before the second game of the series against the Marlins, these elements combined into a new meme-messiah taking the mound to throw the ceremonial first pitch.

The origins of McDonald's purple spokes-thing Grimace go back to the late sixties. The pioneer roadside fast-food chain had already spread the country as a ubiquitous and low-price source of nourishment for workers. To expand the questionable cuisine's market to their kids, new franchises were built with Disney-like playgrounds, complete with a food-themed fantasy mythos in which a heroic Ronald McDonald works with Mayor McCheese and Officer Big Mac to combat Happy Meal–thieving villains.[631] While the Hamburglar was a mere human criminal, the milkshake-stealing Grimace was something far more disturbing—a bulbous, purple, anthropomorphic taste bud, the pleasure-seeking human id turned into a Cronenbergian monster.

Deemed too frightening in the eighties, Grimace returned to prominence in a more desensitized 2023 to promote a purple milkshake honoring his fiftieth birthday. The innocent ad campaign soon took on a viral creepypasta life of its own when TikTok users made short films about how a single sip of the shake transformed them into possessed entities with bulging googly eyes and purple foam bubbling from their orifices.[632]

The Mets scored two in the first and three in the second following Grimace's fatty lob. Jokes that he had possessed the Mets in their refreshingly easy 10–4 win spread online, reawakening the fanbase's fetish for cheap, satisfying non sequitur.

JUNE 18

After sweeping the Padres, the surge continued to Texas. Down 4–6 in the ninth, Álvarez drove in the game-winning runs with a double. The team celebrated in the visitor's clubhouse to Candelita's "OMG."

"We're singing it, we're humming it all the time," reliever Adam Ottavino said.[633]

While the hot bat of Álvarez, Lindor's comfort at leadoff, and anti-individualist commitment were clearly the turnaround's cause, the Grimace cargo-cult continued to recruit. Young fans bought cheap Grimace pullover costumes from Amazon, and hipsters copped a stylish *Grimace x Mets* purple bootleg jersey from fast-acting web retailers.

JUNE 19

As reluctant sports show hosts discussed the relevance of the "Grimace effect," *Shea Station* podcaster Jolly Olive asserted the streak began, instead, with the Pride Month tweet: "the gay Mets are 6–3 btw."[634] "The Gay Mets will take Pride in beating your favorite team."[635] "The Texas Rangers refused to have a Pride Night so the Gay Mets had to fuck 'em up."[636]

The win streak ended at seven on the day the news broke that Willie Mays had passed away at the age of ninety-three in Palo Alto. His number was added alongside Bud Harrelson and Jerry Grote to a growing cemetery of memorial patches for recently deceased Mets on the sleeves of the team's uniform. There was little discussion of Mays' tragic final games in the World Series compared to the magic that team inspired around the memetic *Ya Gotta Believe* slogan—now chaotically revived by combining the embrace of Pride and its new purple genderqueer-icon mascot into "The Gay Grimace Mets Era."[637,638]

JUNE 28

At Citi Field's official Pride Night, some players and staff showed up to batting practice in Pride apparel, including Lindor in a shirt reading "New York Is Love" in rainbow colors, and Harrison Bader in a black Mets cap with a Pride-flag-colored insignia.[639] Drag king Murray Hill threw out the first pitch.

The Gay Mets blew out the Astros 7–2 and celebrated after the game with a self-organized on-field performance of "OMG." Iglesias lip-synched at second base, the still-cheering Pride Night crowd looking on as the rest of the team rushed onto the field giddily to join him mid-song. Even players who spoke no Spanish appeared to have learned the words.

Most remarkably, the team itself—perhaps more liberal than average, although with its share of conservatives—had playfully embraced Olive's Gay Mets moniker. They supplemented the age-old sports tradition of slapping each other's butts after good plays with pirouettes, umpire-sassing, four-way crotch thrusts, and clubhouse kisses.[640] Exceeding the normal homosociality between athletes (often exaggerated by queer-baiting writers), the players, just as the Mets marketers had done by padding Mrs. Met's outfit to make her into a curvy sex icon, appeared to know exactly what they were doing.

JULY 13

It seemed the gayer the Mets got, the more they won. A study of the 2009–10 NBA season by Berkeley sociologists found "early season touch predicted greater performance for individuals as well as teams later in the season," with the touchiest teams—the Celtics and Lakers—topping the league.[641] It was not protest of the wars, race riots, and climate chaos engulfing the world, but something deeper and more personal—an embrace of camaraderie and joy in the face of the right-wing culture war against free expression of gender and sexuality.

They continued cruising in Colorado. Lindor, Alonso, Martinez, and Nimmo returned to form. Severino pitched like he had in pinstripes years ago. Alonso wore Grimace-purple cleats. McNeil started calling himself "Happy Jeff" as he finally started making solid contact.

During the game, Trump, handily beating Biden in every poll, narrowly missed an incel's kill-shot at his Pennsylvania rally. Trump's survival inspired a slew of influencers to endorse him, including far-right billionaire Elon Musk, podcaster Joe Rogan, and a number of players on the Cardinals and Rays, who began mimicking his fist-pounding *fight fight fight!* gesture after hits.

JULY 21

During a Mets loss to the Marlins, a chyron crossed the bottom of the WPIX broadcast announcing Joe Biden was dropping out of the presidential race. Completing a surprisingly competent intraparty coup, Vice President Kamala Harris picked up his dim torch.

Polls immediately turned around for the Democrats, just as the Mets found themselves firmly in the heat of the wildcard race. Even those with no faith in Harris adapted the coconut emoji, a satirical reference to one of her incoherent rambles contrived from her Marxist parents, as a Grimace-like ironic badge of approval for her unlikely ascendance. The comebacks inspired remarkably similar rhetoric on both political and sports-talk radio—*We're so back!* cheered the liberals who had mumbled *it's so over* during sundowning Biden's spring debate.

JULY 24

As Harris searched for a running-mate that could reestablish a genuine link to her progressive base, the Mets rediscovered their own savior in Francisco Lindor. His batting average surged from .210 in April to .290 in June, delivering 23 RBIs in July. During a sweep of the Yankees in the Bronx, Lindor crushed a decisive home run off Gerrit Cole, high-fiving his infant daughters Kalina and Amapola seated beside the dugout before returning to the bench. "They're the future," he had said following Amapola's birth. "Female is future."[642]

The fans who now chanted "MVP" before his at bats, and the players who regarded him as the team's clear leader, wondered alike why the franchise had not officially designated him their first captain since David Wright.

The reticence perhaps had something to do with his second job as the MLBPA's player representative. Before the season, he was central to navigating a revolt from the league's "middle class" of players and newly unionized minor leaguers against the entrenched union leadership they perceived as in the pocket of the top-paid stars. Veterans like Daniel Murphy led the opposition during a contentious March 18 Zoom call, concluding with a vote of no-confidence in union executive director Tony Clark and demands for minor-league organizer Harry Marino to replace deputy executive director Bruce Meyer.

Caught between fellow stars and the rank-and-file, Lindor, who had fought against the previous CBA compromise on luxury tax that reduced offseason spending to inspire the mutiny, acknowledged the difficult negotiations: “This is our union. . . . Ultimately, [Meyer and Clark] do what we tell them to do.”[643] A week after the initial vote, Lindor whipped votes to reaffirm confidence in the established leadership in an OMG-like compromise to push-away the bad vibes of class struggle until the offseason.

JULY 26

The Mets’ injured ace Kodai Senga returned against the Braves. For five innings, he was as dominant as he had been as in the previous Cy Young-contention season. DeMarsico’s SNY cameras panned the jubilant Friday night crowd, showing multiple DIY Grimaces, rally pimps, and Mets-themed furries—anthropomorphic animal fetishists who wear mascot-like “fursuits.” Ron Darling compared the Citi scene to the *Star Wars* cantina.

The next inning, Senga chased a ground-ball dribbler and collapsed with a season-ending calf strain. It quieted the crowd, but most shrugged. We had come this far without him, after all. The 8–4 Mets win sent them half-a-game past the Braves in the standings.

AUGUST 2

The first week of the Paris Olympics reminded Mets fans that, outside of Flushing, the sports world was not so queer-positive.

In a match against Algerian boxer Imane Khelif, Italian contestant Angela Carini resigned after less than a minute, claiming the contest was unfair because her opponent was a biological male. "Four years ago, we lost our way," a Trump ad released that week said. "Men can beat up women, and win medals."[644]

The claim was a hoax. Khelif was born female, raised a woman, identified as a woman, and originated from a country in which being trans had been illegal since a 1966 counterrevolution against its socialist government. But the story exploded as part of the ongoing trans panic's most resonant issue, women's sports, a Trojan horse to push legislation against all trans people, queers, and even cis women perceived as too masculine, like Khelif.

Katia Reguero Lindor summed up the hypocrisy in an Instagram post: "It is absurd that a number of alarmed men believing that she is a trans woman are the same that are silent about the reproductive rights of women (or worse, speak against feminine autonomy). So in cases like these, what they do is get hooked on a misogynistic transphobic agenda while planting themselves as allies to feminism. They are NOT allies. They are still misogynists, and ill-informed to top it off."[645]

AUGUST 5

With the Mets on the road, a small "Planet Over Profit" protest was held outside the Rancid and Green Day concert at Citi Field. A guerrilla performance by a punk band called The Resistance Corporation demanded Citibank divest hundreds of billions from fossil fuels companies like Exxon and BP.[646] Other protests of Citibank locations called for the bank to cut ties with Israel, where, Citi's website boasts, they have the "largest presence of any foreign financial institution."[647] Perhaps assuming the baseball crowd would be less sympathetic than the punks, no similar protests targeted Citi when the Mets played at home.

AUGUST 6

Billy Bean, the second major-league baseball player to come out as gay, passed away from leukemia at the age of sixty. Since 2014, he had visited clubhouses as the MLB's "ambassador of inclusion," encouraging players to be more welcoming to fans and teammates by ditching homophobic slurs.

It was not an easy task. Most of the Mets were receptive when he visited their clubhouse in 2015, but Daniel Murphy later told the press, likely speaking for more than just himself: "We love the people, we disagree with the lifestyle."

"It took me 32 years to fully accept my sexual orientation," Bean later wrote in an invitation to Murphy to talk more, "so it would be hypocritical of me to not be patient with others."[648] In time, the two became friends, and Murphy told Bean his perspective had changed.[649]

AUGUST 15

Slumping since Senga's fall, the Mets attempted to revive their meme magic by having Haliey Welch, known as "Hawk Tuah Girl" for her viral description of an oral sex technique, to throw the first pitch of their home stand against the Athletics.

Fans found the stunt distasteful. The Mets had already earned a reputation as prop comics with their Grimace-dressed fans and OMG sign, and Athletics reliever Austin Adams was one of a few opponents that year who mocked their memeing by imitating the OMG dance after defeating the Mets in a big moment. Many were even relieved that blowing the game put to bed any further talk of the *Hawk Tuah Mets.*

AUGUST 22

The Democrats held their national convention amidst the enthusiasm for Harris and her new progressive running mate, Tim Walz. There was hope they would separate themselves from the deeply unpopular Biden administration, offer economic solutions for the corporate cartels causing inflation in rent and food prices, and make some gesture to the hundreds of thousands who voted "uncommitted" in the primaries to protest Biden's unflinching support for Israel's genocide.

Instead, they promoted only *good vibes* to counter their dour fascist opponents. No vision of how they would expand democracy or reproductive rights was offered, and Trump's lies about an "immigrant invasion" were accepted with promises to *build the wall* themselves. Speaking slots were refused for Teamster president Sean O'Brien, and any Palestinian or trans Democrats. With no serious economic policy for workers, they oriented toward the middle class and small-business owners with convoluted tax credit schemes and deregulation. Their slogan could have been: *Everything that's bad, push it away.*

SEPTEMBER 1

Aura Moody, a member of the Queens Village Republican Club, vowed to sue the Mets for "racial and political retaliation" after she was not permitted to bring her MAGA hat into Citi Field. Signs and attire that are "too political" were barred, security told her.[650] The front office apologized after the game, saying the guard had been "retrained" and that there was no policy against MAGA hats.

When a MAGA-hat-wearing *Post* reporter tested Citi's new political attire policy, she found herself welcomed with extra courtesy by staff, and receiving only gentle ribbing from a few fans no worse than what one might expect if they wore a Yankees hat.[651]

In previous years, during the time of antifascist street brawls with Proud Boys and other Nazis, I'd seen MAGA-hat wearers at Citi heckled, or worse. Now Trumpism had been normalized by the Democrats' acceptance of his policies, and Mets fans and leftists alike had lost any interest on brawling on behalf of the lesser evil.

SEPTEMBER 3

Their threadbare roster pitching with a masterful grit that rivaled the late-nineties Braves, the Mets were on a five-game winning streak and tied for the third wildcard slot. Their opponent the Red Sox, on the other hand, were slumping away from the playoffs after their star Jarren Duran was heard shouting a homophobic slur at a Fenway fan (he apologized and received a short suspension, but his uniform became the top seller at the MLB shop).[652] Despite the series's importance, attendance still averaged below 30,000. Wondering if all the light shows, gimmicks, and memes had distracted fans from the team's actual journey, I told my dad about how some fans on Twitter were reminiscing about Shea's Diamond Vision rally-standard in which a manic anchorman exhorted all New York to rise up in populist anger.

"You know where that's from?" Dad asked.

"Yeah, *Network*."

"Before that. It comes from Jean Shepherd's *hurling invective* bit from his radio show."

I hadn't put together that the beatnik radio monologist, most famous for writing and narrating *A Christmas Story*, who had boosted the Mets as a countercultural happening in early 1962, had also inspired the scene from *Network*. In an early act of culture jamming, he told listeners to crank up their radios and open their windows to allow him to scream non-sequitur threats at people on the street.[653]

The Mets held a 3–1 lead into the eighth. Reed Garrett entered with the bases full and no one out. "They're doing it!" I cried out as the frazzled anchorman appeared on Citi Vision. "They actually brought it back!"

In *Network*, Howard Beale's full monologue begins with a description of the existential despair of postwar individualism: "We sit in the house, and slowly the world we're living in is getting smaller, and all we say is, 'Please, at least leave us alone in our living rooms. Let me have my toaster and my TV. . . . I won't say anything. Just leave us alone.'"

His speech speeds to rant as he describes a political depression apt for the current day: "I don't want you to riot. I don't want you to write to your Congressman, because I wouldn't know what to tell you to write. I don't know what to do about the depression and the inflation and the Russians and the crime in the street."

Beale then rises from his chair, wild-eyed and dripping zealously with sweat: "All I know is that first, you've got to get mad. You've gotta say, 'I'm a human being, goddammit! My life has value!' So, I want you to get up now. I want all of you to get up out of your chairs. I want you to get up right now and go to the window, open it, and stick your head out and yell, I'M MAD AS HELL, AND I'M NOT GOING TO TAKE IT ANYMORE!"[654]

But the Flushing faithful took it a little longer. We exchanged our fear, depression, hopelessness, and anger for the unifying cause of getting through the inning, yelling instead: *Let's Go Mets.*

Garrett got a fly-out, scoring Duran, then a double-play. The Mets kept the lead and went on to win. Dad and I left the stadium joining in the echoing chants of "Let's go Mets" and "Yankees suck." September meaning had arrived.

SEPTEMBER 18

After taking the first two from the Nationals, the Mets were playing their hearts out in a three-way tie with the Diamondbacks and Braves for the second and third wildcard slots. But with only five home games remaining, attendance had barely risen. Their series in Philadelphia the previous weekend, on the other hand, had been totally sold out. Were there only 35,000 believers?

They completed the sweep with a 10–0 win. Once the last out was made, a fired-up Nimmo jogged onto the field, took Steve Gelbs' SNY microphone, and addressed all fans: "We need your help! We need everybody to get out here! We need this place full! This is playoff baseball! This is what you guys want! Let's go! Let's go Mets!"[655]

SEPTEMBER 22

Nimmo's marching order received, Citi Field filled for a weekend four-game showdown with the Phillies. "[It's] about as loud as it's been since 2015," Gelbs tweeted.[656] Mendoza called the energy injection "unbelievable. That's what it should look like, it should feel like, especially when we're playing meaningful games in September."[657]

Suddenly, Mets hats were everywhere in the city, with more fans in public and online celebrating the series in first-person plural. *We* beat the Phillies 10–6. *We* got blown out 2–12 the next day. Sean Manaea came through for *us* on Saturday. A win today will put *us* ahead of the Braves going into the Atlanta series, and *we* can't let them clinch on *our* turf.

The burst of unification intensified when *Batting Around* podcaster Lauren Walker's scalding tweet went viral: "i am glad mets fans are having fun and riding the late season playoff race roller coaster, but there are 162 games in a baseball season and every team on that timeline will experience lots of humor, whimsy, and joy."[658] No, the fan base responded, we saw nothing like our pop-star second baseman, puppet patron saint, or unashamed male love elsewhere. DIY merch and stickers were printed claiming *humor, whimsy, and joy* as the perfect description of the team's incessant Stengelian charm.

Tylor Megill outpitched Zack Wheeler, and *we* had a 2–1 lead in the ninth when Díaz took the mound. He wavered, walking Stott and Marsh. Stott ran. Álvarez's throw was short. Vientos flinched as the ball bounced off the lip of third base straight up for him to grab and hold the runner. The *god of baseball* had heard our *OMG* prayers. Díaz, renewed in his faith, struck out Roger Clemens's son to end the game.

SEPTEMBER 24

I remembered times when I thought that if the Mets were winning, all was right in the world. Obviously, this was never true—but in 2024, such a feeling was impossible. My Twitter feed was a mix of Mets memes and the charred corpses of Gaza. Friends posted exasperated stories on Instagram that depicted the scale of children killed in slide after slide of thousands of tiny pink dots. American activists, soldiers, and journalists set themselves on fire in front of Israeli consulates. The NYPD opened fire on a man for fare evasion in East New York, severely injuring the commuters behind him. Ex-cop Mayor Eric Adams, soon to be indicted for fleecing the city of millions of dollars, praised the officers' discipline. Climate apocalypse loomed over a costly loss to the Braves. Hurricane Helene postponed the remainder of the series, and the Mets fled Atlanta in a cyclonic three-way wildcard tie.

SEPTEMBER 28

The offensive chill of April returned in Milwaukee. Alonso kept batting like a .240 hitter, with few of his 34 home runs coming in crucial moments. J. D. Martinez was hitless in 36 at bats, the franchise's longest hitless streak since the notoriously light-hitting Rey Ordóñez. Lindor returned from a back injury, wincing through his smile. The Mets looked as feeble as they had in their embarrassing opening series against the bully Brewers, losing the series to fall behind the Braves in the standings. The T7LA prepared an update of their I SURVIVED T-shirt of September chokes: 1998, 2006, 2007, 2008, 2016, 2022, *2024.* Trump surged in the polls after working a thirty-minute shift at a McDonald's drive-thru.

SEPTEMBER 30

Chlorine fumes from a nearby chemical plant explosion, apparently unrelated to the broader devastation of Helene, drifted toward Truist Park for the Mets' return to Atlanta. One win in the doubleheader would secure a playoff slot. Two losses would end the season.

Braves rookie Spencer Schwellenbach blanked the Mets until his exit. The Mets scored six in the eighth to overcome the three-run deficit, only to watch Díaz blow the lead in the bottom of the inning. Lindor stroked a two-run homer to put the Mets back up in the ninth. Díaz returned to close it out, slamming his mitt in a gesture that recalled López's mid-season resignation, as Lindor knelt on second with tears in his eyes after making the clinching out. The game reflected "the twists and turns of the Mets season," an awe-struck Gary Cohen remarked. "From 0–5 to *OMG*."[659]

The Mets punted the second game, allowing the Braves to clinch the second wildcard slot. Enemies no more, the players emerged, champagne-soaked from their respective clubhouses, to celebrate on the field together.

OCTOBER 3

Some believed the Mets had come to the playoffs with "house money"—the unearned windfall of a lucky half-season streak. And yet the Brewers could not bully them as they had in the regular season. Jesse Winker, a former Mets killer brought to New York at the deadline, made this clear in the first inning by challenging Brewers shortstop Willy Adames to meet him in the parking lot after the game.

I watched the series in a booth of Lou's Athletic Club in Bushwick. It's a sports bar for punks, or a punk bar for sports, depending on whom you ask. The owners, and most of the clientele, are promenade Mets fans of the variety who shamelessly stay seated during the national anthem. My rotating back-booth crew included metalhead Mets reliever turned illustrator Daniel Herrera, socialist comedian Anders Lee, anarchist gardener Spike, and Cookie Problems, an underground rave DJ. The cast grew each game until the place was packed, chanting, and cheering into the late innings of the decisive game three.

Down 2–0 going into the ninth against ace closer Devin Williams, Lindor drew a walk. Nimmo singled. With one out, Alonso stepped to the plate. All year he had failed in this spot, and doing so now would mean extinction for the Polar Bear. He waited for the 3–1 fastball and poked it over the right-field wall.

Lou's went crazy. Tearful strangers hugged; others leaped upon the pleather booths. It was the first ninth-inning, come-from-behind home run in a decisive postseason game since the New York Giants' Bobby Thomson's walk-off against the Brooklyn Dodgers at the Polo Grounds—seventy-three years prior *to the day.*

A shaken Williams proceeded to hit Winker, who stole second and scored on Starling Marte's single. He let out a primal scream as he slammed his helmet into home plate. The team that had abused equipment in frustration for two seasons was now doing so like a punk rocker smashing his guitar. "Let's rob a bank," Jolly Olive exclaimed in a now-deleted Tweet after David Peterson closed it for the save. "Anything is possible."[660]

OCTOBER 7

The Mets opened the NL Division Series in Philadelphia. Vientos wore sparkling purple cleats. The non-starting pitchers' cheeks were painted with the starter's number each game. Alonso carried a *rally pumpkin* plucked from a Wisconsin patch as an autumnal totem. Even after two weeks on the road, "there's not a single guy that's complained about anything," Harrison Bader told *Fox Sports*. "We're actually having the most fun we've ever had. . . . It's a traveling circus."[661]

Citizens Bank Park, on the other hand, was engulfed with entitled red rage. WFAN host Evan Roberts wore the uniform of Tug McGraw, a Mets and Phillies great, as a peace offering—only to be cursed out alongside his young son all game. Dozens of security guards swarmed to protect the Mets' family section. The anger turned against their own after the Mets won the opener and took an early lead in game two. "These fucking people," Philly hunk Nick Castellanos was captured sneering after being heckled for not swinging at a ball in the dirt. He went on to win the game with a walk-off double.

The mood at Lou's was less troubled by the loss than the psychotic Trump ads running between innings. It implied Harris was part of a global conspiracy, rooted in cosmopolitan cities like New York, to replace the white, or white enough, conservative citizens with rapist, terroristic, immigrant queers, rewarded for their crimes with gender-affirming care in prison. It quieted the bar each time, leaving a moment of disturbed silence in which we silently wondered if Phillies fans, their swing-state votes infinitely more valuable than ours, might be additionally swayed by the hateful propaganda airing as they played the Gay Grimace New York Mets. "Kamala's for *they/them*," Trump's sinister voice concluded the ad. "I am for you."[662]

OCTOBER 9

After the Mets took the first game at sold-out Citi, I biked to game four hoping to see an NLDS win. After a few cups of Grimace Punch at T7LA's tailgate, I asked around for tickets, finally scoring a $200 standing-room seat that I rationalized as a business expense. I entered in time to meet Joe passing out stickers on Shea Bridge—a grim-reaper Grimace holding a scythe dripping with the blood of NL rivals, and Charlie Brown as Pete Alonso, holding his Great Pumpkin in his right hand with three containers of booze in his left. Dozens now swarmed Joe for a sticker, many trading their own homemade merch.

The whimsical DIY atmosphere of Shea had returned. Hundreds of Grimace outfits, homemade or bought, scattered the seats like a hooded, monastic order. The entire park now sang along to Lindor's walk-up song each time he came up to bat, continuing past when the song cuts off into an acapella *talkin' 'bout my girl. My girl!*, only ended by the reaction to the first pitch.

José Quintana pitched strong for the Mets, as Philadelphia's Eugenio Suárez struggled every inning before wriggling, Trump-like, out of every jam unscathed. In the fourth, Bryce Harper scored on a Vientos error, giving the Phillies a 1–0 lead. A kid behind me told his dad not to worry; a comeback was coming, "We just have to wait for the eighth!"

This time, the big moment came in the fifth. The Mets loaded the bases with no one out. The Phillies called on closer Carlos Estévez early to face Lindor. He rocketed a line-drive grand slam into the Phillies' bullpen.

All anxiety vacated joyful Citi. Even the Phillies seemed resigned to their fate as they went down quietly against Peterson in the seventh and eighth. Then it all went black, the Narco beats pumping. A rowdy group behind me yelled toward an elderly man next to me in a Phillies cap, seated alone. "You like the trumpets?"

He turned around and pointed to his ear, showing them his hearing aid. I tapped his shoulder and pointed to Mr. and Mrs. Met, happily reunited, blowing their prop trumpets. "It's funny, isn't it?" I asked, attempting to spin the heckles with friendliness. He shrugged.

Díaz walked the first two batters. People around me were now cursing out Díaz, and Mendoza for taking out Peterson. The Phillies fan whispered to me, "If Estevez can give up a grand slam, so can Díaz."

"Oh, we know he can!" I responded.

Díaz fell behind the next hitter. Slowly, the grumbles were overpowered with a rising chant of "Let's go Díaz." As if hearing them, he struck out the next three batters, ending the series by blowing a 101-mph fastball past Kyle Schwarber.

The Mets stormed the field in celebration. Some went to the mound to congratulate Díaz, but most ran directly to second base to embrace a crying Lindor. "I think I've said at least twenty-six *I love you*s so far," he later told a reporter during the clubhouse celebration.[663]

Iglesias emerged with the OMG placard, leading the fans and team to dance and sing the song together as they had on Pride Night. The Phillies fan shuffled past me. "I hope everyone treated you well tonight," I said to him.

"There was that one guy," he replied, "but for the most part I find Mets fans to be good people."

Already choked up, this sent me over the edge. Citi Vision showed Nimmo, alone on the field scanning the crowd, crying as well.

OCTOBER 12

In the four-day break before the NLCS began in LA, Mets fans surveyed the wreckage outside their purple canopy of joy.

Another devastating hurricane had ripped through central Florida. The roof of Tropicana Field, home of the Tampa Bay Rays and first-responder staging, was destroyed. Israel extended its war to Lebanon, and Jets coach Robert Saleh was fired after wearing a Lebanese flag on his sweater.

Harris continued repeating her flimsy line about "working tirelessly toward a ceasefire" as she campaigned with Republican Liz Cheney, the daughter of one of the most hated politicians in America. Polls in every state moved toward Trump.

NASA warned that a solar storm could knock out all power on Earth on the day of the first NL Championship Series game between the Mets and Dodgers. It instead caused only a faint orange and blue haze of aurora borealis in the city's sky.

OCTOBER 14

By most metrics, the Dodgers were the best team in baseball in 2024, and the best team in the National League for decades. Their prestige, backed by the immense wealth of New York–based global investment behemoth Guggenheim Partners, had bested Cohen that offseason. Even with many of their starters injured and Ohtani slumping, they embarrassed the Mets in game one with a 9–0 shutout.

Lindor, a distant runner-up behind Ohtani for NL MVP, led off game two with a home run. When he was intentionally walked to load the bases in the second, Vientos "took it personally" and hit a grand slam. Manaea and Díaz held on to even the series.

The 7–3 win proved the pennant was now winnable. Mets fans, perhaps for the first time, began *rooting for the Yankees* as they outmatched the Guardians in a comparatively boring ALCS. All narrative force pushed toward a second Subway Series, and total redemption for the Mets and everything good remaining in a world spiraling toward barbarism.

OCTOBER 18

Game three was a replay of the noncompetitive shutout opener. Ohtani finally broke his postseason drought with a massive blast into the upper deck. Then he led off game four with another shot into the bullpen.

As the optimism meter swung back to *so over*, the *power of friendship* narrative turned into paranoid theories that the *fix is in.* Ads throughout the series previewing an Ohtani vs. Judge World Series provided more evidence that the MLB had already determined the Mets would not advance, as Evan Roberts alleged.[664] A more desperate speculation spread across social media that the chasmic run differential was the result of a complex plot in which the Dodgers were being pitched livelier balls, switched out each half-inning to deaden the Mets' bats.

Otis Williams' Temptations sang the team to the field with "My Girl" for game five. With Lindor's optimistic anthem running through their heads, the Mets fought from start to finish to stave off elimination with a 12–6 win.

During a live postgame interview with David Ortiz and Derek Jeter, Alonso reported the team had been playing every game as must-win since June, and they would cling to the magic for the partying flight back to LA: "Grimace is on the aux . . . playing OMG and holding the pumpkin at the same time."[665] Ortiz then spotted Mrs. Met and called her over, kissing her on the cheek and inviting her home. Mr. Met jogged over enraged, trying to steer her back from Big Papi. Disgusted, Jeter ripped off his mic and walked off the field.

OCTOBER 20

I spend the afternoon in Queens' Highland Park watching the Trans-Girl All-Star game. The ad-hoc teams are called the Watersports and the Bones, named for the transphobic theory that future archeologists will identify transwomen athletes as men based on their skeletons.

Bones infielder Zephy Barragán, one of Lou's regulars, invited me to the game. The Red Sox are her favorite team, with the Mets an increasingly close second. Baseball play and fandom had always been a source of community for her, one she worried of losing after transitioning. "What would Mookie Betts think of me?" she wondered.

"Hit the ball, doll!" yelled a Watersport from the bench. The pitcher wore a yellow Boston City Connect jersey, one of a few players representing a team other than the Mets. Several wore Mercury Mets jerseys and hats, a sci-fi-inspired cult 1999 promotional alternate whose astrological logo bares resemblance to the transgender insignia. A Bluetooth boom box pumped emo, pop-punk, dream-pop, and New York hardcore walk-up songs. Play was chaotic and sloppy in the early innings, tightening up after a fourth-inning BBQ break. Some passersby stopped to study the scene before moving on without comment. Where else but New York, I wondered, could there be a large enough trans community to find dozens to play pickup hardball—itself an increasingly rare sight.

Zephy and I arrived after the game to Lou's, packed near capacity for the dual NL and WNBA championship games. As the Minnesota Lynx took a 6–0 lead over the New York Liberty in the first quarter, Dodger

Michael Kopech took the mound with a giant red crucifix stitched to his glove. The Mets eked out an early lead on a walk, poor fielding, and an infield hit. Ohtani stroked an effortless RBI single in the bottom of the inning to take it away.

Since leaving Brooklyn, the once blue-collar Dodgers had become the team of capitalist excess and inevitability. Their top-to-bottom lineup of hard-hitters put runs on the board nearly every inning, and every time the Mets set up their guerrilla offensive to even the score, another artilleryman from their vast bullpen arrived to cut them down. McNeil struck out with the bases loaded on a ball in the dirt. Winker flew out with the bases loaded again in the sixth. A blowout's worth of runners were left in scoring position, with Candelita burning out on the bench.

Mets and Libs fans cheered together as Breanna Stewart came to the free-throw line down two in the final seconds of the fourth quarter, and Alonso came to the plate hoping to start a rally in the eighth. Simultaneous celebration and groaning erupted as Stewart made her clinching shots, and Alonso struck out. On a third screen, few noticed the Jets blowing a late-game field goal.

The Dodgers scored three times more before the ninth, putting the game and series beyond reach. This was no choke, cheat, or act of God. LA's 46 runs were record-breaking for a postseason series, as were the 42 walks gifted by exhausted Mets pitching. The best team in baseball outran their perseverance, draining their last reserves of house-money. Nimmo consoled Manaea as he cried watching the Dodgers celebrate the pennant. The pitcher likely spoke for more than himself after the game when admitting he had "hit a wall."[666]

OCTOBER 21

"PARTY'S OVER," the *Post* headline read the day after the Mets' season ended, "No More Grimace, No More Magic, and Forget the Subway Series."[667] While I had briefly (between NLCS games two and three) entertained the perverse fantasy of besting the Yankees, I never allowed myself to really believe it, allowing me to drown all disappointment in the incredible season's afterglow.

The flood of uncharacteristically sincere comments from the Mets returning to clear out their lockers indicated they felt the same. One came from Harrison Bader, who had played in the ALCS with the Yankees two years prior, but said the 2024 season contained "the most sacred moments" of his career. "I wasn't just a Met, I was a 2024 Metro and if you know you know. What a gift."[668]

There was some debate about what he meant by this—Metropolitan? Metrosexual? My theory is that Bader was referencing clubhouse lexicon for the season's baptismal experience. He was one of the guys hired by an eccentric billionaire to dress as the Mets during their dismal malaise. After the miserable early season, Cohen's threatened blow-up, Strawberry's sermon, and the firing of López, the team decided in their clubhouse struggle session to commune with the franchise's historic character, and actually *become the Mets.*

Accepting both the serious and satirical nature of that mission, they pushed for the impossible of a worst-to-first miracle, while accepting their more likely fate as the butt of millions of jokes by making the joke their own. By having fun winning together, *or* sucking together, they leaned into the comic aesthetics of "OMG," Grimace, and masculine affection to turn the season around. The team's historical spirit was rediscovered as Candelita's prayer turned faithful as the *Ya Gotta Believe* mantra. Players insisted to the media they actually liked the silly song, themselves stunned how quickly they had gone from embarrassment at wearing the uniform to a team that loved each other as if spiritual teammates since 1962.

Mets historian Jay Horwitz recognized the feistiness of 1986 in their late-season and playoff comebacks, and Ron Swoboda compared Carlos Mendoza to the player-friendly guerrilla-platooning of commander Gil Hodges.[669,670] Lindor was steadfast and progressive like Seaver. Vientos overcame the pressures of Darryl-like hype. Winker appeared like a belligerent Ray Knight. Severino cheerleaded like Pedro. Alonso stoically fought for his legacy ahead of contract-year uncertainty like Carlos Beltrán. Jorge López, if given a second chance, could have been Tug McGraw. Cleon Jones identified in them the 1969 "spunk," the underdog character always waiting to be unlocked, which he summarized with the motto often repeated by David Wright: "Once a Met, always a Met."[671]

OCTOBER 25–30

For Mets historian Greg Prince, the closest reference for 2024 was 1999—a season that had "everything but a pennant and a Series and a parade."[672] The team that year, too, re-embraced the ironic humor of its character, falling just short of the Subway Series. The momentum carried into 2000, when they emerged as rebels *with a cause*: to defeat the Braves of racist Rocker and the Yankees of murderous Clemens.

As the 2024 World Series between the Yankees and Dodgers began, a debate raged online about what the Mets' cause truly was. The discourse began with a Twitter poll by the Democratic Socialists of America asking, "Which team represents the working class?" The Mets won with 61 percent, compared to 21 percent for the Yankees and 16 percent for the Dodgers.[673]

Some literati Yankees fans sneered at the result. "The Mets did not capture the heart of the city so much as it did the hearts of the gentrifier class: media elites, political staffers, lawyers for good causes, Brooklyn transplants, Twitter addicts," *New York Magazine* writers Kevin T. Dugan and Simon van Zuylen-Wood wrote in their piece "Real New Yorkers Root for the Yankees." "Though not working class themselves, these fans cultivate a relationship with the team as a way to channel and cheer the city's underdog spirit."

It was the Yankees who truly represented an authentic working class, they continued—manual laborers who identified with the "alpha swagger" of Gordon Gekko, Rudy Giuliani, Jay-Z, and the NYPD in a coalition between "the plutocrat living on Fifth Avenue" and "his doorman who lives in Washington Heights . . . because rooting for the Yankees is an aspirational act." They quoted Bhaskar Sunkara, *Jacobin* editor and *The Socialist Manifesto* author, as saying: "The Yankees are both the elite team of capital and team of the working class. Squeezed middle class Mets fans try to carve out their own path in vain."[674]

"When you switch on game one of the World Series Friday night," the essay concluded, "feel no shame cheering for Judge and the Yankees, who represent everything this Leviathan city can be."[675]

Despite the anger the argument provoked from leftist Mets fans, I had to admit their thesis was close to my own. The teams' dialectical counter-branding intentionally encourages the common misunderstanding of class that substitutes one's actual economic position for aesthetics, diverting the class war into a culture war. The Mets are the team of the New Left—a dropout culture for antiauthoritarian middle-class youth, whose sincere radicalism mostly degenerated to a managerial, class-neutral progressivism after the sixties. The Yankees, on the other hand, champion a type of populism represented well by Thomas Hobbes' Leviathan—a singular monster, accumulated from all classes and identities, whose despotic rein is legitimized solely through unbeatable strength. While from a Marxist perspective the actual class composition of the two fan bases is probably negligible, most would likely qualify the latte-sipping Mets fan typing woke screeds about the Gay Mets all day as more bourgeois than the Bronx-born cafe owner in a Yankees cap, even if I am working for a wage, while his season tickets are bought from the profits produced by his employees.

My main problem with the leftist Bleacher Creatures, however, is their failure to take the argument to its depressing logical conclusion. If the Mets' fan base resembles the idealistic middle-class voting base for Harris, the Yankees' corresponds to that of Trump and Vance's pseudo-workerist Republican Party.

And just as Trump's Madison Square Garden rally confirmed the profound racism, sexism, and authoritarian cruelty of that coalition, Yankees fans reminded Series-watchers of their own ogreish entitlement and supremacism. In game two, hundreds of them watching remotely were captured in a viral video cheering Ohtani's shoulder injury. In game four, three left-field fans collaborated to brace Mookie Betts' wrist and pry a caught foul from his glove. The fans were ejected, but lauded as heroes across the fan base.

Even Dodgers-haters cheered the Yankees' embarrassing collapse to lose the Series in game five. As the election approached, everyone I knew, even those who despised Kamala Harris, hoped the same would happen to Trump.

NOVEMBER 6

In the end, Sunkara and company were right.

Although Harris's Metsian campaign polled as more likable, trustworthy, and competent, Trump won with record percentages of Black, Latino, low-income, and union support. Millions pulled the lever for Musk and Trump's casino-capitalist promise of a golden era of wealth, trickling down from fossil-fuel profits and squeezed from an undocumented underclass disciplined through threats of deportation or imprisonment. Millions more who voted for Biden four years prior could not stomach voting for the administration that had abandoned the working class, refused to stop arming a genocide, and labeled anyone opposing the war as enemy agents; they stayed home, or left the top of the ticket blank.

The 2024 Mets existed as a consolatory vector of metropolitan humanity's timeless frustration—programmed invective hurled toward the conformism of straight society. Once the season ended, so too did this joyful and spiteful moment of communion. Contrary to the sentiment of "OMG," not everything bad can be so simply tossed away.

Could they have gone much further? Their successful turnaround came as much from teamwork as the "power of friendship"—uniting around the union struggle within the MLBPA, rallying around the Latin pop song of an underrated teammate in a clubhouse where Spanish was once unwelcome, and embracing their LGBTQ+ fans. But because these concerns never ventured far beyond the bounds of baseball, there never emerged a purpose so catalytic as Tom Seaver's "if the Mets can win the World Series, then we can get out of Vietnam."

Such a politicized catalyst could have come from pro-queer players like Lindor supporting Imane Khelif and other athletes bullied by the anti-trans movement, or denouncing the homophobic and racist ads running during their playoff games. Or Harrison Bader could have proved his solidarity for the release of hostages held by Hamas in Gaza by signaling support for the massive Israeli protests demanding their return via a ceasefire.

But in a generally depoliticized climate, speaking out like this would have taken immense bravery. The sports establishment, especially in baseball, tends to only tolerate political statements from athletes like

Seaver or Dom Smith in the midst of mass and popular movements. In 2024, when these movements were suppressed by police and the Democrats' failed centrist strategy, it's likely they would have ended up censored like Carlos Delgado, or blacklisted like Paul Robeson and Colin Kaepernick. It was not the Mets' fault, then, that they fell short. In the fall of 2024, progressivism, like their pitching staff, *hit a wall.*

In the days following the election, many friends who had donned solidaristic safety pins, pussy hats, or black masks when Trump won in 2016 quietly rolled their eyes at the result as they would a MAGA hat at Citi Field. Some form of resistance would come to authoritarianism, we knew. And this time we would not fall into the cruel optimism of supporting the Democratic Party, whose feigned progressivism and ultimate disinterest in winning, made them appear as little better than a controlled opposition to the Republicans. One might as well root for the Washington Generals against the Globetrotters.

Uncertain of how horrific the next years would be, we instead planned to recommit to the political activity that blossomed during the pandemic in our workplaces, homes, and neighborhoods—solidarity networks of mutual aid and rapid response that could mobilize to protect one another from ICE raids, abortion prohibition, legislation against queers, economic tyranny, and police-state terror to come. We spoke of these plans in vague and cautious terms, very similar to Lindor when he was asked after the final NLCS loss how he would bring the spirit of the 2024 Mets into the next season: "You have to build. You have to fight for each other. You have to create that bond and that trust. And like I said, *fight for each other.*"[676]

POSTSCRIPT

Baseball as It Ought Not Be

> You historically have gotten knocked down a lot as a Mets fan. The goal is that future generations of Mets fans, or specifically this generation of Mets fan, doesn't need to live that way.
>
> —*David Stearns, May 2025 interview with Louisa Thomas for The New Yorker*

> The amusements that captivate a man are the exact measure of his mediocrity . . . writing or baseball, who cares? The idea of success, once freed from its simplest desires, is inseparable from complete upheaval on a global scale. The remaining permissible successes can only resemble failure.
>
> —*Guy Debord and Gil J. Wolman Potlatch, Bulletin d'information de l'Internationale lettriste 22,* September 1955

Early in the 3002 season, the New New York Mets' new sleazeball owner, Abner Doubledeal, comes across a game between workers of a pizza shop and an interplanetary messenger service in Central Park. A crowd gathers to watch Planet Express's pitcher, a one-eyed mutant, born in New York's underworld ruins, named Turanga Leela. Because her limited depth perception causes her to hit every opposing batter, the crowd cheers her on through what is technically a no-hitter. Seeing a new gimmick to boost attendance at a rebuilt Shea, Doubledeal signs her on the spot.

A wide variety of bizarre aliens have played in the majors over the previous centuries, but Leela becomes the first woman. She proves a fan favorite through the miserable season, that the preserved head of Bob Uecker calls the Mets' latest "crime against humanity," and whose slogan, draped outside Shea, reads BASEBALL AS IT OUGHT NOT BE. A silver lining emerges during the final game, when a far more competent woman named Jackie Anderson is signed to the Boston Poindexters, and finally makes contact with one of Leela's inside pitches to hit a game-winning grand slam.[677]

In this 2002 episode of *Futurama*, the historic flaw of all Rickeyist political optimism for baseball is revealed in Metsian slapstick. The joke isn't that the Mets still suck, it's that all the idiocies of American society have been rebuilt 1,000 years from now upon the ruins of our own New York, as if nothing had been learned. The Mets fit perfectly in this animated eternity because they, like *Futurama*, are a lefty ironic bit—a cartoon satire of baseball's conservatism, appealing to cynical hipsters, with some capability of playing a progressive role in the ongoing cycles of creation and destruction.

As I complete this similar project in early June of the 2025 season, I am tempted to hazard my own prognostication of what the rest of the season, and baseball's future, may hold.

The Mets have regained their division lead as Juan Soto slowly returns to form during Pride Month, and resistance to Trump's authoritarian agenda finally emerges around the county with riots against ICE raids in LA, and the rise of socialist candidate Zohran Mamdani (a Mets fan) as favorite to become New York's next mayor. If there's any truth to my alchemic recipe for Mets victory (unification of fans and team behind a common mission legible with deep politics), it is hard to imagine they will go any further than 2024 unless they distinguish themselves from last year's failed progressivism by signaling their support for whatever other effective resistance to the present state of things manifests. If the Mets do end up winning their first World Series in my lifetime, absent any meaningful connection with a broader social upsurge, you can safely consider that aspect of the book either a failed experiment in Marxist sabermetrics, or playful fan fiction, like the queer fans currently shipping Soto as nonbinary and Brett Baty as a lesbian.

What I will predict for certain is that we will see, within our lifetimes, immense changes throughout this social order. Our own ongoing contest against the global capitalist machine will soon reach a major climax as the epochal crises of economy, climate, and basic survival for growing numbers of those pushed to the margins accumulate. Most imagine this transition will be apocalyptic, with some film portrayals depicting the Mets' destruction to heighten its barbarity. In *Avengers: Endgame,* one character sighs he "misses the Mets," who have apparently fallen victim to Thanos's Malthusian cull of the world's surplus population. In the ecological disaster flick *Sharknado 2: The Second One,* climate change causes the titular tornado of sharks to rip through Citi Field.

But no matter what catastrophes await, humanity will likely live on, as will our games. If capitalism survives too, baseball could take the *Futurama* course—remaining a business based on greed, exploitation, and exclusion—or the utopian vision of Christopher Nolan's *Interstellar* (2014), in which humanity has fled our dying planet for the American suburbs re-created in baseball-diamond-encrusted off-Earth colonies. A more dismal possibility from the postapocalyptic video game *Fallout 4* predicts baseball will be remembered as a martial death match, in which bats were weapons, gloves bullet-shields, and baseball cards tallied kill counts.

Or perhaps we will see a version of baseball from the 1887 sci-fi novel that inspired the Players' League: Edward Bellamy's *Looking Backward.*

It's set in a world in which society has organized as a singular team, and the idea of selling ourselves to another to play games has been defeated alongside the wage-labor system of industrial capitalism. Baseball could live on much as the spectator sport it is today, only managed democratically by players and fans who remember our version of the sport like the child-labor factories of Dickensian London, or the gladiatorial bouts of Ancient Rome. Alternately, mass spectatorship could disappear altogether in a reversion to baseball's amateur-era origins of collectively-organized pickup games. With the primary objective of exercise, pleasure, creativity, and egalitarian camaraderie restored, baseball would be celebrated alongside the Bill of Rights, jazz, and apple pie, as one of America's most enlightened inventions.

Until then, the future of professional baseball lies in the mitts of the players themselves. For the militant tendency of the post-1968 MLBPA, the horizon has always been increased player control of the game. With the union's power center tilting away from stars toward thousands of newly unionized minor leaguers after the labor awakening of 2020, this goal is more possible today than at any moment since the baseball revolt of 1890.

That these turning points came in years of broader social upsurge indicates that even us lowly fans have a role in inspiring the militancy required to reappropriate the sport from the magnates. We each play our position, after all, and we can expect no more resistance from another than whatever we can accomplish in our own node in the circuit board. Perhaps you are a gig worker, a tenant, a business owner, a punk drifter, a movie star, a mother, or a designated hitter. For my own part, I am a writer and a Mets fan, and this book's task has been to rewire readers' brains to enjoy baseball in a more radical way.

Invented by the middle class, baseball became a game that could be watched from either the perspective of the boss, or that of the worker.

One fan becomes a fantasy GM who desires only glory and curses all failure in "you're fired" fantasies. The other identifies with the greats, journeymen, and chokers alike, seeing baseball as a quotidian workplace drama—a shared experience of making choices and struggling through a life that does not fully belong to us.

To experiment with this latter method, I encourage readers to go to Citi Field. Do your best to ignore the constant sound effects and thousands of screens, and notice how Mets fans, more than any other team, are drawn to the breakdowns, neurosis, weirdness, and humor of the game. Watch how the constant ebb and flow of negative, positive, and bored energies circulate between crowd and team—a rolling emotional register far more dramatic than its vulgar manifestation in "the wave." Summon the courage to sneak past the ushers and sit close to the field for an up-close view of baseball's negativity in its most visible manifestation: the anxiety swelling behind the players' stone faces; the pitcher's career hanging in the balance with every throw; the hitter hoping to break the game open with every swing.

From this communal vantage, the abstractions of statistics and standings are confronted by the reality of what we are really seeing—not a game between two opposing teams, but a common *human* struggle, *within* and *against* the economic, legalistic, and mechanical structure of the game itself, and its role as opiate for the physical and existential pain of wage labor.

Former Mets reliever Daniel Herrera, for example, told me that he, like many other teammates, lost their ability to have any true "team loyalty" after the experience of being bought and sold as a major-league commodity, only to be tossed away after injury.[678] Opposing fans of Constantinople's Green and Blue chariot teams came to a similar realization during a sixth-century race at the Hippodrome. Enraged by Emperor Justinian's cruelty toward the athletes, factionalism was set aside to launch a sports riot that spilled out of the 150,000-seat arena to become the largest insurrection in Byzantine history, ending the imperial "bread and circuses" mode of sport until the nineteenth century.[679]

For the social order to change, this type of disillusionment in the establishment's ability to structure our thoughts and desires into opposing fandoms is needed today on every level. This does not mean we can simply abandon all identity—so long as the political parties, business unions, and sports franchises are controlled by the capitalists as a means of reproducing their rule, player and fan alike are locked in their domed stadia. We can at least root together for the same thing in this *BoreDome*—a Ruthian home run that breaks the mindless repetition of the game, punctures a hole in the enclosure, and allows a collective escape to sunnier fields.

This destructive urge is why the utopian workers' movement of the 1880s, and the New Left a century later, loved the working-class-coded Mets, and why we, their children, still watch the long-running tragedy today. The Mets are a team bursting with all the desperation, psychosis, pain, chaos, and cruel optimism for a better future that persists through civilization's sunset. We watch the catastrophe unfold, refusing to fully admit our doom, searching in the minutiae for any appearance of a path to the World Series, to the real enemy, to an ultimate *October* that redeems every moment of our long struggle.

We know that messianic path may never come, and that we are desperately behind as the season grows late. But we watch, wait, and try to believe, nonetheless, as we cheer for the colors we've pledged to always be true—the hard-hat orange of the international working class, and our blue Earth.

ACKNOWLEDGMENTS

Love and thanks to everyone else who helped me pull off this absurd miracle, especially my agent Ian Bonaparte, and Maya Raiford Cohen, Joseph Gunther, Suzanne Lander, Rola Harb, Alessandra Bastagli, Ben Schrank, Alexis Nowicki, Jane Handa, and everyone else at Astra House.

Research help from the patient archivists at New York Historical Society, the New York City Municipal Archives, New York Public Library, Society for American Baseball Research, and Nicole Ward of the Greentree Foundation. Additional assists from Robert B. Ross, Shemon Salam, the Batting Around Clubhouse, Research and Destroy NYC, Matt Peterson, the Tipping Pitches podcast, Richard Staff, Nick Hirshon, Daniel Herrera, Andrew Battle, John Thorn, and Noah Kulwin.

From the fandom: Greg Prince, Joe, Kaitlyn, Darren and everyone else from the 7 Line Army, the Queens Baseball Convention, and Jay Horwitz.

Thanks to my patient readers Milica Iličić, Jarrod Shanahan, Ross Wolfe, Al Bedell, and James Payne.

Final thanks to Stuart Gittlitz for raising me with the New Breed spirit.

ENDNOTES

INTRODUCTION

1 Karen Kelly and Evelyn McDonnell, eds., *Stars Don't Stand Still in the Sky: Music and Myth* (New York University Press, 1999), 157–158.

2 Andy Battle, "The City of Blind Windows," *Spectre*, part 2, November 28, 2022, https://spectrejournal.com/the-city-of-blind-windows-2/.

3 C. L. R. James, *Beyond a Boundary* (Duke University Press, 2004), 153.

4 Jay Horwitz, "Bill Pulsipher Shares His Story," *Mets Insider Blog*, Medium, February 27, 2023, https://metsinsider.mlblogs.com/bill-pulsipher-shares-his-story-7eceb661662b.

5 Roger Angell, *The Roger Angell Baseball Collection* (Open Road Integrated Media, 2013), The Summer Game, Part II, The "Go!" Shouters. Ebook.

6 Tony Collins, *Sport in Capitalist Society: A Short History* (Routledge, 2013), 94.

7 Noam Chomsky, "Why Americans Know So Much About Sports but So Little About World Affairs," *Alternet*, December 1, 2022, https://www.alternet.org/2014/09/noam-chomsky-why-americans-know-so-much-about-sports-so-little-about-world-affairs.

8 *Batting Around*, podcast, "Chris Sabo's They Live Goggles with Richard Staff," August 10, 2022, https://soundcloud.com/battingaround/chris-sabos-they-live-goggles-with-richard-staff.

9 Tony Collins, *Sport in Capitalist Society: A Short History* (Routledge, 2013), 26.

10 Roger Kahn, *The Boys of Summer* (Signet, 1973), 99.

11 Lauren Berlant, *Cruel Optimism* (Duke University Press, 2011), Introduction. Ebook.

CHAPTER 1: THE METS

12 Peter Morris, William J. Ryczek, Jan Finkel, Leonard Levin, and Richard Malatzky, eds., *Base Ball Founders: The Clubs, Players, and Cities of the Northeast That Established the Game* (McFarland, 2013), New York Base Ball Club. Ebook.

13 George B. Kirsch, *Baseball in Blue and Gray: The National Pastime During the Civil War* (Princeton University Press, 2007), 115–116.

14 Mark Ribowsky, *A Complete History of the Negro Leagues: 1884 to 1955* (Citadel Press, 1997), 13.

15 William J. Ryczek, *Blackguards and Red Stockings: A History of Baseball's National Association, 1871–1875*, rev. ed. (McFarland, 2016), Chapter 8 notes. Ebook.

16 Morris et al., *Base Ball Founders*, Mutual Base Ball Club: Epilogue. Ebook.

17 "Sport-Pastime Notes," *Brooklyn Eagle*, December 26, 1886, 6, https://blyn.newspapers.com/image/50334204.

18 Washington Irving, *Salmagundi* (New York: G. P. Putnam's Sons, 1874), 183–184.

19 Bill Lamb, "John Day," Society for American Baseball Research, January 4, 2012, https://sabr.org/bioproj/person/John-Day.

20 Mike Roer, *Orator O'Rourke: The Life of a Baseball Radical* (McFarland, 2005), 106.

21 Justin McKinney, "That Time Former New York Giant 'Dude' Esterbrook Walked from New Orleans to Baltimore," *BaseballObscura*, Medium, June 13, 2018, https://medium.com/@BaseballObscura/that-time-former-new-york-giant-dude-esterbrook-walked-from-new-orleans-to-baltimore-d38c5cdb376f.

22 Bill Lamb, "Metropolitan Park (New York)," Society for American Baseball Research, March 10, 2021, https://sabr.org/bioproj/park/metropolitan-park-new-york/.

23 Michael Shapiro, *Bottom of the Ninth: Branch Rickey, Casey Stengel, and the Daring Scheme to Save Baseball from Itself* (Henry Holt, 2009), 39.

24 Peter Golenbock, *Amazin': The Miraculous History of New York's Most Beloved Baseball Team* (St. Martin's Griffin, 2002), Chap. 1. Ebook.

25 John Thorn, *Baseball in the Garden of Eden: The Secret History of the Early Game* (Simon & Schuster, 2011), Chap. 8. Ebook.

26 Harold Seymour, *Baseball*, vol. 1, *The Early Years*, repr. (Oxford University Press, 2011), 327–329.

27 David Stevens, *Baseball's Radical for All Seasons: A Biography of John Montgomery Ward*, American Sports History Series, no. 12 (Scarecrow Press, 1998), 122.

28 Brian Di Salvatore, *A Clever Base-Ballist: The Life and Times of John Montgomery Ward* (Johns Hopkins University Press, 2001), 187.

29 Robert B. Ross, *The Great Baseball Revolt: The Rise and Fall of the 1890 Players League* (University of Nebraska Press, 2016), Chap. 3. Ebook.

30 Roer, *Orator O'Rourke*, 122.

31 Edward Bellamy, *Looking Backward: From 2000 to 1887* (Applewood Books, 2000), 115.

32 Edwin G. Burrows and Mike Wallace, *Gotham: A History of New York City to 1898* (Oxford University Press, 1999), Chap. 43. Ebook.

33 *Sporting News*, October 20, 1888, 2.

34 *Sporting News*, November 10, 1888, 2.

35 Stevens, *Baseball's Radical*, 122.

36 Albert Goodwill Spalding, *America's National Game: Historic Facts Concerning the Beginning, Evolution, Development and Popularity of Base Ball, with Personal Reminiscences of Its Vicissitudes, Its Victories and Its Votaries* (American Sports, 1911), 270.

37 Robert P. Gelzheiser, *Labor and Capital in 19th Century Baseball* (McFarland, 2006), 128, 154.

38 Robert E. Weir, *Beyond Labor's Veil: The Culture of the Knights of Labor* (Pennsylvania State University Press, 1996), 303.

39 Bill Lamb, "Edward B. Talcott," Society for American Baseball Research, accessed July 24, 2025, https://sabr.org/bioproj/person/edward-b-talcott/.

40 Ross, *Great Baseball Revolt*, Chap. 5. Ebook.

41 Stevens, *Baseball's Radical*, 149–150.

42 Stevens, *Baseball's Radical*, 141.

43 Burrows and Wallace, *Gotham*, Chap. 62. Ebook.

44 Roer, *Orator O'Rourke*, 138–140.

45 Robert B. Ross, email interview with author, X.com, May 2, 2025.

46 Tony Collins, *Sport in Capitalist Society: A Short History* (Routledge, 2013), 71.

47 Peter Mancuso, "Jim Mutrie," Society for American Baseball Research, February 22, 2022, https://sabr.org/bioproj/person/Jim-Mutrie/.

48 "Old-Time Ball Player Dead: T. G. Esterbrook, Who Played with the Metropolitans, Injured by Jumping from a Train," *New York Times*, May 1, 1901, https://www.nytimes.com/1901/05/01/archives/oldtime-ball-player-dead-tg-esterbrook-who-played-with-the.html; McKinney"

CHAPTER 2: YANKEE INSURRECTOS

49 Bill Lamb, "Andrew Freedman," Society for American Baseball Research, January 8, 2012, https://sabr.org/bioproj/person/andrew-freedman.

50 Glenn Stout and Richard A. Johnson, *Yankees Century: 100 Years of New York Yankees Baseball* (Houghton Mifflin Harcourt, 2002), 11–13.

51 Stout and Johnson, *Yankees Century*, 15.

52 Glenn Stout and Richard A. Johnson, *The Dodgers: 120 Years of Dodgers Baseball* (Houghton Mifflin, 2004), 51.

53 John Garvey, email interview with author, February 13, 2024.

54 Scott Longert, "The Player's Fraternity: They Fought the Good Fight," Society for American Baseball Research, April 18, 2023, https://sabr.org/journal/article/the-players-fraternity-they-fought-the-good-fight/.

55 Edmund F. Wehrle, *Breaking Babe Ruth: Baseball's Campaign Against Its Biggest Star*, Sports and American Culture (University of Missouri, 2018), Chap 1. Ebook.

56 Stout and Johnson, *Yankees Century*, 86.

57 Anthony Pignataro, "John McGraw, Baseball, and Lynching Souvenirs," personal website, November 8, 2021, https://anthonypignataro.com/2021/03/29/john-mcgraw-baseball-and-lynching-souvenirs/.

58 Bill Francis, "Scientists Explored Secrets Behind Ruth's Epic 1921 Season," National Baseball Hall of Fame, accessed July 24, 2025, https://baseballhall.org/discover/scientists-explored-secrets-behind-ruths-epic-1921-season.

59 Roaring 20s News (@Roaring20sNews), "Babe Ruth: Any lad can make a hitter of himself," Twitter (now X), June 18, 2023, https://x.com/Roaring20sNews/status/1670383447595012096.

60 Lee Lowenfish, ed., *Branch Rickey: Baseball's Ferocious Gentleman* (University of Nebraska Press, 2010), 122.

61 Robert Fredrick Burk, *Much More Than a Game: Players, Owners, & American Baseball Since 1921* (University of North Carolina Press, 2001), 3.

62 Michael Roberts, "The Roaring Twenties Repeated?," *Michael Roberts Blog*, April 19, 2021, https://thenextrecession.wordpress.com/2021/04/18/the-roaring-twenties-repeated/.

63 Robert H. Zieger, ed., *The CIO, 1935–1955* (University of North Carolina Press, 1995), 33.

64 "'Beginnings of Organization' by Hermann Schlüter From the Brewing Industry and the Brewery Workers' Movement in America. International Union of United Brewery Workmen of America, Cincinnati. 1910," Revolution's Newsstand, February 24, 2025, https://revolutionsnewsstand.com/2025/02/23/beginnings-of-organization-by-hermann-schluter-from-the-brewing-industry-and-the-brewery-workers-movement-in-america-international-union-of-united-brewery-workmen-of-america-cincinnati/.

65 Friedrich Engels to Friedrich Adolph Sorge, December 31, 1892, at "Letters: Marx-Engels Correspondence 1892," Marxist Internet Archive, https://www.marxists.org/archive/marx/works/1892/letters/92_12_31.htm.

66 Friedrich Engels to Hermann Schlüter, March 30, 1892, at "Letters: Marx-Engels Correspondence 1892," Marxists Internet Archive, https://www.marxists.org/archive/marx/works/1892/letters/92_03_30.htm.

67 Ed Sherman, "Unraveling the Mystery of Babe Ruth's Called Shot," *Sporting News*, October 27, 2021, https://www.sportingnews.com/us/mlb/news/babe-ruth-called-shot-charlie-root-yankees-cubs-book-ed-sherman/1w29vd8i39z0x1iho1uj8ciqdt.

CHAPTER 3: BUMS

68 Friedrich Engels to Hermann Schlüter, March 30, 1892, at "Letters: Marx-Engels Correspondence 1892," Marxists Internet Archive, https://www.marxists.org/archive/marx/works/1892/letters/92_03_30.htm.

69 Jeremy Brecher, ed., *Strike!*, 2nd pr. (South End Press, 1973), 180.

70 Louis Adamic, *My America, 1928–1938* (Harper & Brothers, 1938), 405.

71 Adamic, *My America*, 405.

72 Robert H. Zieger, ed., *The CIO, 1935–1955* (University of North Carolina Press, 1995), 231.

73 Zieger, *CIO*, 352.

74 Zieger, *CIO*, 236.

75 Irwin Silber, *Press Box Red: The Story of Lester Rodney, the Communist Who Helped Break the Color Line in American Sports* (Temple University Press, 2003).

76 Burton Alan Boxerman and Benita W. Boxerman, *George Weiss: Architect of the Golden Age Yankees* (McFarland, 2016), Chap. 1. Ebook.

77 Richard Goldstein, "Lester Rodney, Early Voice in Fight Against Racism in Baseball, Dies at 98," *New York Times*, December 24, 2019, https://www.nytimes.com/2009/12/24/sports/24rodney.html.

78 Carl E. Prince, *Brooklyn's Dodgers: The Bums, the Borough, and the Best of Baseball, 1947–1957* (Oxford University Press, 1996), 41.

79 Peter Golenbock, *Bums: An Oral History of the Brooklyn Dodgers* (Summer Games Books, 2014), Chap. 1. Ebook.

80 Prince, *Brooklyn's Dodgers*, 105.

81 Glenn Stout and Richard A. Johnson, *The Dodgers: 120 Years of Dodgers Baseball* (Houghton Mifflin, 2004), 108.

82 Prince, *Brooklyn's Dodgers*, 32–34.

83 Lee Lowenfish, ed., *Branch Rickey: Baseball's Ferocious Gentleman* (University of Nebraska Press, 2010), 354.

84 Lowenfish, *Branch Rickey*, 326.

85 Jules Tygiel, *Baseball's Great Experiment: Jackie Robinson and His Legacy* (Oxford University Press, 1983), 39.

86 Robert Fredrick Burk, *Much More Than a Game: Players, Owners, & American Baseball Since 1921* (University of North Carolina Press, 2001), 79.

87 Tygiel, *Baseball's Great Experiment*, 38.

88 Lowenfish, *Branch Rickey*, 415.

89 James S. Hirsch, *Willie Mays: The Life, the Legend* (Scribner, 2011), Chap 5. Ebook.

90 Burk, *Much More*, 93.

91 "Summer 1996: The MacPhail Report of 1946," Society for American Baseball Research, accessed July 24, 2025, http://roadsidephotos.sabr.org/baseball/MACPHAILREPT.htm.

92 David Falkner, *Great Time Coming: The Life of Jackie Robinson from Baseball to Birmingham* (Simon & Schuster, 1995), 164–165.

93 David Roediger, "Labor in White Skin: Race and Working-Class History," Verso Books (blog), July 13, 2017, http://www.versobooks.com/blogs/news/2596-labor-in-white-skin-race-and-working-class-history; Zieger, *CIO*,

94 Leo Durocher and Edward Linn, *Nice Guys Finish Last* (University of Chicago Press, 2009), 205.

95 Maury Allen and Susan Walker, *Dixie Walker of the Dodgers: The People's Choice* (University of Alabama Press, 2010), 179.

96 Allen and Walker, *Dixie Walker*, 169.

97 John Pastier, "Brooklyn Dodgers Attendance in 1947," Society for American Baseball Research, July 20, 2022, https://sabr.org/journal/article/brooklyn-dodgers-attendance-in-1947/.

98 Lowenfish, *Branch Rickey*, 7.

99 Wendell E. Pritchett, *Brownsville, Brooklyn: Blacks, Jews, and the Changing Face of the Ghetto*, Historical Studies of Urban America (University of Chicago Press, 2003), 113–114.

100 Chris Lamb, *Blackout, The Untold Story of Jackie Robinson's First Spring Training* (University of Nebraska Press, 2004), 166.

101 Tygiel, *Baseball's Great Experiment*, 62.

102 Lowenfish, *Branch Rickey*, 468.

103 Jackie Robinson, *I Never Had It Made: An Autobiography of Jackie Robinson* (Harper Collins Publishers, 2003), 111. Ebook.

104 Tygiel, *Baseball's Great Experiment*, 343.

105 Ronald A Smith, "The Paul Robeson–Jackie Robinson Saga and a Political Collision," *Journal of Sport History* 6, no. 2 (1979): 5–27, http://www.jstor.org/stable/43608951.

106 Steve Crabtree, "The Gallup Brain: Americans and the Korean War," Gallup, March 20, 2025, https://news.gallup.com/poll/7741/gallup-brain-americans-korean-war.aspx.

107 Prince, *Brooklyn's Dodgers*, xi.

CHAPTER 4: MEADOWLARKS

108 Theodore Steinberg, *Gotham Unbound: The Ecological History of Greater New York* (Simon & Schuster, 2014), 217.

109 Terry Pristin, "Home Is Where the Auto Parts Are," *New York Times*, September 17, 2006, https://www.nytimes.com/2006/09/17/nyregion/17willets.html.

110 Eugene A. Santamasso, "The Design of Reason," in Helen Amy Harrison, ed., *Dawn of a New Day: The New York World's Fair, 1939/40* (Queens Museum, 1980), 30.

111 Steinberg, *Gotham Unbound*, 219.

112 Robert A. Caro, *The Power Broker: Robert Moses and the Fall of New York* (Alfred A. Knopf, 1974), 571.

113 Richard M. Flanagan, *Robert Wagner and the Rise of New York City's Plebiscitary Mayorality: The Tamer of the Tammany Tiger*, 1st ed. (Palgrave Macmillan, 2015), 7.

114 Eleanor Beardsley, "Tivoli Gardens Beckons on Denmark's Summer Nights," *NPR*, August 15, 2012, https://www.npr.org/2012/08/15/158870832/on-denmarks-summer-nights-tivoli-gardens-beckon.

115 Durocher's 1947 ban from baseball officially related to his affairs with Hollywood starlets and associating with gamblers, but his steadfast support for integration was its likelier cause.

116 James S. Hirsch, *Willie Mays: The Life, the Legend* (Scribner, 2011), Chap. 6. Ebook.

117 Joshua Prager, *The Echoing Green: The Untold Story of Bobby Thomson, Ralph Branca, and the Shot Heard Round the World* (Pantheon Books, 2006), 204.

118 Prager, *Echoing Green*, 181.

119 "A Miraculous Home Run Wins the Pennant for NY Giants," History Channel, November 16, 2009, https://www.history.com/this-day-in-history/the-shot-heard-round-the-world.

120 Don DeLillo, *Pafko at the Wall: A Novella* (Scribner, 2001), 54.

121 Maury Allen and Susan Walker, *Dixie Walker of the Dodgers: The People's Choice* (University of Alabama Press, 2010), 181.

122 Prager, *Echoing Green*, 228–229, 251.

123 Michael Meeropol, ed., *The Rosenberg Letters: A Complete Edition of the Prison Correspondence of Julius and Ethel Rosenberg* (Garland, 1994), 234.

124 Prager, *Echoing Green*, 253.

125 Red Smith, "Thomson Authored an Unlikely Ending," *ESPN*, November 9, 2003, https://www.espn.com/classic/s/smith_on_thomson.html.

126 Prager, *Echoing Green*, 251.

127 Andy Battle, "Runaway: A History of Postwar New York in Four Factories" (PhD diss., City University of New York, 2019), 64–65, https://academicworks.cuny.edu/cgi/viewcontent.cgi?article=4488&context=gc_etds.

128 Wendell E. Pritchett, *Brownsville, Brooklyn: Blacks, Jews, and the Changing Face of the Ghetto*, Historical Studies of Urban America (University of Chicago Press, 2003), 113–114.

129 Michael Shapiro, *The Last Good Season: Brooklyn, the Dodgers, and Their Final Pennant Race Together*, 1st ed. (Doubleday, 2003), 250.

130 John Drebinger, "Dodgers Capture 1st World Series," *New York Times*, October 5, 1955, https://www.nytimes.com/1955/10/05/archives/dodgers-capture-1st-world-series-podres-wins-20-he-beats-yanks.html.

131 Hirsch, *Willie Mays*, Chap. 17. Ebook.

132 Peter Golenbock, *Bums: An Oral History of the Brooklyn Dodgers* (Summer Games Books, 2014), Chap. 1. Ebook.

133 Pritchett, *Brownsville, Brooklyn*, 113–114.

134 Hirsch, *Willie Mays*, Chap. 5. Ebook.

135 Robert Fredrick Burk, *Much More Than a Game: Players, Owners, & American Baseball Since 1921* (University of North Carolina Press, 2001), 135.

136 Golenbock, *Bums*, Chap. 3. Ebook.

137 Burton Alan Boxerman and Benita W. Boxerman, *George Weiss: Architect of the Golden Age Yankees* (Jefferson, North Carolina: McFarland & Company, Inc., Publishers, 2016), Chap. 10. Ebook.

138 Boxerman and Boxerman, *George Weiss*, Chap. 10. Ebook.

139 Arlene Howard, *Elston and Me: The Story of the First Black Yankee* (University of Missouri Press, 2001), 37.

140 Jules Tygiel, *Baseball's Great Experiment: Jackie Robinson and His Legacy* (Oxford University Press, 1983), 298.

141 Andy McCue, *Mover and Shaker: Walter O'Malley, the Dodgers, & Baseball's Westward Expansion* (University of Nebraska Press, 2014), 130.

142 Peter Golenbock, *Amazin': The Miraculous History of New York's Most Beloved Baseball Team* (St. Martin's Griffin, 2002), Chap. 7. Ebook.

143 "How a Fan's Protest Led the Minnesota Twins to Remove a Statue of Their Former Owner," *All Things Considered*, NPR, June 21, 2020, https://www.npr.org/2020/06/21/881477671/how-a-fans-protest-led-the-minnesota-twins-to-remove-a-statue-of-their-former-ow.

144 Andy McCue, *Mover & Shaker: Walter O'Malley, the Dodgers, & Baseball's Westward Expansion* (University of Nebraska Press, 2014), 159.

145 McCue, *Mover & Shaker*, xi.

146 Battle, "Runaway," 92–94.

147 Peter Marquis, "Complicating the Blame Game: New York Politics, Baseball Fans and the Dodgers' Move Out of Brooklyn," *Revue française d'études américaines* 151, no. 2 (2018): 206–226, https://doi.org/10.3917/rfea.151.0206.

148 Hirsch, *Willie Mays*, Chap. 17. Ebook.

149 Roger Kahn, *The Era: 1947–1957, When the Yankees, the Giants, and the Dodgers Ruled the World* (First Diversion Books, 2012), Notes. Ebook.

150 Robert Moses, "Moses Says Baseball Beats All Other Sports—but It Needs Integrity," *New York Herald Tribune*, August 3, 1958, 1.

151 Jack Newfield and Paul De Brul, *The Permanent Government: Who Really Rules New York?* (Pilgrim, 1981), 3, 74.

152 Burk, *Much More*, 126.

153 Branch Rickey, *The American Diamond: A Documentary of the Game of Baseball*, with Robert Riger (Simon & Schuster, 1965), 166.

154 J.G. Taylor Spink, "'Third Major Must Come Soon'—Rickey," *Sporting News*, May 21, 1958, 1.

155 Lowenfish, *Branch Rickey*, 553–570.

156 Stanley Woodward, "Stadium, Yes or No," *New York Herald Tribune*, January 8, 1961, 1.

157 William Shea to William H. Pierre, October 9, 1957, box 16, folder 186, Robert F. Wagner Personal Papers for 1950 to 1964, New York City Municipal Archives.

158 Lowenfish, *Branch Rickey*, 565.

159 George Vecsey, *Joy in Mudville: Being a Complete Account of the Unparalleled History of the New York Mets from Their Most Perturbed Beginnings to Their Amazing Rise to Glory and Renown* (McCall, 1970), 16.

160 Vecsey, *Joy in Mudville*, 18.

161 Donald Grant to Robert Wagner, October 9, 1957, box 15, folder 181, Robert F. Wagner Personal Papers for 1950 to 1964, New York City Municipal Archives.

162 Golenbock, *Amazin'*, Chap. 8. Ebook.

163 Golenbock, *Amazin'*, Chap. 8. Ebook.

164 Dan Daniel, *Sporting News*, August 26, 1959, 1.

165 Jonathan Lethem, *Dissident Gardens* (Random House, 2013), Part II, Chap. 1. Ebook.

166 W. M. Akers, "Shea Stadium Is Gone, but Its Impact on Ballparks Lives On," *Sports on Earth*, September 26, 2014, https://web.archive.org/web/20141106115638/http://www.sportsonearth.com/article/96537676/shea-stadium-construction-1960s-robert-moses.

167 "Organized Professional Team Sports—1960," in US Congress, Senate Committee on Judiciary, *Hearings*, vol. 15, (US Government Printing Office, 1960), 68.

168 Lee Lowenfish, *The Imperfect Diamond: A History of Baseball's Labor Wars*, 1st Nebraska paperback pr. (University of Nebraska Press, 2010), 175.

169 United States Congress Senate, *Hearings, Volume 15*, (U.S. Government Printing Office, 1960), https://books.google.com/books?id=mZ-rRADfew0C&pg=RA1-PA66&lpg=RA1-PA66&dq, 66.

170 Jerry Holtzman, "Big Timers Clearing Decks for Expansion," *Sporting News*, August 10, 1960, 1.

171 Holtzman, "Big Timers," 4.

172 Lowenfish, *Branch Rickey*, 576.

173 Lowenfish, *Branch Rickey*, 577–578.

174 Rickey, *American Diamond*, 200.

175 Warren Corbet, "Rickey's Folly: How the Continental League Forced Baseball Expansion," Society for American Baseball Research, February 22, 2023, https://sabr.org/journal/article/rickeys-folly-how-the-continental-league-forced-baseball-expansion/.

176 Louis Effrat, "New National League Team Here Approves Mets as Its Official Name," *New York Times*, May 9, 1961, https://timesmachine.nytimes.com/timesmachine/1961/05/09/issue.html.

177 Lindsey Nelson and Al Hirschberg, *Backstage at the Mets* (Viking Press, 1966), 54.

178 Nicholas Hirshon, "'God Bless Joan Payson': The Surprising Coverage of the First Woman to Buy a Sports Team," *International Journal of the History of Sport* 40, no. 10–11 (2023): 936, https://doi.org/10.1080/09523367.2023.2264775.

CHAPTER 5: THE NEW BREED

179 Robert W. Creamer, *Stengel: His Life and Times* (University of Nebraska Press, 1996), 222.

180 Louis Effrat, "Mets Beat Yankees in First Meeting of Clubs on Ashburn's Pinch Single," *New York Times*, March 23, 1962, https://www.nytimes.com/1962/03/23/archives/mets-beat-yankees-in-first-meeting-of-clubs-on-ashburns-pinch.html.

181 Creamer, *Stengel*, 297.

182 Peter Golenbock, *Amazin': The Miraculous History of New York's Most Beloved Baseball Team* (St. Martin's Griffin, 2002), Chap. 11. Ebook.

183 Sean Deveney, *Fun City: John Lindsay, Joe Namath, and How Sports Saved New York in the 1960s*, 1st ed. (Sports Publishing, 2015), 68.

184 George Vecsey, *Joy in Mudville: Being a Complete Account of the Unparalleled History of the New York Mets from Their Most Perturbed Beginnings to Their Amazing Rise to Glory and Renown* (McCall, 1970), 62.

185 "1962 NY Mets Adapt the Brooklyn Bum by Bill Gallo—Sporting News Original Art," Lelands, April 2018, https://lelands.com/bids/1962-ny-mets-adapt-the-brooklyn-bum-by-bill-gallo---sporting-news-original-art.

186 David Koeppel, "Robert Lipsyte Won't Mourn the New York Times Sports Section," Intelligencer, *New York*, July 2023, https://nymag.com/intelligencer/2023/07/robert-lipsyte-wont-mourn-the-new-york-times-sports-section.html.

187 Vecsey, *Joy in Mudville*, 40.

188 Golenbock, *Amazin'*, Chap. 11. Ebook.

189 Golenbock, *Amazin'*, Chap. 12. Ebook.

190 Roger Angell, *The Roger Angell Baseball Collection* (Open Road Integrated Media, 2013), The Summer Game, Part II, The "Go!" Shouters. Ebook.

191 Arthur Daley, "What's with the Mets? Deceptive Appearances Unexpected Strength in Need of Work," *New York Times*, April 02, 1962, https://timesmachine.nytimes.com/timesmachine/1962/04/02/84787244.html.

192 Angell, *Roger Angell Collection*, The Summer Game, Part I, The Old Folks Behind Home. Ebook.

193 Vecsey, *Joy in Mudville*, 43.

194 Leonard Koppett, *The New York Mets: The Whole Story* (Macmillan, 1970), 46.

195 Jonathan Mahler, *Ladies and Gentlemen, the Bronx Is Burning: 1977, Baseball, Politics, and the Battle for the Soul of a City*, 1st Picador ed. (Picador: Farrar, Straus and Giroux, 2006), Kindle Locations 1896–1902. Ebook.

196 Creamer, *Stengel*, 278–279.

197 Golenbock, *Amazin'*, Chap. 15. Ebook.

198 Jack Gould, "TV Review: Coverage of the Mets' Game Is Discussed," *New York Times*, April 14, 1962, https://www.nytimes.com/1962/04/14/archives/tv-review-coverage-of-the-mets-game-is-discussed.html.

199 Angell, *Roger Angell Collection*, The Summer Game, Part II, The "Go!" Shouters. Ebook.

200 Angell, *Roger Angell Collection*, The Summer Game, Part II, The "Go!" Shouters. Ebook.

201 "Let's Go," Dictionary.com, January 19, 2021, https://www.dictionary.com/e/slang/lets-go/.

202 "Fight. Let's Go! Join the Navy," Hoover Institution, accessed July 24, 2025, https://digitalcollections.hoover.org/objects/35214/fight-lets-go--join-the-navy.

203 Dan Reilly, *The Original Mr. Met Remembers: When the Miracle Began* (iUniverse, 2007), 17.

204 Creamer, *Stengel*, 301.

205 Koppett, *New York Mets*, 45.

206 Angell, *Roger Angell Collection*, The Summer Game, Part II, The "Go!" Shouters. Ebook.

207 Howie Rose, *Put It in the Book! A Half-Century of Mets Mania*, Kindle (Triumph Books, 2012), I Confess. Ebook.

208 Stuart Gittlitz, email interview with author, Jan 31, 2024.

209 Lindsey Nelson and Al Hirschberg, *Backstage at the Mets* (Viking Press, 1966), 77.

210 Angell, *Roger Angell Collection*, The Summer Game, Part II, The "Go!" Shouters. Ebook.

211 Jimmy Breslin, *Can't Anybody Here Play This Game?* (Open Road Integrated Media, 2010), Chap. 4. Ebook.

212 Peter St. Clair, "Baseball and Marxism in Brooklyn (and Boston)," *Brooklyn Rail*, May 6, 2014, https://brooklynrail.org/2014/05/field-notes/baseball-and-marxism-in-brooklyn-and-boston.

213 Nicholas Hirshon, "'God Bless Joan Payson': The Surprising Coverage of the First Woman to Buy a Sports Team," *International Journal of the History of Sport* 40, no. 10–11 (2023): 933, https://doi.org/10.1080/09523367.2023.2264775.

214 Leonard Schecter, "Bring Back the Real Mets!," *New York Times*, September 7, 1969, https://timesmachine.nytimes.com/timesmachine/1969/09/07/89372042.pdf.

215 César Brioso, *Last Seasons in Havana: The Castro Revolution and the End of Professional Baseball in Cuba* (University of Nebraska Press, 2019), 182.

216 Brioso, *Last Seasons*, 191–192.

217 Koppett, *New York Mets*, 59–60.

218 Dana, "A Look Back at the Beatnik Riot," *Village Preservation* (blog), Greenwich Village Society for Historic Preservation, April 25, 2011, https://www.villagepreservation.org/2011/04/25/a-look-back-at-the-beatnik-riot/.

219 William J. Ryczek, *The Amazin' Mets, 1962–1969* (McFarland, 2008), 50.

220 "Jean Shepherd—a Day With the 1962 Mets," WOR radio broadcast, June 4, 1962, posted December 7, 2018, by Comrade Dobler, YouTube, https://www.youtube.com/watch?v=nep7DuwCfPg.

221 Geoffrey Hoover and Tatiana Hoover, "The New Breed: The Story of the Fans of the '62 Mets," posted June 8, 2012, by TORGHOOVER, YouTube, https://www.youtube.com/watch?v=PjqcVwCx_9U.

222 Hoover and Hoover, "New Breed" YouTube video.

223 Burton Alan Boxerman and Benita W. Boxerman, *George Weiss: Architect of the Golden Age Yankees* (McFarland, 2016), Chap 2. Ebook.

224 Boxerman and Boxerman, *George Weiss*, Chap 2. Ebook.

225 Creamer, *Stengel*, 302.

226 William J. Ryczek, *Crash of the Titans: The Early Years of the New York Jets and the AFL* (Total Sports, 2000), 159–160.

227 Jim Snedeker, "Mayor's Trophy Games," Ultimate Mets Database, accessed July 24, 2025, https://www.ultimatemets.com/mayorstrophy.php#1963.

228 Nelson and Hirschberg, *Backstage at the Mets*, 136–137.

229 Vecsey, *Joy in Mudville*, 87.

230 Greg Prince, "The Happiest Recap: 157," *Faith and Fear in Flushing* (blog), October 18, 2011, https://www.faithandfearinflushing.com/2011/10/18/the-happiest-recap-157/.

CHAPTER 6: ONE-DIMENSIONAL MASCOT

231 Matthew Silverman, *Shea Stadium Remembered: The Mets, the Jets, and Beatlemania* (Lyons Press, 2019), 20.

232 "Welcome to Shea Stadium: 1964 Mets Yearbook," Mets Heritage, Mets Virtual Vault, June 21, 2021, https://www.metsheritage.com/item/welcome-to-shea-stadium-1964/.

233 Marshall Field, "This Day in Mets' History: Happy Birthday, Casey Stengel," *Amazin' Avenue*, July 30, 2018, https://www.amazinavenue.com/2018/7/30/17617690/mets-casey-stengel-history-birthday-new-york-manager.

234 Leonard Koppett, *The New York Mets: The Whole Story* (Macmillan, 1970), 77.

235 Cleon Jones, *Coming Home: My Amazin' Life with the New York Mets* (Triumph Books, 2022), 58–59.

236 Will Sammon, "Mets Celeb Seymour Weiner, Age 97, Has Heard Your Jokes—and He Loves Them," *The Athletic*, April 26, 2024, https://www.nytimes.com/athletic/5446444/2024/04/25/mets-seymour-weiner-hot-dog/.

237 Bruce Watson, "The Summer of Our Discontent," *American Heritage*, Summer 2010, https://www.americanheritage.com/summer-our-discontent.

238 Alan Gilbert, "My Pal Andy Goodman's Murder Made Him a Civil Rights Martyr," *Daily Beast*, September 20, 2024, https://www.thedailybeast.com/my-pal-andy-goodmans-murder-made-him-a-civil-rights-martyr.

239 Kenneth O'Reilly, *Racial Matters: The FBI's Secret File on Black America, 1960–1972*, repr. ed. (Free Press, 1991), 164.

240 Louis E. Lomax, "The Road to Mississippi," *Ramparts* magazine 23, special issue, 1964, https://www.crmvet.org/info/64_lomax-csg-r.pdf.

241 Lomax, "Road to Mississippi."

242 Malcolm X, "The Ballot or the Bullet," speech in Cleveland, OH/Detroit, MI, April 3, 1964/ April 13, 1964, https://www.icit-digital.org/articles/malcolm-x-on-the-ballot-or-the-bullet-april-12-1964

243 Joseph Tirella, *Tomorrow-Land: The 1964–65 World's Fair and the Transformation of America* (Lyons Press, 2014), 255.

244 Tirella, *Tomorrow-Land*, Chap. 20. Ebook.

245 Tirella, *Tomorrow-Land*, Chap. 20. Ebook

246 Tirella, *Tomorrow-Land*, Chap. 7. Ebook.

247 "Mets Are Stopped Again by Wether; 2-Game Series with Phils Put Off—Cubs Here Today," *New York Times*, April 22, 1964, https://www.nytimes.com/1964/04/22/archives/mets-are-stopped-again-by-wether-2game-series-with-phils-put.html.

248 Janet Biehl, *Ecology or Catastrophe: The Life of Murray Bookchin* (Oxford University Press, 2015), 92.

249 Tirella, *Tomorrow-Land*, Chap. 21. Ebook.

250 George Lipsitz, *A Life in the Struggle: Ivory Perry and the Culture of Opposition*, Critical Perspectives on the Past Series (Temple University Press, 2011), 82–83.

251 Robert A. Caro, *The Power Broker: Robert Moses and the Fall of New York* (Alfred A. Knopf, 1974), 1008.

252 Caro, *Power Broker*, 1012–1013.

253 Jarrod Shanahan, *Captives: How Rikers Island Took New York City Hostage* (Verso Books, 2022), 108–109.

254 Biehl, *Ecology or Catastrophe*, 93.

255 Kareem Abdul-Jabbar, *Becoming Kareem: Growing Up On and Off the Court*, 1st ed., with Raymond Obstfeld (Little, Brown Books for Young Readers, 2017). Part 2, Chap. 16. Ebook.

256 Shanahan, *Captives*, 108–109.

257 Herbert Marcuse, *One-Dimensional Man: Studies in the Ideology of Advanced Industrial Society* (Routledge & Kegan Paul, 1964), 7.

258 Dan Reilly, *The Original Mr. Met Remembers: When the Miracle Began* (iUniverse, 2007), 32.

259 Reilly, *Original Mr. Met*, 33.

260 Robert B. Ross, *The Great Baseball Revolt: The Rise and Fall of the 1890 Players League* (University of Nebraska Press, 2016), Chap. 2. Ebook.

261 Robert Sandomir, "Ever the Optimist, Mr. Met Keeps His Head Up," *New York Times*, Jan 5, 2012, https://www.nytimes.com/2012/01/06/sports/baseball/ever-the-optimist-mr-met-keeps-his-head-up.html.

262 Reilly, *Original Mr. Met*, 40.

263 Reilly, *Original Mr. Met*, 42.

264 Gaylord Perry, *Me and the Spitter: An Autobiographical Confession* (Saturday Review Press, 1974), 21.

CHAPTER 7: STORMING HEAVEN

265 Bill Madden, *Tom Seaver: A Terrific Life* (Simon & Schuster, 2020), Chap 3. Ebook.

266 George Vecsey, *Joy in Mudville: Being a Complete Account of the Unparalleled History of the New York Mets from Their Most Perturbed Beginnings to Their Amazing Rise to Glory and Renown* (McCall, 1970), 139.

267 Madden, *Tom Seaver*, Chap. 2. Ebook.

268 Madden, *Tom Seaver*, Chap. 4. Ebook.

269 Mort Zachter, *Gil Hodges: A Hall of Fame Life* (University of Nebraska Press, 2015), Chap. 20. Ebook.

270 William J. Ryczek, *Baseball on the Brink: The Crisis of 1968* (McFarland, 2017), 176.

271 Ryczek, *Baseball on the Brink*, 86.

272 Harry Enten, "Americans See Martin Luther King Jr. as a Hero Now, but That Wasn't the Case During His Lifetime," *CNN*, January 6, 2023, https://www.cnn.com/2023/01/16/politics/martin-luther-king-jr-polling-analysis/index.html.

273 Eldridge Cleaver, "On Civil Disobedience with Violence: The Death of Martin Luther King; Requiem for Nonviolence," in David Dressler, ed., *Readings in Criminology and Penology* (Columbia University Press, 1972), 444–445.

274 Glenn Stout and Richard A. Johnson, *The Dodgers: 120 Years of Dodgers Baseball* (Houghton Mifflin, 2004), 304.

275 "Here Is the Speech Martin Luther King Jr. Gave the Night Before He Died," *CNN*, April 4, 2018, https://www.cnn.com/2018/04/04/us/martin-luther-king-jr-mountaintop-speech-trnd.

276 Bill Francis, "National Tragedy Brought Baseball to a Halt for Two Days in 1968," Baseball Hall of Fame, n.d, https://baseballhall.org/discover/martin-luther-king-jrs-assassination-brought-baseball-to-a-halt-in-1968.

277 Art Shamsky, *After the Miracle: The Lasting Brotherhood of the '69 Mets* (Simon & Schuster, 2019), Chap, 8. Ebook.

278 Cleon Jones, *Coming Home: My Amazin' Life with the New York Mets* (Triumph Books, 2022), 236–237.

279 William J. Ryczek, *The Amazin' Mets, 1962–1969* (McFarland, 2008), 241.

280 Shamsky, *After the Miracle*, Chap. 22. Ebook.

281 Ryczek, *Baseball on the Brink*, 94.

282 Frederic J. Frommer, "How Baseball's Response to RFK's Death Inspired Some Players to Fight Back and Sit Out," *Washington Post*, June 6, 2021, https://www.washingtonpost.com/sports/2021/06/06/rfk-death-mlb-players-boycott/.

283 Frommer, "Baseball's Response to RFK's Death."

284 Zachter, *Gil Hodges*, Notes. Ebook.

285 Brad Snyder, *A Well-Paid Slave: Curt Flood's Fight for Free Agency in Professional Sports* (Plume, 2014), Chap. 4. Ebook.

286 Ryczek, *Baseball on the Brink*, 205.

287 Robert Fredrick Burk, *Much More Than a Game: Players, Owners, & American Baseball Since 1921* (University of North Carolina Press, 2001), 147–150.

288 Robert Fredrick Burk, *Marvin Miller, Baseball Revolutionary*, Sport and Society (University of Illinois Press, 2015), 136.

289 Burk, *Marvin Miller*, 136–137.

290 Zachter, *Gil Hodges*, Chap 21. Ebook.

291 Madden, *Tom Seaver*, Chap. 6. Ebook.

292 Ed Hoyt, "Donn Clendenon," Society for American Baseball Research, September 22, 2021, https://sabr.org/bioproj/person/donn-clendenon/.

293 Doug Feldmann, *Miracle Collapse: The 1969 Chicago Cubs* (University of Nebraska Press, 2006), 232.

294 Shamsky, *After the Miracle*, Chap. 6. Ebook.

295 Feldmann, *Miracle Collapse*, 164.

296 Feldmann, *Miracle Collapse*, 165.

297 Roger Angell, *The Roger Angell Baseball Collection* (Open Road Integrated Media, 2013), The Summer Game, Part V, The Leaping Corpse Ebook.

298 "1969: We Have Liftoff in Queens," *New York Times*, March 27, 2019, https://www.nytimes.com/2019/03/27/sports/baseball/mets-1969-season.html.

299 Shamsky, *After the Miracle*, Chap. 8. Ebook.

300 Jerry Rubin, *Do It!* (Simon & Schuster, 1970), 59, 125.

301 Steve Komm and Alan Smitow, "A True History of SDS Convention," July 1969, https://archive.org/stream/convention-report-sds-1969-07/convention-report-sds-1969-07_djvu.txt.

302 Paul Heideman, "Half the Way with Mao Zedong," *Jacobin*, May 23, 2018, https://jacobin.com/2018/05/half-the-way-with-mao-zedong.

303 Ellen Willis and Nona Willis Aronowitz, *Out of the Vinyl Deeps: Ellen Willis on Rock Music* (University of Minnesota Press, 2011), 176.

304 Dean Latimer, "Decomposition," *East Village Other*, October 22, 1969, 19, https://archive.org/details/sim_east-village-other_1969-10-22_4_47/page/n19/mode/2up?q=mets&view=theater.

305 Shamsky, *After the Miracle*, Chap 14. Ebook.

306 Paul Lukas, "Cubs, Mets Black Cat Incident as Told by Chicago's Batboy," *Sports Illustrated*, September 6, 2019, https://www.si.com/mlb/2019/09/06/chicago-cubs-new-york-mets-black-cat.

307 Devin Gordon, *So Many Ways to Lose: The Amazin' True Story of the New York Mets—the Best Worst Team in Sports*, 1st ed. (HarperCollins Publishers, 2021), The House That a Well-Connected Lawyer Built. Ebook.

308 "BaphometsNYC," BaphometsNYC, accessed July 24, 2025, https://nybaphomets.bigcartel.com/.

309 Howie Rose and Phil Pepe, *Put It in the Book! A Half-Century of Mets Mania*, Kindle. (Triumph Books, 2013), Miracle. Ebook.

310 Rose and Pepe, *Put It in the Book!* Miracle. Ebook.

311 Leonard Koppett, *The New York Mets: The Whole Story* (Macmillan, 1970), 228.

312 "Metsomania: Young Fans Get Tickets After a Night-Long Vigil and Unscheduled Romp in Shea Stadium." *New York Times*, September 27, 1969, https://www.nytimes.com/1969/09/27/archives/metsomania-young-fans-get-tickets-after-a-nightlong-vigil-and.html.

313 Shamsky, *After the Miracle*, Chap. 14. Ebook.

314 Hank Aaron, *I Had a Hammer: The Hank Aaron Story*, with Lonnie Wheeler, (HarperCollins, 1991), 280.

315 United Press International, "Tom Seaver Says US Should Leave Vietnam," *New York Times*, October 11, 1969, https://www.nytimes.com/1969/10/11/archives/tom-seaver-says-u-s-should-leave-vietnam.html.

316 Leonard Koppett, "Orioles Rated 'Logical' Favorites Over Mets as World Series Opens Today," *New York Times*, October 11, 1969, https://www.nytimes.com/1969/10/11/archives/orioles-rated-logical-favorites-over-mets-as-world-series-opens.html.

317 Madden, *Tom Seaver*, Chap. 6. Ebook.

318 Ryczek, *Amazin' Mets*, 255.

319 Madden, *Tom Seaver*, Chap 6. Ebook.

320 Angell, *Roger Angell Collection, What is Days and Nights with the Unbored34?* Ebook.

321 The Conspiracy, "Mets Fans for Peace," Grove Press, 1969, Broadsides, SY1969 no. 2, New-York Historical Society.

322 Madden, *Tom Seaver*, Chap 6.

323 Kelly Candaele and Peter Dreier, "Tom Seaver's Major League Protest," *The Nation*, September 11, 2020, https://www.thenation.com/article/society/tom-seaver-vietnam-protest/.

324 Vecsey, *Joy in Mudville*, 235.

325 Latimer, "Decomposition."

326 Koppett, *New York Mets*, 245.

327 Jones, *Coming Home*, 14.

328 Jones, *Coming Home*, 15.

329 Jones, *Coming Home*, 16.

330 Shamsky, *After the Miracle*, Chap. 20. Ebook.

331 Shamsky, *After the Miracle*, Chap 20. Ebook.

332 Ryczek, *Amazin' Mets*, 264.

333 "1969 World Series, Game 5: Orioles @ Mets," posted September 25, 2010, by MLB Vault, YouTube, https://www.youtube.com/watch?v=WbCWUehZKVU.

334 Vecsey, *Joy in Mudville*, 226.

335 Katie Charles, "After Dark," *New York*, February 8, 2008, https://nymag.com/anniversary/40th/strategist/43900/.

336 Ryczek, *Amazin' Mets*, 264.

337 "1969 World Series New York Mets Win," posted January 8, 2017, by My Footage, YouTube, https://www.youtube.com/watch?v=qt17oOSScMQ.

CHAPTER 8: SHAME STADIUM

338 William J. Ryczek, *The Amazin' Mets, 1962–1969* (McFarland, 2008), 264.

339 Nicholas Hirshon, "One More Miracle: The Groundbreaking Media Campaign of John 'Mets' Lindsay," *American Journalism* 34, no. 1 (2017): 2–25, https://doi.org/10.1080/08821127.2016.1275246.

340 "The Great Silent Majority (Full Version)," posted on July 29, 2010, by Richard Nixon Foundation, YouTube, https://www.youtube.com/watch?v=TpCWHQ30Do8.

341 Peter Golenbock, *Amazin': The Miraculous History of New York's Most Beloved Baseball Team* (St. Martin's Griffin, 2002), Chap. 22. Ebook.

342 Golenbock, *Amazin'*, Chap. 22. Ebook.

343 Mort Zachter, *Gil Hodges: A Hall of Fame Life* (University of Nebraska Press, 2015), Chap. 23. Ebook.

344 Tug McGraw and Joseph Durso, *Screwball* (Houghton Mifflin, 1974), 147.

345 Jack Scott, *The Athletic Revolution* (New York: The Free Press, 1971), 112–113.

346 Paula Schleis, "Kent State Shootings: Jeffrey Miller Despised Violence. He Died in a Hail of Gunfire," *Akron Beacon Journal*, May 3, 2020, https://www.cincinnati.com/in-depth/news/history/2020/05/03/kent-state-shootings-jeffrey-miller-died-protesting-despised-violence-national-guard-may-4-1970/3059124001/.

347 McGraw and Durso, *Screwball*, 14.

348 McGraw and Durso, *Screwball*, 154.

349 Golenbock, *Amazin'*, Chap. 25. Ebook.

350 Zachter, *Gil Hodges*, Chap. 23. Ebook.

351 Karen Kelly and Evelyn McDonnell, eds., *Stars Don't Stand Still in the Sky: Music and Myth* (New York University Press, 1999), 157–158.

352 Ryczek, *Amazin' Mets*, 264.

353 McGraw and Durso, *Screwball*, 148–149.

354 Jeremy Varon, "Killing the Field of Dreams: George W. Bush, Empire and the Politics of Misrecognition," *Fast Capitalism* 1, no. 2 (2019), 7, https://doi.org/10.32855/fcapital.2005.02.

355 Leonard Koppett, *The New York Mets: The Whole Story* (Macmillan, 1970), 267.

356 Zachter, *Gil Hodges*, Chap. 23. Ebook.

357 Rob Edleman, "M. Donald Grant," Society for American Baseball Research, September 21, 2024, https://sabr.org/bioproj/person/M-Donald-Grant/.

358 Robert Fredrick Burk, *Much More Than a Game: Players, Owners, & American Baseball Since 1921* (University of North Carolina Press, 2001), 176.

359 Golenbock, *Amazin'*, Chap. 12. Ebook.

360 Burk, *Much More*, 177.

361 Devin Gordon, *So Many Ways to Lose: The Amazin' True Story of the New York Mets—The Best Worst Team in Sports*, 1st ed. (HarperCollins, 2021), Gilly and Yoge. Ebook.

362 James S. Hirsch, *Willie Mays: The Life, the Legend*, 1st Scribner paperback ed. (Scribner, 2011), Chap. 35. Ebook.

363 Hirsch, *Willie Mays*, Chap 35. Ebook.

364 McGraw and Durso, *Screwball*, 23–25.

365 Golenbock, *Amazin'*, Chap. 26. Ebook.

366 McGraw and Durso, *Screwball*, 26.

367 Hirsch, *Willie Mays*, Chap. 36. Ebook.

368 Hirsch, *Willie Mays*, Chap. 36. Ebook.

369 Tom Wolfe, "The 'Me' Decade and the Third Great Awakening," *New York*, August 23, 1976, https://nymag.com/article/tom-wolfe-me-decade-third-great-awakening.html.

370 Jerry Herron, "The Amazing Mets and Structuralist Activity," *The Antioch Review* 39, no. 3, January 1, 1981, https://doi.org/10.2307/4638455, 302.

371 Hirsch, *Willie Mays*, Chap. 36. Ebook.

372 Jerry Herron, "The Amazing Mets and Structuralist Activity," *Antioch Review* 39, no. 3 (1981), 314, https://doi.org/10.2307/4638455.

373 Hirsch, *Willie Mays*, Chap. 36. Ebook.

374 William K. Tabb, *The Long Default: New York City and the Urban Fiscal Crisis* (Monthly Review Press, 1982), 31.

375 Hsiang-Shui Chen, *Chinatown No More: Taiwan Immigrants in Contemporary New York* (Cornell University Press, 2018).

376 Ila Jane Borders and Jean Hastings Ardell, *Making My Pitch: A Woman's Baseball Odyssey* (University of Nebraska Press, 2017), 41.

377 Gordon, *So Many Ways*, Tom Terrific and the Midnight Massacre. Ebook.

378 Paul L. Montgomery, "Night and Day, Mets Are Blacked Out," *New York Times*, July 15, 1977.

379 "The Mets' Fans Guess Is . . . ," *Daily Record*, April 8, 1979, C3, ProQuest (2371778772), https://www.proquest.com/docview/2371778772.

380 "An Amazing Era: The New York Mets 25th Anniversary [1962–1986]," posted on November 1, 2021, by MAJOR LEAGUE BASEBALL ON VHS, YouTube, https://www.youtube.com/watch?v=B24nz5H0694.

CHAPTER 9: THE ROBO METS

381 *Meet at the Apple*, podcast, "How Did Howie Rose Become a Mets Fan, Come Up With 'Put It in the Books' and MORE!" July 18, 2024, https://podcasts.apple.com/us/podcast/how-did-howie-rose-become-a-mets-fan-come-up-with-put/id1732076793?i=1000662641053.

382 Thomas Barthel, *Abner Doubleday: A Civil War Biography* (McFarland, 2010), 88.

383 "The People's Team: 1980 Mets Yearbook," Mets Heritage, Mets Virtual Vault, June 21, 2021, https://www.metsheritage.com/item/the-peoples-team-1980/.

384 Cindy Thomson, "George Foster," Society for American Baseball Research, March 5, 2021, https://sabr.org/bioproj/person/george-foster/.

385 Jean Baudrillard, *America* (Verso Books, 1989), 110.

386 Jeffrey Toobin, "Madoff's Curveball," *The New Yorker*, May 23, 2011, https://www.newyorker.com/magazine/2011/05/30/madoffs-curveball.

387 Davey Johnson, *Davey Johnson: My Wild Ride in Baseball and Beyond*, with Eric Sherman, 1st ed. (Triumph Books, 2018), Chap. 6. Ebook.

388 Johnson, *Davey Johnson*, Chap. 7. Ebook.

389 Alan Schwarz, *The Numbers Game: Baseball's Lifelong Fascination with Statistics*, (St. Martin's Press, 2004), Chap. 4. Ebook.

390 Martin Porter, "The PC Goes to Bat," *PC Mag*, May 29, 1984, 209–213.

391 Lou Oddo, "Experience," LinkedIn accessed July 24, 2025, https://www.linkedin.com/in/louoddo.

392 "Crunching Numbers in 1984: Mets Info Guide," Mets Heritage, Mets Virtual Vault, June 17, 2021, https://www.metsheritage.com/item/crunching-numbers-in-84/.

393 Darryl Strawberry, *Darryl*, with Art Rust Jr. (Bantam, 1991), 129.

394 Strawberry, *Darryl*, 127.

395 Strawberry, *Darryl*, 137.

396 Johnson, *Davey Johnson*, Chap. 20. Ebook.

397 Associated Press, "Pittsburgh Cocaine Trial: Baseball's 2nd Biggest Scandal: One Year Later," *Los Angeles Times*, March 12, 2019, https://www.latimes.com/archives/la-xpm-1986-09-21-sp-9304-story.html.

398 Strawberry, *Darryl*, 141.

399 Strawberry, *Darryl*, 115–116.

400 Peter Golenbock, *Amazin': The Miraculous History of New York's Most Beloved Baseball Team* (St. Martin's Griffin, 2002), Chap. 36. Ebook.

401 "Get Metsmerized! 1986 Mets Hit Record," posted on March 5, 2010, by endlessgreg, Youtube, https://www.youtube.com/watch?v=hpvufrpAhls.

402 Strawberry, *Darryl*, 135.

403 "Scouting; Shea's Hatches Battened Down," *New York Times*, September 17, 1986, *https://www.nytimes.com/1986/09/17/sports/scouting-shea-s-hatches-battened-down.html.*

404 George Vecsey, "Sports of the Times; Mugging Our Heroes," *New York Times*, September 21, 1986, https://www.nytimes.com/1986/09/21/sports/sports-of-the-times-mugging-our-heroes.html.

405 George Vecsey, "Sports of the Times; The Mark of the Fans," *New York Times*, September 19, 1986, https://www.nytimes.com/1986/09/19/sports/sports-of-the-times-the-mark-of-the-fans.html.

406 "Mets' Magic, and Mayhem," editorial, *New York Times*, September 19, 1986, https://timesmachine.nytimes.com/timesmachine/1986/09/19/247186.html?pageNumber=34.

407 Dwight Gooden and Ellis Henican, *Doc: A Memoir* (New Harvest, 2013), 88.

408 William E. Geist, "About New York; The "Mayor Discovers Baseball," *New York Times*, October 17, 1986, https://www.nytimes.com/1986/10/17/nyregion/about-new-york-the-mayor-discovers-baseball.html.

409 Michael Sergio (@Sheajumper), "Mets fans, re: my '86 jump," Twitter (now X), February 19, 2023, https://x.com/Sheajumper/status/1627296568306016256.

410 "Mets WALK-OFF Game 6 of 1986 World Series! | FULL INNING," posted January 5, 2025 by New York Mets, YouTube, https://www.youtube.com/watch?v=5UWSXVReu6k.

411 Gooden and Henican, *Doc*, xviii.

412 Mookie Wilson, *Mookie: Life, Baseball, and the '86 Mets* (Penguin, 2014), 207.

413 Cindy Thomson, "George Foster," Society for American Baseball Research, March 5, 2021, https://sabr.org/bioproj/person/george-foster/.

414 Ira Berkow, "Sports of the Times; The Foster Cloud," *New York Times*, August 12, 1986, https://timesmachine.nytimes.com/timesmachine/1986/08/12/issue.html.

415 Gooden and Henican, *Doc*, 80.

416 Reagan Library, "President Reagan's Remarks on the New York Mets Winning the World Series on November 12, 1986," posted on September 5, 2017, by Reagan Library, YouTube, https://www.youtube.com/watch?v=ao57mZBoTh8.

417 Dudley Clendinen, "Gooden Lawyer Seeks to Settle," *New York Times*, December 17, 1986, https://www.nytimes.com/1986/12/17/sports/gooden-lawyer-seeks-to-settle.html.

418 Gary Sheffield, "Do You Believe Me Now?" *Players' Tribune*, June 12, 2020, https://www.theplayerstribune.com/articles/gary-sheffield-baseball-racism.

419 Gooden and Henican, *Doc*, 99.

420 George Vecsey, "Sports of the Times; Gooden Case: Another Look," *New York Times*, December 22, 1986, https://www.nytimes.com/1986/12/22/sports/sports-of-the-times-gooden-case-another-look.html.

421 George Vecsey, "Out of the Strike Zone," *New York Times*, December 15, 1986, https://timesmachine.nytimes.com/timesmachine/1986/12/15/528886.html?pageNumber=47.

422 Wilson, *Mookie*, 208.

423 Sam McManis, "Gibson Returns, Isn't Amused: Orosco Apologizes After Admitting He Blackened Cap," *Los Angeles Times*, March 10, 2019, https://www.latimes.com/archives/la-xpm-1988-03-05-sp-261-story.html.

424 David Cone, "It Was Justice—Not Luck," *New York Daily News*, October 5, 1988, 57, https://www.newspapers.com/image/397011302/.

425 Roger Angell, *A Pitcher's Story: Innings with David Cone* (Warner Books, 2002), 162.

426 Golenbock, *Amazin'*, Chap. 35. Ebook.

427 George Vecsey, "The Mets' Quiet Man," *New York Times*, April 13, 1988, https://www.nytimes.com/1988/04/13/sports/sports-of-the-times-the-mets-quiet-man.html.

428 Strawberry, *Darryl*, 51.

429 Bob Klapisch and John Harper, *The Worst Team Money Could Buy: The Collapse of the New York Mets* (University of Nebraska Press, 2005), 193.

430 Strawberry, *Darryl*, 279.

431 Klapisch and Harper, *Worst Team*, 79.

432 Klapisch and Harper, *Worst Team*, 15.

433 Daniel Engber, "A Woman Accused Three New York Mets of Raping Her in 1991. They Weren't Charged. She Was Forgotten," *Slate*, January 13, 2020, https://slate.com/culture/2020/01/mets-rape-accusation-spring-training-1991.html.

434 Engber, "Woman Accused Mets."

435 Engber, "Woman Accused Mets." In his retrospective of this largely forgotten chapter of Mets history, Engber reported the victim never recovered and committed suicide in 2011.

436 Joe Sexton, "Baseball; Coleman's Tarnished Met Career Is Finished," *New York Times*, August 27, 1993, https://www.nytimes.com/1993/08/27/sports/baseball-coleman-s-tarnished-met-career-is-finished.html.

437 Larry Getlen and Kate Briquelet, "Ex-Mr. Met Spills on Being the Massive-headed Mascot," *New York Post*, April 13, 2014, https://nypost.com/2014/04/13/ex-mr-met-spills-on-being-the-massive-headed-mascot/.

CHAPTER 10: CITY OF SHADOWS

438 Robert Fredrick Burk, *Much More Than a Game: Players, Owners, & American Baseball Since 1921* (University of North Carolina Press, 2001), 269.

439 Burk, *Much More*, 281.

440 "Hawaiian Punch Mets' Agbayani Homers to Stardom," *New York Daily News*, January 11, 2019, https://www.nydailynews.com/1999/06/20/hawaiian-punch-mets-agbayani-homers-to-stardom/.

441 Tim Kurkjian, "The Replacements," *ESPN the Magazine*, August 29, 2002, https://www.espn.com/magazine/kurkjian_20020829.html.

442 "New Meaning to Hardball During Strike," *Daily Press*, November 2, 1994, https://www.dailypress.com/1994/11/02/new-meaning-to-hardball-during-strike/.

443 "New Meaning to Hardball," *Daily Press*.

444 Mark Maske, "After the Strike, Baseball's Disgusted Fans Decide to Strike Back," *Washington Post*, January 6, 2024, https://www.washingtonpost.com/archive/politics/1995/04/30/after-the-strike-baseballs-disgusted-fans-decide-to-strike-back/07c1f121-3de0-4887-8609-45c8c35d876e/.

445 CNN Sports, "April 28, 1995 showing their displeasure at the recent baseball strike, 3 fans jump a Shea Stadium fence with 1 out in the top of the 4th inning and begin . . . ," reposted Ebook on April 28, 2021, by Davenport Sports Network, Facebook, https://www.facebook.com/watch/?v=4249715078413342.

446 *Seinfeld*, "The Label Maker," NBC, January 19, 1995.

447 "Reed Crosses Back Met Gets Invite to Union Meeting," *New York Daily News*, January 12, 2019, https://www.nydailynews.com/1998/03/02/reed-crosses-back-met-gets-invite-to-union-meeting/.

448 Matthew Silverman, "The Minor Signing of Rick Reed That Became a Major Impact," *Rising Apple*, November 17, 2019, risingapple.com/2019/11/17/mets-rick-reed-career.

449 Zach Helfand, "Is Stealing Baseball Signs Really So Bad? Bobby Valentine Has Some Thoughts," *The New Yorker*, February 13, 2020, https://www.newyorker.com/sports/sporting-scene/is-stealing-signs-in-baseball-really-so-bad-bobby-valentine-has-some-thoughts.

450 George Orwell and Dervla Murphy, *Down and Out in Paris and London*, Penguin Modern Classics (Penguin Books, 2020), 103.

451 Bobby Valentine, *Valentine's Way: My Adventurous Life and Times* (New York: Permuted Press, 2021), Chap 20. Ebook.

452 Bill Madden, *Steinbrenner: The Last Lion of Baseball*, 1st ed. (HarperCollins, 2011), Chap. 15. Ebook.

453 Drew Silva, "Yankee Stadium's Bleacher Creatures Agree to Put a Halt to Homophobic Chant," *NBC Sports*, October 17, 2010, https://www.nbcsports.com/mlb/news/15542.

454 Joe Torre and Tom Verducci, *The Yankee Years* (Anchor Books, 2010), Chap. 1. Ebook.

455 Matthew Callan, *Yells for Ourselves: New York City and the New York Mets at the Dawn of the Millennium* (Inkshares, 2019), Chap. 11. Ebook.

456 Tony Collins, *Sport in Capitalist Society: A Short History* (Routledge, 2013), 119.

457 Mike Piazza, *Long Shot*, with Lonnie Wheeler (Simon & Schuster, 2014), 173.

458 Paul Lukas, "Uni Watch's Friday Flashback—When New York Mets Bet on Black in Their Uniforms," *ESPN*, October 20, 2015, https://www.espn.com/mlb/story/_/id/13934889/uni-watch-friday-flashback-new-york-mets-bet-black-their-uniforms.

459 Bob Klapisch, "Mojo Risin'," *ESPN the Magazine*, July 10, 2012, https://www.espn.com/espn/magazine/archives/news/story?page=magazine-19990906-article33.

460 Jeff Pearlman, "At Full Blast," *CNN Sports Illustrated*, December 23, 1999, https://web.archive.org/web/20000817193712/http://sportsillustrated.cnn.com/features/cover/news/1999/12/22/rocker/.

461 José de Jesus Ortiz, "Astros' Venezuelans Watch Country's Political Unrest," *Chron*.com, April 17, 2002, https://www.chron.com/sports/astros/article/astros-venezuelans-watch-country-s-political-2100399.php.

462 "Ex-Met, Fellow Venezuelan Alfonzo 'Surprised' by Castro Comments; Guillen Suspended," *CBS News*, April 10, 2012, https://www.cbsnews.com/newyork/news/ex-met-fellow-venezuelan-alfonzo-surprised-by-castro-comments-guillen-suspended/.

463 Callan, *Yells for Ourselves*, Chap. 11. Ebook.

464 Callan, *Yells for Ourselves*, Chap. 12. Ebook.

465 Piazza, *Long Shot*, 225.

466 Buster Olney, "Baseball; Steinbrenner Says Met Outcry Takes Focus Off Their Losing," *New York Times*, July 11, 2000, https://www.nytimes.com/2000/07/11/sports/baseball-steinbrenner-says-met-outcry-takes-focus-off-their-losing.html.

467 Piazza, *Long Shot*, 227.

468 "New York Mets—Who Let the Mets Out? (2000 Theme Song, David Brody and Z100 Exclusive)," posted on May 4, 2023, by Laurence Lau, YouTube, https://www.youtube.com/watch?v=f1iTQbQ0tjM.

469 Mike Puma, *If These Walls Could Talk: Stories from the New York Mets Dugout, Locker Room, and Press Box* (Triumph Books, 2021), Introduction. Ebook.

470 Bobby Valentine, *Valentine's Way: My Adventurous Life and Times* (Permuted Press, 2021), Chap. 27. Ebook.

471 Torre and Verducci, *Yankee Years*, Chap. 4. Ebook.

472 Piazza, *Long Shot*, 235.

473 Madden, *Steinbrenner*, Chap. 19. Ebook.

474 Peter Hamill, *The Subway Series Reader: Mets-Yankees 2000* (Simon & Schuster, 2000), 61–62.

475 Piazza, *Long Shot*, 217.

476 Valentine, *Valentine's Way*, Chap. 27. Ebook.

CHAPTER 11: FULL AUTONOMY

477 Mark Cowling and James Martin, eds., *Marx's "Eighteenth Brumaire": (Post)Modern Interpretations* (Pluto, 2002), 48.

478 Christina Gough, "MLB Fans Political Affiliation in the U.S. 2020, by Team," *Statista*, June 13, 2022, https://www.statista.com/statistics/1174866/political-affiliation-mlb-fans/.

479 Peggy Noonan, "The Loyal Opposition," *Wall Street Journal*, October 27, 2000, https://web.archive.org/web/20050205203708/https://peggynoonan.com/article.php?article=26.

480 Michael Duffy, "Peggy Noonan," *Time*, November 5, 2015, https://time.com/4101184/peggy-noonan/.

481 Mike Piazza, *Long Shot*, with Lonnie Wheeler (Simon & Schuster, 2014), 244.

482 Howie Rose (@HowieRose), "As promised, here's why a tape measure home run was described," Twitter (now X), September 21, 2022, https://x.com/HowieRose/status/1572597627614801922.

483 Tim Britton, "The 11 Greatest Broadcast Calls in Mets History," *The Athletic*, accessed July 24, 2025, https://www.nytimes.com/athletic/1878334/2020/06/18/the-11-greatest-broadcast-calls-in-mets-history/.

484 Robert Silverman, "When MLB Star Carlos Delgado Fought Post-9/11 Jingoism," *Daily Beast*, September 11, 2021, https://www.thedailybeast.com/when-mlb-star-carlos-delgado-kneeled-against-post-911-jingoism.

485 Mike Puma, *If These Walls Could Talk: Stories from the New York Mets Dugout, Locker Room, and Press Box* (Triumph Books, 2021), Chap. 1. Ebook.

486 Tom Ley, "Why Is ESPN Doing George W. Bush's Dirty Work For Him?" *Deadspin*, September 11, 2005, https://deadspin.com/why-is-espn-doing-george-w-bushs-dirty-work-for-him-1730067091/.

487 Mark Kreidler, "Delgado's Protest No Longer Unnoticed," *ESPN*, July 23, 2004, https://www.espn.com/mlb/columns/story?columnist=kreidler_mark&id=1845388.

488 Jack Curry, "Leiter Says He's a Pitcher, Period," *New York Times*, September 17, 2004, https://www.nytimes.com/2004/09/17/sports/baseball/leiter-says-hes-a-pitcher-period.html.

489 Brendan Lemon, "Letter From 'Out' Editor," *ESPN*, May 2001, https://www.espn.com/page2/s/outletter/010523.html.

490 "In and Out with the Mets," *Page Six*, May 20, 2002, https://pagesix.com/2002/05/20/in-and-out-with-the-mets/.

491 Jessica, "Unconfirmed Rumor of the Day: Mike Piazza & Sam Champion's Love Nest," *Gawker*, July 28, 2005, https://www.gawkerarchives.com/114713/unconfirmed-rumor-of-the-day-mike-piazza--sam-champions-love-nest.

492 Rafael Hermoso, "Baseball; Piazza Responds to Gossip Column," *New York Times*, May 22, 2002, https://www.nytimes.com/2002/05/22/sports/baseball-piazza-responds-to-gossip-column.html.

493 Piazza, *Long Shot*, 307.

494 Andrew Marchand, "Wild Turk Tears Into 'Chicken' Guerrero," *New York Post*, April 9, 2001, https://nypost.com/2001/04/09/wild-turk-tears-into-chicken-guerrero/.

495 Jonathan Mahler, "Building the Béisbol Brand," *New York Times Magazine*, July 31, 2005, https://www.nytimes.com/2005/07/31/magazine/building-the-beisbol-brand.html.

496 Ian O'Conner. "Confidence Is Randolph's Calling Card," *USA Today*, October 4, 2006, https://web.archive.org/web/20090226135841/https://www.usatoday.com/sports/columnist/oconnor/2006-10-04-oconnor-randolph_x.htm.

497 Pedro Martínez and Michael Silverman, *Pedro* (Houghton Mifflin Harcourt, 2015), 269.

498 Martínez and Silverman, *Pedro*, 272.

499 Adam Rubin, *Pedro, Carlos (and Carlos) and Omar: The Rebirth of the New York Mets* (Lyons, 2006), 9.

500 Murray Chass, "The Minaya Touch Turns the Mets into Off-Season Players," *New York Times*, January 10, 2005, https://www.nytimes.com/2005/01/10/sports/baseball/the-minaya-touch-turns-the-mets-into-offseason-players.html.

501 Mark Hale, "Delgado, Omar Had Language Barrier," *New York Post*, March 5, 2005, https://nypost.com/2005/03/05/delgado-omar-had-language-barrier/.

502 Mahler, "Building Béisbol Brand."

503 Rubin, *Pedro, Carlos*, 284.

504 Martínez and Silverman, *Pedro*, 284.

505 Michael O'Keeffe, "He's the Fans' Man! News Readers Agree: Pedro's King of NY," *New York Daily News*, April 9, 2018, https://www.nydailynews.com/2005/08/28/hes-the-fans-man-news-readers-agree-pedros-king-of-ny/.

506 Dave Zirin, *Welcome to the Terrordome: The Pain, Politics, and Promise of Sports* (Haymarket Books, 2007), The Death of Super Mario. Ebook.

507 Rubin, *Pedro, Carlos*, 101.

508 Tyler Kepner, "Pedro Martínez Tells His Story," *New York Times*, May 3, 2015, https://www.nytimes.com/2015/05/03/sports/baseball/pedro-Martínez-tells-his-story.html.

509 David Wright and Anthony DiComo, *The Captain: A Memoir* (Dutton, 2020), Chap. 8. Ebook.

510 Milton H. Jamail, *Venezuelan Bust, Baseball Boom: Andrés Reiner and Scouting on the New Frontier* (University of Nebraska Press, 2008), 9, 53.

511 Zirin, *Welcome to the Terrordome*, The Death of Super Mario. Ebook.

512 Tim Weiner, "Low-Wage Costa Ricans Make Baseballs for Millionaires," *New York Times*, January 25, 2004, https://www.nytimes.com/2004/01/25/world/low-wage-costa-ricans-make-baseballs-for-millionaires.html.

513 Adam Welch, "Millions Strike, March in Massive May Day Protests," *Industrial Worker*, June 2006, https://archive.iww.org/category/campaigns/issue-oriented-campaigns/may-day/index3.

514 "Sheffield Criticizes Baseball for Not Recruiting More Black Players," *ESPN*, June 6, 2007, https://www.espn.com/mlb/news/story?id=2894650.

515 Dave Zirin, "Sheffield Strikes Out on Latino Players," *The Nation*, June 29, 2015, https://www.thenation.com/article/archive/sheffield-strikes-out-latino-players/.

516 David Waldstein, Kevin Draper, and James Wagner, "Fans Didn't Like the Way Jeff Wilpon Ran the Mets. Neither Did Some of His Relatives," *New York Times*, December 6, 2019, https://www.nytimes.com/2019/12/06/sports/mets-wilpons-sale-cohen.html.

517 Richard Staff and Allison McCague, "Mets Editorial: The Mets Don't Know How to Handle Their Players," *Amazin' Avenue*, June 7, 2018, https://www.amazinavenue.com/2018/6/7/17436354/mets-reyes-cespedes-Beltrán-seaver-alderson-wilpon-callaway.

518 "Randolph Backs off Racial Comments, Criticism of Cable Network" *ESPN*, May 21, 2008, https://www.espn.com/mlb/news/story?id=3406079.

519 "Mets Fire Randolph; Peterson, Nieto Also Dismissed," *ESPN*, June 17, 2008, https://www.espn.com/mlb/news/story?id=3447973.

520 Bill Madden, "Mets an Utter Disgrace for Handling of Willie Randolph's Firing," *New York Daily News*, January 12, 2019, https://www.nydailynews.com/2008/06/17/mets-an-utter-disgrace-for-handling-of-willie-randolphs-firing/.

521 Devin Gordon, *So Many Ways to Lose: The Amazin' True Story of the New York Mets—the Best Worst Team in Sports*, 1st ed. (HarperCollins Publishers, 2021), The Legend of Endy. Ebook.

522 Gary Sheffield, *Inside Power: A Memoir*, 1st ed. (Crown, 2007), Forty-Million-Dollar Slaves. Ebook.

523 Keith Hernandez, *Shea Good-Bye: The Untold Inside Story of the Historic 2008 Season*, with Matthew Silverman (Triumph Books, 2009), 290.

524 Richard Sandomir, "Demolition Takes Shea Stadium Piece by Piece," *New York Times*, October 24, 2008, https://www.nytimes.com/2008/10/24/sports/baseball/24mets.html.

CHAPTER 12: ATROCITI FIELD

525 "The Dark Knight—the Hero Gotham Deserves | Super Scenes | DC," posted on December 28, 2024, by DC, YouTube, https://www.youtube.com/watch?v=7pVaGNOp5Vc.

526 Howard Megdal, *Wilpon's Folly: The Story of a Man, His Fortune, and the New York Mets* (Bloomsbury USA, 2011), Indivisible. Ebook.

527 Megdal, *Wilpon's Folly*, Indivisible. Ebook.

528 Jack Curry, "Mets Will Not Be Affected by Losses to Madoff, Wilpon Says," *New York Times*, December 18, 2008, https://www.nytimes.com/2008/12/18/sports/18iht-METS.1.18780736.html.

529 Megdal, *Wilpon's Folly*, Fakin' It. Ebook.

530 Megdal, *Wilpon's Folly*, The Trustee for the Bernie Madoff Victims. Ebook.

531 "Who Has Been Hurt by the Recession in New York State?" Office of the State Comptroller, February 2010, https://www.osc.ny.gov/files/reports/special-topics/pdf/economic-recession-nys-2010_0.pdf.

532 Ryan Ahern, Edith Kealey, and Kinsey Dinan, "A Snap Shot of Enrollment and Participation in the Supplemental Nutrition Assistance Program in New York City," NYC Open Data, Office of Evaluation and Research, Office of Research and Policy Evaluation, NYC Department of Social Services, September 2022, https://data.cityofnewyork.us/api/views/4c8i-cnte/files/852decc7-3ebf-4abb-9b9b-e2a14f16517c?download=true&filename=SNAPParticipationNYC-110722.pdf.

533 Patrick Markee, "State of the Homeless 2012," Coalition for the Homeless, June 8, 2012, https://www.coalitionforthehomeless.org//uploads/2013/03/StateoftheHomeless2012.pdf.

534 Jerry Crasnick, "New York Mets' Injury Issues Go Far Beyond the Disabled List," *ESPN*, May 18, 2017, https://www.espn.com/mlb/story/_/id/19404194/new-york-mets-injury-issues-go-far-disabled-list.

535 Andrew Keh, "Contending Braves Give the Mets a Reason to Play Hard," *New York Times*, September 16, 2011, https://www.nytimes.com/2011/09/17/sports/baseball/contending-braves-give-the-mets-a-reason-to-play-hard.html.

536 Megdal, *Wilpon's Folly*, The Grand Bargain. Ebook.

537 Loren Goldner, "Theses for Discussion," Libcom.org, December 5, 2011, https://libcom.org/article/theses-discussion-loren-goldner.

538 *Family Guy*, "Halloween on Spooner Street," Fox, November 7, 2010.

539 Steve Eder, Richard Sandomir, and Alison Leigh Cowan, "A Mets Owner and Claims of Consumer Fraud," *New York Times*, December 3, 2012, https://www.nytimes.com/2012/12/03/sports/baseball/a-mets-owner-and-claims-of-consumer-fraud.html.

540 Tom Ley, "The Citi Field Amway Store Has a Juice Bar That Doesn't Sell Juice," *Deadspin*, June 18, 2013, https://deadspin.com/the-citi-field-amway-store-has-a-juice-bar-that-doesnt-5989262/.

541 Steve Kettmann, *Baseball Maverick: How Sandy Alderson Revolutionized Baseball and Revived the Mets* (Grove Atlantic, 2015), The Google of Baseball. Ebook.

542 Kettmann, *Baseball Maverick*, The Madoff Mess. Ebook.

543 R. A. Dickey, *Wherever I Wind Up: My Quest for Truth, Authenticity, and the Perfect Knuckleball* (Penguin, 2012), Ch. 21. Ebook.

544 Daniel Herrera, in-person interview with author, September 12, 2024.

545 "Piazza, New York Catcher," by Stuart Murdoch and Stevie Colburn, on Belle and Sebastian, *Dear Catastrophe Waitress*, Rough Trade Records, 2003.

546 Daniel Herrera, in-person interview with author, September 12, 2024.

547 *The Dark Knight Rises*, directed by Jonathan Nolan (Warner Bros., 2012), https://archive.org/stream/TheDarkKnightRisesScriptByJonathanNolanAndChristopherNolan/The+Dark+Knight+Rises+Script+by+Jonathan+Nolan+and+Christopher+Nolan_djvu.txt.

548 "Curtis Granderson; a Legacy of Respect," *MLBPA Players* (blog), January 31, 2020, https://www.mlbplayers.com/post/curtis-granderson-a-legacy-of-respect.

549 "The Citi Field Sheas," 7 Line, April 1, 2013, https://the7line.com/blogs/the-7-line/36068097-the-citi-field-sheas#.

550 Richard Sandomir, "Mets Resolve Suit with Executive They Fired When She Was Pregnant and Unmarried," *New York Times*, March 14, 2015, https://www.nytimes.com/2015/03/14/sports/baseball/mets-settle-case-with-executive-who-cited-discrimination-over-pregnancy.html.

551 "'Sell the Team' Billboard from Disgruntled Mets Fans Goes Up Near Citi Field," *New York Daily News*, April 9, 2018, https://www.nydailynews.com/2015/03/27/sell-the-team-billboard-from-disgruntled-mets-fans-goes-up-near-citi-field/.

552 Shannon Shark, "Let's Compare the 2014 Mets Loyalty Oath with the 2019 Pete Alonso Letter," August 1, 2019, https://metspolice.com/2019/08/01/lets-compare-the-2014-mets-loyalty-oath-with-the-2019-pete-alonso-letter/.

553 Juliet Eilperin, "Obama Lays Out His Foreign Policy Doctrine: Singles, Doubles and the Occasional Home Run," *Washington Post*, April 15, 2023, https://www.washingtonpost.com/world/obama-lays-out-his-foreign-policy-doctrine-singles-doubles-and-the-occasional-home-run/2014/04/28/e34ec058-ceb5-11e3-937f-d3026234b51c_story.html.

554 Tom Verducci, "The Dark Knight of Gotham," *Sports Illustrated*, May 20, 2013, https://vault.si.com/vault/2013/05/20/the-dark-knight-of-gotham.

555 Two Boots Pizza (@twobootspizza), "Did you know the V for Vegan pizza has been a staple at Two Boots Pizza since its debut in Manhattan?" Instagram, January 15, 2025, https://www.instagram.com/twobootspizza/p/DE2igIJvmFm/.

556 SNY (@SNYTv), "On Baseball Night in New York, Terry Collins joins the show," Twitter (now X), February 15, 2022, https://twitter.com/SNYtv/status/1493759548334641156.

557 Michael Powell, "Driving to Work with Keith Hernandez, the Real Mr. Met," *New York Times*, October 02, 2015, https://www.nytimes.com/2015/10/02/fashion/mens-style/mets-keith-hernandez.html.

558 Michael Powell, "Mets' Latest Run-In with Chase Utley Changes the Focus of a Series," *New York Times*, October 11, 2015, https://www.proquest.com/blogs-podcasts-websites/mets-latest-run-with-chase-utley-changes-focus/docview/1721193203/se-2.

559 Corey Kilgannon, "A Leg-Breaking Slide Has Fans Old and New Rushing to Meet the Mets," *New York Times*, October 12, 2015, http://nytimes.com/2015/10/13/nyregion/a-leg-breaking-slide-has-fans-old-and-new-rushing-to-meet-the-mets.html.

560 Tyler Kepner, "For the Mets, Pennies Saved Add Up to a Pennant Earned," *New York Times*, October 22, 2015, https://www.nytimes.com/2015/10/23/sports/baseball/after-madoff-fraud-mets-altered-approach-for-pennant.html.

561 Jesse McKinley, "Cuomo Cancels Fund-Raisers at Mets' World Series Games," *New York Times*, October 29, 2015, https://www.nytimes.com/2015/10/30/nyregion/cuomo-cancels-fund-raisers-at-mets-world-series-games.html.

562 Alan Schwarz, *The Numbers Game: Baseball's Lifelong Fascination with Statistics*, 1st ed. (St. Martin's Press, 2004), Chap. 10. Ebook.

563 "Ode to the Mets," on The Strokes, *The New Abnormal*, RCA Records, 2020.

564 Matthew Trammell, "Long Live Shea Stadium," *The New Yorker*, March 15, 2017, https://www.newyorker.com/culture/culture-desk/long-live-shea-stadium.

565 "Trump Inauguration Speech (FULL) | ABC News," posted on January 20, 2017, by ABC News, YouTube, https://www.youtube.com/watch?v=sRBsJNdK1t0.

CHAPTER 13: BACK IN BLACK

566 Paul Schwartzman and Michael E. Miller, "Confident. Incorrigible. Bully: Little Donny Was a Lot Like Candidate Donald Trump," *Washington Post*, April 11, 2023, https://www.washingtonpost.com/lifestyle/style/young-donald-trump-military-school/2016/06/22/f0b3b164-317c-11e6-8758-d58e76e11b12_story.html.

567 "'Old Man Trump' ~ Woody Guthrie," WoodyGuthrie.org, accessed July 24, 2025, https://woodyguthrie.org/Lyrics/Old_Man_Trump.htm.

568 Robert Fredrick Burk, *Much More Than a Game: Players, Owners, & American Baseball Since 1921* (University of North Carolina Press, 2001), 270.

569 J. Ratsky, interview with author via Signal, May 12, 2025.

570 Natasha Noman, "Bernie Sanders' Big Bro, Larry, Serves up Some New Insight on His Kid Brother," *Mic*, December 31, 2015, https://www.mic.com/articles/131472/bernie-sanders-big-bro-larry-serves-up-some-new-insight-on-his-kid-brother.

571 Sydney Ember and Matt Flegenheimer, "Bernie Sanders Is Still Sad About the Dodgers," *New York Times*, January 30, 2020, https://www.nytimes.com/2020/01/30/us/politics/bernie-sanders-baseball.html.

572 Bernie Sanders (@BernieSanders), Twitter (now X)

573 Igor Derysh, "Joe Biden to Rich Donors: 'Nothing Would Fundamentally Change' If He's Elected," *Salon*, June 19, 2019, https://www.salon.com/2019/06/19/joe-biden-to-rich-donors-nothing-would-fundamentally-change-if-hes-elected/.

574 Peter Dreier, "Sean Doolittle, Baseball's Left-Wing Lefty, Retires," *The Nation*, October 12, 2023, https://www.thenation.com/article/culture/sean-doolittle-baseball-conscience-retires/.

575 Alan Feuer and Liam Stack, "New York City Considers Temporary Graves for Virus Victims," *New York Times*, April 6, 2020, https://www.nytimes.com/2020/04/06/nyregion/mass-graves-nyc-parks-coronavirus.html.

576 Maritza Vasquez Reyes, "The Disproportional Impact of COVID-19 on African Americans," *Health and Human Rights* 22, no. 2 (2020): 299–307, https://www.ncbi.nlm.nih.gov/pmc/articles/PMC7762908/.

577 Roudabeh Kishi, Hampton Stall, Aaron Wolfson, and Sam Jones, "A Year of Racial Justice Protests: Key Trends in Demonstrations Supporting the BLM Movement," Armed Conflict Location & Event Data, May 25, 2021, https://acleddata.com/2021/05/25/a-year-of-racial-justice-protests-key-trends-in-demonstrations-supporting-the-blm-movement/.

578 Larry Buchanan, Quoctrung Bui, and Jugal K. Patel, "Black Lives Matter May Be the Largest Movement in US History," *New York Times*, July 3, 2020, https://www.nytimes.com/interactive/2020/07/03/us/george-floyd-protests-crowd-size.html.

579 "Welcome to the Party: The George Floyd Uprising in NYC," *It's Going Down*, June 24, 2020, https://itsgoingdown.org/welcome-to-the-party-the-george-floyd-uprising-in-nyc/.

580 Andy Battle, "The City of Blind Windows," *Spectre*, part 2, November 28, 2022, https://spectrejournal.com/the-city-of-blind-windows-2/.

581 Dennis Young, "All Mets, Braves Stand for National Anthem on Opening Day at Citi Field," *New York Daily News*, July 24, 2020, https://www.nydailynews.com/2020/07/24/all-mets-braves-stand-for-national-anthem-on-opening-day-at-citi-field/.

582 Alex Smith, "Mets' Dominic Smith on MLB players Kneeling During National Anthem: 'For Me, Taking a Knee Just Isn't Enough,'" *SNY*, July 21, 2020, https://www.sny.tv/articles/mets-dominic-smith-on-mlb-players-kneeling-during-national-anthem-for-me-taking-a-knee-just-isn-t-enough-.

583 Shannon Keating, "Cops Kneeling with Protesters Isn't the Solution," *BuzzFeed News*, June 4, 2020, https://www.buzzfeednews.com/article/shannonkeating/cops-kneeling-hugging-protesters-george-floyd-protests.

584 Tobi Haslett, "Magic Actions," *n+1*, August 20, 2021, https://www.nplusonemag.com/issue-40/politics/magic-actions-2/.

585 Bob Nightengale, "'Starting to Hit Home': Percentage of Black Players in MLB Still Low, but There Are Signs of Growth," *USA TODAY*, August 14, 2020, https://www.usatoday.com/story/sports/mlb/columnist/bob-nightengale/2020/08/14/mlb-black-players-signs-of-growth-100th-anniversary-negro-leagues/3366480001/.

586 "BaseballGenerations," BBG Foundation, accessed July 24, 2025, https://www.baseballgenerations.com/bbg-foundation.

587 "Dom Smith on His Experiences with Racism in America | New York Mets | SNY," posted on June 28, 2020, by SNY, YouTube, https://www.youtube.com/watch?v=aOvlL0pSkMM.

588 Stephanie Apstein, "How Dom Smith Used His Voice for Mets to Seek Social Justice," *Sports Illustrated*, September 17, 2020, https://www.si.com/mlb/2020/09/17/dominic-smith-new-york-mets.

589 Stephanie Apstein, "How Dom Smith Used His Voice for Mets to Seek Social Justice—Sports Illustrated," *SI*, September 17, 2020, https://www.si.com/mlb/2020/09/17/dominic-smith-new-york-mets.

590 Apstein, "Dom Smith Used His Voice."

591 "Breonna Taylor and the Limits of Riots," Spirit of May 28, accessed July 24, 2025, https://web.archive.org/web/20211101000000*/https://www.sm28.org/articles/breonna-taylor-and-the-limits-of-riots/.

592 Shams Charania (@ShamsCharania), "Full release from the NBA and NBPA: Social justice coalition being formed," Twitter (now X), August 28, 2020, https://twitter.com/ShamsCharania/status/1299387471990591488.

593 Lorenzo Reyes, "Donald Trump Followers Chant 'LeBron James Sucks' Against Lakers Star at Pennsylvania Rally," *USA Today*, November 3, 2020, https://www.usatoday.com/story/sports/nba/lakers/2020/11/02/donald-trump-rally-goers-chant-lebron-james-sucks-pennsylvania/6130977002/.

594 Claire Wang, "Wage Theft, Tip Withholding: Chinatowns' Workers Unionize En Masse for Better Conditions," *NBC News*, September 21, 2021, https://www.nbcnews.com/news/asian-america/wage-theft-tip-withholding-chinatowns-workers-unionize-en-masse-better-rcna2040.

595 *Tipping Pitches*, podcast, "The Minor League Theory of Value (Feat. Harry Marino)," February 24, 2022, https://tippingpitch.es/2022/02/24/the-minor-league-theory-of-value-feat-harry-marino/.

596 Lily Rothman, "Where Is the César Chávez of Minor League Baseball?," *Slate*, April 3, 2012, https://slate.com/culture/2012/04/minor-league-union-thousands-of-pro-baseball-players-make-just-1100-per-month-where-is-their-cesar-chavez.html.

597 Emma Baccellieri, "Minor League Baseball Union: How a Group of Players Sprung a Union on MLB," *Sports Illustrated*, September 22, 2022, https://www.si.com/mlb/2022/09/22/minor-league-baseball-union-daily-cover.

598 Bill Fletcher Jr., phone interview with author, March 20, 2024.

599 Thornton McEnery, Josh Kosman, and Julia Marsh, "Bill De Blasio Is Trying to Kill Mets Sale to Steve Cohen," *New York Post*, October 28, 2020, https://nypost.com/2020/10/28/bill-de-blasio-is-trying-to-kill-mets-sale-to-steve-cohen/.

600 Manny Gómez, "Chris 'Mad Dog' Russo Makes Shocking Charge Against Mets Owner Steve Cohen," *NJ.com*, June 7, 2023, https://www.nj.com/mets/2023/06/chris-mad-dog-russo-makes-shocking-charge-against-mets-owner-steve-cohen.html.

601 "Steve Cohen on New York Mets Ownership: I View It as a Civic Responsibility," *CNBC*, April 3, 2024, https://www.cnbc.com/video/2024/04/03/steve-cohen-on-new-york-mets-ownership-i-view-it-as-a-civic-responsibility.html.

602 New York Mets (@Mets), "Back in Black—July 30," Twitter (now X), July 15, 2021, https://x.com/Mets/status/1415672924514570252?s=20.

603 Deesha Thosar, "Manager Luis Rojas Supports Mets Minor Leaguers Who Protested Insufficient Wages," *New York Daily News*, September 20, 2021, https://www.nydailynews.com/2021/09/19/manager-luis-rojas-supports-mets-minor-leaguers-who-protested-insufficient-wages/.

604 Evan Drellich, "Steve Cohen's Mets Spending Spree and the Ramifications for the Rest of the League," *The Athletic*, December 22, 2022, https://www.nytimes.com/athletic/4026971/2022/12/22/mets-steve-cohen-spending/.

605 Stephanie Apstein, "Mets Spring Training: Max Scherzer Glad Despite 'Steve Cohen Tax,'" *Sports Illustrated*, March 12, 2022, https://www.si.com/mlb/2022/03/12/mets-leaders-grateful-despite-steve-cohen-tax.

606 Peter Dreier, "Baseball's Labor Wars," *Dissent*, March 30, 2022, https://www.dissentmagazine.org/online_articles/baseballs-labor-wars/.

607 Baccellieri, "Minor League Union."

608 Tim Britton and Will Sammon, "How The $445 Million Mets Crashed and Burned," *The Athletic*, December 6, 2023, https://www.nytimes.com/athletic/4854008/2023/09/21/mets-mlb-season-record-trajectory-performance/.

EPILOGUE

609 "DIRECTOR'S CUT: Bartolo Colon 'Bartolo Day' With the 7 Line Army in San Diego," posted on May 7, 2020, by The 7 Line, YouTube, https://www.youtube.com/watch?v=YDvX8gVicdc.

610 Margeaux Marks, email interview with author, September 5, 2024.

611 Katia Reguero Lindor (@RegueroKatia), "I'm usually all for triggering male fragile egos," X.com, April 5, 2024, https://x.com/RegueroKatia/status/1776418169684382043.

612 Allison McCague, email interview with author, October 21, 2024.

613 "Dwight Gooden's Number Retirement Speech," posted on April 14, 2024, by New York Mets, YouTube, https://www.youtube.com/watch?v=tTSSuLq98UU.

614 Aaron Bandler, "Teams Express Support for Israel Following Hamas Terror Attack," *Jewish Journal*, October 13, 2023, https://jewishjournal.com/community/363715/teams-express-support-for-israel-following-hamas-terror-attack/.

615 "GENOCIDE IS NOT A GAME! THE BRONX STANDS WITH PALESTINE!," Google Docs, April 22, 2024, https://docs.google.com/document/d/1Fz5I0SDp4P26Y9B53CMqVaQKjGMS48wbiAul6yJ98wc/edit.

616 Adalah NY, "New York Mets called on to cancel settlement fundraiser," *Electronic Intifada*, November 4, 2009, https://electronicintifada.net/content/new-york-mets-called-cancel-settlement-fundraiser/998.

617 Eric Koreen, James L. Edwards III, and Jason Jones, "MLB City Connect Series: All 20 Uniforms Ranked, Including the 2023 Gear," *The Athletic*, June 17, 2024, https://www.nytimes.com/athletic/4633605/2023/06/28/mlb-city-connect-uniforms-ranked/.

618 Andrew Tredinnick, "Will NY Mets Fans Return to Citi Field? They Speak on One of MLB's Biggest Attendance Drops," *North Jersey Media Group*, May 23, 2024, https://www.northjersey.com/story/sports/mlb/mets/2024/05/23/ny-mets-attendance-has-dropped-by-more-than-21-percent-to-begin-2024/73801718007/.

619 Joe, email interview with author, August 2, 2024.

620 Foul Territory (@FoulTerritoryTV), "Did Steve Cohen just hint at the Mets selling at the trade deadline?" X.com, May 15, 2024, https://x.com/FoulTerritoryTV/status/1790930797966295122.

621 Will Sammon and Jenna West, "Former Met Jorge López Clarifies Ill-Fated Interview Comments, Calls Himself 'The Worst Teammate,'" *The Athletic*, May 30, 2024, https://www.nytimes.com/athletic/5530119/2024/05/30/jorge-López-mets-interview/.

622 "Francisco Lindor Explains Calling Team Meeting After Mets' Disastrous May Crescendos | SNY," posted on May 30, 2024, by SNY, YouTube, https://www.youtube.com/watch?v=RimgjW8hIKg.

623 SNY, "Francisco Lindor Proud of Mets Despite NLCS Loss, Looks Ahead to New Standard for Organization | SNY," posted on October 21, 2024, by SNY, YouTube, https://www.youtube.com/watch?v=LVpKzQ5_tYA.

624 SNY (@SNYTv), "'You know what, they say we suck, we suck. Let's suck. Let's go suck together. Let's go have fun sucking,'" X.com, October 2, 2024, https://x.com/SNYtv/status/1842046694675886482.

625 Jeff Passan, "Why the Mets' 2024 MLB Playoff Run Is Start of Something Big," ESPN, October 21, 2024, https://www.espn.com/mlb/story/_/id/41916472/new-york-mets-run-2024-mlb-playoffs-world-series-future.

626 "Darryl Strawberry Has His Number Retired by the Mets! ll Ceremony!)," posted on June 1, 2024, by MLB, YouTube, https://www.youtube.com/watch?v=3DMHdla-0kQ.

627 New York Mets (@Mets), "Happy #PrideMonth! Baseball is for everyone," X.com, June 2, 2024, https://x.com/Mets/status/1797294402945036366.

628 Swimqueen16 (@Swimween16), "Degenerate organization," X.com, June 2, 2024, https://x.com/SwimQueen16/status/1797326085975097573.

629 Dan (@kinerfalefa), "THE NEW YORK YANKEES: GAY FOR A DAY ONLY," X.com, June 19, 2024, https://x.com/kinerfalefa/status/1803429786846437488.

630 Will Sammon, "Mets' José Iglesias Wrote a Song Called 'OMG' and Players Are Obsessed With It," *The Athletic*, June 21, 2024, https://www.nytimes.com/athletic/5579159/2024/06/21/mets-José-iglesias-song-omg/.

631 John F. Love, *McDonald's: Behind the Arches* (Bantam Books, 1986), 309–310.

632 Callie Holtermann, "On TikTok, Grimace Milkshakes from McDonald's Inspire Scenes of Horror," *New York Times*, June 29, 2023, https://www.nytimes.com/2023/06/29/style/grimace-milkshake.html.

633 Sammon, "Mets' Iglesias Wrote Song."

634 Jolly Olive (@Jolly_Olive), "the gay Mets are 6–3 btw," X.com, June 13, 2024, https://x.com/Jolly_Olive/status/1801443396722012435/.

635 Jolly Olive (@Jolly_Olive), "The Gay Mets will take Pride in beating your favorite team," X.com, October 5, 2024, https://x.com/Jolly_Olive/status/1842610801720348820.

636 Jolly Olive (@Jolly_Olive), "The Texas Rangers refused to have a Pride Night so the Gay Mets had to fuck em up," X.com, June 17, 2024, https://x.com/Jolly_Olive/status/1802870737457279249.

637 David Propper, "Grimace Turns Into LGBTQ Icon as McDonald's Mascot Makes a Comeback," *New York Post*, June 16, 2023, https://nypost.com/2023/06/16/grimace-turns-into-lgbtq-icon-as-mcdonalds-mascot-makes-a-comeback/.

638 Matt Stieb, "The Gay Grimace Mets Will Ram Pride Night Like a Big Purple Truck," Intelligencer, *New York*, June 27, 2024, https://nymag.com/intelligencer/article/gay-grimace-mets-pride-night.html.

639 New York Mets (@Mets)," Celebrating Pride, June 28, 2024, https://x.com/Mets/status/1806799444848824731.

640 Shea Station (@Shea_Station), "Mets win," X.com, July 22, 2024, https://x.com/shea_station/status/1815559743303266436.

641 Michael W Kraus, Cassey Huang, and Dacher Keltner, "Tactile Communication, Cooperation, and Performance: An Ethological Study of the NBA," *Emotion* 10, no. 5 (2010): 745–749, https://doi.org/10.1037/a0019382.

642 Andrew Crane, "Francisco Lindor Didn't Get Full Day Off After All on Day of Daughter's Birth," *New York Post*, June 18, 2023, https://nypost.com/2023/06/17/francisco-lindor-didnt-get-full-day-off-after-all-on-day-of-daughters-berth/.

643 Mike Puma, "Mets' Francisco Lindor Wants to See MLBPA 'Improve,' Not Remove Leaders," *New York Post*, March 20, 2024, https://nypost.com/2024/03/19/sports/what-francisco-lindor-had-to-say-about-internal-mlbpa-war/.

644 Alan Dawson, "Donald Trump Brings Imane Khalif Into Pre-US Election Rhetoric," *World Boxing News*, November 4, 2024, https://www.worldboxingnews.net/2024/11/04/donald-trump-imane-khalif-us-election-rhetoric/.

645 dianna (@runwildkian), "Katia Reguero Lindor, the woman that you are," X.com, August 2, 2024, https://x.com/runwildkian/status/1819479336178659370.

646 Protest_NYC (@Protest_NYC), "Outside Citi Field, where tens of thousands have gathered for a Green Day," X.com, August 5, 2024, https://x.com/protest_nyc/status/1820584059711508594.

647 "Israel," Citigroup, accessed July 24, 2025, https://www.citigroup.com/global/about-us/global-presence/israel.

648 Billy Bean, "Opening Up About Mets Visit, Murphy Comments," *MLB*, September 26, 2024, https://www.mlb.com/news/billy-bean-opening-up-about-mets-visit-murphy-comments.

649 Jim Buzinski, "Billy Bean Is Now Friends with Daniel Murphy, Who 'Disagreed with Gay Lifestyle,'" *Out Sports*, March 6, 2018, https://www.outsports.com/2018/3/6/17084216/billy-bean-daniel-murphy-mlb-gay-lifestyle/.

650 Dean Balsamini, "Trump Fan Sues Mets for $2M Over MAGA Hat Ban at Citi Field: 'Emotional Distress,'" *New York Post*, September 21, 2024, https://nypost.com/2024/09/21/us-news/trump-fan-sues-mets-for-2m-over-maga-hat-ban-at-citi-field-emotional-distress/.

651 Deirdre Bardolf and Matthew Sedacca, "Post Reporters Attend Mets Game Wearing Trump MAGA Hat and Pro-Kamala Gear—Here's How They Were Treated at Citi Field," *New York Post*, September 21, 2024, https://nypost.com/2024/09/21/us-news/post-reporters-attend-mets-game-wearing-trump-maga-hat-and-pro-kamala-gear-heres-how-they-were-treated-at-citi-field/.

652 Ryan Morik, "Red Sox's Jarren Duran Has Top-Rated Jersey on MLB Shop After Anti-Gay Slur," *Fox News*, August 14, 2024, https://www.foxnews.com/sports/red-soxs-jarren-duran-has-top-rated-jersey-mlb-shop-after-anti-gay-slur.

653 Eugene B. Bergmann, "Jean Shepherd—I'm as Mad as Hell," *Shepquest* (blog), March 1, 2014, https://shepquest.wordpress.com/2014/03/01/jean-shepherd-im-as-mad-as-hell/.

654 "Peter Finch Is Mad as Hell," posted on February 26, 2025, by Turner Classic Movies, YouTube, https://www.youtube.com/watch?v=M96UAUJWW3Y.

655 Grant Young, "Brandon Nimmo Sends Strong Message to Mets Fans," *New York Mets on SI*, September 19, 2024, https://www.si.com/mlb/mets/news/brandon-nimmo-sends-strong-message-to-mets-fans-grant9.

656 Steve Gelbs (@SteveGelbs), "A huge two out double by Francisco Álvarez plates another two," X.com, September 21, 2024, https://x.com/SteveGelbs/status/1837613678528438641.

657 Tim Healy (@timbhealy), "Carlos Mendoza on the Citi Field crowd today: "Great. Unbelievable. That's what it should look, it should feel like, especially when we're playing meaningful games in September,'" X.com, September 21, 2024, https://x.com/timbhealey/status/1837636236409708627.

658 Jolly Olive (@Jolly_Olive), "Still cant believe this tweet. Still loved how all Mets fans came together on this one," X.com, October 21, 2024, https://x.com/Jolly_Olive/status/1848466379076411789.

659 "From 0–5 to OMG | the Story of the 2024 Mets Regular Season," posted on October 1, 2024, by New York Mets, YouTube, https://www.youtube.com/watch?v=R0_itwVkrDQ.

660 Shea Station (@Shea–station), "[no text]," X.com, October 3, 2024, https://x.com/shea_station/status/1842030930392703047.

661 Deesha (@DeeshaThosar), "Introducing Harrison Bader's new term for the Mets' success on the road," X.com, October 6, 2024, https://x.com/DeeshaThosar/status/1843008071448322174.

662 Donald Trump, (@RealDonaldTrump), "KAMALA SUPPORTS TAXPAYER FUNDED SEX CHANGES FOR PRISONERS," Instagram, September 20, 2024, https://www.instagram.com/realdonaldtrump/reel/DAI3nriuPxw/.

663 "Francisco Lindor on NLDS Victory and Mets Next Steps: 'I Want to Win It All,'" posted on October 10, 2024, by SNY, YouTube, https://www.youtube.com/watch?v=Uw0m8YNHs2M.

664 Evan Roberts, (@EvanRobertsWFAN), "Would be a shame if the Mets saw this," X.com, October 17, 2024, https://x.com/EvanRobertsWFAN/status/1846949137255719230.

665 "Mets DEFEAT Dodgers, Game 5 Reaction: David Ortiz, Derek Jeter, Alex Rodriguez," posted on October 19, 2024, by FOX Sports, YouTube, https://www.youtube.com/watch?v=tBXG9Hl8ydI.

666 Mark W. Sanchez, "Sean Manaea Gave Everything to Mets—Until He Had Nothing Left in Game 6 Dud," *New York Post*, October 21, 2024, https://nypost.com/2024/10/21/sports/sean-manaea-hit-a-wall-when-mets-needed-him-most-in-game-6-flop/.

667 Mike Puma, "Mets Run Out of Playoff Magic as Dodgers Send Them Packing in Crushing Fashion," *New York Post*, October 21, 2024, https://nypost.com/2024/10/20/sports/mets-run-out-of-playoff-magic-as-dodgers-send-them-packing/.

668 Harrison Bader (@aybaybader), "When I think about the 2024 Mets I dont even know where to begin", Instagram, November 2, 2024, https://www.instagram.com/p/DB43ZMRRbVO/?hl=en.

669 Jay Horwitz, "This Squad Resembles '86 Mets," *Mets Insider Blog*, Medium, November 14, 2024, https://metsinsider.mlblogs.com/this-squad-resembles-86-mets-4056ae5099a3.

670 Jay Horwitz, "Who Does Carlos Mendoza Remind Me Of?," *Mets Insider Blog*, Medium, November 15, 2024, https://metsinsider.mlblogs.com/who-does-carlos-mendoza-remind-me-of-7ceadde8428b.

671 Jay Horwitz, "Cleon Jones Sees Similarities to '69 Mets," *Mets Insider Blog*, Medium, November 15, 2024, https://metsinsider.mlblogs.com/cleon-jones-sees-similarities-to-69-mets-7ab648b02640.

672 Greg W. Prince, *Faith and Fear in Flushing: An Intense Personal History of the New York Mets* (Skyhorse Publishing, 2009), 207.

673 DSA North Star (@DSANorth Star), "Which team represents the working class?" X.com, March 24, 2024, https://x.com/DSANorthStar/status/1847375341045895188.

674 Bhaskar Sunkara (@sunraysunray), "The Yankees are both the elite team of capital and team of the working class," X.com, October 18, 2024, https://x.com/sunraysunray/status/1847419666404131098.

675 Kevin T. Dugan and Simon van Zuylen-Wood, "Real New Yorkers Root for the Yankees," Intelligencer, *New York*, https://nymag.com/intelligencer/article/world-series-yankees-mets-fans.html.

676 "Francisco Lindor Proud of Mets Despite NLCS Loss, Looks Ahead to New Standard for Organization | SNY," posted on October 21, 2024, by SNY, YouTube, https://www.youtube.com/watch?v=LVpKzQ5_tYA.

POSTSCRIPT

677 *Futurama*, "A Leela of Her Own," Fox, April 7, 2002.

678 Daniel Herrera, in-person interview with author, September 12, 2024.

679 Alan Cameron, *Circus Factions: Blues and Greens at Rome and Byzantium*, special ed. for Sandpiper Books (Clarendon Press, 1999), 278–285.

INDEX

Photo credit: Elizabeth Day

About the Author

A. M. Gittlitz is an organizer and writer focusing on counterculture and radical politics. He is the author of *I Want to Believe: Posadism, UFOs and Apocalypse Communism* and co-host of *This Wreckage* podcast. He lives in Ridgewood, Queens, but can be often found Tuesday nights at the Vegan City food stand at Citi Field.